PRIVATE LESSONS

IN THE CULTIVATION

of

MAGNETISM OF THE SEXES

*Teaching the Development and
Wonderful Enlargement
of those*

POWERS *and* INFLUENCES

*That Nature has Invented to
Aid Every Human Life*

INSTRUCTION
By
EDMUND SHAFTESBURY

ISSUED BY
THE RALSTON SOCIETY
CLEVELAND, OHIO
1948 Edition

THE MAGNETISM BOOKS:

INSTANTANEOUS PERSONAL MAGNETISM

GROUP A—CONSISTS OF THE BOOKS:
MENTAL MAGNETISM
OPERATIONS OF THE OTHER MIND
SEX MAGNETISM
ADVANCED MAGNETISM
UNIVERSAL MAGNETISM—Volume I
UNIVERSAL MAGNETISM—Volume II

Printed in U. S. A.

Dedication

To:—

All men who appreciate the women of
their homes; and to

All women who are willing to aid the
men of their homes to appreciate them;

This course of study is respectfully
DEDICATED

DEPARTMENTS OF SEX MAGNETISM

First Department—
"USES OF SEX MAGNETISM"

Second Department—
"BASIC LAWS"

Third Department—
"SIX SENSES"

Fourth Department—
"THE ATTRACTIVE FORCE"

Fifth Department—
"SEX INFLUENCE"

Sixth Department—
"GETTING TOGETHER"

6

Seventh Department—
"HEART INTERESTS"

Eighth Department—
"FIVE MAGNETIC LAWS"

Ninth Department—
"COMMONPLACES"

Tenth Department—
"MAGNETIC MARGINS"

Eleventh Department—
"CHARMLAND"

Twelfth Department—
"SHADOWS IN BONDAGE"

Thirteenth Department—
"MAGNETIC CONSORTS"

Fourteenth Department—
"WRECKAGE"

Fifteenth Department—
"MAGNETIC PASSION"

Uses of Sex Magnetism

S the subject of personal magnetism is every year claiming a large degree of attention from the thoughtful public, its myriad uses demand a scientific explanation. It was once thought that personal magnetism was a born gift; but, when it was learned that this quality depended on the simplest acquisitions, the opinion changed.

The foundation of magnetism is attraction.

That which attracts is magnetic. A young man who has courage and displays it discreetly, attracts admirers; while, on the contrary, another young man who is a coward will repel friends. The driver of an automobile who runs over a child and then puts on speed and hurries away, merits the contempt of the world; and no personal quality of a high degree even, could overcome or out-balance the low estimate in which his character is placed. If he were a selling agent, he would find no patrons among those whom he solicited. If he were a clergyman he would soon preach to empty pews. If he were a lawyer, his clients would drop him. Yet, on the other hand, if he had stepped in front of a moving car at the risk of his own life, and had pulled a child from danger and death, his star would be in the ascendant. He would have influence, and success would be attracted to him.

Personal magnetism is the power that attracts the world, or some persons in it, to an individual. It has many phases. It may be a charm of manner, or a subtle influence of nervous fire, or an electric intensity, or some pleasing method that wins; but whatever draws people and does not repel them, is personal magnetism. Its advantage over merely acquired ways, is that it is permanent; other people do not soon tire of it; and they do not find out that it is an empty thing, like studied politeness, or a genial smile. These are valuable assistants, but they are not magnetism of themselves. They are tools of that power.

It is true that a happy disposition will be preferred to one that is sour and crusty; but with nothing behind the happy disposition it is soon a source of monotony. A woman who had married a man because she felt sure that he would always be kind to her, said at the end of a year: "I get so tired of his easy, thoughtless good nature. His smile is a grin, and it haunts me wherever I turn. I see it in front of me at the table, around the corner of the door, in the sitting room, and everywhere. I want a man, not a pleasant smile."

The strong man behind the smile would have been satisfying; but the smile on the face of the weak character is not enough. He was kind to her, and nothing more.

Politeness adds to the power of magnetism, but it is not magnetism. A cordial greeting, and a polite manner will win more flies than vinegar. The selling agent who has good manners, a pleasing way, and excellent address, has the tools of magnetism; and, if he has no more, he will not sell many goods. The film of his surface character will be punctured very quickly, and through this the discerning buyer will catch the real power behind.

The agencies that help make magnetism effective cannot be omitted; but they cannot take the place of the subtle force. They occupy the unique position of being necessary, and yet not being the power they aid. To cease to employ them, will cause failure in the uses of magnetism, and yet alone they accomplish nothing real in the battle of life. A young man who had found a young woman whom he liked exceedingly well, determined to win her. He at first sought to impress on her mind the fact that he was a gentleman. To do this he had to undergo a complete revolution. His manner of dress, of talking, of conducting himself, and all his methods were subjected to a complete change from the basis up to the very top; and this caused his friends to wonder what had come over the fellow. The bettering of himself in these respects helped him very much in the place of his employment. He grew of more value to those for whom he worked, and rose in his position until his salary was doubled.

The young lady all the time was unconscious of his admiration for her. She did not know why he had been making desperate efforts to improve himself. She thus exercised a magnetic influence over him, although she had very little of what is called personal magnetism. It was the young man magnetizing himself. Nature carries on this process for the double purpose of bringing the two sexes together, and of aiding in civilizing the world at the same time. It is a rule of Sex Magnetism that the more a man is compelled to appreciate a woman, the greater will be the effect on the general quality of the race.

The reason is plain.

When a boy has begun to touch the threshold of puberty, he may not be aware of the fact; but he is casting side glances at the girls. When the mention or presence of a girl will bring blood to his face, he is on the verge of young manhood. He does not even think much of the girls, but they are nevertheless exerting an influence over him, of which they are as unconscious as he is. He is not as careless in his dress, if he is to meet a girl at a party, as he would be if he is to meet only the boys of his play hours.

It has been said truly that nature might get along with one sex. The claim has been made that woman, because she brings forth the race, must have respite from her duties; but the sturdiest children come from women who toil hardest at that time. Even the Indian mothers were on the march at the time of childbirth, in a large number of cases. The act of parturition is a simple one when closest to the habits of nature.

There is no objection on this ground. But if there were, it would have no weight; for the power that is able to make the two sexes is amply endowed with the ability to bring results in any way that is most suited to its purposes. If reproduction were all that nature desired, she could have made one sex, and have given that sex all the means whereby the race could be brought forth with even less inconvenience than is experienced at the present time. As some plants are one-sex structures, capable of reproducing their kind; and as other plants are bisexual, capable of impregnating themselves; so the human species could have been made in either way, and have carried on the work intended in as effective a manner as men and women do now.

There are almost unlimited reasons why there are men and women in the world.

The more the subject is thought of, the more these reasons loom up and compel admiration for the design that is clearly seen behind all creation.

It would be out of the scope of this book to discuss the greater number of these reasons; as all that is necessary to the present course is to understand some of the things that result from sex attraction. Progress is decreed everywhere in the universe. There are some scientists who teach that all existence is a circle; that the sun in its career will draw all its planets to itself, expand into thin gas, and begin all over again through the basis of a nebular birth. Nothing but theory has been advanced to sustain this view; and the theory has not one tangible or probable fact on which to rest.

As opposed to this theory is a long line of facts that have been enacted in the past history of the earth, and of which there is an absolute certainty. It is known that the world was crude and rough in its condition and in its peoples a few thousand years ago. It is known that there was no civilization until within the last twenty or thirty centuries; and then only among a small percentage of humanity. It is known that there has been a gradual average improvement, not only in the earth itself, but in its inhabitants; until in this age, in which you live, there is a decided advance in every direction.

In lands where each sex has come to regard each sex with a higher degree of respect; and especially where women have been lifted out of the physical to the ethical standard, there has been a rapid growth of the better impulses of the race. This is called the racial influence of sex appreciation.

But as a nation is the composite structure of its parts, so a general movement for the advancement of a large mass of people must have its basis in individual influences. There is no such thing as the improvement of a whole people as such. If one person is made better, and another person is made better, and other units are made better, the race will improve in proportion as these units become numerous. There is no one power so capable of carrying on this improvement as the power of Sex Magnetism.

This quality is diverse and many-sided.

We have seen that it will bring greater care to the young man in his habits of dress and manner and culture than any other influence. He does not plan his improvement with deliberation so much as with an instinctive drifting of his conduct. He seems to know that the girl expects him to assume a better plumage. This is true in the bird habits of the forest. The female may be wooed by many male birds; and the one that is most attractive to her in feathers, in song and in physical power, is the proud winner. He, too, seeks the most attractive of females; and thus their offspring will average slightly better than their ancestry. The weaker birds are side-tracked; many never propagate; and many are killed in fights. The fittest survive. This is nature's purpose.

The same instinct is handed down to humanity.

When once there is a girl in prospect for a decent young man, he assumes better plumage, cleaner habits, and a more manly conduct. If he is unworthy, like many of the sons of the idle rich, he will visit houses of prostitution long before he is fit for such uses, and his manhood will become mushy and degraded. The very stimulus that nature has implanted in the race is dulled and lost. There will be coarseness in fine clothes; bad eyes in a weak head, and a disrespect of women in a debauched body. Many a boy still under the last year of his teens has become old in this wickedness; which fact carries with it the lesson that parents should know what their boys are doing.

There is a good, or a bad influence, always at work.

Leaving aside all such cases, and bringing these lessons home to the decent classes, we will proceed on the plan that has been founded by the Creator and that bears the divine stamp in every part of its wonderful workings. The first step in this plan is the power that comes over a young man or young woman at that period when they are swayed by the developing sex-growth within themselves. Up to the age of puberty, they are making their bodies; and after that early age is passed, just as they are embarked in the second line of life's journey, they are conscious of a revolution going on within them. It is not best then that they be separated, for the society of the man is handsome, he has a good stock in trade for most girls. If the girl is sweet and beautiful, she has her stock in trade likewise. The fortunes of men buy beauties, and the fortunes of women buy handsome men. If their holdings are great enough to have a foreign commercial value, women are able to buy titles. Not all the disasters to the past international marriages of this character can deter the next ten thousand rich girls of America from buying more foreign titles.

As a general rule, to which the exceptions are few and far between, there is no happiness in the exchange of money for beauty, or money for handsome looks, or money for titles. When Sex Magnetism is lacking, there is absolutely nothing to hold the contracting parties to a state of bliss. When this power is present, there is no counter influence short of death that can separate them.

In order to understand that peculiar power that is known as Sex Magnetism, its first primitive work must be seen, and that is the tendencies it creates in the boy's mind and in the girl's mind when it first affects them. It is, as has been just stated, primitive; but it is a power. It is Sex Magnetism in embryo. It is not a dream, for it is real; but it sets in motion many dreams and creates many fancies.

Its first object is not its permanent love. The fledgling is merely trying its wings.

If the world could seize upon and hold that better impulse that is born with such power, all would be well. The hard knocks of fortune, the struggles to keep body and soul alive, the attacks of disease, the results of bad diet and worse cooking, and the vicissitudes that confront the young man and the young woman aside from the strange visitation at this period of life, all work against its development. So there comes the interim in which the character drifts down stream.

Later on where there is a new stirring of the causes that arouse an interest in the opposite sex, and when the time of fulfilment is nearer in view, the same power renews its work. Loves comes with force then and may abide. Now is the one great opportunity to build well and wisely. Left to themselves the young couple would take on the physical condition of union and all the better forces would be lost. In nature the man must meet competitors, and the woman must have rivals. To overcome these, the man will prove his superiority, and the woman her greater charms. Again the fittest survive. Weaklings and scraggy women are lost sight of in the onward march of progress. But in the conditions of modern civilization, genuine Sex Magnetism is necessary in the making of a correct choice, and in the retaining of the union during a life time.

This subtle force begins as an instinctive influence; then comes the interim of commonplace significance; and again arises the power of attraction and love.

If you can tell what it is in either sex that makes the mind seek to devise methods by which the other party may be attracted, you can get an insight into what Sex Magnetism is. The old man woos with his statement of assets and liabilities; as the sex feeling is lost or weakened. "I have money, and I have real estate," he says. The girl has read in novels that it is better to be an old man's darling than a young man's slave, and so she may be drawn by the commercial offering. But it is not magnetism, and there is no happiness in store for either of them. He will be restless and discontented, and she will be waiting for the kind promise of nature to take back its own.

In middle life the man measures up the faculties of his betrothed, if she is about his age; or he estimates how much happiness youth and perhaps beauty can give him. It requires much more Sex Magnetism and of a different kind to cement two such persons together in a bond that will not break at the first shock. Such marriages have held, but only when the magnetism is of the most positive kind, as will be seen in the later departments of this book.

The best magnetism is in that period of life when the man is between twenty-five and forty years of age; and the woman is between twenty and thirty-five. The foundation of Sex Magnetism is more vital in those periods; and, once laid and laid well, it should survive until the last trumpet has sounded. If it has taken hold of the life of a man between the ages of twenty-five and forty, and of a woman between the ages of twenty and thirty-five, and is genuine Sex Magnetism, it will endure forever. Marriages may have begun before those ages, or after them; but the power once alive at or about such periods is the genuine attractive force of Sex Magnetism. When there is a real bonding of two lives earlier or later, it depends on two other kinds of Sex Magnetism, apart from the natural instinct that has been provided by the Creator for the happiness of the world. All these matters will be taught in their turn in this book.

Enough has already been said herein to show that the purpose of nature in setting up this power instinctively is to make the two sexes attractive to each other; but, as they are not created solely or chiefly to reproduce the race, there must be a still deeper purpose; and that is found in the small but effectual improvement in the personal conduct of each as long as the sex power sways them.

The interim between the first fancy of the boy for the girl, and the girl for the boy, is attended by a falling away from the reach of this influence, and it is at this time that the practical character is forming, for good or for bad. The sooner the young man returns to his appreciation of the opposite sex, the sooner will he, if normal, lay the foundation of a substantial ambition which will have for its object two things:

1. The means whereby he may be able to provide for a wife.

2. The improvement in his personality whereby he may be able to attract the girl he cares for.

It has happened in countless thousands of instances that, where a young man has been absorbed in some young woman whom he has not won, he has made the best out of himself. The law of the "survival of the fittest" is at work in his veins and he does not know it. Nature is teaching him refinement, which is civilization. She is teaching him to add to his attracting qualities, to add to his mental calibre, to add to his moral worth, and to make himself a better man in every respect; all of which are steps in the civilizing of the race.

The young man who does not make rapid love is the most in earnest. If true to instinct he will be several years finding the words with which to state his proposal. In the mean time the girl, if she is true to instinct, will not make herself common property for anyone who may seek her smiles. She will not be forward, but will be patient and let nature work in her the definite knowledge that she most desires to possess, the understanding of her own heart.

He may hear her say that she admires an athletic young man. He will not allow her to guess that he has heard and felt the wish; but he will begin the next day to build up the muscles of his body. Or she may have said that she liked an intelligent man; and he will devote himself to mental improvement. Or she may have said that she appreciates one who can rise in business and become a successful man. All his thoughts and all his energies forthwith will be put into that one line of advancement.

These things have been said by girls to young men, and they have borne their good fruit in abundance.

Now why is it that, after a woman has accepted a man and he is apparently sure of her love and loyalty, he loses much of his ambition, and becomes gradually indifferent to his conduct and personal power to attract her? The reason is that he has won her and supposes that she will not discard him after once accepting his offer of marriage. Another reason is, in some cases, that the responsibilities and expenses of the approaching marriage are more than he is able to cope with. He wishes he were out of the engagement. On him comes the burden of earning the support of two, and the cost of a home; when he has never been able to do much more than support himself. He even fears that there may be three to support, and relatives, visitors and friends to share his hospitality with him; perhaps doctors, nurses and other attaches; or what if his wife should desire a servant? These are fearful thoughts for a young man who has hardly laid aside a dollar a week in the past.

If he becomes indifferent to his engagement, the result is a lapse back to the cruder days when he was careless in his attire, in his manners, and in his ambition. It would have been far better for him to have delayed the proposal.

The wisest woman is she who prefers to hold her answer back for years rather than plunge into an engagement that may be broken, or into a marriage that cannot endure. Love is not a guide to action of this kind. Love has no standing in the practical part of the transaction. If love were a real thing, it would survive the disasters and storms of wedlock. But it is draggled in the sea and is laughed at when the end comes. The man who is ardently loved today may tomorrow invite hatred from the lips he kissed tonight. It is an easy step from the better to the harder condition; and an almost impossible step from hate to affection. Such is human nature. The blow that wounds the tree may not kill it, and may be forgotten in the healing process that follows; but the scar is there to show where it fell. There is but one cog when love turns to hate, and it slips into it as readily as the ball rolls off the icy cliff; but there is no cog that can be adjusted to bring back the wheel of life and shift hate into love. The change works but one way.

Let therefore the girl wait until she is a young woman, and the young woman wait until she is sure of her future, before she makes her reply. As soon as he has won her, after the glow of victory which is attended by vows and promises to himself and to her, he will begin to lose ground. It is the certainty that he has achieved his great purpose of breaking down her doubt or her opposition, that will take away from him the purpose of making himself attractive to her in the grander ways that he otherwise would seek. He may be neat in his dress, but he will gradually drift into careless habits and deficient conduct. His speech and vocabulary will sink to the level of his real character, if he is thrown much in her company. "You are so different from what you were three months ago," she may say to him.—"Then you do not love me now?"—"Oh, yes, I do; but I wish you were just the same as you were before we were engaged."—"What ways have I become different?"—"I cannot tell. There is something that is not the same."—"Then you are tiring of me."—"No, I am not."—There the conversation on that subject ends. But there is the turning point in the lives of both of them. It is the first chiding, gentle and without malice; but direct and full of meaning.

It would be much better for both of them if there could be a drifting back to former conditions. The young man probably has love for her, such as love is under the circumstances; but the keen edge has gone from his ambition to make himself attractive except in the few outward ways that are prompted by common decency. The thing to do is to break the engagement and continue the friendship. This can be done without taking up a life of flirtation, such as girls and young men like to if they are made free from the irksome bonds of betrothal. As long as they have a genuine appreciation of each other, they should be close friends, but no more until times change for the better in their personal history.

We are constantly going back to the primeval forest when

the law of the survival of the fittest was shaping the destiny of the species. The birds were wooing and waiting. The best male won the best female; and this occurred in practically every instance, so exact was that law.

After the winning was accomplished there came the steady onward moving of the law, for the best was not assumed. Birds are less scheming than human beings. Many a girl never drops her slack habits until she thinks some young man admires her. Then she has both her Sunday attire and her Sunday voice for him; while she may have commonplaces for her brother, her father and her mother. The better conduct is assumed and unreal in ninety-nine cases out of every hundred; yet there is an influence going on for improvement in both sexes as long as there is doubt as to the decision. To assume a habit that is better than you are naturally addicted to, will in time raise your real character toward that habit. Most men are boors by nature. When left to themselves they drift down the stream in all sorts of bad ways. There is no power on earth that can refine them but the desired love of a woman who has come within the radius of their attention.

This law of human nature is well established.

There are countless thousands of instances being enacted every day in the year where young men make themselves appear better in dress and manners for the sake of un-won sweethearts, than they would otherwise appear before their own families or friends. Girls likewise are cured or partly cured of their boorish habits by the same nature. Here is a rather pretty face, but there is chewing gum in the mouth and slang on the lips most of the time. Those lips some young man would have the right to kiss for a time; and that mouth he hopes some day will say "yes" to his proposal. An indescribable feeling of joy comes to him when he gazes for the first time on lips and mouth; but, some morning when he is passing the house and, unobserved, sees the cheek bulging with a wad of chewing gum, and hears the lips utter the slang of the bowery or young ladies' seminary, he shrinks from the prospect that awaits him. She catches a glimpse of his form disappearing in the distance and wonders if he saw and heard. In tears she finds her mother, who soothes her and advises her to drop the cheap and boorish habits. This she does. He calls as usual, and she tries to find out what he knows; but he is silent. He is not the same. Then she frankly admits the fault, declares that she will never again use slang or chew gum; and this promise she keeps for many days after they are engaged. Her mother warns her that she has gone back into the old habits; but she is armed with the reply, "What difference can it make now? Harold and I are engaged." Surely it could not make any difference, as it seemed to her, but the marriage never came. He was too shrewd to be caught by an assumed refinement.

Yet had the engagement been kept in abeyance for a few years, the effect on her nature would probably have been permanent. It is a fixed law that an assumed virtue or good habit will in time make a real character. Some people find fault because so many persons go to church and become members, who are not sincere. It is true they are hypocrites and that they do not seek religion for the spiritual good it will do them; but for social or commercial ends. Yet the very hypocrisy they are practicing at the start, if continued long enough, will form a new character. Assume a virtue if you have it not, is an old bit of advice that bears more good fruit than bad.

The laughable thing about love is the assumption of all the better traits by both sexes. This influence begins its work in the teens as soon as love gets its start; but, if there is no betrothal then, and the parties drift wide apart, they will, in other affiliations, put in practice the same law. A young man who fell violently in love when he was sixteen, and who was rejected, became the object of much ridicule because of his shoddy appearance soon after and his careless conduct for several years. Yet when he was twenty-five he again fell in love; this time with a different kind of woman; and she held him back for six more years, during which time he became a gentleman to all appearances and piled on good manners galore, good clothes, and refined speech. So strong was the control she held over him, and so well did she keep his wooing adjusted between doubt and the prospect of success, that he had time enough to actually re-mold his whole character. His earning capacity was increased, and his genuine ability was enhanced in every way. This case is a typical one of its class. The reason why the class is limited is because most girls bite at the first bait, and the wooing is over. The true girl and real woman will be wooed most of the time; the actual winning being held back to the very last day possible and not break the fish line.

It is in this progress of uncertainty that the world has made all its progress toward civilization. The statement seems strong, and it has been challenged thousands of times as being untrue; but the ablest minds that have at first doubted the accuracy of the conclusion have, after thorough examination and analysis, been convinced of the remarkable truth held in the assertion.

There is reason for it.

The most important fact in life is the existence of the two sexes. No one doubts that. Such a form of creation was not made solely or chiefly for reproducing the race; for it would be much more economical in nature to have mono-sex beings.

The next most important fact in life is the understanding that brings two human beings together. This has thus far in the history of mankind consisted in the wooing and the winning of the other sex. In the human species the male does the wooing when civilized; otherwise the female attends to it. In the brute creation the female makes the desire known that she wishes a mate, and generally adopts tactics of a demandatory kind to bring about the consummation.

In the savage epochs the female was a mere slave. She was either captured, or else subdued by a blow on the head that rendered her unconscious until the ceremony was performed. In survival of the fittest, both of physical supremacy and superior animal cunning, the savages paved the way to civilization.

When woman was fit to be wooed, a change of method was ordained by nature. The physical prowess no longer makes the standard of choice. Neither is the intellectual woman to be preferred. By intellectual is meant one who has acquired knowledge from school books. She is often, if not generally, unprepared for the duties of the household, which is the kingdom where woman reigns supreme, and of which she ought to be proud to be queen. The wife is she who has a large fund of common sense, excellent judgment and a practical touch with life itself. To these qualities let her add Sex Magnetism, and her place as well as her happiness will be secure for a long and honorable career.

But the fact that is most interesting is the power exerted

over a whole species, through many individuals, in that interim between the first attentions and the final agreement to accept each other. It is now a well-proved conclusion that civilization owes its progress to the attempt of two persons of opposite sex to attract each other through their own efforts at personal improvement.

It has been shown that this improvement takes place primarily in personal appearance, as in the plumage of birds. Then it takes place in personal conduct. Finally it takes place in personal betterment as in the increase of mental, physical, and earning powers. There is not the slightest doubt as to the correctness of these assertions. Being true, it is due to the race that advantage be taken of the law that underlies such facts.

The woman or girl who accepts the love of a man too readily blocks to some extent the progress of that man. There is no reason why she should accept it until she is certain that marriage is near at hand as a probability, and that marriage ought to take place. "My daughter is eighteen. She is going to be married next autumn," said a mother.—"But ought she to be married so young to that man?" The mother thought it was all right, as she expressed it; but secretly did not want her daughter to grow up to be an old maid, and she took pride in thinking that the girl was popular. Another secret wish of her heart was that the young man would be of help to the family, as the father was not earning much at that time. So the wedding took place, the young man was unable to support his wife and himself, a child was born, debts flooded the parental cottage and the end was the return of the daughter to her parents with the child, and the separation of the couple. The husband drifted away to the West and has not been heard from. There are half a million young couples today situated almost exactly in the same way, and conditions favor the increase of this number.

The man was unable to make himself a power in the world; the burden was more than he could carry and he did the best thing he could when he gave up the fight; and a life is wrecked in the West, while shame and misery fill the parental home in the East. This case is a common one.

Parents are to blame if they hasten marriage. Waiting has its advantages to all parties concerned; to the young people and to their families. In fact the longer they wait, the better will be their chances for a successful marriage in after years. Very few if any long courtships have ended in separation, either by law or in private. The census is not complete in our own records; but of a list of six thousand cases of marriage after five years of courtship, we cannot find one case of separation by divorce; and only four cases of disagreement and falling apart from quarrels. This is a most remarkable fact.

It seems that all causes and influences conspire together to teach the advantages of long courtship. But there is the much more potent fact that, as long as the female can be wooed and keep her lover anxious for her approval, so long can she exert the most powerful of all influences, his progress in every direction. The sum total of such cases is the advancement of civilization. A woman therefore has it in her hands to make herself the greatest of all powers in human history.

A volume of ten thousand pages might be written to sustain the tremendous value of this one teaching.

It is true that, if a young man knows he is being held back by the desire to keep him in line of progress, he might rebel at such treatment. Let him rebel. It is better to make a failure of the wooing than of the marriage. But the woman who has possession of this course of study, if she is fit to handle so great a problem, will have sense enough to keep the volume and the facts from him. Two persons who are not man and wife should not study this course, for one is sure to hold suspicion against the other. After marriage, both husband and wife and all young persons old enough to understand what is taught, should study together, or in common.

Parents owe a duty to their daughters to tell them the necessity of exerting a better power over some young man than has ever before been exerted over him. To do good in the world is important. Charity is not the best good, for it mends broken ware. Prevention is far superior to charity. Both have their place; but prevention makes charity unnecessary. Which do you prefer: to heal the diseased lungs, or to keep the lungs from being diseased? To ameliorate the condition and suffering of the divorced woman, or to show her the way to a happy and permanent marriage?

In addition to these advantages, there is the grander fact

that all progress toward civilization is the sum total of the countless cases where women have been the cause of men making themselves more attractive and more manly; and the latter have exerted a counter influence on women. It is not a one-sided power. Many a man by preparing too soon has caused his fiance to become lax in her habits and weak in her resolution to improve herself.

But the question may be asked, Is that Sex Magnetism?

It is one of the aids to it. It is not the secret itself. It is one of those qualities that cannot be omitted if Sex Magnetism is to hold sway. The soil in which the rose vine grows is not the rose vine itself, nor is the vine the flower. One thing is necessary to another. There must be a place for a garden; soil in the garden, nutrition in the soil, the vine in the ground, growth and a fine condition in the vine, and finally the flower comes. So with Sex Magnetism. It must have all the aids that any power requires in its operations. No agency for success stands alone. The electric current runs along the wires, the wires extend from place to place, and the instruments generate and direct the power, while there is a use for it in some established methods of adoption, or it runs to waste.

The great dividing line between the anxiety to know the mind of the other sex, and the reception of that knowledge, makes two hemispheres of the sexual history. In one there is doubt, eagerness, desire for success, and the constant improvement that will increase the attractions that are calculated to win. When a man in that interim will not better himself, his body, his apparel, his mind, and his usefulness in life, then the woman makes the saddest of all mistakes to venture on the unknown sea in the same lifeboat with him. If his improvement ceases before he has received his answer then it will fall flat and dead after marriage. The same is true of the woman. If she, before the proposal, and while she is anxious, neglects to maintain a constant improvement, then she will be a dead weight to him as a companion. There will be no success in the marriage. This is certain.

It is the bounden duty of each sex when the matter is pending thus, to know what the other party is doing. The rules are nature's laws, and may be briefly stated:

1. The man should not propose until he is close to that

condition that will make marriage possible; that is, he must be prepared for all its conditions before he proposes.

2. The woman should not accept or even encourage too much the addresses of the man until a successful marriage is possible in a very short time after the acceptance. The betrothal then marriage, or the parties may drift wide apart.

3. Before the man proposes and after he has shown an interest in the woman, he should ascertain to a certainty if she is seeking to improve herself in order that she may be the more attractive and the better assistant to him in case of marriage. If she is doing nothing in this line, then she either does not care for him or is not worth his caring for her. This test is infallible.

4. Before the woman accepts the man and after she has shown an interest in him, she should ascertain to a certainty if he is seeking to improve himself in order that he may be better prepared for the vicissitudes of marriage and that he may be the more attractive to her. If he is doing nothing in this line, then he either does not care for her or is not worth her caring for him. This rule is certain and never failing. It is the safe way of knowing what to expect in after life when it is too late to avert disaster and suffering.

Most courtships and weddings are artificial.

They are cut-and-dried affairs, being steered by old women who love to pose as match-makers. Such marriages end badly for the most part, and the old women do not care then. They have fired the train of misery and seek no excuse.

On the other hand the liberal freedom with which girls and young men meet, court, are accepted, and deliver themselves over to each other, is as wrong as anything can be. "I have faith in my daughter and she is old enough to look out for herself," says the mother, and she does not know nor does she care to know that her assertion is the most stupid of all the things that emanate from her mind. She cannot be cured of it, for it is part of her mental calibre. But there are mothers who know better. They know that daughters should not be delivered over to their young lovers forthwith there is an attachment between the two. If they do not want to know, then they do not want to know that there in the city of New York, two hundred and fifty thousand daughters in one profession, the first of all professions, as old as the race itself. Nor do they know, what all doctors well understand, that the average of pure girls at the time of their marriage, not including the foregoing profession, is less than nine in a hundred; meaning that ninety-one in every hundred girls not in the profession are, when they are married, or reach the age of twenty, if unmarried, what they ought not to be. This is the product of that loose system that permits girls to deliver themselves over to the men who court them or show them attention.

This fault must be remedied before there can be the holding back of the will in courtship; for the man who can go beyond wooing will stop wooing.

The girl who is left alone with the man, as is the custom in the families of boors in America, regardless of social or financial rank, can never employ such an agency as Sex Magnetism, unless she is able to put into execution the greatest of all human laws:

Deliver over to the man neither your acceptance of his proposal nor your own self in the body, until that hour when holy marriage may be at hand.

Let the ceremony come first.

An expert analyst of the conditions that make divorce so common and estrangement after marriage so much more frequent than ever before, says: "The one underlying fault is the freedom with which the two sexes meet each other and accept each other. There is unpreparedness in every way."

Of course where this book enters the life of a couple already married, its work will proceed along different lines. There is no wooing then, and the direct uses of Sex Magnetism will be necessary. Then, more than at any other time, will this power be needed. At the present consideration the following plan of procedure is set forth:—

1. All betrothals should be delayed as long as possible, or not permitted until actually necessary.

2. Marriage should be delayed as long as possible.

3. Improperly made engagements, as shown under the tests thus far stated, should be broken forthwith.

4. Where marriage has taken place and there has been a separation, but no divorce, the parties should be brought together by the powers of Sex Magnetism.

5. In marriages where the parties are living together, but with a dislike for each other, all the powers of this magnetism should be employed to bring about a liking for each other.

6. In all marriages where there is not peace and harmony, Sex Magnetism should be employed to maintain such conditions and increase, if possible, the happiness of both.

7. In the case of every man or woman not engaged who desires to be married, this power should be employed to bring about such an end.

8. In the case of every man and woman who is not married, or who has been married and death has taken away the partner, and who will never enter the bonds of matrimony in the future, there is a distinct calling and a full measure of happiness as shown in the present course of study. For them there is a place in nature and in the world. They are not separated from the sex relationship merely because they are apart.

While the one foundation law of progress has been given much attention in this opening department, it is not the real work itself. It simply shows the special design that is behind all sex distinctions and all sex affiliations. It is one of many influences that are at work in this connection.

Mere improvement is not enough. It is not sufficient that a man makes himself a better man and a woman rises higher in her standards under the power of the sex attractions. These are the purposes of nature in making two sexes; and a deeper purpose is that of the unfolding of intricate lines of happiness and bliss in a state of harmony between the opposite sexes.

Nature has decreed one man for one woman. This law of nature cannot wisely be violated.

In the brute creation this law may or may not be obeyed; it follows an instinct that animals obey. In the savage state, this law is sometimes obeyed, sometimes reversed, and often held of no consequence. But we are dealing with a chosen age and a chosen people: the fruits of a true civilization. What belongs to beasts will make a man beastly. What belongs to savages will make a man savage. What belongs to a high ethical standard will make a man noble and estimable.

FIRST TESTS OF TEMPERAMENTAL UNFITNESS.

It is the most important of all things in this world to prevent marriages that are sure to bring unhappiness. The results follow in the children, and no doubt lead to countless miseries that might easily be averted if even so small a step as the first tests were taken during the period preceding and following the engagement. There is a subtle law at work, and it may be read without fail in the following rules:

Rule 1.—If, prior to the engagement, and after the parties show an interest in each other, there is a personal improvement mentally, physically and ethically in which both participate, it is well; but, whichever party fails to make such improvement, is not suited to the other.

Rule 2.—If, in the days of the immediate engagement, such improvement halts in either party, there should be an end of the betrothal.

Rule 3.—If, after the period of the engagement and prior to the marriage there is a long lapse of time, say not less than two years, and either party ceases to maintain improvement mentally, morally and physically, there is temperamental unfitness, and the marriage should never take place. Perfect attraction is sure to sustain an unflagging interest.

It makes no difference how good a "catch" either party may be, the parent or the persons involved who would insist on the consummation of the contract, thinking that after the knot is tied the parties cannot help themselves, will find the results far more disastrous than the broken engagement.

Which is more to be deplored, a disappointed love affair, or a wretched marriage?

BASIC LAWS

ALL LIFE is controlled by laws. If the laws are not made by man, they are established by nature or by a higher power from which nature derives its existence. To be lawless is to be out of the universe. Before birth, the processes by which life is brought into being are fixed and unalterable. During the span of human existence, there are physical, moral and ethical laws at work, the adoption or rejection of which make harmony or penalties that all the while attend the passing on from the first to the last mystery of the epoch. When death comes, other laws take the body and send it back to nature.

When man undertakes to make laws for the world in which he lives, he either expresses in his own words the truths that have always existed or else he seeks to shift the work of nature from a wild activity to a lesser form of energy. Thus the human body, left to the common embrace of earth, would soon be dissolved; but man tries to hold its dissolution in abeyance for centuries by preservatives and close sealing. He merely delays what is inevitable. In everyday life, foods are perishable; but they may be kept in safety for years under shifted uses of the same laws of decay.

The most erratic and the wildest of all forces that play between the sun and its planets, is the unknown but ever-present power of electricity. Left to itself it is not only useless to man but is a source of danger. It is unknown because human intelligence has never been able to understand of what it is composed or whence its origin. By the operation of natural laws it leaps from one conductor to another, seeking temporary rest, only to be hurled out again by some new excitement. Yet man has studied some of the laws which govern it, and he is now preparing to use it as his companion. He makes no new laws, but gives old ones a new occupation. He knows what may be expected of it in varieties of activity; and, as a result, there are many laws now relating to it that were not known a few years ago.

Everything proceeds under some law.

So unstable a thing as human conduct would seem to be exempt from government; especially such government as man writes in his moral and penal codes; but there is no escape from the fixed plan of nature.

The body is physical. It has free rein in nearly all its activities and enjoys personal liberty, but it pays some penalty for every infringement of the laws of health. Under the hard usage of the wear and tear of freedom, the body lasts less than three score and ten years on an average. When a man comes to die at that age, he feels that he has lived long; and he does not know or believe that he is paying the penalty of continual personal liberty. As it is a well proved fact that the body is intended by nature to last for 120 years, and to maintain all its faculties whole and strong for more than nine-tenths of that time, the willingness to give up life earlier is only evidence of the indifference of the human mind in the matter.

Poverty is the natural penalty of similar indifference. For every hour of pinching want there are in the background more than a hundred violations of the laws of living. To use more than you need is waste. To want what you do not need is waste. Most people do not need eighty per cent of what they want. This law applies to every phase of living. When your means are such that you can have more than you need, and all you want, then you must make friends with the future and lay aside a sinking fund on that account. In the meantime, live within your present and future income, if that is possible. Of all the inmates of the poorhouses and similar institutions, fully ninety per cent. are there because they were indifferent to the laws above stated. Poverty is a crime, not against the laws of man, but against the laws of nature.

On the other hand, the man who is sure of maintenance for himself and those he should take care of, and who knows that he has an excess of wealth, should spend it freely until the excess has been used in giving employment to honest workers of good habits. The man who builds a beautiful home and splendid gardens, is the greatest of all human benefactors, if he employs only worthy labor; but if he gets results by distributing in the form of wages his excess wealth among the classes that drink and carouse, he is exchanging honor for filth. It is the duty of every employer to know that he does not pay the bills of debauchery.

There would be more happiness in the world if this law were observed. There would be more happiness in the world if those who cannot afford all they want, would learn the lesson that they can get along with about twenty per cent. of what they desire. The earning capacity of the world, if divided according to its total average, will not bring to humanity any more than they all need; and if one gets more, others must take less.

Once money was almost wholly unknown among the happy classes. Today there are parts of Vermont where money is hardly ever seen. One wealthy woman told the author that she had spent ten cents during the past year. It came to her in the form of a silver dime, and altogether by accident; its presence made her uneasy, and so she spent it. Yet she had a very large house, always comfortable and warm; ample furniture, plenty of clothes for herself, her children and grandchildren; milk, butter, cream, eggs, flour, wood, maple sugar, grain, poultry, turkeys, beef, lamb, pork, pure water, pure air, horses and carriages, and conveniences of every kind, more than ample for her wants; and she was happy, supremely happy, in the enjoyment of these comforts and luxuries. She had books, music, a piano, and other evidences. She said she exchanged in one year two thousand pounds of butter for the piano delivered at her door free of all cost.

She possessed the temperament for living successfully in the country. Most people do not possess this temperament; and they are abject failures there and elsewhere. The country and the country alone produces the great men of all time and all nations. To challenge this law is to fly in the face of nature; like the giant who thought himself mightier than the electric current that killed him when he grasped it.

Most people do not employ their full earning capacity.

Most people do not save what they earn over and above their actual needs.

FIRST BASIC LAW

The total earning capacity of the world is equal to the total actual needs of humanity.

By earning capacity is meant the ability to secure from nature enough to provide clothing, shelter, food and enjoyment during the entire period of life. It is a law of nature that there should be no excess. If one person wins too much in his case, some other person fails to that extent. It is for this reason that freedom and personal liberty are allowed the race, and that those who squander their health, their faculties, their substance, their powers, their time, and their possessions, should be marked by the grimy hand of poverty; be felled by disease; or reap the unrest of discontent. But he who is willing to follow the law is justified in winning all the excess he may, provided he observes the next command.

SECOND BASIC LAW

All persons should study their actual needs and reduce their expenditures to their level until they acquire an excess.

The application of these Basic Laws to the cultivation of Sex Magnetism will be shown as we proceed. It is enough at this stage of the study to make the laws themselves clear and easy to comprehend.

The excess referred to is not that of money so much as property. Money is helpful for what it buys, not in itself. For centuries there were generations of people living in luxury who had no money and saw no money. When they became old and feeble, they lived on in the same enjoyment of their property and its annual yield; and they had no need of laying aside a bank account for a rainy day, as the saying goes. Money laid aside is not useful unless you have somewhere to spend it and convert it into necessaries and comforts in time of want. An old man, spending his life's savings among strangers or away from home, is a sorry sight. He becomes the victim of every scheme and caprice that can be employed against him. The accumulation of property and comforts, of place and companionship, of love and home, are better than the mere laying aside of funds to meet the distress of fading life. From the day when first the hands begin to earn something, down through all the years of earthly existence, there should be one theme for every man and woman; starting in boyhood and girlhood, and never ceasing to hold the center of attention; and that theme should be the acquisition of a home; a real home; a home with land on four sides of it; a home with light on four sides of it; a home with air on four sides of it; a home with growing nature on four sides of it; a home where children may some day be born, and rise up into the next generation to care for and protect those who made this abode possible. That is the best sinking fund against a "rainy day." To own a home is the greatest goal of all human ambitions. It wonderfully reduces expenses. There are no rents to pay. If the house is in harmony with the earning power of the owner, the taxes will not be one per cent. of that capacity, and so will be practically nothing.

Under the Second Basic Law every boy and girl, every young man and young woman, every mature person just beginning to obey the rules of nature, will soon find an excess coming. Let its first uses be towards a home. Never mind if you do not need the home. Never mind if you think you will never need the home. Go ahead and get it.

Do not seek a large house. This is a mistake. One room is better than none; two rooms are better than none; three rooms are better than none. Many a family lives in a one-room house today; many a family began married life in a one-room house, and did not graduate from it until the excess amply warranted. Of all those who began married life with houses larger than they can afford, ninety-seven per cent. were driven from them by creditors. Which is better: to stay pride and adopt the laws of life; or set a pace that will bring ruin in its path?

Marriage should not be tolerated until there is a home in which both parties are willing to live. If the woman is proud and desirous of showing her schoolgirl friends that she is rising in the world when she becomes a wife, then she will become a drag to her husband and the marriage will fail. Better a separation before the ceremony than after. True marriage is an outward voyage, not an ascent, and should not be a descent in fact. The seas are level. They may be rough with billows that rise and fall; but their average is on the level.

The breaking of the Second Basic Law is the most prolific cause of the awful awakening that follows the weddings of to-day. The young man who has made himself appear well-to-do, owes for his clothes that have helped him to win the wife; and the latter, using the squeezed pocketbook of a hard working father, has dressed in her butterfly apparel, only to confess to the burdened groom that he must in the future provide such things for her, as she is now his lawful wife. There are days and weeks of silent weeping. There are menacing misgivings in the husband's mind as he tries to extricate his mind from the abyss into which it has been plunged a tangled mass of thought. Why did he marry? He asks this question a thousand times, but never answers it. They struggle along for a while. Others assist in supporting them. The same clothes are worn throughout the year. The expenses are more than he can bear. They fall in debt. Then the end comes. It may take years to find the first stepping-stone in a pair of lives that began wrong. Had they started right, every part of the journey of effort would have been filled with a happy ambition.

To those who are not yet married, we say, Go back to the Second Basic Law. To those who are married and cannot sustain the cost, we say, Go back to the Second Basic Law.

What is that Law?

It tells you that you should reduce your expenditures to the level of your actual needs until you begin to accumulate an excess. There are many things you have that you do not actually need. Keep them if possible, but do not add to them. Your food bill costs you three times what it should, as may be ascertained by membership in the Ralston Health Club. Your clothing is above your actual financial rank. If you dress for comfort and health, that is enough; but if you must please your neighbors, then the penalty will be pinching want. If you cannot pay for more than one room, take that. If the locality is too costly, go farther out. The walk will not hurt you, for walking is the one best means of physical health. Come down, come down, come down, all the time, until you reach that level where you can live within your income.

It is a wonderful fact, how few things you really need in

this world. Take the view of the philosopher, and throw off the influences that set your mind in other beliefs. If you are swayed by the taunts of your friends or acquaintances, you will always remain their slave. You need very few things. You have now more than you really have use for. Get to your level as soon as possible.

The age is living too fast. The race is living too fast. The conditions of marriage are mostly intolerable on this account. There was never a period in the history of humanity when marriage was so weak a bond, and when the sexes are drifting apart so easily and in such numbers as now. Fifty years ago, they sundered by tens and scores, and created a sensation each time. Today they sunder by thousands and are always on the expectant list. There is a radical wrong somewhere, and it is not difficult to discover it: the age is living far above its means. Men in the lower ranks, men in middle ranks, and men of means, all find marriage too expensive for them; and the rich are unfitted for marriage in proportion as they idle away their days and nights in useless waste of time and substances.

It is needless to talk of remedies.

History repeats itself, and the same story of the physical revolutions that have been enacted in the past will always be told as long as the earth is what it is.

To attempt to improve mankind as a whole, is wasted effort. Only stern necessity drives people to their senses, and they remain there just as long as the stern necessity abides. Then they drift with the stream that is easiest.

But there are a few persons, perhaps one in a hundred or a thousand, who wish to know and better understand the laws that are working changes in the conditions of living; and it is to them that this course of training is directed.

Every man and woman sheds some influence that is sure to help those whom they hold most dear. Such an influence may be sent forth by parents who will teach the following facts and principles to their children:

1. It is not good for one sex to be alone in mature life; but it is better to be alone than be together in a dismal failure.

2. Man needs woman, and woman needs man; but only

under conditions that can result in happiness and a successful life for both.

3. The greatest magnet that can draw man and woman together and permanently hold them, is true home life. There must be a home, one that is owned by both, and it must be made the central theme of interest to both from the first thoughts of union until the last breath of life is taken.

4. Boys and girls, and young men and women should be made to think of the acquisition of a home as the foremost thing to live for. All other ambitions should be secondary to this.

It is never too early to begin these teachings. They will bear sure fruit as the years come on. Let it be understood that it is far more honorable to own a home all free from debt, than to win laurels in any profession. There should be sermons on the importance of owning a place that can be called home. Renting, or living in part of a building, is not and never can be the magnetic attraction that is to cement two lives together.

These doctrines have been taught in private for thirty years. Parents who then were associated with our classes in the study of magnetism as a power to better human life, were induced to make a trial of these influences over their children at the age that was most pliable; and more than two thousand were thus brought under this law. What was the result?

Take a typical case:

A boy not over ten years old was often asked what he was to become when he grew up to be a man. He had only a vague idea of his future. His mother and father had told him that he should be the proud owner of a home of his own, even if it had but two rooms. This idea was kept before him as often as necessary to fix it in his mind; and the boy talked of having a home some day, and of its size and shape, and what it would contain as well as the gardens that would surround it. He drew plans of several that suited his fancy. He observed the cottages that he passed, noted how they were built and had something to say about them. When he earned a small sum of money, he laid it away for his home As he entered into the years of youth he found the subject still more interesting. Opportunity came frequently to lay aside money for the coming home, and he eventually had a goodly sum that otherwise would have been wasted. He did in fact own a small cottage when he was twenty-one, and in this he placed a girl wife that has since grown to maturity with him; and their small home has passed into other hands, while they have come to a grander residence.

This is a typical case.

It was repeated in nearly every instance where the same interest was taken by the parents to impress this one great fact on their children.

Never has there been a divorce or marriage separation among the parents or children of those families. When the love of home and the ambition to own one shall have been instilled in the minds of the young, then a magnetic power begins to draw the sexes together, and will eventually hold them so tightly that nothing but death can part them.

You may say this is very good doctrine for the next generation; but how can it help those who are now old enough to marry or are already married? Let us dispose first of the children. Suppose there are ten thousand families where this course of training enters; and that there are on an average of one child in every ten families; there are then one thousand children into whose minds can be instilled the love of a home and the ambition to own one. Of this number, according to past experiments, fully ninety-nine per cent. will adopt the teachings, and thus there should be given to the world in years to come nearly a thousand marriages that will abide as long as life shall last. What grander work can any one do than that?

Even if only one home can be made happy in the future where otherwise it might be wrecked, some good has been done. True homes produce the truest men and women, the best citizens, and the most exalted nations.

But in the cases of those who are now of marriageable age, the incentive to establish homes is closer at hand. The Second Basic Law must be brought to them in all its meaning and power. It is wise to postpone marriage until both parties to the prospective union are in full harmony with that law; for, if they refuse to be led by it, they will never dwell in content while married.

In the third class, which includes those who are already married, it seems too late to instill the doctrine of home-getting if they are fixed in opposite views; for a wrongly made marriage can never be brought to the basis of a true beginning. It spends as it goes, and gets behind in its expenses rather than ahead. If there remains any desire to reach a better condition, the later laws of Sex Magnetism, as set forth in this book, should be adopted.

No attempt is being made in these studies to urge a restricted plan of living which will bring discomfort or ill health. This statement that most persons want much more than they need, can be readily proved. It is centuries old. There is a minimum condition of necessaries that can be ascertained by careful examination into one's habits and possessions. The mind that cannot perceive that minimum is not qualified to battle with the world.

That minimum is to last only as long as it is required to keep down the expenses that stand in the way of owning a home. When they are met, and when you are able to live within your income, then your wants may be allowed to expand. Things that you do not need may be bought if you can afford them.

What is there wrong in this teaching?

That it will be opposed is assumed at the start. But is there an error in it? What truer law can be laid down than that a person should live within his income? Of course it is possible to live within an income, and save nothing. Here the opposition will make its chief objection; for it will not agree to reduce all the wants to the minimum of actual needs, as too much self-denial is necessary. But the law is a natural one, and will always exist.

Why is a home a bond of magnetism between a man and his wife?

It is part of a woman's hope, if she is normal in mind and heart, to become the queen of a home that is owned either by herself or by her husband; or, better still, by both jointly. She is glad to have a larger dominion than her neighbor; but this is the beginning of her downfall. When a woman wants to shine for the benefit of the neighborhood, or seeks something as good or better than those who see her from day to day, she is breaking one of the best commandments ever given to humanity. There is but one true criterion, and it reads: Your needs are measured by the demands of your life, and by nothing else. Your life demands that you keep your health perfect, and acquire knowledge.

The desire to become the queen of a home is born in every real woman. The glare of false conditions will lessen or extinguish that desire; and the emptiness that follows it is utter misery. No woman can be happy unless she is making a home more attractive every day. In this world money and power do not bring happiness. The most contented classes are in the middle ranks. The rich know very little of actual pleasure. There are flickering moments of triumph when some dress excites the admiration of others, or some dinner advertises the money ability of a host and hostess, or some box at the opera is gay with jewels and gowns; but these moments are followed by sinking spells of abject suffering, only to be lightened by the prospect of the next function. The palatial mansion is not a home to that class. It is too artificial, too much in display, too empty of home affiliations.

On the cheek of some humble woman at work in her two-room cottage is stamped the joy of the wife. In the front room, the couple live in comfort, despite the fact that it is kitchen, dining room, parlor, sitting room, and reception hall; yes, and conservatory, for there at the window two plants shed their radiance of companionship. The other room is the bedroom. It is not much of a house, but it is a bigger home than the palace of the financier. There is more home in that two-room dwelling than can be found in any mansion worth a million dollars. And some day it will be moved aside while a four-room house is going up; which, in its turn, will give way to a ten-room house. The progress of right living is wedge-shaped; it is always widening as it proceeds. But woe unto the person who begins at the big end of the wedge, as many try to do; for the goal is a point.

If a man is able to win a home, no matter how small, he should be careful not to invite to it as his wife a woman who thinks the residence too humble. She belongs to another class. If the man is poor the wife should be poor also. Love may level ranks, but common sense keeps them level. The wife should know just how poor her prospective husband is, before they are married. She should be willing to start at the lowest rung in the ladder of progress and have the satisfaction of knowing, in later years, that she has climbed the whole length clear to the top. Thus the couple will begin aright and on the same plane. When a man is on the lowest rung of the ladder and his wife is one or more rungs higher up, they will not be companions; nor will they pass each other until she takes the fall that is inevitable.

If the home is a magnet of attraction between man and woman, it should precede marriage whenever possible. Sex Magnetism teaches this fact.

If it is to be such a magnet, it must be the center of attraction for both parties. The gravest mistake made by a man is his indifference regarding the ambitions of his wife. What interests one should interest the other. This rule works both ways. The business, profession, or enterprise in which he is engaged should at all times receive the encouragement of the wife; nor should he deny her the full knowledge of all his undertakings. On the other hand the things that the wife takes an interest in should receive the support and cordial attention of the husband. Foremost in her mind and heart, is her home. He should be able to discern with his own eyesight all the things, large and small, that enter into her day's work, especially in the way of adding to or bettering any portion of the house.

The husband who comes and goes from a home as he would from a hotel or boarding house, cannot expect to find his wife contented. The bond of magnetism is lacking. Attraction and control are the two channels by which all magnetism does its work; and they are not sustained by empty influences. The real must at all times confront both parties. If the husband is handsome, that is real, but not alone sufficient. If the wife is beautiful, that is real, but not alone sufficient. A married couple having nothing but good' looks for each other would go hungry, both for food and for the necessaries of existence.

The body must be fed; so must the mind and the heart. When these three receive their nutrition, then magnetism is at its greatest advantage. The mind must be fed by ambition, or a goal for which to live. The heart must be fed by a mutual interest. Home is the basis of all that is most dear in this life. In it are found the sweetest and tenderest relationships. Nothing can take its place. A rented tenement, or house, or room, will never arouse in either man or woman the interest that centers in a home, no matter how small or humble.

A man without an ambition has no magnetism of any kind, and never will possess any until he finds some goal to attract his mind. A woman without an ambition is likewise a floating raft, useless to herself and to her husband in the true sense of the word.

A married couple who have no common interest in anything will never possess magnetism of any kind, and no training can develop results on soil that is a total desert.

These facts should be fully understood. Nothing added to nothing produces nothing. Nothing added to something, adds nothing. Something added to nothing is impossible. The sun is a magnetic force capable of making the garden bloom into beautiful flowers; but if the garden is empty of plants or nutrition, there is no power in the sun that can produce something from nothing. The mightiest influence of all life would thus be wasted. So with magnetism.

The body must be fed and kept whole.

The mind must be fed and kept whole.

The heart must be fed and kept whole.

A man with a well-fed body and an empty mind, like the usual husband in the ranks of the idle rich, is incapable of exerting magnetic control over anybody. The same is true of the woman.

A man with a well-fed body and a full mind, but with an empty heart, is incapable of exerting magnetic control over anybody. Many well-to-do learned men are found in this rank. They are selfish and cold. Some women have good bodies, full minds and empty hearts.

It is the triple combination that lays the basis for magnetism:

A body that is at its best.

A mind that has some ambitions and goal for which it thinks and plans and studies and works.

A heart that has something in which it holds chief interest together with a person of the opposite sex, is well fed, if the matter of interest is worth while. What a man and woman both love, and what they can think of all the time, plan for, and work for, is sure to feed their two hearts; and, if they themselves come together, they are capable of exerting a great degree of magnetism each for the other. But their bodies must be at their best; and their minds should be fed with ambition and a definite goal.

When the sun's rays fall day after day on a flower garden, they feed only the plants and the nutritive earth. Let the plants be ruined bodily, or the earth lack richness, and all the magnetism that nature can extract from the sun will go for nothing. It is effort falling on useless matter.

THE TRIPLE LAW

The human body must be at its best; the human mind must have a definite and permanent ambition; the human heart must possess some life interest in common with a person of the opposite sex; and, when all three of these conditions exist, then Sex Magnetism is possible in the highest degree.

Keep in mind always the flower garden that is brought into beauty and glory by the magnetism of the sun. Remember that the plants must be there and in good physical condition; and that the soil must be nutritive. Remember that the human body may be at a gross disadvantage or at a fair advantage; that the mind may be weak or silly or drifting; and that the heart may be warped by selfishness to such an extent that it is impossible to share its interest in anything with anybody else. These faults are not only serious but fatal to the grand scheme of living. They must be overcome; first by study; and at length by practice of their opposites.

"I love what my husband loves," does not atone. "Love me and you will love my dog," is the price of a silly heart. Many a man has forced himself to love the dog of the woman he desires to marry; and then he awakens to the nausea of it all, after it may be too late.

The thing that is to claim the heart interest of persons of the opposite sex must be large in its meaning, must be of lifelong purpose, and must be capable of constant improvement and betterment. It must be great enough to hold two hearts and two minds and two lives; and a woman's dog can never do that. Nothing less than a home will answer the requirements.

"I want a husband who will love me for myself alone," says the expectant wife. This means that she is to be loved regardless of what she has in mind, in heart, or in her faculties. While book learning is not essential to wifehood, it is never a burden; but, far above book learning, is common sense and good judgment. She herself alone without common sense and good judgment would not be lovable very long. She may be pretty, and even beautiful; but what the man will fall in love with eventually in a beautiful woman or in a homely one, is what she has in addition to herself alone; what she has of sense ánd judgment in her mind, and what she has in her heart. We would a thousand times prefer to be married to a homely woman of the right sort of mind and heart than to a sweet thing with a wrong sort of mind and heart. No woman is long loved for herself alone.

The same is true of the man.

He must be something more than himself. It is true that the possession of wealth takes the place of that something that is added to the man's self, but the best woman likes the mind that battles with the world and wins an ultimate victory, and the heart that is alert in its interest in her daily existence. Wealth is never a substitute for brains, nor for kindness.

THIRD BASIC LAW

Marriage must sooner or later stand face to face with practical life.

It is natural that the maiden in her teens should be a dreamer. In proportion as her prospects are far away, they seem more entrancing; and just as near as they advance toward her, they take on the hard substance of a world full of vicissitudes at every step of the way. It is sweet to dream. The girls who are given the opportunity to grow up to gray-haired age on a mental diet of novels, never awake from their fanciful estimate of life. They have castles, luxuriant gardens, singing brooks, golden fountains, and a kingly suitor always at their feet; and they never know the facts.

The shock is severe to most women after they have passed from the dreamland of hope to the reality of actual wedlock. One by one all the finer things are lost sight of, and the residuum is practical life. This condition should be understood before the betrothal. There are duties in the home and duties out of the home, not one of which can be evaded if the machinery of the new existence is to remain in working order. When the bride discovers these facts she is appalled by the seriousness and the commonplace character of the situation. There should have been a stage of preparation prior to the first steps toward the engagement, so that both parties might have had some definite knowledge of the fate that awaited them.

We have seen that a home in which both husband and wife take an absorbing interest, is a magnet that holds the two sexes together.

We have seen that a mind filled with a lifework, or goal, or ambition, is attractive to the opposite sex, and that a heart having a purpose in common is likewise magnetic in its influence. These are great realities. They have an abiding value.

It is also true that the ability to measure up to the requirements of practical life, is an attractive force that aids in bringing two persons together. Life as it must be lived, and in its most successful form, is practical. It is not ideal, if by that term is meant something beyond the actual facts.

To be ideal is to be right.

To be practical is to be as near right as circumstances permit.

When true success is achieved in life, the ideal and the practical come together and blend into each other.

There are constricting influences that are all the time narrowing one's efforts and checking the progress of ambition; and it is a wise and keen mind that can adjust actual conditions to their assaults.

Such a mind is magnetic. It should be developed in both the husband and the wife. It is the opposite of the silly, weak, aimless, dreaming mind that is unable to combat with the world. To develop it in its best usefulness, both the husband and the wife should study the influences of their own existence and the expenditures compared with the income. The husband should give up all his outside investments as long as there is not enough money to pay bills and lay aside fully ten per cent. for a future home. The largest source of wastfulness is in the personal expenses of the husband. It is true that he could spend as he pleased before marriage, but things are changed since the wedding, and there are two to share the earnings of one. Heroic self-sacrifice is necessary.

The wife should, in aiding at this crucial period, give up all foolish requisitions on the exchequer. She may suffer at the closeness necessary; but times will be harder before they are better if she does not also practice self-denial. The two parties ought to have a perfect understanding, and live up to it. Loyalty at this time will prove a magnet that will hold them together better than bickerings and complaints. A common and mutual budget, showing both sides of the account, and placed daily in writing, is beneficial. When one party begins to deceive the other, then all magnetism flies away, and the rocks are ahead.

The wife has her friends, and her relatives to make suggestions as to the many ways in which to spend money. A strict refusal to let them into her secrets, is her duty to her husband. He has many of his old companions who will want to share some of the old ways with him; but he must possess the mind and will of a man who loves his wife, and so cling wholly to her in preference to all the world. This is being practical, for it is making the best of a bad situation, where every cent has weight, and every dollar is a giant. It is strictly necessary if the marriage is to succeed.

Any advance preparations that are made for the actual conditions that must be confronted, are immensely helpful. The man should try to ascertain if he is able to restrict himself as he will have to do later on; and the woman should practice the same financiering. If the burden is too severe for either to endure, then the wedding should be postponed; for the possibility of adding children to the household is a heavier drain on the income than any other one item.

Practical life requires actual contact with the conditions that must exist. It also requires perfect confidence each with the other. There should be no secrets as between them that relate to the struggle to get along; but there should be absolute secrets from all other persons no matter how closely related they may be. If parents of means wish to help the couple, they will see for themselves what the facts are, unless there is an attempt to live beyond the income, and this show of success that is false, often deters well-to-do relatives from contributing to the little budget. A certain couple set up housekeeping by agreement on a minimum basis, spending as little as possible, and having in view only the bare necessities. Both parties had relatives who could spare liberal amounts to assist them. When the meagre supplies and the very plain meals were in evidence, there were generous contributions from both families. Of these, about ninety per cent. was laid away by agreement; and ten per cent. was at once invested in things for the house. In the course of another Christmas there were more checks with the same result. In the meantime the husband, by attention to business, bettered his own income; and the couple were soon able to own the house which they called home. This was twenty-two years ago; and the family is today in the triumph of their existence. They were loyal each to the other; they had their secrets from all their friends and relatives, but no secrets from each other relating to the conditions of their own affairs. If a man has had anything in the past that he is sorry for, it will only serve to weaken his hold on his wife's affections for him to expose it to her. It is past and it should remain buried. Most young men sow wild oats; let the field stay unharrowed. The real degree of loyalty to her since he has known her, is the only measure by which he is to be estimated. What he was before he knew her, is not always best to disclose. The same is true of her. The chances are that she has had suitors; has been a flirt; may have been engaged; for these are the first steps in the history of most girls who are left to themselves. If there is any fact to conceal from the world in that past of hers, let it be kept concealed from her husband. If he is true, he will not want to know. But if he begins to pry, he should be told in plain words that she has nothing to tell him. It would be a mistake to say that she does not wish to tell him. It is right to declare that she has nothing to tell him. She should not create a suspicion about herself. There are many cases of divorce that have had their first incentive in the desire to get away from a wife who has confessed to errors of her girlhood. While these are not legal grounds for separation, the husband who once loses faith in his wife is sure to drift away on some cause or other.

But from the time when the two first meet and become interested in each other, they should be loyal; loyal in thought, in deed, in purpose, and in every throb of the heart. It is not loyal to pretend to better financial condition than the facts will sustain. It is not loyal to deceive, however lightly. It is not loyal to waste time, money or opportunity that may help to bring comforts after marriage.

Practical life includes all these things, and also involves the many duties that pertain to marriage and to the outside world after the new relationship has been established.

What these duties are may be divided into two classes.

1. The duties that husband and wife owe to each other both personally and in the home itself.

2. The duties that husband and wife as such, owe to the world at large.

You see that marriage involves new obligations. The loss of old friends need not be permanent, but they should not to any extent divide the attention needed in the home. The first duty is to cut loose from all else except the two following demands:

1. Until the income is ample to provide for the home, there should be uppermost in the mind the increase of the earning capacity on the part of the husband, and the increase of the efficiency on the part of the wife; letting everything else remain subservient to these matters. All social and all extra affairs, no matter how simple or how harmless, should stand aside until this basis is well established. Friendships should not be broken, but should be held in abeyance.

2. The couple should center their whole interest in each other except as already stated. This does not mean that they are to be in each other's way, or make themselves weak by a display of affection that is superfluous. A husband is interested in his wife whose every act is for their common good, as in the affairs of home. He can show his interest by work, by helping, by planning and executing, even if she is not in his presence. If she shows a preference for his companionship, there is every reason why he should be at hand to take away some of the weariness of being alone.

The fact to be impressed on the reader of these lessons is that there should be no divided interest. Constant billing and cooing, or holding hands after marriage, is not the right kind of interest. It is true that, under normal conditions, the wife enjoys actual attentions such as she had in courtship; while

the husband dislikes to render them in such fulness; but these
are phases of human nature. It is a wise husband who does
not neglect his wife in these matters; and it is a wise wife who
avoids too much display of affection for her husband. Thus an
average is found by the exercise of judgment.

1. The wife who is a real woman wants many personal
attentions and caresses each day.

2. The husband who is a real man wants very few personal
attentions each day; the fewer the better; but he may love his
wife as much as she loves him.

Nature decreed thousands of years ago that "the male gives
and the female receives." This accounts for the fact that a
man dislikes to be caressed, while a woman enjoys each attention. If there is no suspicion of something unusual in the act,
a wife enjoys nothing better from her husband than to have
him slip up behind her and put an arm about her waist, draw
her close to him, and steal a kiss. She does not forget it, either
at the time, or in after years.

There is too little of such interest in married life.

But the undivided interest that is referred to is that which
involves all the thoughts and all the acts of the day, in and
out of the home. They should be for the wife or for the
relationship that exists; and her thoughts and plans should
likewise be for the husband or for the relationship. that exists.
A new world must be entered into when marriage takes place.
The old ways, the old habits, the old haunts, the old thoughts
and the old expenditures should be cut off by a cleaver as
sharp and quick as human determination can devise. The lack
of such methods accounts largely for the great proportion
of failures in wedlock that the records show today. Divorces
are piling up faster than ever before, and there are many more
un-divorced separated couples than there are those that have
been through the courts.

In the last one hundred marriages from a certain list taken
at random for the purpose of ascertaining the drift of wedlock at the present time, all the marriages referred to having
occurred in the past five years, thirty-eight have been broken
up by separation, a number of which have been ended by divorce
for non-support, and others are waiting the time when they can
afford this modern luxury. In the last ten years the records

show a great increase in marriage failures, far exceeding any increase known in the past. The inquiry is being made on every hand, What is civilization coming to?

A better inquiry is, Can this condition be remedied?

The peace of mind of the individual, the sources of happiness in the home, the welfare of children, and the future of the race itself all demand that a remedy be found.

Basic Laws show the truth, and the truth is all that is needed to make things right, if it is adopted.

Which is better, to plunge recklessly into a condition for which neither you nor your mate may be prepared; or to start in the proper manner and make marriage a success?

Practical life can be studied and understood long before the ceremony; but if such knowledge is not had in time for that event, let all efforts of mind and heart be directed as soon as possible to learn the lesson now.

FOURTH BASIC LAW

The influence of the senses is stronger than the power of magnetism.

The principle opens up so large a field of investigation that a separate department will be devoted to its consideration. On its face it may not be understood. Magnetism in human life is no more powerful than magnetism in the physical world. The sun is the most energetic of all powers, and its energy is magnetism. It is able to hold all its planets away from it by the pushing force of its peculiar rays. Once the world was told that centrifugal force kept the orbs at their distance from the center of the system; and that centripetal force held them within certain bounds; but more is known of magnetism at the present day, and it is now clearly established that the rays of the sun, always proceeding outward and in the direction of each planet, pushes it away from the great center.

This is illustrated by the theory of the absence of gravity. If you were to be in space where no gravity existed, the tiniest push of the finest feather would set you in motion, and you would travel in a straight line to the end of the universe if no other power intervened. The earth is in space. A volume of sun rays is always pushing against it; and it must be true that the earth would keep on moving away from the sun as long as the sunlight continued to push it.

Another power intervenes.

It is the magnetism of the sun.

This is illustrated by the fact that, if you are on the roof of a building and let go, you will drop down to the earth. The latter is the gift of the sun, and holds some of the sun's magnetism, and this is called gravity. Nothing can get too far away from the sun. The substance of the planet is held by the magnetism of attraction, working always against the pushing power of the sun's rays; and the distance of the planet from the sun is determined by the character of such substance which gives it greater or less resistance to these two influences.

As the earth is the gift of the sun, all that it contains is constantly under control of that great orb.

The senses are the practical channels of life.

They are created to enable man to communicate with his fellow beings, carry on his work, secure his living, and have knowledge of life itself. There are six senses:

1. The sense of hearing.
2. The sense of sight.
3. The sense of feeling.
4. The sense of smell.
5. The sense of taste.
6. The sense of knowledge.

The last named is usually omitted from the list of physical senses, on the ground that it is mental. But animal life, as in the lower forms of creation, are all endowed with the power to know something, and mental sensations are invariably connected with those that are purely animal.

The simplest form of the operation of magnetism coming from the sun is seen in the growing plants. The roots taste, the leaves see, the branches feel, the flowers have fragrance, and there is in the germ a knowledge of its mission and purpose; for, if it is commanded to bring forth roses, it will not make the mistake of bringing forth heliotropes. Each cell is laid for roses, each strand is woven in the structure of roses, and a wonderful intelligence has charge of the whole process.

A human being has the six senses above mentioned.

He has been a long time endowed with them, was born with

them, and has come to recognize them as the masters of his life. So strong are they, that they are able to defy all the powers of magnetism. What is called personal magnetism is never able to set aside the sway of these senses. The only course to be pursued, therefore, is to make peace with the six senses. How this is done is told in another department of this course of training.

FIFTH BASIC LAW

The developing course in personal magnetism must be mastered before Sex Magnetism can be made useful in human life.

In the Magnetism Club, which consists of various courses of training in this line, there is one book that should precede all other works. It is called the book of development in general; but is known as the course in the cultivation of personal magnetism, or the exercise book of the Magnetism Club. All these names mean the same thing.

In all announcements relating to this course of training there is the statement that the developing system must either precede or attend the study of Sex Magnetism. While the two systems can be studied together, the former should be kept ahead of the latter. The purpose is to give the body all its electric and magnetic endowment before it is brought into the higher uses set forth in this volume.

If the developing course has been completed before this book has been received, then it is advisable to review it from beginning to end. If it is procured at the same time the present work is obtained, then the two should accompany each other in the following plan:

Ten or more pages of the developing course should be mastered in advance of the same number of pages in this book. The first course will be thus finished before the present course is ended, owing to the larger size of the latter.

The SIX SENSES

EFORE SEX MAGNETISM can hold sway in human life there must be peace with the six senses, as already suggested in a preceding department of this course. The analogy of the sun's influence and magnetism over plant life has been used in order to illustrate the meaning of the conflict between the physical condition of the plant and the energy of the power at work upon it. The six senses determine what a man or woman is; and they are stronger or weaker as these senses indicate in their measure of the person.

Human life is like a flower garden.

It may be beautiful, or overrun with weeds.

In the garden there must be soil capable of yielding growth. There must be nutrition of a degree of value sufficient to sustain life and to advance it. There must be the plant itself, having life and vigor. The weeds must be kept down and the plant must be cultivated, trained, given its best opportunities for development, and such care and attention as will insure a wholesome and healthful specimen when in its best condition.

Constant watchfulness is necessary.

If there is no soil in the garden, all the magnetism of the sun will be wasted. It will be as nothing. If there is no nutrition in the soil, the sun cannot employ its magnetism to assist the plant. You see how valuable the practical things are in the exercise of this mysterious and wonderful power that makes life and buoys it up above the surrounding earth. If the plant is dirty, if it is covered with moss, or attacked by bacteria, or scale, or pests of any kind, all the magnetism of the sun is not sufficient to save it.

Sex Magnetism is the grandest thing in the world.

It is capable of bringing more happiness to humanity than

all other causes and influences combined. Its powers are limit-less and far reaching. It sweeps all things before it.

But Sex Magnetism, grand as it is, pales before the influence of the six senses, and becomes a wasted energy on that account. You cannot place a less estimate on the value of the sun's mag-netism because it is useless in a garden overwhelmed by faults and weeds. No more can you undervalue the power of Sex Magnetism when the six senses combat it at every turn.

What does this mean?

Some truths will be told you that may not be pleasing, but they are necessary and you should not only read and adopt them, but you should compel every member of your family to read and to adopt them.

THE SENSE OF SMELL

The starting point in the relation of marriage is getting acquainted. The girl and the boy may have known each other since childhood, or they may have grown up to the early twenties before they met. Whether in the teens, or the twen-ties, or the thirties, or later in life, they found each other, they got acquainted somehow. When he was ambitious to merit her approval, he became suddenly neat and put on as much of a show of refinement as he could understand, considering the opportunities he had enjoyed along that line.

So fearful was he that she might see him in soiled clothes that he became extra neat even in his working garb. What had been his holiday suit was now used in his daily labor; and new raiment was purchased for Sundays. His shoes that had never had a shine while he knew only his mother and sisters, were bright most of the time, and especially brilliant on the occasions when he called upon his girl, He did not eat onions for two days before those events; and, sooner than he at first thought, he was compelled to omit onions altogether, for they did not appeal to the romantic yearnings of his sweetheart.

Why omit onions?

Because, after they have entered the human stomach and begun a series of changes under the influence of the gastric juices, they are not the same agreeable things they were when in the air. Their first assumption of odor resembles a hemlock

bark tannery; their second, a piece of cheese ready for the
moving pictures; and their third, a defunct mollusk. Yet what
husband or wife today omits onions? What man or woman
during active courtship eats onions?

The pretty girl who knows that she is pretty, who is desirous of making a good match for herself, never thrusts disagreeable smells on the attention of the young men whom she is
asking into her parlor. Her beauty is magnetic, and nature
made it so; for nature is the first and greatest teacher of Sex
Magnetism. Her eyes with their shapely lashes and soft glances
that stir the heart to its unrest, are magnetic. Her lips are
magnetic, and their earliest kisses when hot with love are con-
querors of the world; but those same lips, charged with a fetid
breath, would drive Caesar to Helvetia.

It is not the period of planned and diplomatic courtship
that needs attention here; but that more unfortunate period of
marriage that follows the allurement. How much part does
the sense of smell play in breaking the bonds of matrimony?
How much part does it play in dispelling the illusion that
courtship throws over the prospects of wedlock? Across the
street is a young girl whom we have watched for years. She
got married after a year or more of courtship. In two months
she was back again home, living with her mother, and arrang-
ing to get a divorce. From her habits prior to marriage it
was fair to assume that she herself was the cause of the falling
apart, although he will be the respondent in the proceedings.
When he courted her, and then only, she was neat and careful.

Let us get down to the unsavory facts about the sense of
smell.

A young lady was very desirous of marrying a young man
of great ability; but his rival managed to place some foul
matter on the shoulder of his coat, where the lady had learned
to recline her head. He at the time was suffering from a severe
cold, and the odor escaped him. But she lost none of it. The
result was that she just naturally lost her taste for him. They
were not married to each other; but found other mates. The
point of this incident is to show the influence of the sense of
smell on the hearts of those who otherwise would be attracted
to each other.

What freedom does wedlock bring?

The freedom to neglect the body in the most abominable manner and to compel husbands and wives to endure odors that no other relationship would tolerate; or else to seek a remedy in separation, or at least isolation, as is the case with those who can afford to do so.

The hair yields both a sour smell and dandruff. When neglected it becomes rank to the nose and unsightly to the gaze. The man can readily avoid the odor by keeping his hair trimmed short; but both faults may be overcome in man and woman by the use of any mild soap; or, better still, by a thorough washing once every five to seven days with some kind of tar soap, spending not less than five minutes in rubbing in the soap. Then there should be rinsing in hot water, followed by another rinsing in warm water, and finally in cold water until no smell of the tar remains. This will also benefit the scalp, make the hair healthy, and promote growth of the hair itself.

With this simple remedy at hand there should be no further cause of complaint as to this branch of the body.

The ears are next in evidence.

They collect dirt and hold to it tenaciously. They also run out a yellow wax that hardens at the surface and clings to the lining at the opening. When carefully mixed with dirt this wax assumes a rich golden brown. Then it begins to smell. A woman claimed that she was able to identify her husband in the dark by the smell of the wax in his ear. Husbands have been also privileged to do as much for their wives. There is no use in studying Sex Magnetism as long as this industry is carried on. Get rid of the wax first.

ANTISEPTIC WASH

A very good wash can be made at home for five cents a quart. Get a piece of alum about a half inch in diameter, and put it in a quart of rain water, to which add and stir in a piece, or the powder, of sulphate of zinc, about the size of half the alum. The actual cost of the two is less than a cent. Take a point of cloth, dip it in the wash, and insert it in the ear. Follow this with a drop or two of sweet oil as hot as can be born. Do this once a week, or as often as the wax appears. It will protect the hearing as well.

The same wash of half the strength will serve as an aid to keep the skin about the eyes clean and healthy.

The eyes under neglect become inflamed about the lids, and often are unpleasant both to the gaze and the smell. The wash just referred to will protect them and keep them in good condition.

But the nose. That is a different organ.

It has, when it does not possess a case of catarrh, a phlegmatic state. Bits of congealed mucus are within and sometimes almost outside. Catarrh itself becomes very offensive under neglect. It is estimated that ninety per cent. of men and women have this trouble, and neglect it. The remedy is deep breathing of a scientific character such as is taught in the Ralston Health Club.

The mouth is naturally the most prolific source of smells of the upper part of the body. It had three contributors to its fund of odors:

1. The teeth.
2. The stomach.
3. The alimentary canal.

It was a cause for divorce in ancient Rome to have a bad breath. Women even were given their freedom for this cause, as well as men. One of the most magnetic men of modern times lost his betrothed because she came within reach of the odor of his breath, due to bad teeth. The woman fainted, and would see him no more. What is the use, therefore, of seeking the power of magnetism when it is not equal to the power of the sense of smell? If the sun's magnetism, the most energetic in the world, is not able to overcome the bad condition of the plant, why should the magnetism of humanity be expected to combat successfully the ill conditions of men and women?

Not one person in ten thousand has sound teeth. No matter where the fault may lie, the fact remains; and if any husband or wife wishes to lay the foundation of magnetic control over the other, the teeth must be made endurable. Those that are hopelessly bad should be taken out; those that can be filled should be so dealt with; and those that are sound should be kept sound. A most excellent mouth wash is the antiseptic solution which we have described a few paragraphs back in this department. It consists of alum and sulphate of zinc, and can be put up for less than five cents a quart. The teeth can be made very clean with it; all disease germs are destroyed; the gums are kept in good condition; and decay will be wholly checked.

Daily attention is important.

A good four-rowed bristle brush for daily use on the teeth is necessary. It should be employed every morning on rising; every noon after the meal; every evening after the evening repast; and at night just before retiring. By this care the mouth may be relieved of its distressing odor.

The second cause of foul breath is the stomach. If indigestion occurs, the remedy is to overcome that trouble. It is due always to a wrong food selection.

The third cause of bad breath is the alimentary canal. This for the purposes of the present discussion, begins at the stomach and proceeds through the abdomen. The food in it should move forward at a certain rate of progress; and when this is retarded there is stagnation and decay in advance of the time intended for a healthy body. As the intestines connect with the circulatory system of the body at many stages, the decayed food and refuse is drawn into the blood and carried to the heart, the lungs and the throat, where the foul odors are set free. Few persons know that much of the odor of the breath comes from this source.

The remedy is in lessening the amount of food taken, omitting all rich food, all dessert of every kind, all fried foods, all pastries, and all meats; depending on eggs, milk, cream, butter, toast, old bread, fruits and vegetables. This diet has been tried and the result has invariably been the sweetening of the body and the breath when its fault is due to this cause. That such foul odors come from the intestines is easily proved by injecting onions in the lower end of the alimentary canal; the odor will in a short time be very strong in the breath; and the same is true of any material that may be so injected.

Having got rid of the odors of the sour hair, the waxed ears, the nose and the mouth, the next step is to pass down the neck to the main part of the body. Sometimes the neck itself is not clean, but this affects the sense of sight rather than of smell.

When the flesh has gone for several days without bathing it will ferment at the surface. This sends out an odor that is quite disagreeable. Then the armpits yield up another quota of odors by their sweating. Pads are worn that are guaranteed to cover the smell over and so conceal it; but they do not remove it. It is there all the time, and the husband soon learns to locate it, and also to locate his wife by its aid. There is not much sense in putting the lid down over a bad smell.

Women are sometimes very sensitive about their armpits. They shrink from the society of all persons except their husbands; and to them they freely give out the full amount. "I bathe every night," says a fat, small woman, "but the odor remains just as strong." She was told to try the ingestion of her food as described in the books of Ralston Health Club. This she did, and never once did she have odor at the armpits or elsewhere.

When the sweated surface of the body gives out a ferment, soap and hot water will remove the fault. But when the armpits are too active, there is no remedy but ingestion of food. All other means have been tried and have failed; but ingestion has never had a failure.

Its effect is marvelous.

Similar advice may be given for the care of the body as far as the pores are to blame; but the middle portion is the seat of excretions and accompanying odors, and it can be kept under control only by soap and hot water. It is not necessary for us to specify what we mean; but there is abundant testimony that both sexes are careless in this particular and need to be cautioned. The husband must not forget that his almost nude body is close to his wife at night, and that any offense he may give by negligence is sure to belittle him in her esteem; for, no matter how low down in the scale of dirt she may be, there is some instinct of decency left in her nature, and it must be recognized.

Husbands are careless about cleaning themselves when at the water closet; and wives may be open to the same charge. Their clothing holds evidence of this neglect, and the odors, while concealed from the general public, are reserved for the privacy of married life. These are not stray instances, but are commonplace affairs in wedlock. Think of the awful drop from the illusion of courtship to the realism of marriage; and then find an answer to the question why people do not care as much for each other after they have been married, as they thought they did before. "My husband is so filthy in his person that I dread the time when we must retire together at night," writes a young wife who was once a beautiful bride and whose husband when in public looks neat and rather handsome, even now. It is a typical case.

Once a week bathing is too long a span for the body's cleanliness, as there are evidences of ferment and odor, as well as dirty conditions in two days under the most favorable circumstances. Nor is there any human being who can go twenty-four hours without some of these evidences. The legs and loins have a disagreeable odor in twelve hours; and, in summer, in half that time. The cleanest people bathe in warm weather every morning and every evening. Others bathe once every twenty-four hours with advantage to the marriage state. Those who bathe every forty-eight hours carry odors part of that time. What then can be said of the once-a-week habit of bathing? There are six days of odors waiting for the opposite sex; and if they are in harmony, it is a case of exchange.

While it would require a great exercise of the will power to better this habit, the remedy must be applied before there can be any progress in Sex Magnetism; for that study is based on the law that body must be at its best all the time.

The feet develop odors in a few hours. The wedding night of a bride who had bathed in the early morning and who had developed a strong foot odor by the time they retired, was one that brought a shock to the husband. To him the girl had been most beautiful and dainty; and he could not understand how so energetic and so disagreeable an odor could be generated from ten little toes. The habit of bathing the feet and legs every morning and night, even if they are only rubbed with a wet towel, is necessary if the full respect of both parties is desired.

Not only will neglect in the care of the body bring bad odors; but carelessness in the use of the clothing will also cause the same result. Grease, dirt, food, oils, and nastiness from many sources are collected on the outer clothes and give out an unpleasant smell to one who approaches them closely. In addition to this both sexes go too long before changing their underclothing. The latter will gather the ferment and urea from the skin and retain them until they pass to a secondary stage of decay. If the sense of smell is so dulled that there is no repugnance to such conditions, then the nervous system needs refining in order to understand and employ so great a power as Sex Magnetism.

Owing to conditions peculiar to her sex, a wife is compelled to carry odors that she deplores as much as her husband. But these may be reduced to a minimum. They are largely the penalty of too much indoor life and too much food of a wrong kind. It has been proved in thousands of cases in the past thirty years that outdoor air and gentle activity will lessen the loss of fluid each month, at about the rate of one per cent. a month, if much time is spent in the air accompanied by some degree of activity as walking or attending to a flower garden, or in any way. Some women have been taught to take their work from the house to the open air. There are many things that are done indoors that can be as well performed in the open air, such as sewing and small duties; while some women take their larger work to a porch.

Perfect digestion, which means the disposal of all the food without waste except in the natural way, lessens the same trouble. Meat is always a prolific cause of odors and excrescences of various kinds, in excess of what ought to be the case. Pastry, fried foods, and any rich diet will cause odors that are unnecessary. The practice of thorough ingestion, and the consequent decrease of the amount of food taken daily, will make woman a cleaner individual.

We refer to refined women, and those who want to be refined.

There are some who are negligent, and have no desire to be otherwise; and they include the handsomest of ladies sometimes. Not a few of them dress in the neatest and most elegant fashion; but their neatness ceases with their outward display. They assume that the public has no interest further, and that any private nastiness of under conditions belongs strictly to the privacy of home. The husband is expected to have the same respect for the woman every day in the month, who neglects herself always; and she wonders why she has not the same magnetism for him that she had before marriage. A case in point shows the effect of the shock on the male mind when it comes all at once. A young lady who was noted for her neatness and special tidiness, even to the extent of being called over-neat, was engaged to be married to a very worthy young man of good family and means. One summer when her parents were away, he made the suggestion while they were on an automobile trip a few hours from her home, that they be married at once, as a clergyman was at hand with whom he had been acquainted for some time. She did not wish to miss so good an opportunity for entering wedlock, and soon gave her consent; risking greater matters for an unfit preparation. The details were arranged and they continued on their trip to a hotel where they remained over night. They were legally man and wife. In the morning he left her and refused to see her again. In court he testified that he had been sickened by conditions more foul than those that belong to the female sex by nature; and, although this was not legal ground for divorce, it entered into the general testimony. The fault was not with nature, but with a young woman who did not think it necessary to be careful in her habits.

Such negligence is too common.

It is true that there are many women who are refined, and who are as cleanly in all parts of the body and in the underclothing as the cleanest and neatest woman can possibly make herself. These lessons are for the others; and they dwell in every rank of life. Poverty does not stand in the way of cleanliness. In the middle ranks, as a rule, are the most tidy women. Some sections of the country are noted for their cleanly people; others for the opposite. The exterior of body, the hair, the ears, the nose and the breath are all indicators of the character in this respect.

THE SENSE OF SIGHT

While the married couple have access to the disagreeable odors that are associated with the body, and which for the most part are concealed from the public, there is a more general exposure of carelessness to the eye in open view after marriage than is seen before.

This is due to the fact that the private relationship turns to license between themselves, and sooner or later is free with intimate friends and members of the families to which they belong. A young man who had always been very careful of his habits, and a young wife of the same previous experience, found it easy to forget their past neatness in dress and care of the body; and in a few weeks after the ceremony, they were lounging about with disheveled hair, unwashed faces and hands, and unkempt clothing. This practise started with one of their Sunday morning risings, when they were weary and did not think it worth while to dress for breakfast. It was noon time when they were attired for receiving their relatives. After this experience there was a gradual falling away from the habits that are proper in the public eye.

It is useless to contend that man and wife should observe the care in their dressing and conduct that they are required to maintain even before their parents. Some license is necessary; but it should not be of a nature that will repel respect.

The hair should be made tidy as soon as circumstances will permit on arising in the morning. Going about like a fright is not magnetic. The face should be kept clean; and the hands, above all, should receive constant attention. No wife enjoys a husband with soiled hands and deeply dirty finger nails. There should never be discolored hands or fingers, and the nails should be both trimmed and cleaned at all times. These hands of your husband pass the food at the table, handle your fine clothes, and come in contact with yours. You want them clean. All the more reason why you, as a wife, should have clean hands, clean fingers and immaculate nails.

Many women have soiled skin about the hair where it joins the flesh of the face and neck. Some have dirty ears, and there are too many with wax stored away there, but not out of sight. The soggy eyes, red lids, and coal-dusted corners close to the nose, are evidence of neglect in some form. A runny nose, either loose with thin catarrh, or creamy with stagnant influenza, is unattractive. It does not look well, and has no inviting qualities.

Men have these same faults in equal or greater degree.

Women who have not eaten proper food have bad complexions and they seek to cover over the blemishes with powder or rouge. This cover does not tend to effect a cure of the trouble; and generally adds to it by closing the pores and cutting off the circulation. It is amusing to note the many things and the hours of hard work a woman will employ in getting the blemishes from her face, or in covering them up; all the while forgetting that the source of the trouble is a bad diet, lack of fresh air in abundance, and rapid eating in place of slow ingestion.

There are holes at the toes and heels of your stockings.

The public will not see them. If you go to the shoe store to be fitted with new shoes, you will wear whole stockings. But in the privacy of married life you think it makes no difference. It does make a great difference, for thereby your measure is quietly taken by your mate, and the slight sneer is a straw that tells which way the wind blows.

Men's clothes go unmended, and are too often slouchy in appearance and soiled on the surface. Dr. Johnson, who wrote the dictionary, was a famous man, and his habit of separating his soup so that part of it went into his mouth and the rest over his clothes, was looked upon as one of the curiosities of English literature. But it is not magnetic even with a dictionary to endorse it. Most men wear soiled coats at the dining table for the companionship of their wives, and they save their clean coats for the companionship of their friends; like the perfect lady who carried two handkerchiefs with her; one for show and the other for blow.

Women become very slack in the care of their underclothes, allowing buttons to fall off and stay off, and depending on pins for holding the apparel on. They look in a mirror, taking front and back views, and if there is nothing wrong that the public can behold, they are content to go forth into the outside world; but when they are at home and less appareled, they bristle with pins in the presence of their husbands. Torn clothing also is in view. The mending that is needed is postponed until the plot of the pending novel is carried past its agonizing crisis. Then the wife wonders why her husband has so little real affection and respect for her. Magnetism is founded on facts, on practical sense, on good judgment and on those better qualities of mind and heart that denote a superior person.

"I was led to marry my husband because he seemed to have grand ideas, and I thought he was as much of a man as he made me believe he was," said a wife who walked out of the house never to return. "I found myself living with a bad smelling, bad appearing, and shambling fellow that was far below the standard he set in his speeches to me before we were engaged."

All persons who wish to improve, can do so. All that is necessary at the start is to wish to improve.

The finer qualities of mind and heart can be cultivated, for that has been the one impulse that has brought the world to the better plane it now occupies.

The man who does not keep his shoes whole and polished, or otherwise in good condition, is not refined. This seems a trifling matter, but it has its influence over others. The soiled collar, or the dirty shirt, or cuffs, or handkerchiefs, will also have an influence over those who see them. There is no more reason for a man going abroad with his shirt front smeared than for his appearing in public with smear on the end of his nose.

People may claim that they do not have time to keep clean. They have an abundance of time, for they waste small periods all day long, and have many opportunities morning, noon and evening for the brief minutes that would suffice to maintain a better condition of things. More than this, they are careless. Let them be more graceful and less awkward in their movements, and they will have less dirt to remove. The habit of lifting fluids on a spoon to the mouth in such a way that part of the fluid misses its destination, is inexcusable. These very men, if they were pitching a baseball, would make a reasonably good aim over a distance of seventy feet or so; and to say they cannot find the mouth that is less than two feet away, is an error of calculation.

Clumsy, awkward people need to take up the study of grace and refinement. A man is a gentleman because his manners are gentle; not because he was born of a family that stands well in the community. If a woman is to choose between a boor and a gentleman, all other things being equal, she will prefer the gentleman ten hundred times in a thousand. Of course the man selects a wife because she is known as a member of the "gentler sex." If she shall prove to be a rampant, rough, inelegant woman, he is repelled by her ways rather than attracted by them. No magnetism that can be taught or acquired can overcome the influence of conditions that drive away respect.

THE SENSE OF HEARING

It has already been explained in what ways the sense of smell and the sense of sight may disintegrate magnetism, and cause a separation instead of an amalgamation of the two sexes.

The sense of hearing plays an important role in the same regime.

This is confined largely to the use of the voice in conversation. There are disagreeable voices, and disagreeable words. Of the two, the latter may be more direct and better met than the former. All high pitches are unpleasant for the reason that their vibrations double in number every second of time as each octave is raised. A woman who uses a pitch an octave too high, as most women do, will soon prove distressing to the husband who must listen to her voice. Then the habit of raising the pitch in conversation always excites the flow of words, and she talks three times as fast as the man would like to have her.

He does not know the mechanical reasons for the harsh effect on his ear and brain. All he knows is that her voice is not as charming as once it was.

Such moods as seriousness, earnestness, calmness, sound judgment and the like always lower the pitch of the voice naturally. Pitch is not loudness or softness; but is the place of the voice in the musical scale. Thus a soprano voice is a high pitch, and a bass voice is a low pitch. A tenor for a man is too high for conversation, and a soprano for a woman is likewise too high. An octave below should be cultivated. There is no high-pitched voice of a man or woman in existence that can carry magnetic tones; there never has in the history of the world; and there never will be. Song tones are magnetic under some circumstances; but never speaking tones when above a certain pitch.

Speed of talking is also distressing when much indulged in. It evinces nervousness in the speaker, and arouses nervousness and irritability in the hearer. There is a natural reason for this effect. The tone of the voice is a vibration of the body of the air which strikes the ear; and, in course of an hour, millions of these vibrations pound the sensitive nerve in the brain. The later becomes exhausted of its vital fluid, and this depletion either induces sleep, or else irritation; generally the latter. One continual tone will bring insanity or catalepsy to the listener.

Each note in the scale of conversation or of song taxes the brain power in a special way. Two notes, employed in the same conversation or song, would only become half as exhausting to the brain of the listener as one note. Four different notes would become only one-fourth as exhausting as one. Thus, if a person were to converse in one note of the voice for an hour, the wearying effect on the listener would be the same as if that person talked with two notes for two hours, or with four notes for four hours, or eight notes for eight hours.

One note is often used by talkers, especially those who are mere talkers, lacking magnetism, and the result is sure to drive away all friends except those who remain friends for policy and nothing more. A woman who wants to hear the "news" from another woman will lay aside her dislike for the woman and listen; then, after the talker has gone, the victim ejaculates "cat" and thus sizes up her supposed friend.

High pitch voices and rapid talking are wearying to those who listen and also to those who talk. The effect is reflex on the nervous system of the latter. Prostration follows to a greater or less extent. Women who have doctored for this loss of vitality, and have found a cure impossible, have at length been told the plain truth; and those who have not been offended beyond repair, have adopted the advice of experts and, having lowered their voices an octave and reduced their speed to the limits demanded by magnetism, have found a complete cure of supposed neurasthenia.

The matter involved in the use of the voice in an unpleasant way may or may not be disagreeable itself; but is naturally the offspring of a character suited to the tones employed. You can set it down as certain that a woman who talks in the high pitch has an unpleasant disposition. One who talks rapidly may be merely nervous. Both characteristics are opposed to magnetism.

THE SENSE OF TASTE

One would hardly believe that the use of this sense played a part in the present study. It is an old saying that the way to a man's heart is through his stomach; meaning that the woman who knows how to cook or have cooked for him the dishes that are most appreciated by him, will win his affections.

But is this true?

The work at hand is on the negative side in this department, and the sense of taste is to be discussed from the viewpoint of being disagreeable. The wife is expected to kiss her husband. Most wives prefer this, or to be kissed by their husbands, rather than to omit this custom. But there is a decided objection to the taste of tobacco on the male lips. While refined men, or gentlemen, do not chew tobacco, many smoke, and their lips are strong with the flavor of the cigar. A man who really loves and appreciates his wife, will refrain from this habit. He may ask her if she objects to the taste of tobacco; and she says "No" rather than offend him; but the fact is, she much prefers to have him stop his smoking. There are wives who seek to keep their husbands at home evenings by inducing them to smoke indoors rather than be absent. They are sacrificing their own pleasure and some veracity in thus making the invitation. One woman says, "I tell my husband that I feel unhappy when he is not smoking in the house; and I would not for the world let him know that the smell and taste of tobacco are disagreeable to me. If I had it to do over again, I would marry a man who did not smoke."

On the other hand the wife may offend by being remiss in her duty to have proper food set before him. Whether she cooks it or not, she is the one person who is responsible for the quality of the food that he must eat. He cannot

go into the kitchen himself. The wife has a right there, and
her duty to her home requires that she be there whenever
necessary.

There must be a morning meal for him. He has his work
to do and she has hers; or, if she is above the need of toil,
she has still greater duties, and they consist in the management of her home. To whatever extent she neglects this great
responsibility she must answer if not to him, then to her own
after life. Widows are becoming four times as numerous as
widowers. The dining room is the great execution chamber
of modern civilization. Last week a personal friend died of
acute indigestion; the week before, three prominent men in
one city died the same evening of acute indigestion; and the
week before that two men died of the same cause in the same
city. In the past year the greatest percentage of any one cause
of mortality in the United States was in the one malady, acute
indigestion. There are not two men in any thousand whose
stomachs are in normal health. Some form of gastric derangement is found in practically all men.

The wives are to blame.

There is nothing that will so irritate the mind and the
nerves as indigestion. It eats, cuts, scrapes, tears, pinches and
tortures the whole nervous system. No human being is so
well endowed with calmness and poise of temper that he can
withstand the agony of indigestion. The pain is blind. It
may not be present in the stomach; but the man wonders why
he is so easily angered at trifles. He is not in a mood to
endure the least bit of trouble or annoyance. Many a husband who has vowed never to speak a cross word to his wife
has been obliged to hold back the rising temper with both
hands on the reins. Then the wife seeks to know the cause,
and jumps at him for an explanation. One look, one thrusting aside for a second, one ejaculation; and the harmony of a
happy home is broken. The wife cries. The husband does
not know what made him cross. The wife has no way of finding out. He may say that he does not feel well. She knows
that is true. He cannot tell her that the dinner has distressed
him, for he is not himself thinking of that as the cause. The
pastry was delicious, and the fried potatoes most agreeable;
while they were being eaten. The accounting to the stomach

is an after consideration in the matter of pleasure of this kind.

Except in acute forms, indigestion is blind. It hurts the heart by the formation of toxins that cramp or stifle the action of that organ. It may be known only as a heavy feeling somewhere. Or there may be difficulty in getting a deep breath; or heat in the head; or a dizzy feeling; almost everywhere except in the stomach itself is the result felt.

If a wife undertakes to do the cooking she should adopt only the plainest and most wholesome foods. Most women, after failing in the bread, the toast and meat, will construct a baking-powder cake of two-pound calibre, and rest on that as the *piece de resistance*. This means that the husband must forego all hope of having nutritive food for his meal, and take his chances on "angel cake" or some other venture. If the angel cake "falls" and he calls it "devil cake," which is the synonym of "fallen angel," she will not understand his felicitation, and war may be declared at once.

Of all the irritability in the home, ninety-nine per cert. of it would be eliminated if there were no indigestion; if the food were plain and wholesome; and if the cooking were proper. Many unkind remarks have been due to this one cause. Many headaches, nameless pains, "blue" spells, dull and gloomy hours, and quick retorts have had their origin in the blind forms of stomach trouble. They are called blind because they do not indicate where the trouble is. The stomach may be wholly free from pain or distress and yet a nervous, "touchy" feeling may take possession of the body and mind.

The importance of mastering and preventing this condition is at once seen, for there can be no content and no happiness where there is irritability. The wife who is fretted has a hard struggle to keep her temper in the presence of ordinary annoyances; but to add to her burden the irritability of her husband who is suffering from indigestion is to place upon her a serious handicap in the effort to smile and be philosophical. Wives are human and cannot rise above a sea of discouragement.

The stomach of a person in good health may digest bad cooking or foods that are unfit for nutrition, and yet the nerves may be made very sensitive by the process. A person may walk on tacks and arrive at his place of destination, but his feet will be sore, and anything that scrapes the sore places will disturb the even tenor of his mind. The same experience as to the stomach occurs every day and every night. The appetite is more keen at the evening meal, and more food is desired; the result being that there is more to be digested. What should be the lightest meal of the day and should consist of only the simplest foods, is turned into the heaviest repast of the twenty-four hours. To this error is added wrong food selection and cooking that interferes with digestion; furnishing a combination that can have but one result: the setting up of nervous irritability.

The man who is made irritable by blind indigestion is not to blame for his condition. The fault is wholly the wife's. She will not admit it. Most women when told that it is their duty to study the laws of food selection and the proper way of cooking food, or of having it cooked, become either angry or sarcastic. They refer to all such suggestions as coming from cranks. Here is the case of a most estimable lady whose husband died quickly of acute indigestion due to her errors in food selection. Even that event did not take the stupid conceit out of her head. A year later a very dear friend died at her table of acute indigestion; and that event did not deter her from her errors. Nothing could have the slightest influence on her mind. Recently a grown son has died at her table of acute indigestion, and still she cooks pies, pies, pies, and serves them; and she cooks hot bread, hot rolls, hot muffins, and has them every day on her table. Three deaths are traceable to her obstinacy, and it is certain that she does not charge her conscience with any of them.

A wife whose husband had died of acute indigestion because of pastry and fried foods, and hot bread, was told the cause of the death. She got very angry and requested the informant to mind her own business; and the informant was a close neighbor. Later on when a lady acquaintance fell dead of acute indigestion at the very table where the husband had died, the woman awoke. She has five children, and their faces showed the pinching done by pie crust and fried foods and hot bread; and now they are coming into better blood. This woman is one in a thousand. You cannot move the 999 to remedy their food selection and their cooking, or to instruct their cooks, if they have them, to change their methods. The old ways are very firmly established, and no woman will take the trouble to learn aright.

To this danger is added the adulteration of all foods, and of almost all baking powders; and the fact that women today prefer to prepare baking-powder foods rather than get down to the basis of the period when health was prevalent, and baking powders were unknown.

Many husbands have tried to encourage their wives in the study of the laws of food selection, only to be met with scoffing, or scolding, or tears. Then that ends the discussion. Few husbands will order the right thing to be done, even in their own homes. They must eat what is set before them, and they cannot have a voice in what they eat. They go forth in the morning to earn the support of the family, and they come to their meals in a spirit of meekness accepting what they get, and letting nature work in them as best she can. They have imperfect stomachs; some of them have horrible stomachs; and there are many hundreds of thousands of men today who are cross as bears, irritable and touchy, because they suffer from indigestion due to wrong food selection and bad cooking. The most attractive forms of cooking are almost always the worst. It is a strange contradiction.

No person should live to eat.

The alluring piecrust that looks and tastes so nice, breaks up good blood and makes none in its place. Food is bad enough when it will yield no nutrition; but it is much worse when it destroys the best elements of the blood.

Is the stomach the road to a man's heart?

Here are two verdicts:

One husband says: "I married a woman because she could make the most delicious cakes and pies. I thought she was a fine cook. Before I was married I had never known what it was to have indigestion. Since then I have suffered tortures, have become ugly and profane, and I am at last rid of the whole affair by separation."

Another husband says: "Before I was married I boarded at the home of a woman who was a good cook, but her cooking kept me in a bad condition all the time. I laid the case before a young woman who had not been to a cooking school, but who had studied in books the methods on selection of good foods and of preparing them, and who had learned by practice at home how to cook them. She told me that her father and mother both had been cured of bad stomachs by the sensible methods, and this pleased me. I was invited to call and eat with them. This I did a number of times, and found the change delightful. Our acquaintance ripened into marriage; and after a long period of happiness together we have made up our minds that nothing on earth can ever separate us "until death do us part."

This latter statement has the true ring.

Much as women hate to be told that their food selection and cooking are for the most part on a line with the most barbarous products of the minds of the dark ages, there are now and then a few who wake up in time to save valuable lives and thus do good in the world.

A few more such women are needed.

The marriage problem and the drink problem hinge more largely on the diet question than on any other. It has been proved that nearly all taste for alcoholic drinks follows inflammation of the stomach in an incipient form. When the stomach is given only the plainest of foods cooked in the simplest of ways, then the desire for liquor ceases. When there is an absolutely normal health of the stomach, no man or woman will care for liquor or stimulants in any form. But when there is inflammation, however slight, in the lining of the stomach, then it demands and will have its accustomed alcoholic beverage. "My stomach is in first class shape. I can get along with cold water," said a man some months ago. Later on after eating some hot rolls, fried meats, fried potatoes, and new pie, he said, "I am on fire in my stomach. I have not drank a drop for six months; but if I do not get some whiskey, and get it quick, I shall die." The fire of the hurt stomach could be appeased only by the fire of the liquor. This is the story of alcoholism today. It is not a theory, but a fact, and the proofs of the fact are abundant.

The time will come when sensible women will be willing to study the question of what foods and what kinds of cooking cause indigestion. They would not take up this study if only the lives of their husbands were at stake, for it is not human nature to profit by the lessons taught by death. But when women learn, as they soon will have to learn, that the peace and happiness of their own lives depend on the genial disposition of their husbands, and that a man with a case of blind indigestion cannot long be genial no matter what temperament has been given him at birth, these women who cook according to old standards will mend their ways in this respect.

Little pains are harder to endure than large ones. The constant grinding at the vitality and nervous system by the indigestibility of food, will break up the peace of any family. Religion itself staggers in a man's life at the inroads made on his temper by this same enemy of modern times.

THE SENSE OF FEELING

By feeling as described in this department is meant the physical uses of the body and all its parts. Much that might have been included herein has already been discussed under the sense of taste, referring to physical pain from indigestion. But there are more direct causes of pain and discomfort that are properly a part of this sense.

One of these causes is pain that arises from the drudgery of severe work. The human body of a highly civilized being was never intended for such drudgery. Distinctions in the ranks of people are made for the purpose of providing the labor that can endure the strain of hard work. While it is true that every person, whether man or woman, should be active as much of the time as possible, there is a broad difference between activity and exhausting toil. Work is the only accompaniment of happiness that can be found in this world. But work should be suited to the class and grade of individual. Physical work is essential, for all other kinds are merely occupations of the mind. A man or woman who is physically active eight hours in every twenty-four is laying the foundation for a successful life and a serene old age.

In marriage there may be times when it is necessary for a man or woman to do actual drudgery for a short time. This is honorable, but it should not be performed as a daily duty. The husband should spare the wife and the wife should spare the husband. One of the smallest characteristics of a man is to sit around the house evenings and Sundays and permit her to do many menial duties that he could better do, and which would look better to an impartial observer if done by him. It is wrong to allow a wife to do any physical task of a menial kind that the husband can perform.

There is nothing in the evening paper that will benefit the mind of the man; yet he thinks he must sit for several hours and read it while the tired woman is hurrying about the house trying to finish up her tasks, many of which he ought to attend to. There can be nothing in his nature on which to found Sex Magnetism as long as he will sit while she stands and works. He may be tired with his labor of the day; but she has been at work also, and does for her size and strength more than twice the real toil that he performs. The hours of the artisan have been reduced, but not the hours of the wife.

She must have her turn now.

The man should treat his mate as a more delicate being than himself. In some countries the husband yokes the wife with a cow to a plow, and drives the pair all day long in the hot sun over baked land. She has a decided pull in those countries. But they savor of barbarism. In a refined age the wife should be kept refined and her labors should be made light and of a delicate nature. She should not be idle. There is enough to keep her busy if she is loyal to her home; and the most potent influence that will induce loyalty is the mutual help and constant assistance of her husband.

She never forgets his attentions and his aid.

If he can lighten her burdens, he ought to do so, and she will render to him sooner or later the appreciation that he deserves. As long as she has no hours of respite, he should have none. His practice of spending the evenings away from home is most reprehensible and the sooner he reforms this habit the better it will be for his welfare and future happiness.

There are many physical attentions that the husband can bestow on the wife, but that he omits after marriage. She of all creatures likes to be caressed if she has any respect for him. If he has faults that will repel a sensitive woman, then he should overcome them and begin his courting days over again. The new regime should not be sudden, but by easy stages; for a sudden show of kindness might be taken as a joke. Many a man has said in substance: "You tell me to return to the habits of the days when we courted. To do so, I must kiss and embrace my wife, and talk to her in different tones from those she is now accustomed to. A kind remark made as I would make it to the girl to whom I was about to propose would choke in my throat. I would like to try the experiment of putting my arm around my wife's waist as she stands washing her dishes; but the fear of something after that deters me. How would she take a kiss if I were to give her one on my return from work some evening? This is a fearful question."

It certainly was.

This man who had been educated at college and who had settled down to a very commonplace life, voiced the feelings of the great majority of married men when he gave utterance to these views. But once the ice is broken the kiss will not be taken as a joke, or the embrace as a shock; nor will kind words arouse a suspicion that he is planning some escapade, the effect of which he desires to discount in advance. There was another man who said to his wife, "Ellen, if I were to say to you that I want to turn over a new leaf, that I have been reading some things of late that makes me believe I do not appreciate you as you deserve, would you be glad of it? For instance, if I were to kiss you as I leave for my office, and again on my return, would the surprise be too great? Would you take it seriously?" She understood him, and they began their courting days over again. It was a new life to the woman and she showed in her happier existence.

Gallantry is forgotten after marriage except when a third party is around to witness it. A woman said truthfully, "I am glad to have some one near by when I get in my carriage, for my husband always helps me in then; otherwise he lets me get in the best way I can." This is merely an example of the drift of human nature in wedlock.

There are scores of small attentions that can be paid to the wife by the husband. One man said recently, "Frances, why does my brother display so much gallantry to you?"—"Because you forget to do so," was the reply.

Look at a typical case of this exact kind:

There was a banker who had nearly a million dollars more

than he could ever spend. He had a wife who, although she was forty, was as petite and charming as a girl. He did not think she was in existence if his lack of personal attention to her was to be taken as evidence. His brother, a man about the age of the woman, spent a month at their palatial residence and showed to his sister-in-law so much attention in the presence of her husband that the latter opened his eyes. "Why is it not my duty and privilege to bestow on my wife as much personal attention as my brother is doing?" he asked.

It was a very vital inquiry.

While the absence of courtesies and gallantry is an error, the rough use of a woman is still more reprehensible. A woman should be treated as a lady until she has proved herself otherwise. To hurry past her, to jolt her, to allow a crowd to press against her, and the many little neglects that leave her to herself in public when the gentle guidance of a gentleman is needed for her comfort, is too often the experience of wedlock after the new has worn off. Sometimes she is seen following her husband making long strides to catch a street car. Sometimes she is pushed along the sidewalk by persons passing in opposite direction who elbow her, drive their corners into her ribs or else attempt to turn her body in one direction and her head in another in the scramble to get by.

Such cases are frequent.

She feels these neglects, no matter how much she gets used to them. There are millions of wives today who have given up all hope of receiving gentle care and attention from their husbands; but until the latter change about and become men instead of rough boors, they will not be catalogued in the rank of gentlemen.

THE SENSE OF KNOWLEDGE

The things and facts that a person is conscious of, apart from the experience of the five usual senses, belong to the operation of the sense of knowledge.

Husbands and wives should keep themselves informed of the many events that make up the lives of their mates. "The day I was engaged," says a young man, "I thought of the many dangers that might attend my fiance's daily routine. I thought of how many times she might go out of doors and be in peril from passing horses, and of other exposures that might bring risks to her. Since then I have seen how foolish I was to entertain such groundless fears. Now she can cross the railroad tracks in front of express trains and I would not think of such a thing as danger to her." At one time he was over-anxious; and at another time he had no anxiety at all.

Surely marriage makes a difference.

But to close the mind against the hopes, the wishes and the fears of a wife, is not the way a husband should treat her. Wives, as a rule, have a very definite knowledge of their husband's most common failings and aspirations. But they do not know one-tenth of what they ought to know. A reason for this lack of knowledge is the unwillingness of both parties to confide in each other.

There is wide distinction between questions prompted by curiosity that pry into the doings of either party, and the acquisition of knowledge of the inward moods of a husband or wife. When questions are asked, there is a suspicion that there is mistrust behind them. In good form, socially speaking, it is not allowable to ask questions. The man or woman who tries to be sociable and interesting in conversation by propelling a lot of questions at a visitor, is soon dropped. At times a meaningless inquiry may start a ball rolling in talk, and thus help to make the conversation easy; but the questions are not of moment. It is proper to ask, "How do you do?" But it is not proper to ask, "Are you quite well?" Nor is it proper to ask, "How is business?" Or anything about Jones, or Smith, or Brown, or others. Statements should be made. They should belong to subjects of public and not of private interest. In the best society where brains and sense prevail, these things are regulated very readily.

The same rule applies to husband and wife.

Questions are annoying and generally useless. If either party has something to tell the other, it is best to tell it, and it is a good trait for the other to listen and receive all the information that is volunteered. It is generally the habit of a wife to try to inform her husband of the many experiences of the day; but he does not care so much for them as for the standing of the baseball clubs, and she soon grows tired of talking to him of her doings. Now he makes a serious mistake to avoid hearing all she has to say. If she is gossiping about a neighbor, let him note some piece of work on which she has been engaged, and soon she will begin to explain to him all about it. This pleases her, and she is proud of having such an audience.

In this method the husband becomes diplomatic.

He has not asked any questions. He may have said, "This is pretty," as he takes up some work she has done in sewing or embroidery. That is enough. She will do the rest for a while. Of course this is merely a sample of the way in which he may proceed in any line of thought.

It is surprising to know how many small matters there are connected with each, that the other may express an interest in. The time ought to come when the model husband will know every dress and hat that the wife possesses; and the condition and newness or age of each and all of them. He should have an opinion as to her modes of dress and her taste. Then her duties ought to be the subject of pleasant congratulation. There need not be a running fire of statements, nor a close connection between one subject and another. It is enough that at least one thing is talked of each evening that shows him to be interested in her and her work and efforts.

The adverse criticisms should be omitted. If affirmative praise cannot be given, avoid the subject. If some better way can be devised, let it be done in a manner that will not cause a feeling of discouragement in her mind. If she has been reading a magazine, take it up when she has got through with it, and note some fact in it. Or if she has been engaged in study, let that be talked over to some extent. The thing to omit is segregation; or taking yourself behind a paper and remaining in hiding for hours each evening, while the wife may be but a few feet away, lonesome and lost. The same habit at a dining table is wrong. Some men eat and read the paper at the same time; they do not assist the others at the table, do not help to make others comfortable, and shut off their society from all about them, behind a paper. The whole contents of the daily newspaper is of little value. If you go away for six months and then return and take up all the papers to review, you will be nauseated by their headlines and contents. The nervous, fidgety unrest that prompts a man to want something to interest him all the time, is a low condition of the mind and heart.

In the presence of company before whom you wish to appear refined, you would not read a paper while at the table during a meal; and what is good enough conduct for a stranger is none too good for your wife.

It is at the lull in the work when you are privileged to be in her society in the dining room that you have the opportunity to cultivate in yourself the graces of a better conduct, and the companionship of one who should be dearer to you than the sensational news of the day.

The rule is, ascertain without the use of questions all you can of your wife's wishes, of her hopes, of her fears, of her ambitions, of her pleasures, and of her daily duties and progress. Know her as she is. Do not make the effort all at once after years of neglect; let any new regime come gradually so as not to attract attention and lead to ridicule. It will seem funny to her to find you something like yourself in the days of courtship.

The wife naturally drinks in and absorbs these things about her husband. Partly by instinct and partly by her nature she learns to know her mate better than he learns to know her. But not ten per cent. of the full knowledge is passed between them that ought to be rendered; and, for this reason, it is well for them to begin little by little to confide in each other all there is in the mind and heart that can be of interest. It is not best to interfere with the duties of either by interposing these things; but there are moments as at the dining table, and when they are not tied down to work then they can speak of the things that impart a better knowlege of each other. If the husband is in business, the wife should know of any dangers to his credit, for her words of confidence to the woman who may drop in to see her might bring on the bankruptcy of her husband. We regret to say that this has occurred a number of times to our knowledge. Some remark dropped by the husband to his wife, such as the statement that he had a note to meet in a few days and he would have to hustle to get the money, has been repeated by the wife to a visitor to whom she said that her husband had a note to meet and he did not know how he could pay it; a trifling variation that means nothing to the woman who repeats it. The visitor went forth and told her lady friend that the man could not pay his note; the lady friend told the wife of the creditor that the man would not be able to pay his note.

This brought alarm to the holder of the note, and the result was a run on the business of the man and his failure and bankruptcy.

It is not an isolated case.

More than one husband has been deprived of the credit and confidence of business men by the careless remarks of his wife. The latter has lived to suffer because of the results. Nothing she could do or say would mend the broken vase. All panics are begun in this way; not by wives in most cases; but by some careless remark that has been set in circulation and magnified as it sped on its journey. In the greatest of recent panics, one woman spoke of the fear she had as to her deposits in a trust company. Another woman who had larger deposits in the same company took up the alarm and withdrew from it all her funds, and carried the news to others. In three hours people began to line up to take away their money. The powder was everywhere dry and needed only the application of a little fire and some wind to create the conflagration that covered the nation. In another panic which resulted in a run on a bank, the officials issued a statement which was endorsed by an official of the United States, saying that a woman had called to collect a check which was not drawn on that bank, but on another of nearly the same name in one part. The paying teller, instead of informing her what bank the check was drawn on, merely replied, "No funds." She could have read the reason why in the face of the check itself. But she went back to work in an office where there were hundreds of clerks, many of whom had money in the same bank; and she told them that they would not get their money there as the bank had no funds. Before the people awoke to the facts, nearly a million dollars had been taken out.

Of course the man or woman who will assist in making a run on a bank has not even the first, primitive knowledge or fitness for doing business there or anywhere else.

The public, not only in masses and mobs, but in the supposedly more sensible classes who are able to deposit money in banks, lose their heads, and in so doing add to the damage that they themselves must suffer when they run amuck.

But the question arises whether a husband should conceal all things from his wife because she may not be able to contain the least bit of information as to his business. If he tells her he is prospering, she will need the new dress and bonnet much sooner than otherwise; and if he tells her he is not able to buy them, she may confide in some woman who lives on the same block the fact that her husband is having a hard time in his business. It would be better if an allowance were made her every month for all purposes.

The successes and depressions in business ought to be confided in the wife, but she should be a woman who has no confidants except her husband. The importance of this rule should be made clear to her, with the reasons for its strict observance.

It can hardly be assumed that she is unworthy of business secrets. When she feels the honor of being given them for safe holding she will not drop the careless remark that might undo the business of her husband.

But apart from this line of confidence, there are many personal views, many personal hopes, wishes, fears, desires, prospects and plans that enter into his life of which she generally knows nothing. Without waiting for her to ask, it is better for him to mention some of them from time to time, if she shows a disposition to listen. It is by such methods that she will come closer to him; and, in the same way, she can bring him close to her. There must not be a schedule conference for the purpose. Some wives have no tact; for instance the woman who starts in saying after the evening meal is over: "Come, Fred, I have a lot of things to tell you," and he finds not one of them of any moment, so he takes it as an exaggeration and passes his mind on to other things. The way to do is to let some bit of information come in edgewise, as it were, like a wish, or a statement that does not displace any attention in other matters.

Complaints, criticisms, questions, adverse reports, and the darker side of one's thoughts and feelings, should be omitted whenever possible. No woman likes to hear all the time the ailments of her husband, unless he has one worthy of attention. Of all his pains and ill feelings there is not one that will not yield to sensible habits of diet. He suffers either at the stomach, or in his liver, or nerves, or has a pain in the head, or is irritable; all of which are due to bad food selection and modern cooking. So there is no use talking about a condition that neither party is trying to remedy. Some day this error of diet will take her off, or take him off; and even then the survivor will not seek a remedy. It is like the table of fine pictures; a child was allowed to overturn the ink on one of them, and great effort and expense followed in the attempt to clean it. As soon as it was in fair shape, the child was allowed to tip over the ink on another valuable and beautiful picture. Again the doctor of pictures was given the case, and money was spent freely in curing the results of the stain. When this was effected, the child was allowed to tip over the ink on a third picture that was valuable and beautiful. So this process was continued all through the year and year after year. All their spare money went out to remedy the damage being done to the pictures. The picture-doctor did not complain because he was receiving an income from the habit. One day the woman said, "Frank, what do you think of the idea to stop the child from tipping ink over on the pictures? Would it not save expense, worry, and trouble? You see we have spent money and wasted time in getting these damaged pictures cleaned up, and they are never as good after the cure as they were before. How would it do to stop the baby from turning the ink over on them?"

The husband scratched his head, rubbed his forehead, and a ray of intelligence came into his eyes. "Mabel," he said in excitement, "You are a great woman. We will stop the baby at once."

Now, the baby in this case of simile is merely the habit of neglect; the pictures are the human body; the repairer is the physician; and the husband and wife are the ones who pay the bills, suffer self-denial, and have the hard luck that generally follows unnecessary sickness. The one thing for the mind to find out is that the source of any illness can be ascertained, the running cause can be checked, and the cure made unnecessary by withdrawing the trouble at the fountain head.

A complaining person is lacking in magnetism. There are so many complaining persons at large, that the man or woman who has the good judgment to get cured and to stay cured, will hold the advantage in all dealings with the world.

There are two steps in this fault:

1. The permitting of sickness to enter the home, or become a part of the life of the individual.

2. The disposition to talk about the ill condition of the body. The sense of knowledge should be employed in lines of use-

fulness and with good judgment. It is not useful to talk of complaints, either to visitors or to husband and wife. Some callers are spotted in advance of their coming, and the "Not at home" response is often made because the call means the rehearsal of all the illness that a bad system of living has catalogued in one woman's system. "Mrs. Catlet is coming, and I am not at home. I do not want to know the state of her liver, and I take no interest in her duodenum. Her stomach has gastritis, but I did not do it. She has bronchial troubles, spinal troubles, heartburn, colonitis, and some other unmentionable failings, all of which will make up the visit."

This is a common condition in all branches of life. Poor people bemoan their ill luck instead of turning the vitality of their minds to making something better for themselves. Those in the middle ranks pretend to be in better circumstances than they really are, and they spend their time when making calls in exploiting all their ills and physical failings, unless there is a bit of news worth telling.

What is in bad taste with callers is equally bad between husband and wife, for it is wrong of itself no matter where and when. If there is sickness, there is a fault somewhere which needs mending, and the co-operation of both parties in devising methods for putting an end to the trouble is praiseworthy. Bright things should make up the home talk; and it is better to have substantial ideas to talk about. Idle nothings said pleasantly are no more substance than are the steam and vapor of viands.

Nothing thrives so poorly as emptiness.

Nothing is so unmagnetic as pain, suffering, sickness, disagreeable subjects and complaining tones. These must all be swept away before magnetism of any kind can begin. No person pretends to believe that unpleasant things will attract the good will of another. They not only fail to attract, but also actually take the opposite course; they repel.

The husband who depends on the fact that his wife is bonded to him for life and that she must therefore listen to him, endure him, work and slave for him, make herself abject and humble before him, put up with his numerous failings and uncouth qualities rather than break away from the whole disagreeable relationship, might have pinned his faith on such dependence in the days when women were in the legal class of underlings; but today there is a very short step between her condition of degradation and freedom. She is taking that step in numbers that are appalling. Ere long the husband will hold the wife by some attraction, and not by force of the marriage relationship.

What that attraction is will be known as Sex Magnetism in one of its phases.

There are many men, in fact hundreds of thousands of men, who have no inducement held out to their wives to remain at home except the mere chance of being supported, supposedly of being clothed, fed and housed. Against this meagre asset, are placed all the unattractive conditions made by the men themselves. There must be a complete change in methods, or wives will vanish out of the homes to remain out forever. Where is the woman who, while pinched by poverty or the lack of the ordinary comforts of daily life, is willing to stay in such place a day longer than she is compelled to, when the carelessness or indifference of the husband may drag her still lower by forcing children on her that the home has no place for, and the purse cannot properly feed?

The majority of husbands have some of the brute in them; and a large minority have almost nothing else but the brute in them. To that minority an appeal is useless in this generation. It may be lessened by decreasing the conditions that make such qualities possible and logical.

But to the men who, while not brutal, are neglectful of their wives, who spend their time, their surplus thought and their money away from home, when they are not at work, and who do not offer one genuine personal attention after the first few months of the marriage, an influence may go out that will help them to attract instead of repel their wives.

On the other hand, the women who depend on the bondage of wedlock to hold the relationship intact, and who do not try to furnish meals that will bring health instead of pain and irritability to their husbands, or who are indifferent to the management of their homes, will very soon cease to be attractive. Simple and practical as it is, and devoid of all semblence of romance, it is nevertheless the greatest fact of life that the food that is eaten makes or un-makes the human body. A man is what he eats. He must have the right kind of food, selected by the right kind of knowledge, and cooked in the right way. The modern wife learns at home to make new bread, cakes, pastry, puddings, all kinds of rich things and whatever is indigestible and barbaric, under the belief that the way to a man's heart is through his stomach. In this she is wrong. The boarding-house keeper who fed her boarders to the richest kind of food, made money because she ruined their appetites and tore their stomachs to tatters, so to speak.

The practical and permanent way to a man's heart is to make home a place of comfort to him; and the first step in this direction is to give him freedom from the discomforts, pains and irritability of indigestion. He will be what he eats. Plain food, simple food, cooked in an attractive manner will soon prove that the way to a man's adoration of a woman is through the good health she can give him. There is but one synonym for the condition of hell in physical life, and that is modern food selection and modern cooking.

It seems a matter unworthy of a book like this; but it is the crucial point between misery and happiness.

Now most wives are unwilling to even give the matter a thought, and they wonder why they have ugly husbands who prefer any place to home. Say what you will, the wife who wants her husband to remain at home, can attract him there if she chooses to make the effort. But smiles will not do it; pleasant tones of voice will not do it; having his slippers at his feet will not do it; mending his torn clothes, catering to his wishes, being solicitous about his well being, and the artifices that most women adopt for effect, will not do it; because all the attentions of a wife eager to please will not fight down or drive out of his existence that inflamed stomach that she has been developing for him by her ignorance or indifference to the one most vital problem of married life today.

When will women wake up?

Will it be tomorrow, or the next day, or the next year?

The wife who wakes up first in this revolution will be the first to reap the reward. A man's nature leaps as out of the darkness into the daylight with the return of that healthful feeling that attends good digestion. He seems to be a new man all at once.

Do not make the mistake to adopt some freak fad in food

selection or some silly nut-schedule, or other unusual thing. In the lists of plain foods there are many things that are suited to the stomach, that have been used for generations, and that held sway until the modern French chef began to tell us how to break down the stomach. There is not the slightest trouble in finding what is right and how to get and prepare it, when once the wife makes up her mind to reform the habits of her kitchen. A few simple articles of food, costing less than one-third of what is now paid for groceries and provisions, will bring health. If the husband denies his indigestion, which he may do in all honesty, for it is blind in its first years, then let him be educated up to the standard set in this work. If you, a wife, have this instruction, he will have access to it. He may sneer at it for a while; but there is a way to invite him to peruse its pages without thrusting them at him to his annoyance. His stomach condition may make him "touchy" on this subject as on others.

Men are going to break away from the ties of marriage with great ease in the near future. The courts cannot compel them to support their wives unless they can reach them, and no State court has inter-state jurisdiction. It is estimated that today there are more than one million husbands who are still legally married, but who have gone out of their States in order to evade the courts, and who will not live with their wives. They do not seek divorces, but rest.

A great business man said, "If all the men who will not stay with their wives were to be jailed for non-support, the manufactures of the land would be crippled." A judge said, "I am of the opinion that the real fault is with the wives, but I must obey the statutes and order husbands to support their wives." A man said who voiced the opinion of these run-away husbands, of whom he was one, "I want to live where I can have my meals properly prepared. What is the use of a man dragging himself out all the time just to pay for stuff that no stomach can turn over?"

The conclusions reached at the threshold of this study are as follows:

1. There must be an attractive force in the man who wishes to retain his wife at home or in the marriage relationship, even if he does not choose to make her supremely happy.

2.   There must be an attractive force in the woman who wishes to retain her husband at home or in the marriage relationship, even if she does not choose to add to his contentment and pleasure.

3.   There must be something more than a mere attractive force in the man who seeks to make his wife supremely happy and exalt her state as a wife.

4.   There must be something more than a mere attractive force in the woman who seeks to make her husband supremely happy and give him the bliss which he once thought would come to him with her.

THE ATTRACTIVE FORCE

OMING up out of the valley of a disagreeable discussion into the uplands of a wider and more pleasing realm, we will proceed to state the laws that are established by nature for the benefit and the blessing of marriage. Before they are outlined, there should be a clear understanding of the frame-work of this system of training. It is not a drifting course, but one fixed in the immutable designs of nature herself and the clearly shown purposes of creation.

In all the systems that have been put into form of printed instruction during the past thirty years, there is not one that has a more certain character than Sex Magnetism. It contains every possible means of assistance to men and women who need such aid. It has a basis as strong as the foundations of the solid mountain. On this basis is set a law as full of vitality as nature herself. Above this law is a superstructure as logical in its meaning and value as the castle that holds a kingdom in safety.

Such is Sex Magnetism.

It is not one and the same power with both sexes; but is so made that it operates in one way for woman and in another way for man. It differs for those who are not yet betrothed from its uses when the betrothal is announced. Then again it changes its operative force after marriage. It has its uses for those who are not married and are free from the desire to enter that state. Yet through all these phases there is one direct purpose at work to achieve a certain end.

STEPS IN THE PLAN

1. There is, in the first step, the man who lacks the attractive force.

2. There is, in the second step, the woman who has never yet had or who now lacks the same quality.

3. There is, in the third step, the man who possesses the attractive force, having added it purposely or instinctively.

4. There is, in the fourth step, the woman who possesses the attractive force, having also added it.

5. There is, in the fifth step, the man who possesses something more than the mere attractive force, which has already been referred to.

6. There is, in the sixth step, the woman who possesses something more than mere attractive force.

7. What has been called the attractive force is that impulse taught by nature and explained in the first department of this book, which causes a man or woman to seek every possible way of self improvement in order to attract one of the opposite sex.

8. Prior to the birth of such impulse there is in the non-regnum period of every man and woman a partial or total absence of the attractive force which has been described above.

9. There is also after the consent to marriage has been won, a partial or almost total lessening of the same force of attraction.

10. After marriage there is a further lessening of the attractive force if any of it was left when the ceremony was performed.

THE AFFIRMATIVE PLAN

1. Under the influence of Sex Magnetism it is necessary to restore the attractive force in its full degree in the man, whether it is restored in the woman or not.

2. Under the same influence it is necessary to restore the attractive force in the woman, regardless of the man. These two rules imply that the man or woman are not in the same acquaintance. They mean that any man must build up that force, and any woman must do the same thing; and that it is immaterial whether the opposite sex shall do it or not with relation to the other man or woman involved. It is enough for two if the husband has that force; and it is enough for two if the wife has it.

3. As the attractive force in one sex is not exactly the same force as that possessed by the other sex, it is important that the true uses of this power be understood.

4. When this attractive force has been restored, it should be increased beyond the instinctive demands of nature. This means that there should be something more done to build up an attractive character than is done blindly.

5. This force in its highest degree must hold sway all through the marriage. It served its instinctive purpose when it brought the two sexes to an agreement; but that was not enough.

6. Whether there is marriage or not, every man and woman should possess this extra high degree of the attractive force.

7. In addition to the extra high degree there should be added the direct power of Sex Magnetism as a still greater influence to compel the most complete and satisfying results of the relationship.

Two remarkable facts should be reviewed at this time:

1. The instinctive attractive force is ordained by nature.

2. The reception of the added power of Sex Magnetism is encouraged by nature.

The following tendencies are repeated here in another form so that they may be made more prominent in the mind of the reader:

1. Prior to the awakening of an interest in the opposite sex, there is no impulse toward using the attractive force.

2. After this force has done its work, the tendency is to lapse back to the state of former indifference; but not to the full condition then prevailing.

3. The difference between the former state and that which follows the lapse, is the net improvement of the individual.

4. The sum total of the individual instances of improvement represents the advance that civilization has made. Slight though it may be, it is something.

It has been asserted and proved in many ways that civilization in this way, and in no other way, makes its progress; and thus we see the reason why two sexes are established instead of one.

Before proceeding with this study it is necessary to review all the statements made in the first department of this book. It is important that the philosophy of progress should be understood, as well as the meaning of the sex forms of life. It is a

grand thought that nature should intend to advance the race
and the earth, that the past is less and the future is greater
than the present, and that this will so continue until the plan
of creation as far as this part of it is concerned, is fulfilled and
brought to the climax set for it from the foundations of all
eternity.

In the absence of the sexes there could be no progress.

Selection and the survival of the fittest would be inoperative
laws, lacking the channels of activity. Variation could not take
place, for there would be no mixing of individualities in reproduction.

Variation is the soul of progress.

Having reviewed all that is stated in the first department,
the work now ahead is to grasp the meaning of the term, "attractive force," which has been so much used herein.

There is a well defined reason why a man should seek to make
himself attractive to a woman whom he wishes to win. On the
same ground the woman has a reason for wishing to make herself attractive to the man she wishes to win. There is very
little deliberation of an insincere kind in this attempt at improvement. It has come down to the human species from the
other species that have preceded. We have cited the cases of
the birds in the forest, the better plumage, the better song voices
and the abler bodies have won against all lesser specimens.
Humanity is driven on by the same nature.

The attractive force makes itself manifest through different
channels and in different ways as the race progresses. Once
the better mind would not be considered a point of superiority;
and it is not so regarded today except where it bears practical
fruit. Book learning in either sex is not an agency of attraction. Education may have its drawing qualities among the
educated classes, for a trained mind will not be contented with
one that is ignorant. The woman who speaks grammatically and
spells correctly will not be impressed by a man who is very
backward in these accomplishments unless he has other qualities
in excess to overcome such handicap.

A highly educated man may take a very pretty woman who
rakes English fore and aft; because he thinks he can educate
her in the privacy of married life. A highly educated woman
may take a man of wealth who is unable to recognize the differ-

ence between nouns and fractions, because she believes that she can give him some polish in their spare moments. But, on the other hand, where these extra inducements are lacking, a highly educated man may delay proposing to an ignorant woman until she has had her ambition stimulated to the point of learn-, ing how to use grammar and to spell; and a highly educated woman who is sought by an ignorant lover, may let him know that she appreciates a knowledge of grammar and the use of the art of spelling; and, if he really cares for her as he should, he will set to work and master these branches. It is possible that no other power on earth could so influence him. But for the holding back of the woman, the man might remain ignorant all his life. When he has made the start towards an education he may keep along for years. He certainly could be swayed to any possible extent as long as she holds him back. But if she accepts him, even on the condition that he learns these things, the impulse has gone. Nature steps side as soon as the consent has been given, for the purpose of nature is to bring the two sexes into an agreement.

Now notice how weak is the agreement and the impulse when the man has no trouble in winning the woman, or the woman has no difficulty in bringing the man to her heart. Then notice how shabby is that betrothal where the couple, on brief acquaintance, agree to marry and proceed at once with the privileges that pertain to wedlock. She is, prima facie, unchaste, and he is of her class. There is no attractive force in this animal agreement. Notice how weak is that relationship where the man, meeting the woman without introduction, calling at her home on her invitation, being refused certain favors until they are married, being wed very soon, and attempting to make marriage a success. There are cases where such couples have lived together, but no one of them has ever appreciated the other or held the sex in respect.

It is hardly fair to the students of these pages to assume that such couples have any standing in this work of building a happy life through Sex Magnetism.

The one great thing to be desired is the development of the attractive force. That cannot take place unless there is a period of friendship in which both parties are in doubt as to the minds and hearts of each other. This is necessary. The longer that period lasts the greater will be the development. In the time when a term of years was made essential to an engagement or betrothal, conditioned on the qualification of the male, the result was a race of gentlemen.

When a woman thinks she is being observed by some man she admires, she makes every effort to look her best. If an acquaintance and friendship follow, she will try to appear beautiful as the first step. But if she is not able to succeed in this direction, she will shift to the effort to appear pleasing, which is beautiful in manner and speech. The next garnishment will be intelligence. Much will depend on the character of the man. If he is a college professor, and she is uneducated, or has a very limited education, she will not attempt to talk much. Her face, dress and manner will then be made as attractive as possible. Where a woman has very little to match the accomplishments of the man, she will pose as having been deprived of the advantages of other girls, and will make the confession in all humbleness, thinking to arouse his sympathy. It requires tact to hold a man by such methods. Beauty of face and of manner take the place of much; but a man of good judgment will not be swayed far beyond a plumb line by them. Love falls down before the elements that are unattractive.

Added to the above efforts to seem pleasing, will be the usual neatness of dress and of hair, cleanliness of face and hands, and a general sweetness of body. No department of her being that can be exposed to any of the senses, will suffer neglect. Even if no engagement follow, she will not be the loser by this advance in her refinement. She will be a better woman for the experience.

A man when he has met a woman whom he would like to marry, will make similar efforts but along lines suited to his sex. The first idea that will occur to him is, will the woman think him handsome? To get some help on this problem, he will look in the mirror often and at all places where he can find such an article. When a woman glances at herself in a mirror, she wants to know how she will appear to men who may see her. If she knows she is homely, she will let the mirror alone. When a man looks in a public mirror, he is in love, or else is vain beyond pardon.

If he seeks the admiration of an educated woman, he will

talk as little as possible on subjects that he knows nothing about. If he is not handsome, he will wonder if she cares for a manly man, and if he thinks she does, he will straighten up and look much more ferocious than he is. But the first true sign of love having come into the heart of a man is the care with which he has his shoes shined. They become bright and reflect all the good things in the sky and scenery about him. "Henry is in love," said a business man in speaking of a clerk whom he had in his employ for several years. "How do you know?" was the response. "Because he is polishing his shoes, and that is something that he has not done for a long time except when they are very dingy." "Look here, Henry," said the other, "I hear that you are in love. Has she accepted you yet?" "Dear me, no, not yet. She does not know I love her. I am hoping for the best, sir."

All men in love, until they are accepted, make themselves neater, gentler, more pleasing in speech and manner, and more progressive in every way that may have an influence on the woman desired.

Now come to the marriage state.

The first thing to do, ere this is considered, is to review the second and third departments of this book. In the second department the basic laws must be read until they are fully understood, for they tell the negative story of humanity. They show how far both sexes have fallen from that period of effort when they tried to be attractive to each other. Where is there an attempt to build a home or restrict the expenditures so that the earnings may exceed them and an excess be laid aside?

But the third department, in its discussion of the six senses, shows something more, over which we would like to drop the curtain of charity could it be done and this work proceed. Answer, if you will, the following questions:

1. Today to what extent are you clean in body, hair, eyes, ears, nose, mouth, teeth, neck, chest, armpits, loins, legs, ankles and feet?

2. To what extent are your underclothes clean, and your outer clothes neat and tidy?

3. Is your speech careful, well chosen, pleasing and attractive?

4. To what extent are you well-mannered, observing the

accepted laws of etiquette, taking pains to be polite to every-body even in the privacy of your home and the outward side of your life?

5. To what extent are you refined, polished and gentle in your conduct and words?

6. Are you constantly seeking to aid and sympathize with the one you have professed to love, co-operating in every way to make all duties and tasks easier, and fill every day full of comfort and happiness?

7. For the sake of that person have you added anything to your mental qualifications, increasing your intelligence, building up character, and taking on a higher stature?

8. Have you made your hands more skilled, and developed your faculties in order to be a more useful helpmeet?

9. Do you keep informed of every wish, hope, fear, ambition and duty that enters into the heart of that person?

10. How much time in every twenty-four hours do you turn into selfish uses that might just as easily be devoted to the companionship of that person?

11. Have you read carefully the third department of this book, and have you, as measured by the standards set therein, taken an account of stock of yourself in every detail of that department as far as it may apply to you?

12. Do you recall the period of courtship? In that period did you display more attractive qualities than you now show in your daily life? Can you be perfectly frank in making reply to this inquiry, or is it your desire to evade the matter and try to make yourself believe that you are still as attractive as you thought you were then?

Nature had a purpose in impelling you to attract the other sex in the period of doubt when first you evinced an interest in another. Not alone to win or be won, but to make a new standard of excellence for yourself. Nature felt sure that it was then or never; if you would not improve at that time you never would improve. This is true philosophy.

If you are married, go back to the third department and read all about the six senses, and make a written note of every instance in which you can better your habits. You may say the other sex is not worth it. The request is not made for the benefit of the other sex, but solely for your own good. You have possibly become yoked to a person whom you despise, or over whom you exalt yourself as far more worthy; but remember that private opinions of others are reflections in the mirror of your own life.

If you despise the other sex, never mind that; get the advantage that will come from your own improvement. If nature sought to make you better by taking advantage of the time when you could be induced to try to rise, why not adopt the same principle at another time and rise in spite of the lack of inducement as far as the other sex is concerned.

Study all that is said of the sense of smell in the third department and then apply it to yourself. In case of doubt, give the benefit not to your own conceit but to the sense itself. Make all defective habits over into perfect habits. It may take some effort, but remember that physical activity brings perfect health and long life, as well as good fortune in every way.

Then the sense of sight should be gone over in that third department and an inventory taken of your shortcomings. Be honest with yourself. You may cover up and deceive your outside acquaintances, but not your own honest self. There are scores of ways in which you can improve in this one line alone; and if you find less than sixty defects in your methods in this regard, go back over the whole list until you get them all. Then, even if you do not care for the other sex, go to work for your own good and make a perfect record in the change.

There are the other senses likewise to be reviewed in the third department, and you must be faithful in the reading of them in the ability to discover the neglects. You may perhaps be in a position to hide some things even from your consort, but that must not be your guide. Hide nothing from yourself.

Finally there is the sense of knowledge. The discussion of it contains many things that are needed in your life. Change bad habits and adopt those that will improve you. All magnetism may be acquired in this way.

Now it is not asked of you to become impractical. Ideal existence is not possible. Nothing like the ideal is sought. You are requested to put yourself just where you were when you began your courtship, and where you were in personal habits in the first twenty-four hours of marriage, if you had any refinement at all. Remember that civilization is at stake. No one person can do much to advance the race; but a hundred million persons can assist it to make great strides in a few years.

There are teachings that tell of the excellence of a higher mode of thinking and living; of self-denial beyond all endurance to add to the exaltation of man or woman. Such ideals are not taught here. Keep down to the useful and the practical. They are good enough. Take the measure of what you are aiming to do from the measure set by nature during courtship. You then tried to make the other sex believe that you were better than your past habits gave warrant; now try to make yourself see, in fact, that you can be better than you were yesterday.

Cleanliness and neatness in clothing, in the body itself, and under all circumstances are traits of character that cannot be improved, without at the same time improving the power within you that impels them. These are certainly practical. Is your underclothing and your under-condition such that, in case of accident and you were exposed, the public or the doctors would find you just as you would like to be found? If not, then you have a standard night and day to be lived up to. That is certainly practical and useful. You may say you do not have time to be neat and clean. But you do have time. You may deceive yourself, but you cannot deceive mother nature. She knows. You have hundreds of little minutes that are wasted every day. You talk idly to others who have no claims on your time, and you thus let valuable moments go to waste. You believe that the daily newspaper is a means of education, when in fact it is a means of dethroning reason and inviting suicide by its flaring columns of crime and disaster. Surely you do not wish to flood your mind with the impure news stream of the daily press. Permit scant offerings of the newspaper to enter your mind. The press has no power over the public. It sways no one whose mind is worth swaying. Therefore, do not make the mistake of taking your mental food from such a source. Save the wasted moments for such reading and current history as you can get from the weekly publications of high merit and from the monthly magazines.

Having learned that a moment is a diamond set in hours of gold, spare them to the best aspirations of the mind and heart.

Cut short idle conversation and idle reading.

Then will come the objection that you do not feel like improving yourself; you have won the courtship and there is no reason now why you should be careful in order to retain the good opinion of the other sex. Of course that is laziness. You are now sounding the note that has held people down all their lives. It is the repetition of history to invite poverty and failure by the love of doing nothing that can be evaded. The old advice to never put off till tomorrow what you can do today, shows the trend of humanity all through the past centuries. The man or woman who does not draw prosperity like a magnet is the one who reverses the advice, and never does today what can be put off till tomorrow.

Magnetism is founded on eternal activity of the muscles and of the mind. You can study the habits of magnetic men and women, and you will find, much to your surprise, that they are never at rest; they are not time wasters; they cannot let moments run to waste. Perhaps you do not care to purchase success at the expense of learning how to be active. In that case, it is useless to go further. You cannot reverse nature. Those who are active in mind and muscle by born habit or temperament, are looked upon as naturally magnetic. But it has been proved that the same habits may be cultivated in either way; you may cultivate magnetism and the love of activity will follow; or you may cultivate activity and the magnetic character will be set up along with it. You cannot separate the two.

Therefore, when you say that you do not feel like paying attention to the scores of details that will make you neat and cleanly, bright and attractive, you are sounding the death knell of your future success, unless you have the inherent will power to turn about and make up your mind to do what is right. Once, when in the throes of courtship, you sought self improvement through excessive activity and personal attention to your manners and character, your dress and body. Nature was then behind you pushing you on. Now you must invite nature to come again to your aid.

Suppose you are a husband. You have some male friend of about the same age of your wife, and this friend comes to your house to live for a few weeks. He is not her husband. He is no relation to her. He may or may not be married; that makes no difference; but if your wife is neat, refined and attractive, this male friend of yours will show you how to behave before her. He will be extra neat in dress, person and appearance. He will be careful and gentlemanly in speech. He will be courteous and gallant at all times. He will be considerate and patient if trying circumstances arise. That is the measure that nature sets up within him for him to follow. Not that he is courting your wife, or that he is flirting with her. He may be careful not to see her when you are not present, so there is no reason for jealousy; but he merely acts on the instinctive impulse that comes forth on all such occasions where the man meets the woman to whom he is not married. It is, of course, true that his own wife at home, if he has one, will not receive the gallant attentions that he bestows on the wife of his friend right under the gaze of that friend. It is of course true that, if he were to marry that wife to whom he is showing such politeness, he would cease such extra attentions; but you cannot take away the fact that this wife enjoys such gallantry and evidence of appreciation, and that the man suffers not the slightest inconvenience in rendering them to her. Then the excuse that you do not feel like it, when these matters are urged on you as a daily habit, is only a false reply to the suggestion.

The wife, all other things being equal, prefers to have this man in the house, as every woman enjoys homage; but let him relax his politeness and care of her or himself, let him show clothing that is not neat, let him come to the table unkempt, let him slip up in his refined speech, or otherwise show signs of the marriage habit, and his wife will suddenly despise him. The thin veneer has broken and the same disappointing man is there in the guise of a visitor. If his attentions do not ring true, she will find them out. His hope of retaining the welcome is in a genuine admiration for her, and an honest attempt to be attractive to her. All this may be done without overstepping the hospitality offered by the husband. It is not flirting. If the visitor has designs other than loyal to his friend, he will make them manifest in other ways, and then the wife must either confide in her husband or else cow the invader.

Let the husband himself transfer this visiting gallantry and attention to his own wife, and never relax from it as long as he lives. He would show such refinement to some other wife; why not to his own? He thinks it is not worth while. He sees the woman he is married to, and knows her under all circumstances, and he does not think it worth while to court her over again. Let that part of it drop. All that is asked is to evince the attentions and manliness in her presence that he would yield to the wife of his friend. That is not too much, and it is eminently practical.

Read all of department three in this course and adopt the suggestions there made, as they cover the whole ground of personal conduct.

Then there are some lines of improvement that may not be invited in the usual courtship. While book learning is not always essential to sex influence, it is a means of help; but common sense and good judgment are always necessary. They can be cultivated by the process known in magnetism as asking yourself a constant question, or expressing a constant belief. In acquiring common sense and good judgment the question to be asked as you analyze each idea or each proposed act, is stated below:

"Is it sensible?"

The statement to be made is:

"This is not the best thing to do."

The purpose is to concentrate the mind on the conditions and to select the best course. If the reply to the question is favorable, you have the advantage of the brief analysis; and if the assertion is not correct, then you will have had something in the mind that has turned it about completely. By this process a person comes soon to acquire good sense and accurate judgment. Many men who have won the highest success in life, have had the habit of taking the opposite view of everything from that which is first presented to them; and they then see if they are able to break down this opposition. The mental process is done in a flash and soon is a fixed habit.

Men appreciate evidence of practical, common sense in a

woman whether she is married or single. Women admire the same trait in men. A girl is pretty. Some young man is infatuated with her beauty. His older friends may say, "She is a mere doll."—"She has a baby face."—"She is just pretty and nothing else, and beauty is only skin deep."

It is a very undesirable marriage that has merely the beauty of a wife to cement it; for, as she matures, her good looks will give way to the lack of sound intelligence. The mind that first breaks down, in the average number of cases, is that which has followed the vanishing of a pretty face. Many of the women in the asylums have once been beauties. Sense and fine looks make a good combination; and sense coupled with practical judgment, embellished by native intelligence, is much more desirable than the velvet skin and the bright complexion. Look at the police and court history of many of the noted cases of recent years, and see how many girls of the pretty type have figured in them.

What is called sense and a lack of genial kindness are too often found blended in the same person. While sense is an aid to magnetism it is overcome by harshness and a cold disposition. As sunshine has been found essential to the growth of all life, so the brightness of mind and heart have the same influence over our fellow beings.

Character has power to win, but it loses against bad manners and cheap habits. The greater the real worth of a person, the greater will be the character, and it is doubtful if character is real where the habits are faulty. A very attractive young woman was seen after dinner at a hotel where she had met the son of a prominent millionaire of New York City. He thought he had never beheld so rare and fascinating a beauty before, and he was already beyond control in love with her, when he saw her move her tongue along the entire row of lower front teeth, and clean them. The lip was bulged out as the tongue made its repeated progress in this effort. Her next achievement was to run a long, slender, delicately pink little finger up into her nose for several inches, as he thought, and pull down something that he did not wait to scrutinize. He was gone.

The real man will not chew gum or tobacco or work his mouth in any way when it is not necessary. He will not pick

his teeth in public, or in the presence of any other person;
nor will he suck the teeth at the cavities, or otherwise make
himself appear nasty in personal habits. Of all the nauseating faults of men, none is more disagreeable than these, especially
any action of the tongue, teeth, lips or mouth that can be
seen or heard. One woman was driven crazy by the "sucking"
of cavities in the teeth of her husband. He did this all the time,
and she had been brought up in a family of refinement. Some
natures cannot endure the swinish habits of men.

It is true that a person who has not been well bred would
have no guiding rules to aid in doing right and avoiding
error; but there should be ambition to find out the facts. Get
a book of etiquette, and read it not only once, but a hundred
times until everything is understood and can be adopted easily.
Husbands and wives sometimes agree to find out all they can
for each other, and to make suggestions for the help of each
in all matters of personal conduct. In the rules of etiquette
there are some forms and some customs that vary with the locality; but every person in and out of society should have the latest
local guide in good manners and should take a few minutes a
day for the study of it. There will be an opportunity to practice these rules anywhere, or at least some of them. There
are couples who actually do put them into practice in the homes
they occupy, humble as they are. It was at one time thought
that such couples would never have an opportunity to show their
good manners in the higher ranks; but the latter find them out.
In one case a wealthy woman had occasion to call at the home
of one of the couples referred to, and was surprised to witness
the same methods that she was accustomed to in her own circles.
To her husband she said that she believed they had seen better
days. "Let us find out," he replied, and they gave a dinner to
the poor husband and wife. All the attaches of the mansion
stood about and there was no form that was omitted. Of course,
the guests were not at ease, but they knew what to do and they
did it at all times. The result was a friendship that led to a
business opportunity for the man, and today he is himself the
head of a great house.

It can be set down as an axiom that any person in humble
circumstances who is willing to study and to practice the rules

of etiquette in a lowly dwelling has that something in him that will rise to a better condition.

On the same principle it may be set down as an axiom that any man or woman who, while not seeming to have any use for an education, will improve in spelling, in grammar, in mathematics, in rhetoric, in the English language as a literature, or in any branch of useful learning, will some day rise to a level that will suit the accomplishment.

Among the ordinary ranks of educated people you will be measured largely by the way you pronounce the English language, and by the kind of grammar you speak. Among those with whom you correspond, you will be estimated according to your use of grammar, and your vocabulary. But in the higher ranks you will stand or fall on your knowledge of rhetoric.

Here then are three studies that you should become master in. They may not be exchangeable right away for bread and meat, but they will sooner or later buy something greater than bread or meat. Every person who is ignorant, every person who is fairly well educated, every person who has acquired great learning and has grown rusty in its use, should have near-by every day of the week certain books, of which a grammar, a dictionary, a speller, and a rhetoric are the first four. Some persons carry one of these books with them all the time. There are minutes in every day that are wasted, and that can be put to some use in study.

The fifth most important book is a work on character; the sixth is a work on etiquette, and a seventh is a work on mathematics of some kind, for every person should be quick and accurate in figuring.

Now what will be the difference between adding knowledge and reading the sewerage of the daily press? The latter is more entertaining, just as pastry tastes better than corn meal bread. But the pastry ruins the blood, and the newspaper ruins the mind. There is a difference of value all along the way. The seven books we have referred to will give you a new level. Your own ability will rise to a higher level. It is a rule of human life that every individual sooner or later rises to his actual level, just as a fountain will do the same. A man had a seven-story building, in which he had running water on the first floor only. He carried his pipes farther up the hill and the water rose to supply the second floor. Later on he carried the pipes still farther up the hill, and the water supplied the third floor. In the course of time he went back far enough and up high enough to reach the level of the seventh floor, and he got the source of supply even beyond that so he could add another story or more to the building.

In just this way human values rise and fall.

The young man says, "What is the use of my learning arithmetic? I am not working where they want arithmetic." When he was told that it would not hurt him, he was induced to try it, and he soon found it both harmless and a pleasant study. When he had become skilled in figures, he was wanted at another place where they required the knowledge of arithmetic, and his wages were doubled. This will be the experience of every man and woman who ever expects to be thrown on his or her own resources. A young lady some years ago was advised to take all seven of the branches of training referred to above, and she obeyed. The books were borrowed and so cost her nothing. She had the time and blindly went to work. Then she happened by some good fortune to fall heir to the estate of a rich uncle of the Far West, and her education was useless. But she did not regret it. She felt all the better for the knowledge she had acquired. In the course of three more years the mines failed, and all her fortune was wiped out. She was in debt. At this time, being compelled to live on her labor, she found the education the only means of earning a decent livelihood. Again she did not regret it. When she was rich, her training, all self-taught, enabled her to attend to the duties of her circumstances, and gave her a place among the educated classes. When she was poor, the same training enabled her to subsist and lay aside a fund each year against old age.

But aside from the monetary value of knowledge, there is the making of a better level. It is easily and quickly made. Not much is required to effect a change for the better. Take the case of a young man who had married and who wanted to rise above his level both of wages and of mind. He wrote to a business man for advice. After perusing the letter, the business man told him to learn to spell. "This is a joke," he said, "but I will do it, for I suppose my letter was a freak."

He paid five cents for an old speller. He had an hour or two each evening in which he could study. In a month he challenged his wife to trip him on any word in the book, and she could not. He became an unusually accurate speller. Then as a joke he wrote to the man and took pains to make the letter quite long, asking him what he would next advise. The man said he needed grammar. This was a different proposition; but the young man and his wife both started to learn grammar without a teacher. They had no trouble that could not be surmounted, and in the course of a year they were very good grammarians. Again the young man wrote to the merchant and asked what next he would suggest. The latter had employed the young man's father and had told the younger one that he would be glad to give him advice at any time. The third suggestion was a knowledge of arithmetic; but this was anticipated, as there had been an old book of that kind in the house for some months. It was not long before this same merchant offered a good position to the ambitious student, who was at best nothing but an ignorant knock-about fellow two years before, and who married when he had nothing with which to support the wife. The business man and his protege had a conference after a while and they computed how much the latter had gained by being willing to educate himself instead of remaining at his low level. In place of wages averaging less than fourteen dollars a week, he was able to earn all the year round a salary equal to fifty dollars a week. This was the money value of the self-taught training.

There are millions of young men in this land who are able to raise their own level, but who will not lift a finger to do so. They come home and claim that they have had all the hard work they want for that day. In a line of beggars in New York City last winter, eight men out of every ten showed evidence of a possible intelligence beyond their condition. A lady of wealth had her agents meet these men singly and apart from all listeners, and offered to them books they would need to enable them to learn; but not one man in a thousand would let this be done. They all preferred to sit in the parks, reading scraps of old newspapers and talking about their hard luck; and the well and strong among them refused to aid themselves or be aided except as mere beggars.

For poverty there is a cause.

For ignorance there is a cause.

The men and women who will not take an interest in themselves when their health is such that they are able to do so, should not be fed, especially when the offers of help are made in connection with the offers of food and clothing. Of course a hungry man wants something to eat rather than something to study. But if he can have his food, his clothing and his lodgings all given to him free of charge on condition that he try to make himself more useful, he will refuse the latter part of the tender. In one experiment a man of wealth gave three good meals a day, and lodgings and clothing to a large number of men, and then assembled them in a hall where he had teachers try to arouse in them a desire and willingness to be taught the easiest and simplest things of a useful education; but the men would not listen. Not one would open a book given him.

These facts show why that class is not worthy of help.

A young married man recently killed himself and left a letter in which he said that he had consulted a clergyman who advised him to end his life, as the conditions of modern civilization were such that no man was under moral obligations to live in them. This husband left two small boys and a wife. He was twenty-seven years of age. He had been married five years. Prior to his marriage he had been given an opportunity to receive an education and spurned the offer. After his marriage he showed no disposition to lighten the burdens of his wife who slaved for him more hours than he worked for her. He spent his evenings away from home until ten or eleven o'clock, while his wife was struggling with her cares and children. When the panic came seven young men of his acquaintance who had been to school and had learned their lessons well, had steady work and were laying aside money, while this fellow was idle and took very little interest even then in bettering himself. One of his young men friends said to him one evening, "Tom, you have a chance to get good work if you will fit yourself for it. But you know nothing of the plain branches of knowledge." The despondent young man said he did not know and he did not want to know. Then came the suicide. The clergyman denied having given the advice to kill himself.

There was no evidence of insanity. It was merely a typical case of the class who will not better their minds, and who prefer to remain ignorant and abjectly poor rather than try to rise in the world.

We do not uphold the idle rich, for we have only profound disgust for them and their monkey dinners; but, on the other hand, we do not uphold the poor and ignorant classes who refuse to help themselves when help is offered in a way that will enable them to seek new levels and rise to them. It is not the fault of the wealthy classes that the poor are poor. It is the fault of the poor themselves. This fault can be brought home to that class and very easily identified.

The husband who does not care to better himself by making a new level for himself, has no genuine love for his wife. He may have animal affection and a dog loyalty, but not a manly love. He may grumble at modern civilization and blame it for his poverty, but he forgets that the millionaire who puts a million dollars in a house, really distributes the million dollars. If he did nothing with it he would have it; but when he spends it somebody else has it, and it is the great public. The women who each year spend a billion dollars for dresses that are wholly unnecessary to them, part with the billion dollars. If they did not spend it they would still have it; but, having spent it, the public has it. How many persons do you think get some of the billion dollars that the rich spend for their dresses each year? More than forty millions of people. Now which is best: to keep the money and not let the forty millions of people share it; or to spend it so that it may go into general circulation? After the rich women part with it, what have they in place of the billion dollars? Nothing at all, after the dresses have been worn and given away or discarded. There is a total annual loss of one billion dollars to the wealthy women. But some of the forty million people who share the sum of one thousand million dollars each year, lay away part of it against a rainy day.

This is but one case in illustration of the value of the spendthrift to the world.

It is a lucky thing that the rich spend their money like water. It would be a calamity of the most disastrous character if the rich did not spend their money. It used to be the policy

of governments in hard times to carry on public improvements
so that the idle men might be employed and thus be able to support their families. When a million rich men each year will
maintain constant improvements in their property, they will do
a far wider work and a more beneficial charity in the name of
money-squandering than the cities and States that open up
their treasuries in days of panic. The city of Washington spent
five thousand dollars to give its idle men work one winter,
and less than two thousand negroes got this money in two
days. The city of Philadelphia spent a hundred thousand
dollars to help circulate some money among hungry families;
but this was spent in three days, and the amount that was added
to the circulation went chiefly into the bar-rooms.

In and around that city, twelve months in the year, year
in and year out, rich men spend a million dollars a day in
labor bills for the mere purpose of carrying on private improvements and keeping their estates and property in good
condition; and the excellent thing about this expenditure is
that men who drink and carouse are being gradually dropped
from the payrolls. When the men of wealth will make work
plenty, and give it only to laborers who are sober and industrious, they will do a greater charity than the sentimental women
who feed the idle poor. In the park near Somerville, New
Jersey, a multi-millionaire spends for labor alone between fifteen hundred and two thousand dollars a day. What he gets
in return is a shifting of the land. He has been doing this
for more than ten years. If he were to sell the place today,
he could not get as much for it as it cost him. His expenditure, then, has been a form of distributing his money among
his fellow beings. Had that money been sent to the coffers of
the middle classes it could not have cropped out in the form
of parks, and no one would have been benefited by it.

Permanent employment is the best charity.

Such facts should be borne in mind when a person is disposed to blame poverty on the rich, on the ground that the latter have taken the money from the poor. Today there is a
stampede of money into the country from the city; and the
wealthy classes are taking on the average of forty laborers
with them to each new home. These are given homes without
rent, and work all the year round. Imagine each million dol-

lars that is held by one person to have been distributed among a thousand persons of the middle classes, and you will have a condition that would cut off the support of forty families from permanent labor, as well as the multitude of other expenses that arise in the maintenance of a great estate. Each person who received the thousand dollars would horde it, and it would be idle; or, if it were spent, it would be gone; while the expenditure of the millionaire goes on forever.

It is a glorious thing that in this land today every man or woman who wishes to make a higher level can do so. Just get the seven books referred to and begin to make that higher level. The books can be taken from any public library without cost, or bought at second-hand stores for a few cents each. It makes no difference how poor or how affluent you are; master the seven books; know all there is in common arithmetic, in spelling, in grammar, in rhetoric, in English literature, in character and in etiquette. Just as sure as you make yourself the master of these studies, just so sure will you make for yourself a new level; and just as sure as you make a new level of mental and physical value, just so sure will you rise to it.

It is one of the most gratifying laws of life that every person can make a new level every year, and we might almost say, every month.

But once a new level is made, nothing on earth can keep you down. It is the old case of the fountain-head and the outlet; the higher the former rose the higher the latter forced itself.

Is it worth trying?

A husband who has spare moments, as all husbands have, can put them to no better use than this. The same is true of the wife. If the two do not care to study together; or if one is unwilling to aid or sympathize with the other in any effort, take up the work alone. Make no show of doing this. Just do it as the moments offer themselves. But do not neglect any other duties of home life for the study. The order of action should be as follows:

1. Give your work and duties full attention and make them complete each day.

2. Aid your mate morning, noon and night in any way you can in the performance of the duties that belong to each day.

3. Volunteer to assist such mate in extra matters where there is any possibility of being helpful.

4. Then pay full attention to your personal habits and conduct so that the suggestions of the third department of this book may be fully complied with. Be all you should, refined, neat, careful and alert.

5. After that, take up the studies of the seven books referred to in any order you please.

You have time enough.

By doing these things and making your plans so that you can surely do them, you will become a different person. The difference will be perceived by everybody who knows you. Your life mate will notice it, and then that high respect that precedes magnetism will be awarded you at all times. Mark what we say, there is no higher honor in this world that can come to you than to have earned such consideration.

Is it worth trying for?

Yes, if life has anything in it that is worth trying for, and we think it has.

By these means you can cultivate the attractive force.

If you lack it, you can never develop Sex Magnetism.

It is the soil in which Sex Magnetism grows.

If you cultivate the attractive force and should not go so far as to add Sex Magnetism, you will not have worked in vain, for the latter power is very close at hand to a man or woman who has attained the former.

Suppose you are not married, but are old enough to enter that state, and should not possess this attractive force, its coming to you through your deliberate effort will add a great value to your life. The new level will be high indeed and you will rise to it and thus make yourself the person most fitted for a life mate.

If you are married, then there is all the more reason why you should develop this attractive force, for it will make marriage mean more to you than anything else can except Sex Magnetism.

If you are old and have passed the time of life when you should marry, do not let that deter you from cultivating the attractive force. It is important that you should have it, not that you may take a life mate, but that you may find that affiliation that one sex needs in the appreciation of another. It is not good for a man or a woman to be alone.

Lay this foundation well.

Keep in mind the fact that it is practical, useful and filled with opportunities for rising in the world in every department of life.

SEX INFLUENCES

WO THINGS are assumed as having been accomplished by the time this stage is reached. These may be found described in a general way in the third and fourth departments, and there they should be searched out and analyzed until they are fully understood. They may be briefly summed up in a few words as follows:

1. It is assumed that by this time that you have acquired the attractive force.

2. It is assumed that by this time that you have found a new level.

Such being the case, you are ready to enter directly upon the study of Sex Magnetism. If the two preliminary steps have not been taken as yet, then do not proceed for the present, for there will be nothing gained in overleaping the space between the foundation and the higher part of the system.

Proceed slowly.

There is much to be attained if it is reached by solid steps along the first part of the course. Haste accomplishes nothing in this study.

The purpose in view must be fully known and kept before the mind all along the way. The difference between personal magnetism and Sex Magnetism is also of material importance, and should not be misunderstood. The first or foundation course is known as the cultivation of personal magnetism. This is not the power to hypnotize, but its opposite. It is the power to awaken, to thrill, to win; to obtain a voluntary following from a person whose senses have been quickened instead of dulled; it does not put to sleep, but wakes up and arouses; it makes no slave, but a brighter, better helper. Personal magnetism also teaches self-mastery, self-control, rulership, leadership, and the full strength of life. It gives power; conscious power; tremendous power; a grander manhood, and a more exalted womanhood; an influence that is far-reaching and ever-growing; an influence for any purpose in life. It wins respect. It compels attention.

Such is the foundation course, that which should and must precede this system. It is in the foundation book of the Magnetism Club.

As has always been stated, that foundation course should either come before this, or should accompany it; there can be no omission of it by this time.

It will, if its teachings have been mastered, have conquered in you all reluctance to acquire the attractive force, and to make for yourself a new level in your personal worth.

There is nothing ideal or merely advisory in these steps. They are exactly the steps that any successful man or woman will have to take in whole or in part. They are instigated by nature, and have been so directed since first the dawn of civilization gave promise of a better manhood and womanhood for the race.

All that has led up to this stage of the study has applied only to the improvement of yourself. It has been taught in a negative and an affirmative process:

1. The negative process has been intended to drive out the unattractive qualities such as are described in the third department.

2. The affirmative process has been intended to build up something of greater value, as described in the fourth department, including not only the attractive force, but also the new level.

Think over these two steps, and note their effectiveness along the lines of usual and natural progress. Then you will be ready to make another dividing line, as follows:

1. The two processes, negative and affirmative, have applied solely to your own improvement as an individual of attractive powers.

2. The next step must apply to your helpfulness toward your life-mate.

Here again the distinction is important.

It would not be enough for you to better yourself and your value unless you could bestow that improvement on the person whom you have allied yourself with for life. As a matter of side advice, it is suggested that a mutual desire for the prolongation of both lives should be fostered, and everything done to bring about its fulfillment.

If you are a man it will be doubly important that you do this. It may now be supposed that you have passed the various stages that precede, and that your desire is centered on the health of yourself and wife, provided you are married, or are to be married. If you think your health good enough at present, remember that men who have been sick but little are quick victims of a single severe attack, for they are unprepared for it in mind and will power. They get frightened easily, and a frightened patient is an easy victim of death. It is easy for every well man to keep well, but it is not easy for a well man to remain well without giving attention to his health. While you are well you are in the best condition to make the plan of living that will keep you in health. Prevention is the leading demand today in everything. To be curing something all the time, and mending something day in and day out, is neither wise nor practical sense. The man who locks his house and keeps out the burglars is a much more intelligent man than the one who, after he has been robbed, hunts down the thief. The owner of the horse who locks the barn door after the animal has been stolen is a type of the man who tries in this age of multitudinous sickness to take care of his health after it has gone.

When a husband is well the duties of the wife are many and hard. All his earning capacity is needed to help her and supply the home. When he is sick that capacity is removed, and in place of it there will stalk in the house the costs of medicine and doctor. But the duties of his wife are increased, for the man must be waited on, and his share of helpfulness at home is taken away. Therefore, the man who will not look after his health, but will allow things to take their own course, is very selfish. He is unfair. He thinks of the chances he may have of getting well, but not of the tax and possible breakdown of his wife.

As sickness is always invited by the negligence and faults of someone, it is always a sin that is fastened on someone by the judgment of heaven. It may have its start in a previous generation, but for the most part every bodily ill is due to ignorance and stupidity in food selection, in cooking and in senseless habits. Sickness has always been a sin, despite the fact that the innocent suffer for such wrongdoing as much as the guilty parties. Some day, in a higher civilization, it will be made a crime. But today in nine homes out of ten, in ninety houses out of every hundred, sickness stalks in as an unwelcome visitor, destroying the peace, the comfort and the happiness of all present, making the sick helpless and imposing extra toil on the well, and sapping the finances where they are most weak. Yet there is hardly any attempt to check this lack of sense in the great public. Men and women who are able to manage their financial and business affairs, and who are reputed to possess great powers of sense and judgment, fall down in this one department.

People live in habits, not in thought.

The disposition to let well enough alone is the cause of the deficiency of mind in looking after the health while yet it remains.

People who let well enough alone are like the owner of the horse referred to.

They do not stop to think that the seeds of disease are sown in silence, and when they break forth, as in appendicitis, in paresis, in paralysis, in rheumatism, in diabetes, in kidney troubles and in cancer, as well as in many others, they come so suddenly that there is no chance to fight them; yet, taken when the health was good, they could have been easily averted.

"You are sick unto death," said a doctor to a business man recently. "You could have prevented this a year ago had you given your health thought and care then." "Yes, doctor, I know; but my motto has always been to let well enough alone." So he died for the sake of the motto that would leave every door unlocked in a house until the burglars came; that would allow every infant to play on the car tracks until death came, and that is setting back more than seven homes in every ten that are struggling to rise above the vicissitudes of life's uncertain struggle.

If you are a wife, you should take care of your health for your own sake, for the sake of your husband, and for the sake of your home.

Ill health may come in the form of acute or chronic sickness. In the former condition you become felled at once, and the duties of the household are at a standstill. Your services are lost to your family and to yourself. Others must take care of you, go without sleep and rest, and become more or less unfitted to earn the income that the home needs. If you have some chronic illness, it means an unhappy marriage, for there can be no content where there is bad health. Somebody must pay for it in all sorts of coin—loss of time, loss of opportunity, loss of pleasure, loss of money, and generally loss of temper.

How many young women today who are engaged to marry have a right to enter wedlock? Less than two in every twenty. Their health is such that, although they cover up the facts until they are married, they are sure to begin a series of impositions on their husbands by bringing chronic invalidism to him. The delicate and languid maiden may pose as dainty during courtship, but she stands out clearly defined as an invalid after marriage.

There are not ten female stomachs in a hundred on an average among the classes above the poor that are free from some form of chronic malady. The pastry, soda water, ice cream, candy, cakes and what else that the female loves above her health have all been doing their work for years. There are not ten girls in a hundred who are old enough to become wives who have not been taking medicines or stimulants for years. They cannot resist the temptation to abuse their stomachs. They eat heavy evening meals, no breakfasts of any value, and light lunches; thus reversing all day long the law of nature that food is a fuel to be taken before using, and not after. As a result these girls when married have dull headaches, bad eyes, dirty breath and disordered stomach; and they wonder why, when the husband promised so faithfully to care for and to cherish the wife, he should not have greater sympathy for the sick than for the well. The answer is that men who are old enough to be at large know perfectly well that the headaches, pains and disorders of women are due almost always to a senseless method of eating. Men may not say aloud what they think; but they are today proving by their actions their belief; for husbands are walking out of the marriage state at the rate of hundreds of thousands every year, while other men are refusing to enter it. The reason was given in one case, and it stands as the general reason in nearly all cases: ''I will not marry a girl who is to enter upon a state of chronic invalidism just as soon as she becomes a wife," is the reply of the man of today.

It is easy to study health from a sensible standpoint, and to preserve it; or, if it has been lost, to get it back. The key that unlocks the door of good health is proper food selection and proper cooking; for what a person eats is exactly what that person is. If you ill-feed a valuable horse it will be sick and may die. If you treat a husband just as well as you would treat your horse, then he will have proper food, carefully prepared.

These evidences of unselfishness are essential for the happiness of your home and your existence with the mate whom you have allied yourself with for life.

It is selfishness to become sick, and a charge on the care of others when you can avoid that condition by foresight and attention to the few simple laws of health. If you are alone in the world, living out in the woods as a hermit, then your health is yours alone. But if you dwell in civilized society, or in a state of civilization, your health is both public and private property. It requires but brief reasoning to figure out this result.

This being the case, study daily to keep your mind and your body strong, in order that your life-mate may be helped by your better physical and mental condition.

If your mind goes wrong, as many minds are going in this age of rapid living and carelessness in personal health, then you may do harm to those you love. Be regardful of your mental state. The toxins that are generated by the stomach during indigestion poison the brain and inflame it, or else lead to paralysis and breakdown. One of the most prolific causes of derangement is gas poisoning from the organs of digestion. Paralysis may follow such disorder. This stopping of the nervous fluid or current, is all the time occurring in the body, but the serious consequences are being checked in time by the operations of life. It is safer to remove the cause. The loss of the mind is sometimes a very sudden act, and is traceable to the condition of the stomach. The eyesight follows the stomach in everything. People dread appendicitis, but its control begins and is lost at the stomach. It is just as preventable as is the loss of a leg by removing it from the track in time.

If you permit a condition of constipation to continue, you are risking appendicitis, paralysis, heart failure, apoplexy and blood derangement, as well as headaches and neuralgia. By lessening the amount of food to one-half the usual quantity, omitting all kinds except those that are plain and simple, ingesting what you eat in the most thorough manner before it is swallowed, and otherwise exercising care in all things pertaining to daily existence, you will make these dread maladies impossible.

If you expose yourself to drafts of air, or to cold sidewalks, or to inactivity out of doors in cool or cold weather, or sit on metal or stone steps, or stop to talk to a friend, either in the cold air or at the doorway, or sit at an open window, or cool off too quickly when heated, or drink ice water or other cold drinks, or take stimulants, you will attract disease in some form; and these exposures always discover the weak spots in your health.

In the past year we had knowledge of six cases of paralysis following the opening of car windows to enable somebody to get fresh air; the ones who got it being those in the seats next behind the silly fellow who imagined that air would come into a moving car at right angles with the side of the car itself, instead of slantwise to the seat behind him. The man who rocks a boat is generally young and lacking in common sense; and the man who opens a car window is of the same mental calibre.

Here is a case that occurred last week. A young mother went out of doors on the damp ground without overshoes to protect her feet. She is now dead, and the funeral will occur tomorrow. Where was her mind when she took the chances? What did she owe to her baby? if she owed nothing to her husband or her parents? Is the fact that she is dead, and that she cannot know the sorrow she brought to several lives a warrant for her indifference? When cautioned against the act, she had only a sneer for the sister who gave her the warning.

Such a case, differing only in the kind of exposure, is common. People are taking chances all the time. They have a pity or a cheap answer for those who seek to guide them. Is it because the human mind has much to do before it can attain a condition of ordinary civilization that these neglects of body, of mind and of stomach by exposure, by bad habits and by a fearful diet are so numerous?

Is the mind just entering civilization?

Whatever the cause, the fact remains that homes are all the time being invaded by sickness and the grim figure of death, where there might have been many years of happiness. There is no golden rule of peace when illness is too frequent a visitor in the home. Nothing will so quickly break up the domestic contentment as sickness, even if death waits a while. The boy that sleeps in the icy ground might have been alive and well had his parents been alert in his days of health. The daughter that is lying with upturned face to the sod was a sacrifice. Look back up the years that have gone, and ask yourself how many pies she ate as a sum total, and then try to excuse yourself by saying that you never heard of such a thing as pies destroying the good elements of the blood. You, perhaps, never heard that pastry breaks up the blood faster than any other one cause. It is much more to be feared than the germs of disease; for it has numbered more victims, although its work is principally to deliver the body over to such germs. When the blood has been robbed of its value then the germs appear; and you are made to believe that the germs were the real cause instead of being merely the last agency of the taking off. No person will succumb to germs or to any contagion or malady who has not first laid the foundation by breaking down the blood by a bad diet.

Place the blame where it belongs.

The handkerchief tied about the neck stops the circulation of blood; but the heart failure is the cause of the death that follows. The act of tying the handkerchief is the real instigation and the only guilty agency.

Love for yourself may not prompt you to be careful of your health; but how about the love you bear to others? Are you willing to bring sorrow to the wife, the husband, the child or the parent when your inherent selfishness might easily stop the advance of sickness? Think this over.

You owe it to yourself to do all in your power to add to the peace and happiness of your home life. As sickness is the worst and the most common of all enemies, you should master that foe from this moment until you no longer possess any will power to make you look after yourself. If your wife or husband or family will not attend to their health, you should educate them with as little friction as possible. They dislike to be talked to on the subject, but there is a duty in the work, and you may acquire some diplomatic method of performing it.

This is the beginning of the plan of helping the life-mate whom you have taken.

It is practical work.

After death has come then its value is seen; but, of course, too late. "If you had back your dead child would you watch over her health day in and day out?" was asked of a mother. She said truly, "If I could know how close to the brink we all are I would devote myself to the care of the health of my own body and of my family," and she paused, then continued: "But why are we not able to make up our minds to do this when health is ours?"

Why will humanity see things too late?

There are too many people in the world. Only those who are willing to care for themselves and for others are of any use, and so nature opens the way to eliminate the weak and the careless; and that man or woman is weakest who is most indifferent. Progress is the banner cry of the ages, and progress can be made only by men and women of foresight; all others are in the way. This has been the rule of nature since first life appeared, and it always will be the rule. A few thousand years or a few million years are nothing to nature. She cares not a whit for people who care nothing for themselves. Help yourself and God will help you has been preached for centuries.

Love is not strong enough to overcome indigestion, colds, catarrhs, rheumatism, neuralgia, headaches and the many ills that crowd modern homes. It is useless to seek solace in any promises of affection under such conditions. Love likes vivacity, brightness, sweetness, wholeness, and the rich, red blood of life. It has no affiliation for the bandaged head or the rolling intestines. A man with rheumatism joints will not look well courting a woman whose face is twisted into torture by the toothache. He should wait till he is well, and she should have the tooth treated. When her eyes dance with the pleasure of conscious health, and his limping walk and crutches have been laid away for good, then they can begin their courting history. And what is right during that period is right all the time.

You desire to cultivate Sex Magnetism, for you have this course of study.

But you cannot build a house upon air, nor magnetism upon a bed of false living. You are not true to yourself if you neglect your health, your mind, your body, your faculties or your essential being. All these come into the building up of Sex Magnetism. It is like a grand mansion with a solid foundation.

Now, what has been the foundation thus far laid as taught in the preceding pages? Let us review them:

1. Your personal unattractiveness must be removed, and an affirmative quality developed in its place. This is called the attractive force.

2. Next you are shown the necessity and the way to make yourself of greater value, whereby you will build a new level; and as sure as you live you will rise to that level.

These two mighty steps open up the way to your personal improvement, which should be maintained, regardless of the fact that others may be helped by them. But as sex means two, then there is another step to be taken:

3. You must make your health such that it will aid your life-mate on the one hand, and will not be a drag to her or him on the other; and your own betterment in health you must carry to that life-mate. This is the first effort to reach out beyond your own improvement for the good of the other.

4. You must cultivate a philosophical forbearance.

This is the second step that reaches out towards your life-mate.

The attractive force removes the unattractive characteristics and habits; the new level raises your value; the better health gives more hope to your home life; and now in that home there must come a new philosophy. It is supreme forbearance. It is not to be adopted as a theory, but must be practiced as a fine art. It must be put to the test all the time. There is no credit in bearing and forbearing when all things go smoothly. The real struggle is when you are sorely tempted.

Adversity tests everything.

The difference between character and forbearance is seen in the following instances: A man who is alone and who finds everything wrong becomes impatient; but if he controls himself, that is character. He is to blame to start with. His collar button left him and sought a quiet nook under the dressing case; that was not the fault of anybody, unless he himself was to blame. He confounds his luck, and thus places it in the category of chance. Perhaps this is as near right as it will ever be made. But if he swears or jumps about and throws things, he will not be strong in character. In dressing himself he collides with a pin, and it is run into the ball of his thumb clear to the bone. Again he either has or lacks character.

The same man may have these experiences in the presence of his wife. If he gives way to a burst of temper, with or without profanity, she may cry violently on the first day of such episodes; but she soon learns to pass them by as matters in which she is not involved. But if he, in a temper, should throw a shoe at her, that would not only be lack of character of the right kind, but a very brutal proceeding. He will repent in a flash, take her in his arms, ask forgiveness and be pardoned. That is affection. She rather enjoys the whole affair if it ends in such attention.

But now we come to the more useful quality in married life, which is known as forbearance. The husband gets up in the morning. Something is wrong for which the wife is actually to blame. He does not throw anything at her. He does not swear at her. He does not scold her. He does not make sarcastic remarks. He does not even look as if he minded it. All he does is to take Dora in his arms, kiss her, and tell her that it is all right. She will try to make it all right the next time, and she does. This is forbearance of the true husband, and it is philosophical.

If she makes the same mistakes again, without many mornings intervening, it is stupidity. He should analyze her makeup to see if it is curable stupidity. If it is not, then he must forbear all his life. There is no remedy. If it is curable, he must be diplomatic, for a person who is stupid and who wants to be bright is very sensitive, whereas an incurable case is lacking for the most part in any sensitiveness. A sensitive wife may be a sensible one at the same time, although it does not look so at the first glance. If she is really trying to overcome her fault, she is much more likely to do so with a kiss for chiding than with a harsh complaint. It is much better not to appear grieved or inconvenienced. Deal with her just as you would if it were the second day of your acquaintance with her when you were falling in love.

That is always a safe rule.

Whenever you have any criticism or complaint to make always pave the way by a caress and a kiss. Tell her plainly and kindly, so that she may see the necessity of greater care. If dinner or any meal is delayed, and you must blame someone, select some cause outside of the wife, and let her seem to be the impartial third party. Thus, when a woman was interested in a novel and forgot to have the noon meal ready for her husband, who was in a hurry on account of some important business engagement, he felt keenly the annoyance, but he did not blame his wife. He put the fault on some imaginary man who had accosted him on the way home, and soundly berated him to his wife, telling her how sorry he was that he had kept her waiting. She was suspicious for a long time as to the genuineness of his sorrow, but the hint was taken, and no further delays were caused by novels.

If she has habits that are not to his liking, let him mend his own bad habits first, and then correct her indirectly. This is done by referring to some imaginary girls whom he once knew. As an illustration, a man found his wife constantly "tonguing her teeth," or feeling of them with the end of her tongue, and drawing air from one or two cavities. While this was going on he said nothing; but once when he himself did it he said: "I must stop that, for it is a bad habit, and grows on a person before he is aware. I never knew of girls doing that except once in a while. I recall a very pretty young lady who was a personal friend of mine, who would work her tongue all the time someone was talking to her, and she soon lost all her friends." This was all the young wife needed; she broke up the fault at once.

It is a very excellent plan to agree to assist each other by suggestions. Two heads are better than one. In faults of etiquette a wife may often observe more than a man, and she can coach him frequently if he is willing to be helped. Everything referred to in the third department of this book can be brought up diplomatically between husband and wife, and not cause friction.

If it should so happen that your wife makes a severe dig at some fault of yours, do not get angry. Put into practice the philosophy of forbearance. If she speaks angrily, forbear. If she says mean things, forbear. If she does mean things, forbear. If she flirts with another man, it will be due to some lack of attention on your part. A husband who is a man should be able to hold even a natural wanton by his magnetism. There are many cases proved where pretty girls have married men who were very busy, and who were compelled to leave their wives at home alone all day long. These wives were naturally prostitutes by disposition, and all had been guilty of that crime before they were married; but their husbands had no suspicion of the facts.

In the particular case referred to the women did not break away from their marriage vows. While the cases were separated they were well known from reports of the personal magnetism club members who had been posted to observe them. There are probably thousands of wanton women today who are married, and who have been true to the promises made at the wedding. Some of them are true and loyal, even though sorely tempted at times. It seems that beauty is a bait that draws men about town to its charms, no matter how reluctant a fallen woman may be to offer such bait after once she has found a good home and happy surroundings. In a recent case where a girl of great beauty married a prosperous business man, after she had spent three years in a house of ill-fame, of which fact he was totally ignorant, some enemy of hers made the revelation. He had overwhelming evidence of the truth of the assertion. She knew what had been told him, for she was present at the interview when the enemy made the disclosure. She did not offer any denial, nor did she tell of any conspiracy that had induced her to enter the evil life against her will, nor anything of that kind. The bold truth stood out before the husband, He asked her if she had been true to him since the marriage, and she looked him full in the face and said "Yes."

That was all he ever said to her on the subject. They are still living together, and both claim to have found their marriage a source of satisfaction, barring only the facts stated. A friend of the writer, on being informed of the case, secured the following statement from the husband: "I had no suspicion either before or after my marriage. She is a good wife, and has been from the day I married her. She is refined, cleanly, of sweet disposition, kind at all times, forbearing, active, intelligent, full of health, and a better helpmeet than any wife of my many business friends, as far as I am able to judge. I would lose everything to part from her, and I think I am gaining much by remaining with her."

But he did more. He hired detectives to follow the history of the enemy, and at length, since these lines were first written, he was handed a written confession from that enemy stating that the charges were untrue, and were made solely out of spite at being repulsed in the home of the wife. This confession was itself untrue. The writer suggested that it would be forthcoming as an act of repentance after remorse. The husband is today of the opinion that his wife has always been a true woman, and he is entitled to the peace of mind that this belief brings, for he has been forbearing beyond all expectation.

A good life crushes out a bad past.

Some husbands flare up at the least shortcoming of their wives. The slightest mistakes are beginnings of storms that breap in terrific fury on the household. It is wrong to speak unkindly before others, and certainly wrong to speak unkindly at all. What purpose is served by ill nature.

In moments of irritation, with or without adequate cause, the tongue and the temper should be controlled. Forbear at all times, even when it takes a philosopher's nature to keep good-natured.

The wife has more cause to let her temper get the better of her than the husband. The woman's faults, as a rule, are of the lesser degree. Of course, if she is a card-playing woman, or one that drinks, the sharp line must be drawn at once. No

woman who drinks, or is untrue, or plays cards, except when
her husband is present, and then only occasionally, is fit to
be a wife. These are the three natural causes for separation.
Disloyalty is a Biblical ground. Drinking is the one offence
that cannot be forgiven, for it is more wicked in its consequences than adultery. Ninety per cent of all the crimes in
the code of man are due to the direct or indirect influence of
drunkenness.

In the families referred to there has never been a crime;
no killing, no stealing, no assault, but there has been unhappiness and blackened lives all the way through the awful
history. Insanity will be the heritage of three of the chil-
ren; one of the wives has been temporarily insane three times
because of the conduct of her husband through his habits of
drink; and constitutional diseases are in the blood of all of them.
It is from this drink habit that there falls to the next of kin
the many nervous and blood maladies that defy all attempts
at cure.

The greatest wrong a woman can do is to marry a fellow
that drinks. She should not plead ignorance because he succeeds
in hiding the fault from her. She should ascertain by positive
inquiry that he does not drink. If he has ever had the habit,
and has been cured of it, she should let him alone. There is
too much at stake in the venture.

The habit of drink in a wife is much worse than in a husband; in her case she may be the victim of patent medicines,
as some of the strongest prohibition women have been made
drunkards by the use of such medicines. A husband who weds
a woman of the wine, beer or liquor habit should submit to
emasculation for the sake of saving the next generations of
his line, the disgrace and suffering of being cursed with the
habit of alcoholism and its attendant evils. He will thereby
cut off much misery, insanity probably, and blood taint.

There can be no forbearance against drink habits, adultery
and card playing. The latter is excusable when husband and
wife play at the same game or in the same gathering, but much
indulgence even then is wrong, for it makes a new level down-
wards to which they will both sink in time. It strips the mind
of its keenness, robs life of the ambition to rise to a better
level, and wastes the energy of brain and body in the excite-

ment of watching and using the chances that turn up on pieces of pasteboard. It instills in the blood the love of gambling, for it trains the nerves to enjoy chance and luck without a minimum of skill and thought. All the while the players look with pity on those who do not care to thus waste their time; the players pretend that much acuteness of mind is essential to play well, and in such a gambling game as bridge they even pose as thoughtful during the play.

The dead stare of the eyes after the game tells a different story. Thought has gone out, and much of it has gone out to stay. The mind is never good for its duties after once it has been saturated by the weakening process of the game.

Nature demands nobility of character.

When there is one or more of these three evils in the life of a person; when adultery, drink or card playing is made a second nature in man or woman, then the marriage totters if it has been contracted; and if not, then it should be suppressed at once. There is no use in entering on the contract with a man merely for the alimony the woman needs. But if the wedding must take place, do not bring children into the world to carry on the sins of the parents.

Prevention is better than cure. It is possible in most cases to prevent the misery by refusing to wed the person. But if it is too late for that, then seek through magnetism to end the wrong and stop the habit. This can be done by a magnetic man or woman without having to break up the home.

Forbearance for past wrongs may be a virtue, and undoubtedly is when present conduct warrants it; but forbearance for current wrongs of the kinds we have described cannot be advised, as it means too much harm in the future.

As this training proceeds it will disclose step by step the manner in which a husband may bring an erring wife out of her evil conditions; and a wife may save an erring husband.

GETTING TOGETHER

ITTLE by little this course of training unfolds the possibilities of power over the opposite sex. It is founded as the old maxim would have all human conduct founded, on the rule that he would rule others must first prove his ability to rule himself. For this reason all the faults that stand forth as unattractive in man or woman are eliminated under the guidance of the training set forth in the third department. Having thus made the man or the woman to cease the repelling influence, the next step was to raise the value of the personality to a new level, where circumstances would soon bring the individual life.

The next step was a natural one, that of helpfulness reaching out into the personality of the other party.

Now the step at hand is that which brings them together.

The process can be applied to men and women before they have fallen in love, or while they are engaged, or after they are married, or when marriage is out of the question.

At first thought it would seem strange that Sex Magnetism could exert an influence over those who did not care to marry, or who have no present intentions of entering wedlock. But we teach that there is too much marriage; that more deliberation and less haste are necessary in this era of universal divorce, and that the two sexes owe to each other a duty outside of marriage as great in its way as the bonds of matrimony.

In young manhood and in young womanhood there should be friendships that need not lead to wedlock. Or there may be, in advanced life, similar friendships in which the distinction in sex is respected and the friends are not so associated that a wrong construction can be placed on the acquaintance. Some very plain rules should be observed:

1. If a young man who is not engaged to marry a young woman is friendly to her, he should meet her at her home with

the consent of her parents or guardians, and should at all times have them or other persons present or near at hand. There should never at any time be an opportunity to be alone.

2. If he is engaged to marry her, the couple should not be left alone, although they may be apart from others, as in an adjoining room with the door open. The chaperone system is necessary in Sex Magnetism, for it increases the respect which one sex holds for the other; and in this age the loss or short duration of respect is the cause of so much haste and carelessness in selecting a life partner. Whatever will tend to make betrothals more deliberate and more reasonable will add to the safety and the permanency of marriage; and there is no greater end desired in this era.

3. No young man should escort a young woman on any trip or walk, ride, drive or other departure from home unless there is a chaperone. This rule is observed in all ranks where people are of good standing. It is not merely to guard against indescretion on the part of the young folks, but to compel them to respect the difference between them in nature. The constant cry that a young woman is able to protect her virtue is the advance cry of prostitution. It has always preceded the fall of the honorable girl. But, whether she is able or not to look after herself, the one thing most certain to cause the young man to lose interest in her is a commonness of companionship and cheapness of acquaintance. If they are allowed to wander off alone not all her sweetness, nor all her purity can long hold him away from her side. She is in her muscular powers weaker than he is, and soon the kiss will be forced and the embrace compelled. Then all else is cheap.

4. The woman of the twenties is more sedate, as a rule, or if she is gay and vivacious it is forced or vinegary when the froth has settled. The young man of the teens will not be attracted to her; but she may have companions who are in the twenties. While the same care that has been advised for the younger folks is not essential, she should remember that, just the moment they are given the opportunity to be talked about, they will be discussed; and they will be charged with exactly the things that they have the opportunity to do, whether they do them or not. Scandal is a blessing. If all girls and women were virtuous, then scandal would be a sin of the

grossest kind; but, since ninety girls in every hundred fall from grace before they are married, and since this has been the rule from the time Eve fell, and will remain the rule for some time yet, the voice of the suspicious woman is the voice of safety. It is a blessing that the girl and her young man friend, who have been away for a drive in a buggy in the deep woods, are charged with dishonor in the suspicions and afterwards in the enlarged charges made by liars who know nothing of the facts. The girl will hear of it, her mother will hear of it, and the first venture is generally not a guilty one; so there is time yet to save the girl. This would not be possible under a system of human nature that caused people to refrain from talking unless the wrong were committed on their own doorsteps in the presence of invited guests. Nothing is so valuable to the girl and to the future home as her chastity. Nothing is so easy to take from her when she is young. Nothing is so persistently sought by men. And it is saying what is true when we declare that scandal has been the means of saving nearly all who would have fallen and have been kept in the right path. The real fault is with the parents in believing that the daughter is able to protect herself. The proper rule is to keep the sexes both away from the opportunity.

5. In the trial of divorce cases where the charge of adultery is the basis for legal separation, the old Biblical ground is endorsed. There is no church today, nor was there ever a church that did not permit a divorce for this cause. But it is a difficult thing to prove adultery as a criminal charge. In the civil courts there are but two things that need be proved:

a. The disposition.

b. The opportunity.

Having shown to the court that the respondent possessed the disposition to do this wrong, and that the opportunity occurred, the decision follows. While this would not warrant a conviction in a criminal court where the defendant must be proved guilty beyond all reasonable doubt, it is sufficient in the civil hearing. Now, what does scandal do? It presumes that if a young man takes an interest in a girl, and she in him, they possess the required disposition. If they lacked this she would go her way toward the state of the old maid, and he would go his way. Being interested in each other, and being inclined to get away from the rest of the world, is some evidence of the nature that is in them. But it is not until the opportunity is given them that scandal begins her work. This opportunity may occur in any one of scores of chances to be alone and wholly apart from all intrusion. If the young man is of evil intent, he will lead her away before she is aware of his purpose; while he entertains her with wonderful stories about his honor and prowess in matters that interest girls. It may be some college game, or riding, or driving, or automobiling, or some exploit in the army or navy, or on the plains, or some enterprise that is of large importance to her mind, or other thing that can hold her attention. If he is in the twenties and has had experience with girls and women, he will talk grand thoughts, make grand plans, build hopes that tower over the commonplace routine of her unvarying life, and so lure her on; all the while she is being led to seclusion where opportunity is complete.

6. The man who is several years older than the girl is the more to be feared than one who is nearer to her; although the rule of the chaperone should never be broken. A whole family, or smaller child, or a parent in a room or location near at hand, may suffice as chaperone. But the older man, one who may be from three to thirty years older than the girl, is to be watched in proportion as the difference in the ages is greater. Men who are forty, fifty, and even sixty, make prey of girls in their teens if once they can interest the latter.

7. The woman who is older than the young man may be of a different character. If she is not already bad, she will remain as she is during their friendship. It is a pleasant thing to have a boy in his teens befriended, advised and looked after in an ethical sense by an older woman, if scandal cannot find ground for its active tongue. Always pay homage to scandal. It is your best friend. It can never harm the discreet. If it finds an entering wedge in your life, it will be due, not necessarily to your own wrongs, but to your carelessness and indiscretion. You cannot defy it. You cannot declare that you will do as you please, and people can talk all they please. It is true that the most moral persons are often the most indiscreet, but they suffer in a good cause. It is also true that thousands of girls have been deterred from wrong-doing, as

well as indiscretion, by the fear of scandal. So do not lessen
this most excellent servitor by defying it. No good will come
from boldness in the matter. Men who seek pure wives, as
all men do, will keep away from the woman who has been
maligned, even if she is chaste. If she has been talked about,
she has done something to invite the discussion. There has
never been a case of scandal that was groundless, except
where the identity of a person was lost or mixed with another.
Recently a woman who looked exactly like another woman of
about the same age, was charged with an offense of which
she proved her innocence by showing that she was many hundred miles away at the time. But the allegations were so
direct and so clear that it was supposed another woman of
the same appearance was the guilty party. Detectives found
the other woman. The two were brought into court, and each
in turn was identified as the same person by three accusing
witnesses. But such cases are comparatively rare.

Discretion is always a virtue.

8. There are cases where women in the thirties have held
sway over the hearts of boys; and where women in the forties
have done the same thing; while gray-haired old women, small
in stature and dainty in manners have, without wealth, attracted youths. Of course, most any old woman with wealth
can secure a husband from almost any rank of men, even boys
having taken rich wives and waited for the time of release,
or else spent their fortunes and vanished to distant parts.
Motive is a matter that should be studied in proportion as the
normal conditions are changed. An old man prefers a young
wife to an old one, other things being equal; for youth and
beauty are excellent substitutes for wealth. But the reverse
is not as often true. The boy will naturally shrink from the
old woman, and motive must be sought in order to straighten
out the appearance of crooked design. If such a feeling as
genuine appreciation can exist in the young heart, advice
should be taken before marriage is contemplated. It is
fortunate that such cases are rare; although there are hundreds of marriages taking place every year between young
men or boys and women altogether too old for them.

9. A great discrepancy in age should be looked upon as
suspicious where the older party is rich.

10. There are real friendships between boys and old women in the fifties and sixties who are legally qualified to marry, but between whom there exists no intention more serious than appreciation and friendship. As a rule, there is some reason for such affiliation. It may be some accomplishment of the older person, as where a woman of eighty was a splendid linguist, and had the friendship of a boy of nineteen, who was himself somewhat accomplished in the same line. As soon as he began to take an interest in her ability, he called as often as she desired, and this grew to be so frequent that tongues wagged; but her grand-nephews were chaperones, and nothing real wicked was suggested. The effect on the old woman was to brighten her up, and to cause her to observe herself more closely in dress and manners. They said of her that she had gone back thirty years in her age. The strangest of all things, however, was the fact that when this boy married, as he did in two years, his girl wife cut short the visits to the aged friend. Jealousy plays many odd freaks in a century.

11. The animal nature in a young man rejects the idea of any kind of alliance with an old woman. Yet an old man is a burden to her. No old woman ought to marry an old man. If she cannot get one who is young enough and healthy enough to take care of her infirmities, then she ought to withdraw from the competition. There is no natural reason why some of the young men of the present day should not tie up with an old woman, if the latter is poor and needs care and support. There are no material bodily differences between the woman of thirty and the woman of sixty, except in the face.

Let, then, the young man make friends with the old woman. He will not do himself any harm by doing so, and he will do her a great deal of good.

Never mind the face. Keep the teeth cleaned. Almost all old women and the majority of young men have plates. Let them be kept fresh and in good condition by the use of the alum and zinc wash, which, as has been said, can be made for a cent or two a quart. Then the husband will have the same conditions to face as he would have in the girl-wife on an average. A dentist of national repute has said that, in the next generation, there would be few girls out of their teens who did not wear plates.

There are the same organs in the old woman as in the young. If she is careful in diet and applies the good old common sense in cooking that has come up from the past generations out of which she is a product, then her health and that of her husband will become better as the years pass on. The younger women do not know how to cook well; and most of them do not intend to cook at all. The older women are all natural cooks, and if they are healthy at seventy it is evidence of a conclusive character that they know how to cook for the preservation of the health of themselves and their husbands. In this connection so excellent a judge of human nature as the great railroad king, James J. Hill, who visited in Omaha, Nebraska, on December 9, 1909, the domestic science department of the National Corn Exposition, said to the Director: "For want of good cooking more homes are broken up and more divorces result than from any other cause. Lack of knowledge of this kind is the most fruitful cause of the unwillingness of men to remain husbands, for ill health, arising in the home where good health should be found, if anywhere, is sure to drive them to the divorce courts. The new interest wives are taking in the science of cooking is to be commended."

But cooking schools need civilization.

The young women are not only bad cooks, or none at all, but they are themselves invalids, despite the attempts to color up and to powder up for the visits of their male friends. If a young man wants health and attention at home, he must seek the wife who is two generations his senior; and there are some who are only one generation older who will make splendid wives. His choice among the women of his own age or younger will not be an improvement on this plan; for he will be plunged into a home of chronic invalidism, weak children and expenses of every kind. The cost of maintaining a home with an old wife will be less than one-half, and her desires will lessen his expenses in every way. She will dress more quietly, and have only an interest in her home. She will not stay out afternoons and evenings, nor join bridge parties. She will be temperate and moderate, will have an even temper and pleasing habits.

The final objection is that her temperament may not be as agreeable as that of the younger wife. Much will depend on

how obstinate she may be. If she is fixed in shoddy styles
of dressing, she will give evidence of that fault before marriage. If she has set ways and notions that are stiff and un-
changeable, drop her and seek one who can modify her habits
of mind to suit your wishes. If she has money do not pay
her attention; for you will be charged with mercenary motives, the meanest of all accusations when one person takes
an interest in another.

The unfitness of temperament in husband and wife is the
cause of quarrels. Two bodies conflict in proportion as they
approach each other too often. The difference of feelings and
of methods may be very pleasing where there is a real interest
each in the other. This difference of temperament is a common experience, and its results are much more favorable for
happiness in a marriage between a young man and an old
woman than when two persons of about the same age are wed
to each other.

There are many thousands of marriages between old men
and young women and generally to the disadvantage of the
former. The demands that young wives make on the vitality
of old men are such that long life is impossible. The records
show that of every hundred weddings between young women,
or women under forty, with men over sixty, the average age
of the latter is less than eighteen months. Many die in the
year; quite a number die on their honeymoon; and hardly one
lives four years. This has given the world a race of young
widows. Doctors advise most strenuously against old men
marrying; but if they must marry, let them avoid the woman
who is full of vigor and youth; for it is only a mild form of
suicide. But doctors are agreed that the old woman can wed
the young man, as the results are reversed. The child of an
old man and a young woman is an old child; it will be senile
long before its time. On the other hand, there will be no
child resulting from the marriage of an old woman with any
man.

A young woman who wishes much attention from an old
man will miss her desires. He may become the father of a
child or two, but such events will be desultory even if sought.
There will be a coldness in all his display of affection that
will mar the daily life of the wife. His kisses and embraces

will be weak and chilling. The male is the natural suitor, and when he lacks the red blood of vital energy, the wife will be discontented. On the other hand, the old woman is always a willing recipient of attentions of every kind, especially from a young man who cares for her as a husband should. Age is supposedly weaker than youth, for which reason the feeble, but healthy, old wife of a young man will play in harmony with the difference between the two sexes. A strong wife and a weak husband are a discord; while a weak wife and a strong husband are in accord with the plan of life.

All these suggestions assume that there is to be a disparity in the ages of the parties. Where such difference exists it is better that the extremes should meet in the aged wife and the young husband, rather than in the aged man and the young wife. The latter case is always disastrous. We have had records of more than two hundred marriages of very old women with very young men, and there has never been one case reported as a failure. A certain liking for the enormous margin of years seems to fascinate the man. We have taken the trouble to search out a dozen of these boy-husbands, and have had conversations with them. In one case a lad of nineteen wed a woman of sixty-three. She weighed ninety-four pounds when the ceremony took place, and gained fifteen pounds in two years. She was an adept at housework, was a fine cook, could mend and attend to all the details of the home, and had a high degree of book learning and intelligence. At the date of the engagement she possessed no money and few clothes; but was given an outfit by her sister. She had never been married before, and could, therefore, be set down as a confirmed old maid.

The lad of nineteen married her, as he confessed, because he had no faith in the cooking abilities and household qualities of the girls of his acquaintance. He wanted a home more than he wanted a wife. He earned five hundred dollars a year at the time. Since then he has risen to much better wages. "Forty-four years is a big difference in ages," he said; "but I don't mind it. I am satisfied. If I had it to do over again, I would do the same thing. My wife is a better wife than any of the boys of my acquaintance found that have got married. I think she is neater about the house, and cleaner in every way. I do not know how any woman could be any more attractive than she is to me. I do not know as I love her as people think they love when they court, but I guess I think more of her than husbands think of their wives, if the papers tell the truth.''

In another case a young man of twenty-six married a woman of seventy-four. He had known her about seven years. When married she weighed one hundred and two pounds, and gained thirty pounds in three years. She was an old maid also, and so were her four sisters. They had all been school-teachers, holding their positions for many years. The bride was poor, having lost her savings in stock investments. There was no incentive to wed her for any supposition of money-getting, as she was about to accept the charity of an institution when this young man saved her by making her his wife. It was ten years later that we talked with him about the marriage, and she was then eighty-four years of age; but she really did not look more than fifty, except for her white hair. She had a rather full face, and was the very picture of neatness and elegance. The young husband was certainly very proud of her. In a private conversation he made the statement somewhat as follows: ''I was a rather unsteady boy up to a year before my marriage. I had knocked about a great deal, and was not of good moral habits in every way. I told the woman whom I asked to marry me all about myself, keeping nothing from her. She was very poor, and my wages were not large. But she has made a man of me. I have never spent any evening away from her since the marriage. All errands I have done before coming home at the end of the day's work. She asked of me one favor, and that was for me to not leave her alone in the house after dark; so when I went out I took her with me. She is very lively, and can walk five miles any day, even at the age of eighty-four. She loves the home, and takes an interest in every part of it. Honestly, I do not think there is any difference between a young woman and an old woman as a wife. I never married before this, and she never did. But I was wild, and I know something of the world, and I say it is true that the aged wife who has her health is the superior of the young woman in every way.''

He was at that time holding a responsible position as a

head gardener with an excellent salary, and his home was a dream of comfort and neatness. We took supper with the couple, and she had no notice of the expected company; but the meal would put to shame ninety-nine young wives out of any hundred that might be found. She refused to talk of the discrepancy in their ages, and it was not wise to mention the matter, after a single remark that told her how beautiful the home was in the opinion of the guest, and that it had more attractions than other homes. It was evident that she did not wish to encourage the conversation in that direction. But afterwards the young husband said: "She is glad to have your good opinion of her home, and would advise you to select for your young men friends as good wives as you think she is."

Sensible old women do not try to make themselves look young in their dress. That would be a mistake; but they are justified in making their face as smooth as possible, and otherwise keeping up their general condition. Neatness, cleanliness and charming manners are important; but not flashy colors or reproductions of the display of young girls. There is more reason for an old woman keeping within the limits of good taste in dress than of others; although all females should avoid the dowdy on the one hand and the sensational on the other.

It is our opinion that every young man should pass a state of probation in marriage with some woman who is two generations older than himself. This proposition may not be received seriously, and some readers will think it ridiculous. If marriage with a girl is only a compact for physical union, why make it a legal compact? Why not let matters go on as they are going today? In one city there are two hundred thousand women, mostly girls, who secure their living in this way, and have no legal complications. Their men friends must, in the nature of things, number five to one, or there would be no profit; and this means fully a million men who are untrue either to themselves alone, or to their wives as well as themselves.

This is the record in only one city. There are other cities that have the same ratio. There must, therefore, be millions of men who are immoral. A large majority of these men are married, but are untrue to their wedding vows. They cannot love their wives. It would have been much better for them to have omitted dragging girls from homes of virtue to be stained with the foulness of this kind of deceit; for the husband who is a patron of a house of ill-fame is sure to carry some portion of the stain to his wife. As they did not marry for love, but only for the animal union, they would have been nobler men had they passed the marriage state by. They have done an endless wrong to young women whose lives are thrown into the turmoil of separation and divorce.

Such false marriages cannot long endure.

The defenders of these men claim that they in time reform and become good citizens. They sow their wild oats with their first wives, and during their marriage to their first wives; and then are ready to settle down with second wives and become model citizens. This seems to be the history of a large number of this class of husbands.

Girls who had dreamed when in their youth of happy homes and royal consorts, whose gallantry would shine at every step of the way, are made to stand face to face with the terrible sins of brothel life as it is forced upon them by criminal husbands. These girls fall by the wayside; some by sickness; many by suicide; many by divorce, and many by disappearing. Had they never met these fellows whom the law gave to them, they would have grown up into womanhood and have fitted themselves for some profession or useful occupation, out of which they might have been taken by better men into happy homes. Now their lives are blighted.

Such husbands should pass a state of probation with older women. The latter may live a few years, or many years; but not half as long as their young husbands; and then the latter, having been on probation, will be ready and fit for their second marriage to other women nearer their age. No wrong will have been done to innocent girls. No young lives will have been blighted. No children will have been brought into the world to become half-orphans because their parents have separated. The husband and widower of an aged wife will make the best and most experienced of husbands when he comes to marry his second and younger wife. The latter will be spared both divorce and disloyalty, and will have many advantages that will serve to make her home most happy as long as she lives.

In the absence of the state of probation just mentioned there should be other periods of probation on the following basis:

1. The young man who wishes to marry the young woman, both being in their teens, should wait not less than five years without a definite betrothal. Both should be free.

2. The young man in his teens who wishes to marry a woman who is at least ten years older than he is should wait a year before being engaged.

3. The young man in his teens who wishes to marry a woman at least twenty years older than he is, may do so as soon as he is able to support her; and the older she is than he the more reason there is why he should wed her, if there is a practical assurance of his being able to support her. If she has money and he is poor, the wedding should not be permitted unless it is free from all mercenary motives.

4. The young man in his twenties who wishes to marry the girl in her teens should wait at least three years before they are engaged.

5. The man in the thirties who wishes to marry a girl in her teens should wait at least a year before being engaged, and there should be a freedom from all apprehension as to how the family will be supported.

6. The man above the thirties who wishes to marry a girl in her teens should wait at least two years before they are engaged. If she has money, and he is not well-to-do, then it is better to wait still longer to see if his ambition can be stimulated to better himself.

7. The man in the twenties who wishes to marry a young woman in the twenties, should wait at least four years before being engaged.

8. The man in the thirties who wishes to marry a young woman in the twenties should wait at least three years before the betrothal, and he should be sure he can support a family.

9. A man in the forties who wishes to marry a young woman in the twenties should wait at least a year before being engaged. No man older than the forties should marry a woman under thirty.

10. A man in the thirties who wishes to marry a woman

in the thirties should wait at least two years before being engaged.

11. A man in the forties who wishes to marry a woman in the thirties should not be engaged until they have known each other for three or more years. No man above the forties should marry a woman in the forties or older.

12. When a man is in the sixties he should not marry at all. If he is married, he will by that time be physically weakened, and married life will be taken conservatively. But to pass from the habits of non-marriage to those of marriage is sure to shorten his days.

There can be no objection to a wide difference in the ages of the parties, except that old men and young women are always badly mated, unless they were wed before the age of sixty for the elder side. If old men must marry, they should select with care women who are not too feeble to look after them, and who are not too vigorous to take their vitality. But the line is drawn tightly at sixty in this respect, and fifty-five is a still better place for the division when the man is entering the marriage state.

The greatest mistake that can be made by young men in their teens and in the twenties is to omit an interest in women who are much their seniors. The friendship of such women is worth a vast deal to all young men who are under the age of thirty. This is, of course, on condition that the women are free and have a right to receive such attentions, and that the young men have a right to give them. Married women and engaged women are not included in the list. In every locality and community a young man should have a list of all the un-married and unengaged women who are older than he is; and the older the better. They should then become acquainted with them, and institute social meetings where they can come into each other's companionship attended by a chaperone or in groups of three or more to avoid discussion from outsiders. The greater the regard and respect of the public for the good names of its women the better the moral atmosphere all about.

Every man under thirty needs the influence of women who are older than he is. The custom is the reverse. Mature un-married women are looked upon as wall-flowers and left-overs; but the fact is they have escaped much by their patience. They have seen their girl friends grow up, get married, quarrel, separate from their husbands and go through the divorce courts, or worse, while they themselves have been submissive to the fate that has cast them on the island of singleness. This is no idle theory. Let us look at ten cases that arose under our advice during the past thirty years:

1. The young man was a plumber. His father had been a plumber and had retired to become a stock broker. The young man was making money rapidly when he was twenty-two years old. He had over forty girls from whom he could select a wife. Seventeen of these were in their teens, and some of them were very pretty. Eight of them were a year or two older than he; and the others were from three to fourteen years his seniors. Which one should he select for a wife? He thought he loved a pretty miss of nineteen; but he was rather practical, and paid no attention to his feelings of love. In his dilemma he came for advice, and was told to marry a girl who was eleven years older than he; an account of this woman having been given, as of the others. She really cared for him, and was a good housewife, although he was able to employ help in the home. They were married, and the union proved a great success. They have grown old together, and she is still young to the eye and in her manner.

2. A young man, the son of a grocer, and himself in the business with his father, at the age of twenty-four married a woman ten years older than he was. He had a fine wife, and has been supremely happy all through the wedlock. He selected this woman against his feelings of love for a girl of eighteen. He says: "I do not love my wife. I adore her."

3. Another man of twenty-four, a lawyer who had been in the practice for two years, and who was making a good impression on the public by his honesty and ability, was violently in love with a girl of eighteen, but agreed that he had the will power to take whatever woman should be proved to his judgment the most likely to bring happiness to him. This was a lady of thirty-seven, thirteen years his senior. He had not made known his love for the maiden in her teens, and so was free to wed the woman in her thirties. Just before the wedding he said: "I still love Aggie, but she does not know it, and my wife-to-be loves me, I do believe, most sincerely." Happi-

ness followed the wedding, and he has lived to rejoice at his fate. The younger girl was not worthy of a good man, as her life afterwards proved. She never knew how near she came to receiving a proposal from the man who is now a well-known judge of court.

4. A young man of twenty-five married a woman of thirty-two. They have had five children, and the family is prosperous, and all are in good circumstances.

5. A young man of twenty, inheriting a small fortune and a good business, fell in love with a woman of twenty-three; but was advised to marry an older woman, one who was nine years his senior. This he did, and succeeded in establishing a happy home and a fine family.

6. A man of twenty-eight married a woman of forty-five. They had a child in a year, much to their surprise. At that time she was of dark complexion, and severely wrinkled for a woman not any older. She was thin and slender, while her husband was stout and fair. The child was like its father, and we have often seen the wrinkled mother pushing the baby carriage on the streets of a town as she went forth to meet her young husband coming from his office. She began after a while to take an interest in making her face smooth; the wrinkles disappeared, and she grew younger to the eye for many years.

7. A boy of nineteen, who was in love with a woman of thirty-six, and who had set up an income-producing business of his own, induced her to elope with him. She suddenly left her position as a school-teacher without notice, and was married to the boy. His business prospered to a remarkable extent, and today he is a man of wealth. She still lives, and they have been happy all the time. The seventeen years between them are nothing, as they both declare and believe.

8. A boy of eighteen, who was very much in love with a fine girl of the same age, was rejected. Out of spite he proposed to a woman of thirty, who had been a seamstress in his father's family, and, to his surprise, she accepted him on condition that he marry her before he could change his mind. Under advice he did this. They are living together now, and have been very happy all the time.

9. A young man of twenty was in love with a girl who loved

another. He married on impulse a woman of forty-two. They have prospered, and are living in content at this time.

10. A young man of twenty-seven fell in love with a very pretty girl of eighteen, and they were engaged. After a quarrel, in which she returned his ring, he followed advice and never called on her again. He married a woman who was thirty-nine. They have been happy, and are prosperous at this date, having risen from a humble home to one of opulence.

In all these ten cases there has been a steady flow of success to all the parties. They have not quarreled, and have found the advanced years of the woman side of the affiliation an advantage, instead of being a disadvantage, to the state of wedlock. In many other cases of marriage of young men to woman older by a number of years we have never found a separation or a divorce, or any serious friction in their companionship where there has been a reasonable discretion used in the affairs. When a young man who was drunk was led to a marriage with a woman of the town, he fled from it on coming to his senses. Certain stray cases may be found that are unworthy of entering into the discussion; but there is no case of decent people marrying in which the husband is much younger than the wife where there has ever been a separation; at least, we cannot find such a case in the United States.

Some years ago we came to the conclusion that love was a reason for not marrying. This was contrary to our own belief of many years before. Since then we have submitted our reasons privately to physicians, clergymen, judges of courts where divorces are tried, and thoughtful men and women whose advice might be of benefit. At first thought it seemed contrary to all precedent, and in violation of all rules of human conduct. But proof was abundant that love was blind. This defect in its sight is still admitted everywhere. No person pretends to believe that love can see.

All good citizens should uphold that system that will make marriage the most enduring and the most successful.

If love will not accomplish this result, then it should yield to the rules of good judgment and common sense. If love is founded on good judgment and common sense, then it is the basis of marriage; otherwise it is not.

How many girls are there in their teens or twenties, or at

any age, who, when they are engaged to worthy, but poor, young men will not find a reason for breaking the engagement when some worthy, but rich, men come along? How many girls and women are not interested in the news that a millionaire is about to come in their midst? The fact of being betrothed to another man does not deter them from accepting a sure engagement from one who is rich and equally qualified to make a husband that can maintain a grand home. A football captain from a great university came into the possession of six hundred thousand dollars. He made the statement that every pretty girl who was engaged to be married to young men fully as well prepared for marriage as he was, except as to the money advantages, sought him, and he was interested in knowing how many of them would break faith with their sweethearts. Not one of them had the slightest hesitation if she could be sure of winning the football captain.

Girls who stand no chance of immediately bettering their positions are filled to the top full of energetic loyalty to their promises; but the certainty of securing wealth soon tells the real story. It is a very common remark with such a girl, or with any girl who is engaged, to say: "I would not give a penny for the heart of a girl who would drop a poor man she loved for a rich man she did not love." But the marriages of the poor men who are loved speak for themselves. Most of them are abject failures. Most of them are totally devoid of all love in thirty days after the honeymoon is over. As soon as the drudgery and the neglect begin, it is the end of romance. "Jack will not neglect his little birdie, will you, Jack?" says the confiding bride who is trying to make water and flour stick together long enough to put in the pan to be baked. And Jack says he will not. So he kisses her and goes down town to the poolroom for three hours of smoking and fellow-fun, while birdie is at home, in the midst of dirt and foul air, wondering where she will see the end of the toil that her maiden life never revealed to her. Jack says to himself that it is a good place to get out of for an evening.

Lift the curtain on any home, or on any condition of marriage which has been founded on love rather than on the principles of common sense, and the one girl in a thousand who would not give up the man she loved for the richest millionaire on earth is now ready to do anything to shake off the terrible shackles which her sentiment forged about her life.

It is not surprising that young wives who have left in their faces and bodies any semblance of the old beauty drift to houses or lives of shame, or seek legal separation. There are very few homes today where there is any cementing bond of love or affection where once it was the belief that the love was so strong that each party to the union would do anything for the other; and now the strong husband will not bring up a scuttle of coal for the weak wife, as he must read the evening paper if he stays in evenings; and if he cannot stay in and rest he must go down town, to be with his old pals.

Young wives hate to confess their failures in marriage; but young husbands do a lot of talking when with their old friends.

It can be set down as a safe rule of conclusions that there is not one marriage in ten that was founded on love that has been sustained as well by reason of that love as by the rules of judgment and good sense.

Most, if not all, parents want their daughters to be happy. When asked their opinion as to a choice between two men, one of whom the girl loves and the other of whom she believes to be the more desirable man; or if it comes down to selecting one from motives of love and another from motives of judgment and good sense, the parents will not advise the love match.

A true love match between two persons who are otherwise qualified to marry is the best; but the qualifications come first and love second. The latter will never take the place of those essentials of a successful union that are indispensable to success—good judgment and practical sense. If there is nothing but love as a reason why two persons should marry, it will prove nothing on which to marry. It is the most evanescent of all feelings. It cannot withstand an ordinary storm, and takes wings before adversity. "When poverty comes in at the door love flies out the window," is a very old and very true maxim. But is is not alone poverty that drives it forth; a quarrel will do as much; disappointment in the other party, which is almost universal, will do as much; and the facts stated in the third department of this book will tell why many wives and many husbands, on waking to find the animal habits of their consorts so pronounced, will wonder why they ever entered into the marriage state.

The curtain should never rise.

The kind of love that can endure for a day the habits suggested in that third department is wholly blind, and what is so blind as that can never be a safe guide to any state of existence.

The general rule is that love matches are failures. A general rule is established when sixty per cent. of events are on one side of the account; but it is a proved fact that fully ninety per cent of all love matches are failures from the standpoint of love. Less than one in ten remains a love union.

On the other hand, of all the matches that have been made by long deliberation, by thorough preparation for the new conditions, and by the exercise of a sound judgment, not more than three in a hundred have been failures. Ninety-seven per cent. have succeeded. Here is a rule made clear by the tables of percentages from which all safe rules are derived. If more than ninety in every hundred of the matches that have been founded on love, to the exclusion of good judgment, have been failures, and if ninety-seven in every hundred that have been deliberately founded on good judgment have been successes, then the rule is established beyond all doubts; and these data can be readily verified.

Before a person is committed to the promise of marriage let the information of the first five departments of this book be fully digested and absorbed by repeated readings; and let it sway the mind and personal habits. No mistake can then occur. The later use of the power of Sex Magnetism will add success to success, and bring the grandest of all victories. But those five departments are necessary for the first success, and for the first step in the engagement, if it has not already been taken. This same course of instruction was taught more than a quarter of a century ago, and it has been the guiding light to many happy unions that have been founded on its teachings. Where they have been carefully adopted there has been no failure. The percentage of success has been one hundred. Therefore, you can make no error in following the teachings of the first five departments.

The steps to be taken to determine the availability of the two parties to an engagement are as follows:

1. Deliberation. This means that both parties should know as much as possible of each other in disposition, in habits, in readiness for the duties of home life, and in other qualifications for the union.

2. Preparation. This means that each party should understand that marriage imposes new duties of all kinds for both of them. There are also many vicissitudes that cannot arise until after the state is entered upon. These may be surmised, and many of them may be ascertained by inquiry. The man should have some male friends who can post him; and the woman should have women friends who can furnish her with all the conditions that will confront the new couple.

Deliberation means waiting. The promise to marry ends the first part of the deliberation, and renders ineffectual the greatest of all human laws, which impels those who are in doubt as to the intents of others to raise their own standards of merit so as to win against such doubt. No greater mistake can be made than for the man to offer marriage and ask to be engaged, or for the woman to agree to become betrothed. The knot is tied then and there in many lives. The freedom that comes from a state of non-engagement is both wholesome and healthy. It is the vantage ground of life.

Of all the nuisances in the world of a girl is the young man in his teens who is infatuated with a charming maiden. He is never quite sane, and many such boys have gone insane in the past; no less than six or seven hundred having, in the year 1909, killed young girls who refused their offer of marriage. Most of the boys then committed suicide, showing the insanity of love. The maiden should be kept as much away from the lads as possible. Commonness of acquaintance should be allowed only when some functions of a social nature are being given, where the boys are on their best behavior, and the girls are also at their best. To throw the two sexes together in a common way is sure to invite some silly and wild-brain of a boy to make love at a time when he is no more able to know his own mind than he is the mind of an elephant running amuck.

The analysis of love shows that it is merely the development of puberty, or sexual unfolding.

It is never present where there is a lack of this nature. If you take away the male power, you destroy forever the feeling of love as it exists in the boy or man. This has been abundantly proved. It is likewise true in woman; for there are many cases of operation to remove the ovaries that have been followed by all loss of the love nature that had been strong before.

The passionate song of the poet, as reflected in Burns, or in Byron, is but the same feeling of physical intensity. Neither poet, nor any other of the love poets, could have written their lays of passion immediately after gratification. War and pestilence and the stern realism of life would have then occupied their minds. Had either Burns or Byron or any of the love poets been emasculated, all their love songs would have died out after that event.

In the case of a general, prominent in history, who was also a most gallant and ardent lover, an accident made him a eunuch; and after that occurrence he was unable to feel or display, or even to talk of love. Woman to him was a friend, but no longer a sweetheart.

Boys that play hard or work hard and keep mind and body busy are not often dragged down by a strong love for a girl. Their energies have gone out into their usefulness. In proportion as the mind and the faculties are idle or partly employed will the feeling of love grow into intensity and become an infatuation. Hard-working boys who are not left much alone, or in the companionship of other boys, are free from this disease of the nervous system, for love in the teens is only a disease. The father who cares for his boy should have him educated in all the branches of a common education, and should also take care of his evenings and his spare hours, beginning about the age of fifteen, and continuing until he is of age. This is a tax on the time and the love of the father for six or seven years; but it will pay much better than to let the boy drift away. There are few, if any, boys that would not prefer the companionship of their fathers to that of the lads who hover about them with all sorts of temptations. If the boy is worth saving, he is worth the sacrifice of time that the father may render him in these years of change and development.

The daughter is generally closer to the mother than the lad is to his father; but it is a matter of disappointment to know that mothers do not, as a rule, accept their companionship as freely as they should. There should be hardly a minute when the daughter's occupation is unknown to the mother. If she is at school the mother should know it. Any absence or partial absence should be reported to the home by the teachers, under a private understanding. Any wandering off with other girls should be checked at the very outset. Daughters should be warned of the danger of having girl friends, for the first sins of the maiden life are giving their seed in that companionship.

Mothers have been able to hold the society of their boys, as well as their girls, thus excluding the outward temptations. Some women plan to have their sons escort them; much in the way that the very youthful son of the late Grover Cleveland acted as an escort to his mother. He traveled with her and looked after her interests like a man. There are women who attend church, or evening gatherings, or make visits in the charge of boys not over fifteen to twenty years of age. Thus the mother becomes the sweetheart of the lad.

By proper planning it is possible for women to keep their girls always under their eye. If the practice is begun too late, when the girl is already a fixed companion of several other girls, and the special friend and run-about of one in particular, it will cause too much friction to intervene; but the future of the girl is not safe even then. The miss who is most anxious for the companionship of a good girl is the one who is most dangerous. She is persistent, and helps herself with the boys that float about by the display of the friendship existing between her and the other girl. She is continually making engagements, and calling for her friend to come out with her, or to come over to her house when there is no intention of going there; and so there will arise the clandestine meetings in places that are not wholesome for a pure maiden.

It is a good rule that companionship of boys with boys is not as good for them as the companionship of the boy with his father; that the mother and daughter should be the closest of friends, and the attachment of girls away from home, or of one out of her home even for an hour at a time, or for any interval, is not good for the girl. Let parents make their boys and girls when in the teens their most welcome companions. Begin before puberty is advanced; always in the first months of the sixteenth year, and sooner than that if possible. Cut off all private friendship outside. Keep the girls where the boys cannot make love to them. Do not allow boys to come around the home to see the girls, unless they come to social functions where there is no separation into couples. Keep up a general acquaintance, and put a check at once to all forms of special acquaintance. The two sexes should meet publicly and openly, but never privately at that time of life.

Many years ago, at the advice of physicians and others, parents in a certain city agreed that it was right to explain puberty to their sons and daughters, and to begin when it was first making itself manifest to the young people. They spoke of it as the cause of that peculiar sentiment called love and infatuation. They made it so clear that the boys and girls completely met this love nature as it developed, and what might have driven some of them into hasty engagements was taken in a philosophical manner, and allowed to die with their increase of mental work; for it is a fact in physiology that the harder the brain works the less the heart loves, and the smaller will be the sexual nature. The faults of boys have been cured by healthful studies that were hard and all-absorbing. Give the lad all he can do with his mind, and all the ambition needed to make something of himself, and his error will die out and never return. Such boys become deliberate in their love-making, and are not hasty in marrying. It is only when the sexual intensity sways the mind that bad marriages are made. Reverse this condition, and let the mind sway the sexual nature, and error will cease almost at once, and so will love.

What is better than love will take its place.

The girl whose mind is absorbed in mental progress of a hard character will not fall into a hasty love. It is for this reason that most old maids are intellectual, for they wait and wait, lacking the fire, until they are left in the whirl by the men who know no better than to seek the young face and the doll heart. If men knew themselves better and wanted homes and happiness, they would never look to any women except the old maids. There, and there alone, is the certainty of happiness. The giddy girls, the faces that fade as they pass out of their honeymoons, the inexperienced hearts and hands, make no true wives.

Mental work, hard study and fine intelligence drive out love in young hearts, and deliberation follows. The most intelligent of women are those who are, or were, old maids. They are the most sensible. They have by far the better education. Many of them have been school-teachers; and where the brain is greatly employed the sexual nature is almost wholly depressed, much to the benefit of the mind and body. "Had I to choose over again, were I young and in search of a wife, knowing all I know of the world, my first choice, and only choice, would be the woman of intelligence who had grown up free from all feelings of sexual love, even if she were much my senior," was the statement made by a man of great prominence in the world.

A graduate of Harvard University, who was twenty-one years of age, and who had come into a large fortune, was besieged by many young and pretty girls of the best families. An alliance with almost any one of them would have been to his financial and social advantage, and yet he could not accept such a fate. "I have no wish to marry a girl," he said. "I want an old maid school-teacher. I do not know just who she will be, but I am going out into the world and get acquainted with some woman whose life has been an open book, who has taught school for fifteen or twenty years, and who is in her thirties or forties." He took his time, and eventually found a woman of very sweet face, who was decidedly intellectual. She had graduated from the normal school of the State, and was teaching when he met her. She was thirty-four at the time. No man had ever fallen in love with her. This wife-hunter made himself friendly with her, and called to see her at the home of her parents, where she lived.

The meeting came about by an accident of such a nature that she did not suspect that she was being hunted down like a wild animal in the lair. The visits to the home were not apparently planned, and she merely asked him to call again at his pleasure, if he desired. He did call again, and rather often. In six months it began to be rumored that this graduate of Harvard and man of fortune was making love to a woman almost old enough to be his mother. At the end of a year he proposed, and she refused him, on account of the difference in their ages and her lack of love for him. This refusal made him the more determined, but a second year went by before she agreed to marry him, and then only with the understanding that she did not, and never could, love him. But did she respect him? Yes. Once after their marriage, when he was stricken with fever and likely to die, she realized that there was something in her heart stronger than love that prompted her to a willingness to lay down her own life for his sake. "I do not know what this feeling is," she said. "It is not love, and it seems stronger than adoration, for I have adored him for a long time, and now I regard him in a holier light than that." Whatever the feeling was it mounted higher than love in her life, and she was the happiest woman in the world, as she thought, when he got past the crisis. Stay in the room with him day and night? Yes, she did; and she kept a watchful eye on every moment of his flickering life as the days came and went during which her fate and his were to be sealed in that awful suspense of sickness.

With what wonder she looked back on the night when she said no to his offer of marriage, and kept him waiting a year for his answer!

Now that he was convalescent and out of danger, and the new future with him was opening in all its dazzling brightness, she clasped his hand in hers, and the tears of thankfulness fell over her arm, pale with the fading of her vitality; an arm that a few days later wound itself about his neck and held them together in a passionate prayer that he might have all the happiness her life could give him. He was the most fortunate of men. He has since said that some power higher than his own discernment shaped his life with that woman's. He believes in inspiration, in the sense that a person may be inspired to select a course of conduct, such as he did, and that these strong influences ought to be given scope in every case. He says today, after many years of happiness: "I do not see any advantage in marrying young girls or young

women. I find that wives outlive their husbands in a majority
of cases by ten or twenty years. I knew, from a list I had
of the widows and widowers, that the former were by far the
more numerous. The insurance tables show that the woman
stands a better chance than the man of great longevity. This
being the case, a woman should be about fifteen years older
than her husband. At least, that was my view. In my class
that left Harvard when I did a large percentage of the marriages that have occurred have been failures. Quite a number
are divorced, and some have separated by agreement, others by
quarrels. I shall never be sorry that I made the choice I did.
It proves that there is a bond stronger than love.''

In this department we have presented many views of the
matter of love-making and marriage, of selection and rejection.
In all these views, differing as they do, there is a steady trend
of the law that marriage should be founded on something
stronger than love. The woman who has never faced the fearful
reality of a wrong selection, or who has not yet graduated from
the school of sentiment out into the hard world of experience,
will challenge this law; but those who know will agree with it,
and those who do not know are not in a position to give an
opinion.

If you can tell what that feeling is that will prompt a man
of sixty to cling to his wife of sixty, then you will understand
the meaning of a stronger bond than love; for in his day and
in her day they spent the forces that burned brightly when
the heart was young. They have been together for forty years;
one of the few examples of the binding force that held the
marriage ties strongly when wrecks were strewn along life's
beach as they went on their journey. There is none of the boy's
love in the hearts, or the girl's infatuation that seemed so
lurid when it first broke out. All that has passed. They
never knew such feelings themselves. But they are fast and
secure, heart to heart and mind to mind, and will so remain
until the snows turn to kiss the western sunlight in the winter
of their life, and melt in the warmth of heaven's opening gates.

If you can tell why the eunuch took to himself a wife who
was, like himself, barren and defective in love, but who proved
better than a lover, for he was loyal in every pulsating throb
of his heart, a condition that is impossible in ordinary love

matches, you can understand what is meant by a bond that is stronger than infatuation. What civilization needs is the enduring marriage, not the flash in the pan, the explosion and the putting together of the pieces in new combinations.

Whatever will make wedlock permanent during life is the best for the parties themselves, for their children and for humanity.

ONE more step is now to be taken in the onward march of this work. Reviews are always beneficial, and for this reason it is advisable to re-read all the foregoing departments. It will be seen that there is a logical growth of importance and strength in the plan of instruction. In the beginning of the course we discussed the uses of Sex Magnetism. This laid a general map before the student. Then came the basic law, by which the practical character of life was seen. The third department made clear the common faults that stand in the way of a satisfactory relationship, and that detract from the pleasure of marriage.

In the next step the attractive force was taught as the final exaltation of the personality of each sex.

Thus far the training related to the work of fitting one's own self for the other sex. In the fifth department the first step was taken that reached out toward the other sex; and in the sixth department the reaching out proceeded far enough to select the mate.

This study and training must be kept before the mind under its title of Sex Magnetism. It is intended solely for the man and the woman who are willing to believe that the union of the two sexes, either in marriage or out of marriage, is the greatest institution of life on earth.

The union in marriage is designed for specific purposes.

The union out of marriage is designed for social and beneficial purposes; and it must be so conducted that the two parties to it are not left to themselves, but are a portion of some larger body of people. No opportunity for scandal must be given in any instance.

If the student of these lessons is not of the opinion that the union of the two sexes is the most important affiliation on earth, there will be nothing gained by pursuing the course further. Nor can we take the space to prove the truth of the assumption, except to record at this time the few leading facts in this connection:

1. Every person is the product of two persons—a mother and a father.

2. The mother love is the strongest bond of affection in the world, and is wholly different from marital love.

3. The father love is next in strength.

4. The purpose of these parental loves is to bring up the child, not only in safety, but under such influences as will increase the higher instincts of the next generation, so that it may take its place in the line of progress which is the chief end of human production.

5. In home life alone can parental love manifest itself, and give to the child the nurture and the good influences that will better its nature.

6. As parental loves are the strongest on earth, and as home life is essential to the welfare of the child and of the race, there must of necessity be harmony in the home, and this can exist only when the parents are united together with heart interests.

7. The man or woman who, imbued with other ambitions, thinks that sex union is not the most important affiliation in the world must remember that, prior to maturity, the home stood sponsor for the welfare of the child; and, after the years have been emptied of their ambitions, the home is the one place to which the tired mind and the weary heart must turn.

8. Home life, therefore, must bring up the rising generation, and must throw its protection around the passing generation. Of these facts there can be no doubt.

9. There can be no home life with one sex in the house. Try ever so hard to imagine it, and there will be a void somewhere that cannot be filled. A man may live alone, but he will be a failure to himself and to those around him. A woman may live alone, and she, too, will be sadly deficient in those interests that are essential to happiness. If it is possible for a woman, or for women, to conduct a home, it cannot be so arranged that a man can do the same. He needs woman, whether she needs him or not. While, from the administrative point of

view, women are able to take care of themselves and of a home
without the companionship of man, he cannot be left out in
the cold; and, until all men are extinct, it will be out of the
question to leave home life solely to women.

10. A true man is always turning his mind and his thoughts
to some woman. A true woman is always turning her life to
some man. It matters not how young or how old they may
be there is this swinging of the mind, and of the yearnings to
some one of the other sex. Let this demand of nature be killed,
and no man would seek to climb the ladder of success, nor
would woman care for life. What she may lack now she once
had in fact or in hope, and what she has now that is sacred to
her inner life is centered in some man of the past or present.
It is only when she dies in earthly spirit that her thoughts turn
wholly heavenward.

The white-haired widow sits at her window and watches the
walk up which he came many years ago. It has been nearly a
quarter of a century since he was borne out at the front door,
never to return; but his steps on the walk and his touch on the
knob of the door are eagerly awaited in her dreams of the
days gone by.

The flower that he gave her lies dead with dusty petals in
the leaves of the old Bible, but she slowly turns those leaves
until the broken blossom is revealed to her gaze, and she reads
the words of comfort and of promise on the open pages. In
the twilight she sees his form passing across the hall, and
hears him call to her in tones of affection that fill her heart
with rejoicing. Thus are the memories ever alive.

Regrets are many, but they are only shadows of love.

The man who did not appreciate the woman until she was
gone, and who has been true to her ever since, cannot escape
the feeling of her presence as of old. There are mementoes
that he prizes now, and would not part with for all the gold of
earth. There were paths in which they walked and talked, made
plans and built greater castles than ever they could realize.
The ring he gave her is always before his eyes at evening, and
the book out of which she read to him gives up its thoughts as
freely now as then, but the voice is feeble, and he can scarcely
hear its tones.

These are films of the affiliations that were sweet while they lasted, and that would fill life with bliss could they be renewed.

Such is the nature that dwells within the human heart. Born in the home, of parents that loved the home, reared in the home, gone out from its walls for life's sojourn and battle, and returning at last to its comforts when the fight dwindles down to the vale of peace, the heart cries for the solace that only woman can give to man, and man can draw out of woman's companionship.

The highest authority, the Creator of the race, declared that it was not good for man to be alone, and that declaration has been true ever since it was given utterance.

The greatest blessing in life is happiness, and there can be no happiness until there are two sexes to enjoy it together. No person can ride over the laws of nature. Defiance and conceit prevail for a while, but only a brief while, and in shabbiness and littleness. The severe man and the carouser pretend to find satisfaction and pleasure apart from a true appreciation of the opposite sex, but such experience is short-lived. It narrows the heart and dries up the conscience.

True happiness must be abiding.

In the sixth department there is the coming together of the two sexes, designed to bring happiness in the place of the failures that are now so common as to threaten the breaking up of the home and the debauchery of civilization. Read that sixth department several times, and master all the teachings that precede it in this book; then seek some affiliation with one of the other sex, and establish heart interests at once.

Four classes of people are now invited to set up new lives, based on the laws of Sex Magnetism, as they are already laid down, and are to be further described in this work:

First Class—Those who are married.

Second Class—Those who are engaged to be married.

Third Class—Those who are neither married, nor are engaged, but who are marriageable.

Fourth Class—Those who are neither married, nor engaged, and are not marriageable.

All these should have heart interests of a kind to suit their relationships, but founded on the same laws of Sex Magnetism. These interests are of two kinds:

1. A mutual interest in common.

2. A mutual sympathy.

What is meant by "mutual" is that two persons should agree together in response to each other; and what is meant by the term "in common" is that the same thing should be the subject of the interest of both persons.

The word sympathy means something quite apart from its common interpretation as an expression of sorrow, or a sharing of feeling in the misfortune of another. In this work sympathy is union. The definition given in the dictionary, taken from the two words out of which this word is framed, is "conformity of temperament by which two persons are agreeable to each other."

As illustrations of sympathy showing "a conformity of temperament," the following instances may be cited:

1. When one person is interested in the cultivation of flowers of a special kind, another person who discusses such flowers to an extent that evinces a real interest, and who exchanges information and bits of experience on the same subject, not only once, but often, would display an interest. The thing that is "common" is the special variety of flowers, and the fact that both take an "interest" in it shows a mutual liking, or else an assumed liking, for the same thing. If the assumption is made solely to win the attention and friendship of the other person, and is not genuine, it will be dropped after an engagement or marriage, and the reaction will be worse than a refusal at the start to take an interest in it.

As sympathy is an advanced step in the growth of mutual interest, and must have the same basis to begin with, it will take form when it proves itself genuine and abiding. Thus the interest in the special kind of flowers, and their cultivation, would turn to sympathy when the one person sought to assist the other person in the cultivation, and entered into the pleasure of it as both a science and an art. If the woman enjoys such diversion, and her husband actually enjoys it also, they will possess sympathy along this line. That is, there will be "a conformity of temperament that makes them both agreeable to each other." This is one kind of illustration, taking as a ground-work a worthy diversion.

2. Where the subject is not worthy of the community of temperament, as where a woman loves dogs as she would love

children, the husband would be untrue to himself to join in such an interest. If he loves horses, and she has a similar interest or affection, the subject, while worthy, is not large enough to build a temperament upon. The cultivation of flowers is so close to the first profession of man, and is so near to the heart of nature that the married couple who can enjoy it together would find a community of temperament if there were no commercialism in the practice. When these beautiful children of the heart of God are raised to be sold, those who raise them do not see beyond the dollars.

3. A wife who loves her children, and whose life is centered upon their welfare, can achieve no grander victory in the world than to arouse in her husband a similar love. Such love must be made manifest in works, not words. The father must devote himself to them. He must be with them, teach them, lead them, play with them, study their own inclination, and, above all, take an active and constant interest in their play and their plans. He should listen to them, and let them explain what is in their little minds. Most fathers neglect this duty. The mother love should reach out to the father love, and both should unite in the child, and there find a union of temperament.

4. This question of temperament is a hard one to meet face to face, for nature implants it, and few persons can cultivate it unless they are willing to change their dispositions. Many men, however, have been transformed when a child has blessed their marriage. One word from a friend to a newly-made father set alive the spark that might never have burst into flame: "Now that you have a child, take an interest in it. Love it you will; but show that love by constant interest in it." He could not forget that word "interest." Prior to the event he had been spending his evenings at the clubs and lodges and down town; but that word interest rang in his ears, and he gave up his evenings out, and joined his wife in her world of love for the child. As the latter grew up there was certainly a community of temperament, for both husband and wife made it the center of a mutual love. When the temperament is natural there are scores if not hundreds, of little and great things that can be done that will develop as the new history is enacted.

5. The liking of home life is a matter that should command the most intense interest of two persons.

6. The love of the home itself as an abode is, or should be, the strongest tie on earth; rising in importance above the love of children, for the latter is included in the former. When a husband loves his home, and appreciates all a wife does to make it pleasant, he has a mutual interest in common with her; but when he seeks to take part in its betterment, when he thinks of it in the morning in his first hours, when he gives thought to it as he goes to his day's duties, when, in the intervals of the day, his mind reverts to the abode and the wife there, when, on his return, before he catches a glimpse of its walls, he wonders in what way he can add to the beauty and comfort of its conditions, and when he practices the things he thinks about the home, aiding his wife in her actual work of improving it, then he has a temperament in conformity with hers. As he would not be married if he were not desirous of a true mode of living, it would be a natural, and not an assumed, temperament. All it needs for its development is that he make up his mind to cultivate that temperament. If no other kind is given growth, the love of home should by all means be encouraged.

7. While the cultivation of a love of flowers, a love of children, a liking for home life, and a love for the home itself, are the four most important bases of temperament that are easily unfolded in every true man and woman, there are many other matters of lesser interest about which the mind and heart may center. Music is the theme in some homes, the singing or playing done by the wife being a source of pleasure to the husband, even if he is not able to participate in them; and if he does not at first care for them, he can easily learn to do so, and should be willing to make an effort on the principle that mutual interest and a community of temperament bring two lives close together. There is also the love of any art, or of literature, or of study and improvement, as shown in the fourth and fifth departments, or the building up of a library in the home, book by book, or other matter in which both parties are expected to join mind and hearts. All these, or any of them, serve to effect the end desired.

But there should not be attempts made at feminine things

by the male, or at male subjects by the female. It would not
be sensible for a husband to develop sympathy with his wife
in the direction of dressmaking, although he should be pleased
to respond to any desire she has of showing him how well
she sews and builds dresses. On the other hand, it would not
be sensible for the wife to develop a sympathy for her husband's dental practice, or law practice, or other merely masculine vocation, although it is almost impossible for a wife
to separate her interest from the work which her husband is
engaged in, especially if he is a writer, a clergyman, a doctor
or is in business, for her sympathy generally spurs him on to
his best achievements. A minister who has a wife that did not
enter largely into his church work, or help him in his aspirations, would be remiss. So would a wife who opposed the vocation of a husband.

The difference between mutual interest and sympathy is
important.

Mutual interest is the operation of the mind acting with
another person in relation to a matter in which both find
pleasure and attraction.

Sympathy is a conformity of temperament by which two
persons are agreeable to each other, and proceeds from the
heart. It may begin in the mind in the form of a mutual interest, and advance to the heart in the form of sympathy.

The minds and the hearts of husband and wife should unite.

It is not enough that they agree in mind. They should
agree in heart. If they cannot agree in mind, the time to
ascertain the fact is prior to their engagement, not after they
are married. If they do agree in mind and not in heart, they
should have found it out at the same time. But if they agree
in mind and not in heart, they will be cold to each other,
and their coming and going will be formal and selfish. The
home will lack warmth and cordiality. If they agree in heart,
they will very likely have a mental harmony; but the double
agreement is necessary to a highly magnetic marriage, as we
shall see later on.

As marriage, if not altogether false, is sure to carry with
it the possibility of cultivating a mutual interest and sympathy in the love of children, the liking of home life, and the
love of the home itself, as well as several other broad sub-

jects that arouse the heart as well as the mind, there is no reason why husbands and wives who today are cold to each other and selfish should not turn about and come into the conformity of temperament that will make them agreeable to each other, especially under the developing power of Sex Magnetism.

This conformity of temperament has a peculiar action.

Will you imagine a body from which radiates a light broad enough to reach as far from that body as its own diameter. Then imagine another body having the same radiating light. Now, suppose this light is called sympathy; that one body is the husband, and the other body is the wife; they will radiate a power that will reach from each far enough to include each other. Both will be in the radiation. The wife will be in the light that emanates from her husband, and the husband will be in the light that radiates from the wife. This is sympathy. It is a conformity of interest that makes both agreeable to each other.

All magnetic persons radiate a power that is not light of a visible nature, but is magnetism of a clearly-felt character. If you have taken the foundation course in this study, as set forth in the outlines of the magnetic club, you will have developed this radiating power.

But it will not have influence until you associate it with something that is tangible and practicable. Electricity is a magnetic force of a mechanical kind, yet it is useless until it is made to do valuable work. The test of any power is its ability to aid humanity.

The idea of radiation has been expressed by writers and speakers for hundreds of years, if not thousands. It has always been an old saying that a good woman radiates gentleness and cheer all about her; that a man who is honest radiates confidence among those whom he meets, and similar allusions to the radiating power of a person of influence.

In the study and practice of personal magnetism a force is not only developed, but is actually attached to the personality of the individual that corresponds, in way of illustration, to the actual radiation of light from a luminous body, or heat from one that is warm. A candle sends forth light, and uses the ether within the atmosphere for its medium of passage. A hot object radiates forth heat and employs the air itself. A magnetic body radiates an electric energy within a certain range, intense when nearby, and attenuated beyond its line of intensity. A magnet actually radiates magnetism that attracts, and the object that is attracted has only to come within the scope of its power to be caught and held.

This principle is everywhere manifested.

No attempt is to be made here to review the lessons of the foundation book, as they are too extensive for even a reference. The instruction of the next few pages is along new lines entirely.

But the presence of two mediums of passage for any force is taught not only in the foundation book, but in all works of science that bear upon the universe and its parts.

This planet is enveloped in an almost invisible air, estimated from ten to two hundred miles or more in depth or height. Owing to the attraction of the earth itself, which is a form of magnetism, the air is most dense within the distance of five or ten miles from the surface, being actually heaviest at the ground or sea level, and gradually growing thinner as it rises.

In this way the earth radiates its atmosphere; for the chemical parts of the air are also parts of the chemical composition of the earth itself, and are constantly changing places. The air comes into the solids of the planet, and the latter pass into the air. Here we have a common example of radiation of a mechanical character.

The sun is probably composed of a fire-mass, out of which radiate both light and heat, as well as animal vitality and electricity, magnetism and attraction. All that exists within the body of man, or in the air or ground, must have its source, if not origin, in the central orb, which is called the sun. But its power of radiation is not infinite. If it were, there would be but one sun in the sky. No person who has studied this orb believes that there is any influence going out from the sun beyond the solar system. It would seem wholly impossible. The solar system is comparatively a small space in the sky. To us mortals it is very large, and its diameter of more than four thousand million miles is inconceivably large. Yet, if we were standing on the nearest star beyond our system we would not discern any planet here, and could behold our sun alone, with a background of thousands of other stars, all seemingly jumbled together. As the largest telescope that human genius can invent is unable to detect any planets in other solar systems, so no beholder there can see ours here.

Each system seems separate.

Hence it is true that our sun, mighty as it is in its own realm, has a limit to its powers. It radiates light, heat, animal life, plant life, magnetism, electricity and attraction; and these forces go out to their limit of distance, growing weaker and weaker until they cease, and the solar system is ended, for its limits are reached. Too near the sun the forces would be most intense. Too far away they would be most weak.

Our earth radiates its atmosphere, as has been stated.

But it takes up the light of the sun, and radiates that also. It is very probable that light does not exist in either, but depends upon the radiating power of a tangible object to make it manifest. As it is merely an activity against the nerves of the brain, and as the brain is built of the earth and the sun forces, the power to know light is only a response to some form of radiation.

If the human body did not radiate light it could not be seen.

If it did not radiate heat or warmth, it could not be felt.

When you place your hand upon an object, you recognize its shape and its characteristics, because there is radiation of some kind emanating from it.

Sound is radiation.

It employs the air as its medium of passage. If you are at a distance from a cannon when it is discharged you can hear it, but not so plainly as when you are nearer. If you are many miles away, the sound is fainter. If a person speaks to you, the clearness of the voice is greater with his nearness to you; and at a certain distance it is wholly lost to your ear, because there is a limit to the radiation of sound.

Electrical bodies act upon the same principle, having two methods of discharge, one the direct and the other leakage. The former operates at close range.

The stove sends out its warmth by the same kind of radiation as sound is projected, but has a much closer range. A stove may be too hot six inches away for the hand to be held near it, but is only moderately hot two feet away, while at a rod or more its heat is felt only in the moving currents of the air in the room. It is radiation with the usual limit.

All natural powers follow the same law.

The magnet will act only when some object comes within the range of its greatest intensity. The natural magnet, or lodestone, loses its power in time, and steel and iron magnets are made artificially because they alone are permanent. In the earth, in the far North, is the magnetic mass that attracts the needle of the compass to aid the mariner thousands of miles away, showing a long range of natural magnetism. Just in what way that mysterious force turns the point of the needle and compels it to direct the ship across wide seas, is one of the great marvels of life. Through solids and through liquids, through air and through storms, that silent influence is pulling the needle around to its direction, as though a hand had hold of it. It is not attraction, because it must overcome that agency, even in infinitesimal degree.

The attraction of gravity is just as hard to understand.

Some writers think it is identical with electrical attraction, but the magnetism exerted on the needle of the compass is wholly different from the attraction of gravity. The earth radiates attraction and has influence on the other planets and on the moon, the revolutions of the latter having been stopped by the earth, so that but one face or side of the moon is always towards the earth, no matter how persistently it keeps in its orbit.

In another kind of radiation a human being sheds intelligence from the brain. He also sends forth magnetism from the entire nervous systems of the body. These radiations have three degrees:

1. The range of close intensity.
2. The general range of influence.
3. The negative, or minimum, range.

The last named has no power beyond the body itself, and is classed as non-magnetic, or dead, in influence.

The second degree is general and thin, and the power is not extensive or strong, unless aided by some faculty. It is, however, a power, and exerts an influence that in time becomes effective, even against determined opposition.

The first degree, or the range of close intensity, is capable of reaching a high energy where the conditions and the personality conform to such end. In the foundation course of personal magnetism, which is the book devoted to the cultivation of that power, there are many exercises and other means of developing this radiating energy; all under the general name of personal magnetism. The name is correct, for that is the nature of the power referred to.

It is strictly personal magnetism.

As the student begins to make progress in that course, which is noticeable from the first real work in it, the body at the same time undergoes a change. Magnetism begins to radiate from it. The man or woman who is magnetic, whether naturally or by development, will make this power felt on entering a room. There is something in the presence, in the walk, in the attitude, in the eye and in the voice that impresses this fact on every person within a certain distance of the individual. There are two kinds of radial magnetism:

1. That which is unaided by any faculty.
2. That which is aided by some faculty.

There are two sources of radial magnetism:

1. That which is called natural.
2. That which is developed.

The natural power is said to have resulted from inheritance, which is never true. Then it is said to be born in the person, which likewise is never true. Then it is described as coming natural to a man or woman. All this means that a person becomes magnetic, and does not know how; but the expert knows very well how it came about. Certain habits of the mind, body and emotional system tend to the natural saving of the power. All persons are magnetic, but nearly all of them lose the energy by leakage and wrong methods of caring for the body, the mind and the emotions. Those who, by accident, take proper care of themselves, largely through instinctive common sense, are rapid developers of magnetism.

The natural or accidental possession of this power is never as effective as the cultivated form of it. The lodestone is found in a magnetic condition, but the useful and permanent magnets are made by the art of man. The natural lodestone cannot do the work, bring the results or secure the confidence in its stability that the man-made magnet will produce. It has also been proved that men and women who did not know they were magnetic, or, if knowing it, did not understand its uses, have suddenly lost all control of the very people over whom they have fitfully at times exercised power. In these arts nothing can be left to accident or chance or nature. No florist will leave his garden to nature, for it would be ruined by weeds.

As the methods of developing magnetism in men and women are founded on the processes and laws of nature, just as the flower garden is made; and as they are not left to the care of nature any more than the flower garden is left, the power is wholly natural, while being controlled and directed by the art of man. This is the rule in everything. Electricity originates in nature; but left to nature it runs wild, and does more harm than good. When cultivated by man, and its uses are controlled by him, then for the first time is it reliable and of high value.

The same is true of personal magnetism.

It is the same force as that which is said to be a born gift, but it is of no permanent value unless it is developed and employed by the art of man.

But there are two kinds of radial magnetism—one is unaided by any faculty, and the other is aided by some faculty.

A faculty is any operation of the mind, the body or the emotions that a human being may direct, control or regard as swayed by voluntary purpose. Whatever else occurs of itself is a function. The functions do not aid radial magnetism, but the faculties all may be so controlled that they will aid it to a wonderful extent.

Thinking is a faculty.

The formation of a purpose is a faculty.

The development of a habit is a faculty.

The interest that the mind takes in anything or any person is a faculty.

Sympathy, being one of the emotions, is a faculty.

Temperament is a faculty, for it is controllable, changeable, and can be decreased or increased.

What the hands do, what the body in any of its parts may

do, what the mind does, what the thoughts are, what the habits are, what a person is, as estimated by his conduct and daily life, are the results of voluntary purpose or voluntary neglect, and aid or interfere with the radial magnetism that exists like an atmosphere about the individual.

All radial magnetism is a use of personal magnetism, such as is developed in the book of the foundation course, but is employed in a way that is suited to the results desired. The particular way in which it will be employed is determined by the faculties that aid it and their uses.

In the first place, any man or woman who has cultivated personal magnetism in the foundation course possesses radial magnetism, but is not yet an active agent. By tests that leave no doubt of its extent there is a radial atmosphere of magnetism that surrounds the individual like an enveloping ether. This ether begins to form and to extend itself just as soon as the true work of the foundation course is undertaken. As that course always precedes this, or, at least, accompanies this, and as this present work is not announced to any person who is not familiar with the foundation course, it is always presumed that the student of these pages is the owner of the first course. Constant reference to the latter is necessary, in order to make the training clearly understood.

The radial inactive force is that form of radial magnetism where no aid comes to it from any faculty. This is as nearly as it can be designated, the developing energy resulting from the practice of the foundation course. This energy can be felt, and is readily recognized by any person who possesses it, or by any expert who accosts such a person, and any instrument that measures the nervous vitality of a live body will determine the extent of the radial power when in an inactive state.

A man or woman who is magnetic as the result of practice, or in any other way, has a greater radial atmosphere when the physical or the mental vitality is high, and a more limited atmosphere when some excess or some cause of exhaustion has interfered with it. Thus the loss of sleep, or the suffering of pain, or indigestion, or hard, mental work, or other harmful agency will cause quite a change in the extent of this radial magnetism.

In married life two sources of help and of harm are constantly fighting each other. The husband or the wife who lacks radial magnetism will never be attracted to the other. It has been said that all human beings are magnetic. This is true. Any scientist knows that all substances are magnetic; any lump of earth has some, any dull clay has some, and nothing exists that is empty of this quality; but there are certain substances that are highly endowed with magnetism, and these are so classed because of the difference in their condition over their lesser neighbors in the material world.

It is true also that a girl who has entered upon her maiden stage, and a boy who has entered upon his young manhood, is much more magnetic than at any previous period of his life. The sexual growth develops the radial energy, and this attracts and holds two persons together for a while; and may become so strong and so erratic that it will set aside the judgment. Even insanity has followed its wild career.

Experiments prove that radial energy widens or narrows with each use or misuse of the faculties, assuming that it exists at all. Of course, there are many persons with so small a radial atmosphere that they are classed as unmagnetic. Nature imparts this power to the two sexes at times and under conditions peculiar to them, so that they may become interested in each other. But that form is narrow and limited, and quickly vanishes on the first exhaustion of the nervous powers.

When the normal radial magnetism is added to by the cultivation of personal magnetism it becomes enlarged, and is given a tendency to permanency. At least, it is very difficult to drive it wholly away, while ordinary sexual radial magnetism, or the usual drawing of one sex to another, is quickly wasted or lost.

If personal magnetism is added to normal radial magnetism, and to these two there be added the unfolded influence of Sex Magnetism as taught in this book, there will be a combination that will always endure, and that nothing can break down. It is to such end that this course is tending.

As these powers are continually dependent on the faculties,

and as the latter are always fluctuating, there is a new form of value being created all the time. The following are some of the facts that have been collected and tested under so many conditions that there cannot remain any doubt of their accuracy:

1. A man who has no magnetism and no polish in his manners will not have any genuine attractive force.

2. A man who has polish in manner or politeness, but no magnetism, will please in a surface way, but will not have any wearing qualities. He would be a bore after a short time. Many of the most tiresome men are those who are highly polished, and who know every rule of gallantry. Women like them for the new sensations they may produce in contrast with their husbands and brothers; but there comes very soon the fact that such men are bores.

3. A man who has most highly polished manners and magnetism will not gain in his control over others, for there is a limit to usefulness in method, and people measure magnetism by its practical value.

4. A man who has magnetism, but no polish of manner or politeness, being merely neutral, might win a common mind to his cause; but he would be crude among the better classes where refinement is at par.

5. A man who has magnetism and is positively disagreeable in his manners, will be unable to use his magnetism. The thing to be drawn will be repelled. Thus it is seen that magnetism is the agency of habits and of substantial qualities, and not their master, as far as the possessor is concerned.

6. A woman who has no magnetism and possesses no refinement will not have any genuine powers of attraction.

7. A woman who has refinement and no magnetism will please in a surface way. After a brief acquaintance with her, the man who seeks to pay her attention will wonder why he ever called, and how he can most easily withdraw without giving her offense. Coldness, accompanied by numbness, in a woman is stupid enough, but when it is polished off like shining marble it glares at you.

8. A woman who is magnetic, but lacks refinement, being neither polished nor disagreeable, but just neutral, may win a common fellow, but will not reach with her influence into the ranks of the better classes.

9. A woman who is unrefined, but magnetic, would repel others, for nothing can be attracted by a driving force. You cannot push a man off the steps and prevail on him to continue his course until he returns. He may retaliate, but he will be an unpleasant visitor.

10. It is not generally possible for a trained person who has developed magnetism to retain disagreeable qualities.

11. A man who takes an interest in a woman must of necessity take an interest in something that she herself believes in. He cannot be merely interested in her, for that is impossible. Friendship does not cling to the body as an inert mass, but to something that the body is engaged in, or the mind enjoys, or the emotions are influenced by. You cannot imagine a man in love with a woman who is saying nothing and doing nothing. He and she both may be involved in eager conversation. He is not telling her that she is beautiful and all that, for he passed that stage some weeks before. He and she may be building castles in the air, and they will do their best architecture then. They will have themes that interest both of them. She would not, in the nature of things, intrude a subject that he cared nothing for, and he would be equally diplomatic. If he has magnetism and takes a genuine interest in what she says and does, then there is the exercise of the faculty of interest aiding the magnetism. It finishes it with a medium for its extension. The result is that his radiant energy reaches farther away, and has greater intensity.

12. It is not necessary for two persons to possess personal magnetism, for the power of one will easily include the other. The yielding party is as content, and the controlling party finds the mutual pleasure always present and this is enough. But the magnetism of one person is imparted in large degree for the time being to the other person, if the latter is controlled. Lack of control would end the matter at once.

13. The subject of the mutual interest must appeal to the magnetic party, and emanate from the other; or else it must emanate from the magnetic party, and be in harmony with the wishes and views of the other. If a man seeks to hold a woman's will by his own magnetism, he should first find out what great subject most interests her permanently, not for the time being; and he then should ascertain in his own mind if he can take a

positive interest in that subject. If not, he does her a wrong, as well as himself, to continue the relationship. But if he can become interested in it, then he will retain great control over her by uniting his magnetism with the interest that is mutual. This is a common and practical law of life.

14. If he wishes to introduce to her mind for acceptance some permanent subject in which he wishes her to take an interest, then he should first seek to arouse that interest without using the power of personal magnetism. If she is enthusiastic in her reception of it, then he can secure lasting control over her life by adding to the subject of mutual interest his own personal magnetism. This, too, is a common law of human nature.

15. There come to all persons who are married a crisis in which the ways will part if there is not a community of interest. Their minds and habits have been drifting apart. It may be easy or it may be difficult for them to leave each other. Many cases are not as serious as that. The remedy is in the cultivation of personal magnetism by one or the other of them. Whichever one chooses to do this, should then make the effort to find some subject that both may become interested in, or some mode of living, or some line of conduct, or other matter that is worth great interest; and then it should be combined with the magnetic power, founded on the first six departments of this course. Where the wife, for instance, will not evince an interest in anything, and knows of nothing that can arouse her enthusiasm, while the husband is the party who is cultivating his own magnetism, she may be made, by his aid, to see something that will prove of importance to her. It should be a theme that pertains to both of them, and that can be amalgamated in their home existence.

Eighteen years ago a man wrote as follows for advice:

"I have been married eleven years. My wife and I have got along very well together, but there has never been any real love since the first few months of wedlock. She finds the monotony stupid and says there is nothing in it. What can be done? I have studied and practiced many of the advisory systems for home happiness, but have not benefited myself or my home in any way."

Under advice, after further information, he was told to try

in many ways to ascertain what she would become interested in, while he quietly, and without her knowledge, took up the cultivation of personal magnetism. A year later he wrote:

"I have finished the course in personal magnetism, and have been making progress in the private sheets furnished under the title of Sex Magnetism. I see what is to be done, and have been trying to find out what great subject will interest both of us permanently."

After the lapse of three months he again wrote:

"You ask what progress is being made. I tried birds, pets, animals and flowers as possible subjects. These did not make any impression, although she said she wished she had a conservatory attached to the house, but would not let me spend the money for it. The pets were not of sufficient importance to found a permanent and great interest upon. Unfortunately, we have had no children. She took some interest in charitable work, but that is wholly outside of our home, and has no uniting power with us. We were not church-going people, but have since been attending regularly, and find some mutual interest in this new life, although we are not yet members. But this is not domestic. I one day this spring happened to meet an agent selling rose vines, and I got three climbers. She was not consulted, and I did not know how she would take it, but she seemed to like it. Then I had the grounds graded and the rough places brought down to the level of a floor, and grass seed sown, and privet hedge placed around the land, with paths of cement. At this writing the interest she is taking is very great."

A year later he wrote:

"I raised a fine lawn, and the privet hedge is growing fast. The roses this spring show buds, and she is talking of the time when they will bear. I had two evergreen trees, and some evergreen shrubs set out by the paths, and they have changed the looks of the place very much. The house has been given a new coat of paint, a small porch and piazza have been built to receive the climbing vines, and we are soon to have the showiest place on the street. Last week a real estate agent offered us a price for the home that is twice what it is worth, because he has a client who is very much in love with the surroundings. For that money we can buy a new piece of land and build just the kind of house we want, and add the conservatory.''

Three years went by and he again wrote:

"The new house has been built, the conservatory added, and the grounds have been put in lawns and hedges, with trees, paths and other attractions too numerous to be stated in one letter. As luck would have it, we laid aside some of the purchase price, and yet have a much better place. The location is superb. But there is a man who wants to buy it, and we think we may sell, as there is a decided profit in the exchange. Besides, we see things that could be improved.''

They did sell again at a large profit, and have built a house that they considered perfect in its new ideas and innovations. This third home they have had for many years now, and will not sell it; but the man has found his experience a way by which he became a builder of homes in a growing locality, and this is his business now, with the laying out of grounds as a specialty of attraction. Ten years ago he set out hundreds of small evergreen trees and shrubs and privet-hedge plants, and has been drifting into the nursery business as an adjunct to his builder's profession. His wife is interested every minute of the time.

At this writing there is no healthier and more permanently established marital relationship than that which now exists between them.

They are pleasant companions. They meet each other with a hearty good will, and a cordiality that seems to fit lovers more than old timers. Their home, within and without, is the model of attractiveness and comfort. They have the air of people who are well-to-do beyond the thirty thousand dollars they have laid aside.

In our books in various ways there is taught the doctrine that a law of special design is at work in every progressive human life; and that life is progressive that seeks to carry on, even in small degree, the progress of nature towards a higher status of the race.

Read now, if you will, the first department of this book. Make yourself familiar with the teachings that there might have been one sex if there were not other ends in view than the mere reproduction of the race. By sex influences the generation to come may be made better and more refined and intelligent by taking advantage of the lessons taught by nature during the first meetings of the couples who are destined to come together.

True courtship wields the greatest power in civilization.

The spirit of loyalty to home life is everywhere urged on the race by nature. Where this loyalty is great and abiding, there special design brings rewards to those who thus show their value. There are many such cases like the one we have just quoted at such length. In all of them, without a single exception, where a married couple have refound their hearts after a coldness, and have thereafter built up a home influence of great value to themselves and, relatively speaking, to the world, there nature has visited them with special design, and bestowed rewards they never before dreamed of.

Why was it that the husband referred to, when he failed in many things to arouse an interest in his wife's mind, came upon the rose-seller? Why did he buy? Why did he sow his lawns, and plant the hedges, and make the paths, and adorn the grounds with trees and shrubs? Why, when this was done, did the place attract a price greater than he had paid for it, and so lead him on to higher aspirations? And why did he drift from a clerk-ship with only a fair salary to a new business, in which there was awaiting him a small fortune?

In such an extensive course as Universal Magnetism, the climax of the Personal Magnetism Club, there are many instances of this mysterious power drawing something grand out of the viewless ether that bathes all the earth with its influence. The principle is a plain one:

There is for every man and woman who is truly magnetic, and who conforms to the plan of nature for the improvement of the world, an inexhaustible fund of rewards, and they come in the most unexpected manner. Any person, man or woman, who has passed through the several realms of magnetism with a faithful adoption of the simple truths that all may use easily and freely, and has thus climbed to the top of the upland on the heights as found in Universal Magnetism, will be rewarded. The reward will not be in doubt, but will be clear and certain. The instances are without exception. No person who is earnest will fail, for no one who has been in earnest has failed. There are reports, of which the following is one, that tell the story: "I have found myself passing from a state of the most com-

monplace life full of drudgery and routine toil and duties, up
to the highest planes of earthly existence, and all through the
practice of magnetism. I have done something more than read.
I have given fifteen minutes a day to the practice of it, and it has
not interfered with any other work or duty. When I reached
and graduated from the all-embracing course, Universal Magnetism, then I came in touch with that fund of rewards, as predicted, that showered blessings all along my path. I had constant evidence and proof that there is a boundless deep all
around us, out of which we draw what we will by our magnetic
power."

From all the men and women who have pursued their studies
clear to the end the same proof has come, and we find no exception. No notice can be taken in making up percentages of
those who merely read the studies. It is the practice for fifteen
minutes a day, unremittingly, that develops and employes magnetism at its highest.

But, without ascending the uplands of Universal Magnetism, many persons have caught glimpses of the same wonderful power to draw forth rewards from the great fund around
us. From all sides come proofs of the workings of special design, urged on by Nature herself, in return for honest efforts
made to become a part of her plan of progress.

These facts are cited to give courage to every person who seeks
to make home life attractive, and in some way to interest one
of the opposite sex to take an interest in the same purpose. Find
in your mind the desire, and in your heart the hope of such a
goal, and then add magnetism. The results will be as sure as the
fact that the sun will rise again.

Radial magnetism must be aided by some operation of the
faculties, and mutual interest in a common subject is such a
process. This is the mind in agreement.

The heart must likewise be brought into a similar agreement.
This is done by the development of sympathy.

Much has been said in the early pages of this department
on the nature of sympathy; and it has been defined by the
dictionaries as "a conformity of temperament by which two persons are agreeable to each other." In fact, as found working
in the lives of people, there are the following characteristics of
sympathy:

1. The radial influence that emanates from one person embraces the personality of the other.

2. The radial influence of the other person embraces the personality of the former.

3. The radial influences of both persons overlap each other, and blend two hearts in one being.

The service of magnetism is to bond sympathy.

Without magnetism the radial influences may lapse and disappear, as is often the case. Two persons who have a mutual interest in something in common, and a decided sympathy, find in time their interest on the wane and their sympathy vanished. Lives that might have grown together until death parted them have drifted sadly away from each other, and been wrecked in counter-disappointments. History of this kind is being made every day.

Thus the necessity of personal magnetism is seen in the most important phase of life. Persons who will not study magnetism are not willing to study anything that is beneficial, for it is the one most practical and useful training on earth today. It has no equal in the good it will bring to every man and woman who takes advantage of its laws.

A person who will procure a course in magnetism, and then read it and lay it aside, does not deserve the benefits that accrue from its doctrines. When only fifteen minutes a day will be required both to read and to practice its work, no one has any right to ask to be excused from it. Much of the training is obtained by absorbing the instructions without practice; but they should be actually absorbed, and this is done by re-reading many times. Any law may be put into practice by knowing what it is, and this is true of any teaching.

What is included in the present course is not to be practiced in the sense that the exercises of the developing book are to be practiced; but the doctrines are to be adopted by changing the methods of living. This rule is seen in the suggestions of the third department. Any man or woman who, after reading that department, will still carry the same neglects and bad habits, need not expect any happiness in life; for there is the turning of the ways, either to the left and away from what is essential to attractiveness, or to the right and along the path in which the attractive force is cultivated.

SECOND TESTS OF TEMPERAMENTAL UNFITNESS.

We come now to the application of the next methods of ascertaining the fitness or unfitness of two persons for each other in marriage.

At the end of the First Department in this book, the first tests are made. They are mathematically accurate, and that is the perfection of accuracy. When applied they do not tell an untruth. It is a very easy process to learn how much real power binds two lives together, even by so simple a test as that; or it is the simplest of all evidences for or against a young man, if he maintains or lessens his improvement under the influence of his attachment for a young woman; and the same law applies to her as well.

The next tests come under the theme of mental interests and the deeper theme of heart-interests.

More careful observation is needed; for it is necessary to distinguish between the physical and nervous character on the one hand, and the real temperament on the other. Much is inherited, and more is acquired. The dull, slow body has been quickened under the power of thought; and the highly nervous nature has been given stability by the aid of thought taking the place of habit.

Love, so-called, or that attraction that brings the two sexes together in the better way, if genuine, is always strong enough to supplant habits. If it were not, then the only agency of a better civilization would fall to the ground.

The one giant fault of humanity is that they live in habits rather than in thought.

It is hard to think, and to most persons genuine thinking is painful; for which reason nature sets up the one greatest power in life, sex attraction, or love, if you will, and uses this power to change habits into thought; and, then, through thought, it reaches the heart and establishes heart-interests. This is not only civilization on the upward grade, but it is religion itself in the process of being molded, for it touches chords in life that are never vibrated by any other power.

Under the spell of this influence a man or woman will come into poise of mind and heart, will think new habits and will build new hopes.

Now just at that point where these new habits are being thought out and adopted, and new hopes are shaping themselves, the offer of marriage, if made, should be gently taken under advisement; or, better still, the offer itself should be delayed. Just as long as the two persons can keep each other in doubt and in anticipation of the coming agreement, just so long will it be possible to watch the growth of new habits as the result of new thinking.

FIVE MAGNETIC LAWS

HERE the course mounts to a higher plane, with a constant view of the ground behind and below over which we have traveled. From the first step to the present time there has been a gradual ascent to higher ground; and so the course will progress to the end. Review is evidence both of good scholarship and of interest in the work. When each new department is reached all the departments that have preceded should be carefully gone over in search of truths that are sure to escape the mind on a first reading.

There are five laws that relate to radial magnetism, which was fully described in the seventh department. These laws will constitute the instruction of the present stage.

FIRST RADIAL LAW

Sex Magnetism demands the adoption of a sympathetic voice.

It has already been stated that radial magnetism must be aided by the faculties in order to become effective in the highest degree. The faculties are those operations of the mind and body that may be controlled by the will or the habits of the individual.

The most common and the most useful of all the faculties is that of speech. The voice is the tool both of the mind and of the emotions. The mind takes part in magnetic control, and may become one of the most powerful and successful of all agencies for success in life when trained under the plan set forth in the course known as Mental Magnetism, which is a part of the series of the Personal Magnetism Club.

The voice is also the tool of the emotions, and these are trained in the other powerful course known as Advanced Magnetism, which is another part of the same Club.

When the voice has behind it an unmagnetic mind, it is

most dull and uninteresting. It hardly ever succeeds in holding the attention of others, as is witnessed in many sermons, in the work of teachers, and in ordinary conversation. Interest in a thing arouses some temporary magnetism of the radial kind which dies at once when the interest lags. An important fact when realized by a speaker may arouse in him and in others a certain amount of magnetism which has no life beyond the few minutes the fact is being told.

So skilled is the ordinary mind in this knowledge that one person seeks to secure the attention of another by carrying news, or by gossiping. It is the cheapest and lowest of all grades of radial magnetism. A clerk who wants the good will of his employer may suddenly open fire on his attention with a piece of news that is either startling or valuable to the man. A woman tries at times to make herself agreeable to her husband in the same way. If she lacks magnetism in the conduct of her home, her children will not be controlled very easily, and she uses as a substitute for magnetism the promise of something she is to tell them. They wait for the news with eagerness, and if it is not up to the standard of their expectation, they will give less heed from time to time to these promises.

In place of these old-time methods, it is possible to rule and to win by the aid of magnetism in the employment of the faculties.

There are today too many unmagnetic men in public life, especially in the pulpit. Power to convince and to win men and women is needed, but these unmagnetic preachers go on year in and year out wearying their hearers and wondering why there is so little genuine religion in the heart of the world. No greater wrong can be done the cause than the lack of mental magnetism in so grand a field of work.

The voice is also the tool of the emotions. Of these there are seventy-six in three classes. They are faculties, just as the mental operations are faculties. These emotions are known as the moods and feelings, and as such are made agencies of power under the plan of instruction set forth in the course referred to as Advanced Magnetism. Thus we see two separate, private courses of training devoted to the two realms of life that are behind all magnetism. A few facts may help at this place.

1. Magnetism is a power that can be developed to any

extent by the exercises and habits contained in the foundation book.

2. Magnetism, like any power, must employ as its tools the faculties of human life.

3. The faculties are divided into two classes—Mental and emotional.

4. What a man thinks, plans and decides upon are controlled by the faculties of the mind.

5. What a man feels, hopes for, wishes, loves, hates, seeks, rejects, enjoys, disobeys, adopts and exists in harmony with, are controlled by his moods and emotions, and the faculties by which they are expressed.

6. As all life belongs to these two sets of faculties, and as all power is derived from magnetism, it follows that the great work of the Magnetism Club must include a complete and thorough course of training in Mental Magnetism, and another complete and thorough course of training in the moods and feelings, which is called Advanced Magnetism.

As this present work is one of the series of courses in that Club, its position should be understood in connection with the others. The organization would be a tangled mass of laws and doctrines if they were not classified, each in its place with its goal ahead. To know what the Club is doing, and by what methods its proceeds, is demanded by all its members; and this is the reason why the student is referred to the proper courses for aid in mastering all the work that is outlined.

It is important to know that magnetism cannot work alone, nor can any power. If the architect spends all his life learning the duties and teachings of his profession, he will never perform anything. He has his apprenticeship. When he leaves that stage and goes out into the great battlefield of the world, he must build. At first he will build in one line of activities; then he will be led by his genius into a higher line, and finally he will seek the grandest honors that await him. The same procedure is true in magnetism. The term of apprenticeship occurs while he is mastering the work of the foundation; there he develops the power and the knowledge; but as magnetism is all life itself, it must include the great divisions of life.

The emotions are the first faculties.

They precede knowledge.

What we know we first felt. The brain is the result of reasoning out the emotions, their causes and effects. Had there been no emotions, there would have been no mind.

As our students require this outlining of the plan of the Club in each book, it has always been our custom to make clear what each course means, and its place in connection with the others. The three following facts will now be plain:

1. Radial magnetism must employ the faculties in order to become effective.

2. The faculties of the mind must be made highly magnetic, as is done in Mental Magnetism; and the faculties of the emotions must be made highly magnetic, as is done in Advanced Magnetism.

3. Sex Magnetism, being a form known as radial, achieves its best success when based on the highest development of mental and emotional magnetism.

As all persons are magnetic to some extent, any degree of this power will be helpful, even if these two intervening courses are omitted; but it is important that, sooner or later, every student of the present work shall take the regular courses in the Magnetic Club. As they may be obtained on the co-operative plan at slight expense, there is no reason why the matter should be delayed. There is too much at stake.

That the emotions precede the mind in all the operations of life is easily proved. At birth there is supposedly no intelligence in the child, and the brain is comparatively smooth. The first sensation is the emotion of hunger. Then follow heat, cold and pain; all felt and registered first in the nervous system, and then conveyed to the brain, where impressions are there made on which reasoning will some day be set in motion as a mental faculty.

The desire to be amused and be given attention is an emotion. It takes almost complete possession of the life of a child at an early period, and there are very few persons in after life who lose this desire. It is a crowning emotion.

Hunger creates all the tastes, good and bad, that force themselves into the habits; all the vices of the palate and stomach are the outgrowths of this original desire. Pleasure is all the time being sought. Sweets are more pleasant than plain things, and joy will attend the gift of candy, while anger may accompany the arrival of a piece of bread, in the experiences of the very young infant who has passed the first year of its career.

Men and women like to eat and drink the things that give them pleasure. Ordinary water is unattractive to some tastes, because it contains no element of enjoyment. In the bottles on the shelf are scores and, perhaps, hundreds of liquids that actually give satisfaction to some men and women. Many things are taken into the mouth that convey no food to the body, but that are enjoyed in spite of that fact. Milk is nutritious and necessary; but it supports life, and, therefore, is not a source of pleasure to the taste that expects liquor or champagne, gum or tobacco, candy or soda water, cake or ice cream, puddings or pastry.

All children are born with their mouths open, and they are ready to eat just two seconds by the clock after their birth. This readiness of the mouth to open all the time during life until sickness closes it temporarily, is the source of nine-tenths of all the crime in the world, and practically all the bodily illness and suffering.

Marriage must take into account these facts.

Most husbands either smoke, chew tobacco, drink alcoholic beverages, or like rich cooking. Most wives enjoy the candy box, the sweets of the table, or the products of the soda-water fountain, assuming that they have none of the grosser tastes of men. In any event it is the open mouth all the time, year in and year out.

If no other feeling but hunger were at stake the matter would be quickly settled by the common sense of the mind; but when the wife finds much pleasure in what enters her mouth, and when the husband finds as much joy in what he puts in his mouth, these emotions of the brighter side of life cannot be avoided. They mean often the success or failure of the marriage itself. If the wife sees that rich foods, attractive cooking and pleasing drinks are placed before her husband, she may or may not achieve that result that she most has in mind. Some forms of pastry are enticing; and if an engagement depended on the man's enjoyment of them, he would propose as soon as he had begun to partake, but not an hour afterwards.

The palate is one thing, and the stomach another.

What highly pleases the palate in most cases displeases the

stomach. What is most graciously swallowed is digested with the greatest difficulty. What the palate will hold and act upon with the greatest deliberation and slowness, is a source of pleasure to the stomach.

In other words, eagerness of the palate means reluctance of the stomach.

The wife who can please the stomach will in time secure the greatest hold on the regard and respect of the husband; but the wife that aims to please the palate will lose her happiness.

The stomach likes only the foods and drinks that enter into the construction of the body; all else being a source of displeasure and disease to it.

The palate likes only the things that give joy, and these, as a rule, are enemies to the stomach.

The new wife under the new regime, as taught by the Ralston Health Club, will learn the new combination, which is:

Select and prepare the things that the stomach will like, and that will enter into the construction of the body, and prepare them in such a way that the palate will be eager for them.

This is the new religion of married life, and it is sure to become a part of every well-conducted home in the future because it is right; it has the endorsement of all the best physicians, who care more for their patients' lives than for their purses. Experiments have been made for years, and proof has been abundant that it is possible to prepare wholesome and plain foods that they will be attractive to the palate. Today the reverse is true, for what gives pleasure to the palate does harm to the stomach, and through that organ to the nerves and mind, bringing irritability, weakness, neurasthenia and kindred disorders in clouds to humanity. The greatest sufferers are the husbands of young wives who are experimenting in cooking, and who have learned to make one kind of cake as the missing link between nothing to eat and a pain in the stomach. Bread, potatoes, vegetables and plain foods are beneath their art. Not one woman in ten knows how to properly cook potatoes, the staple of wholesome foods.

In proportion as plain foods are made attractive to the palate without taking from their value, in the same ratio will the desire for rich stuff, stimulants and abnormal things grow less. This is the light in the gloom. It is the hope of the future.

Pain is an emotion.

When there is pain in the nervous system, or when there is irritability in the body, it will creep into the voice. You can speak ever so softly, the color of irritability is there. The wife who gives her husband a case of indigestion will get it back in his irritable nature, and she will blame his disposition. Likewise the husband who will not seek to educate his wife along higher lines of domestic life will receive back from her the voice of irritability. She does not intend to speak in such tones, nor does he, but they cannot help it.

The voice need not be cross to be irritable.

Many a time you will hear a man trying to be agreeable. He will not use a loud voice; in fact, he may have it well modulated, but it will bear the emotion of pain, not conscious pain, but the suffering that is blind, and that breaks forth mildly in irritable nerves. He will be uninteresting. The less he talks the better it will be for him, but he will be looked upon as sulky. The more he talks the less his wife will care to hear him. More than once a wife has said, "Henry, there is something in your voice that I do not like." "Well, what is it, Josie? Have I said anything that has hurt your feeling?" "No." "Well, have I used a cross tone to you?" "No." "Well, what in—what is the matter with you?" "There, there, Henry, you are cross now." And so it goes.

How much magnetism has that husband?

How much is he able to generate in his wife?

Where is the harmony in that home? She will go away to some other room, if she can spare it, and there her eyes will redden with tears that she is too proud to encourage.

Pain lowers vitality, and a lowered vitality means the loss of radial magnetism. If you could see the power of a man or woman who is magnetic as it radiates out from the body at its best, and again when it is weakened by pain or loss of vitality, you would then understand the action on it by pain and weakness. Of course, it is not a visible form of power, but it is as real, or even more real, than any electric energy that takes the form of magnetism, as in the lodestone or magnet from which emanates an attracting force.

As the faculties are aids to radial magnetism, and as pain, weakness, joy and suffering are faculties of the feeling or emotions, they play a part that is most important. The voice, a faculty of the mind in its advanced form, is the expression of the emotions in its primitive condition. The voice came into being in response to the emotions.

The cry of hunger is the emotional voice.

The cry of pain is the same, but in another emotion.

The cry of joy, the shout of laughter, the cry of alarm, of hate, of fear, or hope, of anticipation, of disappointment and many others are all made in different tones, and eventually in different vowel combinations, to which are attached beginnings and ends called consonants, and these become words; so that language is built of emotions expressed in voice. This is the first step in language formation all over the world. If a new race were to be placed on this globe, with no ancestors to give them a mother tongue, their emotional uses of the voice would set up new words, while their attempts to reproduce sounds from nature would make the second step, and their imaginations of various things would constitute the third step.

The basis, however, is the voice of emotions. It begins all other ideas and facts as they grow to become parts of human thought.

By the tones the heart is made manifest. One or two tones by themselves may be so concealed that they will stand as neutral, except to the expert; but the use of words in sentences, as in conversation, will quickly win confidence or repel it when magnetism is lacking. It is only a stupid mind that is deceived by a non-magnetic voice.

Such a voice is mere sound.

When the scores of emotions are fully cultivated as an art, and all their degrees and variations made a part of the practice of a magnetic habit, it will be an easy matter to recognize the emotion that prevails in any other person, whether the latter is magnetic or not. This recognition happens on the principle of the musical string; let it be struck, and it will start in motion its mate in another musical instrument. This is a very common occurrence. If one note of a piano is vibrated, it will set vibrating every harmonic note on the same instrument, such as the seconds, third, fifths and eighths; and it will give a leading tone vibration to its exact mate in any other instrument near by. So a person may sound a note in his voice, and the mate to it will vibrate in an instrument in the same room, even if the latter is some distance away.

Sound is a radial force.

The voice devoid of magnetism is a dead noise. When it is magnetic it is a radial force. When it is charged with an emotion it is the conveyor of that feeling. When it is charged with an emotion and has no magnetism, it touches a similar feeling like a harsh discord, and is not repelled easily; whereas, if it is magnetic and is charged with an emotion, it becomes the controlling agent of the person to whom it is directed.

There are many of the dark, or unpleasant, emotions that are masters of men and women, and that bring disaster to all who are at its mercy. The feelings that sway us ought always to be the nobler and more useful moods, while those that are worthy should be controlled by ourselves, if we would be truly magnetic. For this reason the magnetic person does not allow these dark emotions to get into his voice. He employs only the better moods. More than this, he feels only the better moods.

Magnetism in the foundation course teaches perfect self-control. This mastery gives all the better emotions to the person, and prevents him from using the dark moods, or being moved by them, of feeling them. This is a three-sided victory; the highest kind of self-control.

It is not possible to master another person and be mastered by the very moods that make another person weak.

The great office of magnetism then is to remove all emotions from the voice except those that are pleasing to other persons.

Sympathy is the conformity of two temperaments that cause them to be agreeable to each other. A sympathetic voice is one whose tones are agreeable, assuring, inviting and attractive.

If the husband has magnetism he will have none of the dark moods in his nervous system. When things go wrong he will be able to master them and keep out of his temperament the moods that cause dislike or uneasiness in another. He will not be snappish, or whine, or find fault, or grumble, or be peevish, or get angry, or otherwise make himself unattractive to his wife. Every part of his nervous system will be on the bright side. If she has hard luck in the performance of some of her duties, he will not laugh at her, for he will not be frivolous nor will he chide her, for he will not rebuke; but he will come into her own state of mind as it was when she thought success was at hand, and that feeling will soon be made paramount in her heart again.

How little a man or woman is after the one snappish tone of the voice! It may not last more than a second, yet it will reverberate in the brain of the other party for years. It reveals the littleness of the bond of marriage. Who wants to hear a man or woman whine, even for a second only? What is the feeling towards a person after the fretted temper has had its say?

All these smallnesses are swept away by the noble force of personal magnetism, which will not allow one of them to remain in the system. They are little things, but it takes only one of them to drive out all sympathy out of the voice, and with it there will go much of the respect and confidence that a wife seeks in the husband, and he in her. Sympathy of voice and manner is necessary; but any person can see at a glance that sympathy cannot exist a moment in a voice that is saturated with ill nature.

The voice of sympathy cannot be assumed. The weakest thing in human nature is the attempt to be sympathetic when there is nothing real in the effort. The artificial character of such an attempt strikes on the ear harshly, and grates on the very chords of the heart.

Here is a family that has been suddenly stricken with grief. A man calls to extend his sympathy, but he cannot find the tones of voice that will convey it. His words are all that can be expected, and in print they would pass as correct, or be well received if written in a letter; but when spoken they have nothing that is real in them. The reason is that he lacks that feeling in his own nature.

But in the broader definition of the word sympathy is a conformity of two temperaments. There need be no sorrow. Joy can be shared, and that is what is meant by conformity. Hope may be shared. Any effort to accomplish something that is worth while may be shared by two persons, and the union is then filled with harmony. Selfishness is one of the opposing terms of sympathy. It is a dark mood, an evil emotion. It is killed by magnetism, for the man who possesses this great power drives out of his own life the little meannesses that prevail so much in others. The husband who lacks selfishness can have his mind in conformity with that of his wife, and his heart as well, and their two temperaments will be in absolute harmony.

Did you ever notice the methods of a magnetic person?

Take a husband, if you will, for an example. He does not raise his voice to loudness, nor does he thrust it in everything that occurs, nor compel his wife to hear it too much; but when he speaks she is glad to listen. There is a gentleness, even combined with great magnetic firmness in its tones. There is a musical softness that is not weakness. It flows without effort, and ceases as it flows, easily and at that point where something in response stands on the tongue of the listener. It is a pleasing voice to hear. No one would ever tire of it. It has directness and straightforwardness, yet is not aggressive. It has no challenge. It defies no one. It is inviting and charming. There is a quietude in the man as in his voice. He is strong in feature, and his tones are firm, but they have the simple quietude of the great river that can carry ships of the heaviest burden, yet makes no hurrying motion.

This magnetic man is in perfect poise, is self-constrained, and is never in a mental or nervous rush. He may be very active without being in a hurry. The river that is deepest has the least apparent movement. The river that ripples and dashes over the shallows and creates the sound of rushing waters cannot sustain on its bosom any vessel of size and importance.

We know of such husbands. Their wives think them the most attractive men in the world, and they compare them constantly with all the other men that are attractive, and it is a fact they would not exchange them for the others.

Wives are not as often students of magnetism as are men, and for this reason they are the prey of their emotions, every passing mood making itself felt in their manner and voices. They do not care to tie themselves down to the practice of the extensive work of Advanced Magnetism, where the emotions are brought under perfect control, and where poise and self-containment are cultivated to a degree that exceeds any other accomplishment in all the history of personal training.

But men go easily and eagerly through all those studies, and soon are masters of their emotions. In every hundred male students of Advanced Magnetism where reports of progress have been made it seems that ninety-two succeed to a perfect record, and the eight who do not graduate from it are merely inclined to read the exercises and methods. Reading brings some results, but they depend on the ability of the individual to absorb what is read. Practice is needed in that wide range of human nature, and practice must be indulged in just as there directed if success is desired. Women, as a rule, read and re-read the methods, and lay the work aside, only nineteen in a hundred having reported perfect mastery of the moods and emotions under the system. The nineteen in every hundred have, however, been changed from women of discouraged lives to women of queenly powers over men. On the other hand, the ninety-two in every hundred of the men who have succeeded in achieving perfect mastery over their emotion, and winning the great goals of a supreme power and prosperity in their life work, contrast with the nineteen women in every hundred as a lesson which tells why the weaker sex is weaker.

They lack perseverance.

When a woman has a sympathetic nature and a sympathetic voice, she is in her most attractive mood. No woman of beauty can compete with her. The most entrancing beauty looks weak and doll-like in comparison with her. A man of good judgment in all matters except the charms of women once was nearly caught by as pretty a face as you could ever hope to see in a lifetime. He had money, and she made up her mind that she would win him on that account; so she was as affirmative and as coy in her attractions as her sex could possibly make herself. He was wholly overcome, and was about to propose to her, when another woman, plain of face, neat of dress and pleasing in figure, came upon the scene, wholly by accident. She happened to be a magnetic woman of the highest degree of power, such as graduates from the course in Universal Magnetism. She certainly had the sympathetic manner and voice. The man saw her, and paid but little attention to her, until the pretty maiden began to use the plainer woman as a foil with which to show off her superior beauty by engaging her in conversation. The latter replied plainly, without affectation, and most sweetly. The man was at once struck by the remarkable difference in the two voices; one devoid of that human element, sympathy, the other full of it. The voice soon made the face. The beauty was weak of features in the conversation; the other was fascinating by her charms.

Men and women, the best and the smartest of them, see things through their emotions. They may think they use their eyes, and they do; but their eyes must finally record the impressions in the brain. If there were no other organ of sight but the eyes, nothing would be seen. The brain sets up the real picture. So it is possible to see a plain woman with the naked eye, and by her side a most beautiful, also viewed with the naked eyes, while the brain records the plain woman as the most charming, and the pretty woman as the weakest. This man said: "I did, in fact, think the woman who first entered the room the most beautiful I had ever looked upon. I had seen her several times before, and she was always just as fascinating. But the second woman seemed to me when first she came in to be very plain. As she talked I saw the two faces in my mind. My eyes were as good then as now; yet I saw this plain woman exchange charms with the other. As the minutes went by the first woman grew less interesting, and the second woman began to grow beautiful. At last they had each been reversed, and no longer was the beautiful creature a creature of beauty."

All human beings see with their emotions.

They say love is blind; it sees with its emotions.

The husband who is in love with his wife wakes up soon after marriage and sees her with his eyes. Then he wonders why he ever married her. He must make the best of it, and would not for the world let her know just what his feelings are.

Sex Magnetism intensifies the emotions with which one sees the other. It is right that it should do so. Before we finish this course of training we shall show the necessity of this high state of cultivation of the emotional powers that will exalt women and place man on the pedestal of greater worth.

All else is animal existence.

Life began with emotions. Language began with emotions. All happiness and pleasure began with emotions, and can live only in them. There is nothing in life that is worth having unless it brings content, happiness, hope and deep satisfaction; and all these are emotions. Human beings have all their existence in the faculties, and these are of two classes— one of the mind, and the other of emotions. To hunt in the mind for the pleasure and climax of living would be useless, for it is fruitless of these things. There is nothing in the mental division of life except what we think, and every person who has carried on any process of self-analysis, however simple, knows perfectly well that what we feel is what we really are.

The higher the man or the woman may rise in the scale of existence the more will life be lived in the emotions; not in any of the dark and weak ones, but in the strong and inviting ones, just as is taught in the course of Advanced Magnetism. In that training true life has had its beginning in fact for many a man and woman.

The human soul lives in its emotions. It cannot be taught by the operations of the mind, as it has no mental faculties. This fact has been well proved in all cases where reason has sought to convince men and women of the necessity of a higher life. Religion that appeals to the mind will never make any headway in the world, and the thousands of years of history show this law to be a universal one.

An age of reason is an age of suicide.

All the beauty, all the grandeur, all the sweetness of life must be seen and known through the emotions.

It is in the emotions that sympathy holds sway over other hearts. These make temperament, for that is the sum total of the particular emotions that prevail in one person. The best thing a magnetic husband ever did was to take an account of stock of his wife's temperament; which means that, by the rules of another course, he could ascertain to a certainty every one of the emotions, good and bad, that she possessed. Then, having secured this account of stock, or inventory, he showed her the way to sift out and to part with the dark ones, and to add to the bright ones. This was a healthy process, for her mind, as well as her nervous vitality, were made stronger and brought both to a normal condition.

Temperament is the sum total of the emotions that prevail in one person.

Sympathy is the conformity of two temperaments, so that they are attractive to each other.

Opposing temperaments are attractive only when their bright emotions make the opposition.

When one person has dark emotions that oppose the bright emotions of another person, there will not be accord.

When one person has dark emotions that oppose the dark emotions of another person, no matter whether they are the same emotions or not, there will be discord and quarreling.

In briefer language:

1. Any dark emotions that differ will make discord.

2. Any dark emotions that are opposed to any bright emotions will make discord.

3. Any bright emotions that differ will make harmony.

4. Any bright emotions that agree will make the greatest harmony.

5. Any dark emotions that will agree will make the greatest combination of wrong, as where two or more pals in a gang become conspirators in any line of crime.

The most pleasing fact is that any bright emotions that differ will make harmony. This is due to the peculiar force of the bright side of human nature. Two persons may be wholly different, each from the other, and yet get along nicely together. Some persons teach the mingling of different temperaments. But the well-founded results of many tests show the following laws to be the true measure:

1. Where the temperament is made up largely of some bright emotions, and meets with another temperament that is made up largely of some bright emotions, these two temperaments are in accord only when both possess some of the same emotions that are possessed by each other. This is called the overlapping of similar emotions.

2. Where one temperament has none of the emotions that prevail in another temperament, there will not be a conformity

of temperament, and sympathy is not easily possible without a complete revolution in one or both of these persons.

3. Without a possibility of sympathy there can be no possibility of harmony. The fact that two lives, one male and the other female, are on the bright side of the emotions will not bring them together where there is a total diversity of temperament. There must be some over-lapping emotions; some that are the same in both persons. Let this be lacking, and marriage will be a cold assembling of icebergs, bright, but chilly.

Marriage is a coming together—a union.

Before a man weds a woman, or engages himself to her, he should master the emotions by the methods taught in Advanced Magnetism, and then should develop in himself the power to take an account of stock of his own emotions, and her's also. This can be done to a certainty. By the processes of magnetism all persons who put into practice the methods taught are given the ability to know themselves, and to know others. When the old Greek savant said, "Know thyself," he may have intended to tell people to know their own anatomy, or their own mental powers, but we are sure that he had in mind the knowledge of the temperament within the individual, and this means the knowledge of the emotions.

By temperament in this study is not meant the physiological character, as the nervous, the sluggish and such kinds; but the real make-up of the person through the developed nature within.

It is possible for any man to learn to take an account of stock of his own temperament, and that of the woman whom he seeks to make his wife. It is possible for any woman to learn how to take an account of stock of her own temperament and that of the man who would marry her. It is possible for both to drive out of their lives all control over them of their own dark emotions, and to add to the bright emotions that have been enhanced by magnetism.

But when they have come down to that point of discovery where they learn that they have no temperament in common, nor any portion thereof, then there is the place where their lives should part.

If you are not yet married, but are engaged, delay until

these things may be ascertained. You will never regret it, and you may have before you a lifelong sorrow if you fail to heed this advice.

If you are not yet engaged, but are on the verge of making the promise, stop and wait. Nothing can be gained by hurry, and everything is at stake in the lives of two persons. If you say to yourself that YOU and the other party will not be like others who have made marriage a failure, just count up the millions who have said the same thing, and then have had to swallow the assertion. In a city a clerk who issues marriage licenses was called on by a young man who asked for a license to marry the "best girl in the world." "Hold on there," said the clerk, "you are the seven hundred and fiftieth young man who has taken out a license to marry her since I have been here, and you cannot all have her."

People see with their emotions.

That being true, they should be master of their emotions, and not be ruled by them. The mob is swayed by its emotions, as is the man who kills in a temper. The magnetic man or woman rides above all emotions, and drives them to the harness of his or her chariot.

If you are a man, find out the temperaments both of yourself and the woman. If you are a woman, find out the temperament both of yourself and the man. If there are too many dark parts to your own temperament, withdraw from the prospect until you ascertain if there is a chance of driving away the evil nature. Apply the same test to the other party. Take time to study, to develop, and to know the truth.

There must be a conformity of temperament.

There must be sympathy in the sense described.

As the voice carries in its tones the color and picture of every mood and emotion, the voice should be made the medium of winning and of holding the respect and the good will of the other person.

See that no moods or emotions stand forth in the voice except those that are on the bright side of life. See that these are made stronger day by day, and let their color be conveyed in the voice. Know every tone you utter, and know what it contains. Let it never take care of itself, but always be its master and its directing power. To its use add all the magnetism you can develop. The voice, then, being a radial energy, will bring close to your life the individual who is intended to come there. It may be necessary to break an engagement, or to withdraw from one that is intended; but if you are married, it is too late to dissolve that union. Maintain it at all hazards until the time comes when a higher voice shall set you free. But most marriages that are now discords can be made better than they are; and many may be brought wholly within the harmony of Sex Magnetism. We shall see as this work progresses.

SECOND RADIAL LAW

Sex Magnetism demands that you make yourself believed in.

If you are a man, some woman must believe in you. If you are a woman, some man must believe in you. These are the counterbalancing laws of life. While it is better that the woman who believes in the man shall be his wife, and the man who believes in the woman shall be her husband, the law remains the same in any event. If you are a husband, and your wife merely tolerates you, your usefulness in the household is not very important. If she does not believe in you, there is some reason for it. On the other hand, if you are a wife, and your husband regards you as a very useless piece of furniture, there is some reason for it. The reason may rest in the character of the other party, but this is very unlikely.

Why women marry men is as often a matter of conjecture to the women as to impartial outsiders. What is gained by marriage? If nothing is the value estimated, then there is a reason why this is so. Why men marry women is also a wonder in many cases. The profit side of the transaction is missing, and the loss side is large to both sexes. If the period of courtship could be spent in deliberate study of the two sides of the account, there would be very little chance for the after regrets. Each party would then have time to establish a solid belief in the other, or become worthy of such belief.

One girl married a football player because, as she said, she wanted a man who was a man. Her idea of such a being was a fellow with muscle. After they were married she found that he had nothing else. He was not inclined to work, and his muscle was so energetic that it could not be tuned down to the chores that belonged to home life.

Another girl married a young man because one day she caught him in a uniform of the State militia, and she wanted a brave husband. She did not stop to find out if the uniform made him brave, nor how he came to be a militiaman. She just took it for granted that the uniform was all that was necessary. After the wedding, and some time after the honeymoon was over and forgotten, this same fellow was seen lounging about the house as indolent as the Southern darkey in his days of ease; and the wife wondered how so small a proportion of man could have got so large proportion of uniform into his make-up.

She remarked to a friend that he was the smallest apology for the masculine gender she had ever seen, although physically he was tall enough and broad enough. What was lacking was manliness.

Another girl married a man on account of his good looks. He was handsome, and she liked him for that reason; but she had her misgivings until there were several other girls in the same town who were trying to catch him. So she thought it a victory to take him from her rivals. He was conceited. All handsome men are conceited. Some of them do not intend to be, but they all are. He knew he was good-looking, and he knew that the girls watched him, and all liked his attentions, and he paid them out in such a way that they wanted more. But marriage ended his triumphs. He posed before the mirrors, and bought two new ones. He was of no benefit in the house, and his wife was rather glad when he went out. The other girls cut him, and did not even give him a glance or a bow; but some women rather enjoyed his flirtations, and the end was a divorce for the little wife who wed him because he was handsome.

Another girl married a man because he had money. The advantages of having money are many, especially when there are household bills to be paid. But if the husband has nothing else, the union is rarely ever worth while. Another woman married because her husband had a good business. He kept a little store, the income from which was not much in excess of two dollars a day, and the hours were long. Her needs were not many. After a while she drifted into the store, and liked the variety of action that came from performing the duties of selling odds and ends and seeing the cash drop in the money-drawer. She soon grew to be penurious, but the life suited them both. After a year or more the business grew, and the profits were several times greater. Then she had a better home, and remained in it. But at the start the object of entering wedlock was to secure the income that the man derived from the little business. This mercantile marriage is neither commendable nor objectionable, if their temperaments are alike in the matter. It all depends on temperament.

Some women marry for love, but as a rule they are in their teens or very early twenties. We do not believe that any woman who is much over twenty-one takes love seriously, as it is a puberty affection, arising on the impulse then established. In the sense portrayed by poets and novelists, love is a young person's malady; and when age has added a few more years, it is a high form of respect, or a feeling of exaltation.

Whoever marries for love, and for nothing else, makes a lifelong mistake. If there is something besides love to induce the union, then the presence of this affection is no handicap, as a general rule. But that something else is the main attraction. It is something that compels a wife to believe in her husband, and a husband to believe in his wife; not to trust or to have confidence, but to entertain a regard that is real, and that would be just as real if there were no other persons in the world. A man may have trust in the honesty and virtue of his wife, even if she is a very silly and weak woman. A wife may have confidence in the faithfulness and honor of her husband, even if he is a lazy and worthless fellow in all other respects. To believe in a person is to hold a degree of admiration and satisfying esteem that elevates that person above all others who might have been in the same relationship. A wife should feel that she has married, not the best man in all the world, but the man who was best for her; whose care of her and associations with her make him the one above all others who was best suited to her temperament and heart.

A man should think he has married, not the best woman in all the world, but the one who was best for him. He should find her something more than a mate, something more than a helpmeet, something more than a housekeeper, something more than an ornament.

In what way may he make himself believed in?

It is not his honesty that is at stake. If he lies to her he drops very low, and will not be able to extricate himself from the slough of meanness that he has got into. We do not see exactly how a wife can ever respect a husband who has lied to her. He might lie to others, and she have knowledge of it, and they both might take it as a piece of diplomacy or strategy, or business enterprise, or necessary escape from some contingency that had no other release; for there are wives who even participate in the falsehoods told by their husbands, as may be seen in small stores where both wait upon customers and make untrue representations about their goods. Some men boast too extravagantly, and thus pass easily into falsehoods. Wives overlook such hyperbole, and take no offence if they are not the subjects of it. That is, a man may tell his wife a lie when he is boasting of some adventure, some great deed, some event or transaction in which she is not involved; but if he tells her he has no money when he has plenty, or if he says he posted a letter of hers to her mother when he tore it up, or if he reports that he did not meet his former sweetheart when he had a moments' conversation with her on the street corner, he is making for himself a bed that is not of roses. These falsehoods are base, and show a low character. It is cheap to falsify in boasting or in selling goods or otherwise, but it is evidence of a low grade of character to tell a positive lie to one who has a right to know the exact truth. A man who has a pleasant reason for making an untrue statement is always forgiven; as where the husband has bought a necklace for his wife to be given to her on her birthday, and she discovers some trace of his purchase in the form of an addressed box which he quickly conceals, as he wishes to surprise her most magnificently when the birthday comes; and she asks him point-blank where he got it and what it is for and he tells her it is an old watchchain that he is having repaired, whereupon she proceeds to ascertain the truth, and puts him down as a falsifier, weeping and making ready to pack her things and go home to her mother, when he is compelled, under the law of self-preservation, to show her the necklace, and the bill of five hundred dollars receipted, with her initials engraved, so that there is no doubt about the purpose of the purchase; she quickly forgives him. But he has not the respect for her that she might have secured had she been more of a woman than a child.

Women are more magnetic than girls.

In the last cited case there is nothing in the conduct of the husband to lessen the wife's regard for him. His talk about the watchchain that needed repairing is referred to for some weeks afterwards as a piece of pleasantry. It shows no meanness of character.

He must be honest in word to her, and honest in all acts to her.

If he cheats others and she never suspects that he has cheated her, she will not refuse to believe in him if her temperament is of the same character. The temperament and conscience have much to do with the degree of regard that is entertained for another person. A refined woman would hold in contempt a husband who cheated others, although he was honest to her in word and act. But there are women who do not really know that business lies are wrong; they would go so far as to be smitten with conscience if their husbands were to admit the faults, as of a horse, or of some merchandise that was to be sold.

In the ranks where Sex Magnetism would have any elevating power, no kind of dishonesty, whether diplomacy, strategy, subterfuge or the direct falsehood could be indulged in and respect be retained, and it is in those ranks that this work is to be taken.

Therefore, in order to make yourself believed in, be honest in word and act, omit all exaggerations and untruths, deceive none, be clean in speech and in thought, in body and mind, and be frank at all times.

But something more than honesty is necessary. A person of good habits may be believed in, provided there is further reason for the respect and admiration that are required. Merely good habits will not suffice. A wife says: "My husband does not drink, nor smoke, chew, gamble, swear, lie or have any bad habits." Yet he may be very weak in character and in mind, lazy in body and mean in disposition. One of the most contemptible curs we ever knew was a man who did not lie, chew, smoke, swear, drink, gamble or otherwise offend; but he was always engaged in something mean. He had no friends on account of his unmanly ways. He was what is called a churl. While the chances are that such a man would add some other fault to his meanness, the absence of the great faults is not of itself a guaranty of manliness.

A man who always tells the truth is not, therefore, necessarily a manly person. He who always refrains from dishonest and unclean acts is not, therefore, of necessity manly and noble. Wealth does not add anything to the stature of character. But character itself, founded in all these excellencies that are desirable in the best man, goes a great way toward inviting belief.

Success attracts belief in a person, but the effect depends on the one who beholds the successful individual. To be able to make money in any honest way indicates that the man has exceptional judgment; that he planned wisely and well, and that he knows more than the average of men. Thus success invites some degree of homage. Then comes the question: What is success? If it is the winning of money, it places the man higher up in the scale of usefulness than if he had inherited it; for every woman likes to know that her husband can earn money in large amount, as she fears that he may lose what he inherits. It is better to be able to earn a hundred thousand dollars than to have it given to you. The man who inherits money, and then adds to it, is looked upon as more capable than his benefactor.

But success in this line is not enough.

All the good things in humanity, and the power to win in the world, do not constitute the whole scope of influence which a man should exercise over his wife. They are helps. A bad habit stands in the way of making her believe in you; but it of itself does not entitle you to her belief in you as the one best man for her. You see that bad traits make it impossible, while good traits only help some.

Then what is the secret?

Strength of heart.

What is this quality, and how may it be described?

A man is strong of heart not because of his moral or ethical character, but because of his inherent manliness. He has something about him that is noble. It is partly based on strength of mind, for that depends on good sense and the best judgment. Book learning may not be attended by, or result in, strength of mind. Some persons are well educated who are painfully weak in judgment and practical common sense. The habit of transferring from the pages of school books facts that depend on the exercise of memory does not build up the mind; yet most of the graduates of schools and colleges are no more than memorizers. What they can remember they know, and when they forget it they do not know it. This is not mental strength.

A merely moral man is not necessarily strong of heart. Some people are moral, and offensively so. Their goodness is negative, like the house that held only dead bodies; it was fine in architecture, but did not house living folks or do affirmative good.

The meaning of ethics is irreligious morality. It may be negatively good, like religion; or affirmatively good, like charity. It is freedom from the things that are sins *per se*. It is a help to a strong heart, but is not enough.

Still, something more is needed.

It is that indefinable nature that shows real worth. Words do not easily describe it. A man was accustomed to ask himself what he was good for, and he repeated this inquiry nights before he fell asleep, and mornings after he awoke, making the question the last thought of the day and the first thought of the new morning. It thus became a part of himself, and it next inspired the desire to answer it in the affirmative. "I will be a man of real worth," he would declare. He did not want to be a mere machine to go through the work of the day, year in and year out, for that was nothing but routine slavery to self-chosen tasks. By real worth he did not mean money value, but something more than character, or something added to character; a man within a human frame. He wanted a better mind, a stronger heart for his place in the world, and a nature that would be appreciated among his fellow-beings.

The woman likewise must be strong of heart, must develop good judgment and a fine strain of common sense, so that she rises in value day by day. Her husband does not care to point to her as a thing of beauty and say no more. He may be asked what he would most appreciate in a woman, and would reply: "A grasp of the great responsibilities that accrue in marriage, and a courage to meet them grandly." This reply was once made by a man whose position among his fellow-men was as high as can be attained. He had just the kind of wife he desired. He believed in her, and she in him.

Few men are manly, noble men.

Few women are womanly, noble women.

All may acquire these traits by making up the mind to secure them, and by living daily lives according to their determination. We believe that every page that has preceded thus far in this work is necessary as a means of help in the effort to reach so grand a goal.

THIRD RADIAL LAW

Sex Magnetism demands an active body.

Activity of the body is not merely a distinction from laziness. Many persons are hard workers who are not constantly active in the body. Some work hard with the head, as clerks and business or professional men. Some labor all day long, and like to rest all the evening, or lounge around in an easy manner. This is not constant activity.

No lazy person is magnetic, either in this line or any other.

The person who can work hard for eight or ten hours with the muscles and come home so tired that nothing else can be done in the twenty-four, is not magnetic. The claim is not made here that a person who is all tired out should go on working evenings. There should never be a condition of exhaustion except in war, or in some great calamity in times of peace. In normal conditions the man and woman should so work that there is never any real weariness. We cannot see what kind of labor there is that tires a man or woman all out, if it has been properly performed.

Bad methods produce weariness.

The most graceful person is the laborer who works in a way that will not exhaust him. Suppose he is digging with a pick and shovel; if he is to be very weary after an hour or two, he will either rush abnormally in his activity, or else will do things awkwardly. Magnetism requires that his motions shall be easy, free from awkwardness, devoid of all that is clumsy, and direct instead of wasteful. Some men take six blows or motions to do what a graceful man will do in one. It is lost action that makes the muscles weary.

Work so that you can keep at it indefinitely.

This is one of the laws of magnetism. It conserves and saves the strength.

The man, Lajoie, who was the second baseman of the Cleveland Baseball Club, accepted the most difficult chances in play, and covered more ground than the average player; yet seemed actually lazy. His work is realized only when the results are totaled. He received a salary said to be seven thousand dollars for a season for many years, some estimates placing it much higher. He accumulated a fortune, while yet a young man. When a ball was sent at him, driven with the fury of some terrific blow, he seemed to move towards it in an easy jog, and to absorb it in a swinging catch that is part of the throw he makes to the first baseman to head off the batsman. He has lost no part of the muscular action needed to handle the play. Some other player would run with all his might at the ball, make a dive to secure it, strain himself up into a standing attitude, from which he would throw it, using all the muscular determination that his strong body can summon, and then hurl it with a tensed energy. A dozen such plays in succession would weary him very much, and a hundred would exhaust him, if indeed he could go as far as that number. On the other hand, the graceful player could handle a thousand, and seem to be just as fresh and easy in the last play as in the first.

The muscles should never become exhausted.

Here we find the reason why some people are tired out all the time, and others who do more work are fresh all the time. Weariness takes away all radial magnetism. To be exhausted from any cause is to be played out in magnetism, as well as in brain force and muscular power.

All three go together.

Rest, on the other hand, takes away magnetism.

Only those persons who are always active are magnetic.

But no one must get tired. The laborer is not, as a rule, interested in these studies; yet we have known of ambitious laborers who have developed these powers by book training, and have rapidly risen from their lower level to higher planes in life. One of the first things they have learned is to conserve their strength. They have found the way to keep active all the time, and yet never get tired. They have become graceful, easy, ever doing something, and ever fresh. This is the foundation of muscular magnetism.

If you will take note of any workman, no matter how strange the name of magnetism may seem to him, who works all day in a fresh state of the body, you will find two facts:

1. He enjoys working, and is never weary.
2. He has muscular magnetism.

Such a man should be given an opportunity to get up in the world, for nature has made him a power, and he does not know it. If, on the other hand, you take a man who is awkward, clumsy and hard-working, evincing a strain in every piece of labor he does, and if you can show him how to do the same things in an easy, graceful and languid style, as it seems, he will soon change his methods, and will become like the man first mentioned. Then he will also develop muscular magnetism, showing that this quality is only the result of habits. What is called a gift is merely a natural outflow of the manner in which a person lives or acts. What a man brings into his life by his accidental habits may be trained into another man who adopts the same habits.

We have seen many thousands of magnetic men and women, and we have never seen one who did not acquire this quality by putting into practice the ways of men and women who are naturally gifted with the same quality.

The rule is a natural one, and there is no other way of obtaining a genuine benefit in any department of existence. Another way of stating it is to say that what a magnetic person does, or the way he does things, will give the key to the origin of his powers; and any other man who can do things in the same way will achieve the same kind of results.

There has never been a magnetic man or woman who was not constantly active. Nor will there ever be such a man or woman in the world. The constant activity is a generator of vital energy that turns into magnetism under the process of conservation. It is nature's way, and it is the way of art borrowed from nature. Lack of activity brings a quiet condition into the nervous system. Activity that is wearying uses up all its force as fast as it is made. Activity that continues, and yet that saves some of the energy that it develops soon has an excess of energy on hand.

These rules may seem rather dry as reading, but we have seen men of the highest intellectual ability grasp them with the eagerness of children in the presence of new gifts. They are so important that they may be repeated hundreds of times to advantage, and one more statement of them here will not be amiss:

1. In the first place, what a man's habits are will determine what his powers are.

2. If he has habits that tend naturally to develop magnetism, he will be said to be gifted with that quality.

3. If some other man, whose habits tend to destroy his magnetism, turns about and adopts the habits of the former man, he will soon become naturally gifted with magnetism; and, although this is called training, it is nothing but nature at work in the wrong man to make him right. All the works in the series of books of the Personal Magnetism Club follow this plan, and no other. It answers the question: Can a person become naturally magnetic?

4. No man or woman ever lived who was magnetic who was not at the same time constantly active.

5. Activity must, as a matter of necessity, develop the energy on which it feeds.

6. Persons who work in such a way that they use up all energy they produce as they work are tired when they get through, and are generally weary most of the time they are active.

7. Persons who work in such a way that they use up less energy than they produce, have some excess of energy as a result of their activity. By this means they generate magnetism.

8. As muscular magnetism is the basis of all other kinds, the habits of constant activity under the laws of conservation will make any man or woman very magnetic.

When you see a man who loves constant activity, watch him to see if he saves his strength as he proceeds, or is tired and makes it a hard effort. If the latter is the case, he will be fretted and worn out. If he is blessed with the gift of saving himself, not by doing less work, but by doing as much with less effort, then you will find a man who is magnetic.

The idler is not magnetic.

The lounger is not magnetic.

The loafer is not magnetic.

The waster of time is not magnetic.

The man or woman who works in such a way as to be tired while at work, and exhausted when through, is far from magnetic.

It may be said of you that you have not a lazy bone in your body; but you may be tired all the time and not love activity, although you are active by force of necessity. You are in the right way, as far as being active is concerned, but in the wrong way by reason of the manner in which you are active. Reform that part only, and the results will be exactly opposite those you now experience.

In what way will you be active?

Never loaf. That is the whole answer. Never do useless and hurtful things. Keep going. Rest not, haste not. This is the maxim of greatness. By resting not you keep active; and by hasting not you save energy which becomes magnetism.

These habits are natural with great people.

If you are a husband, you will find hundreds of things to do; little things, most of them; but the house will be all the better for your doing them. Do not be afraid to help your wife and your children if you have them. If there is too much serious work for your good, take up some form of physical play; not the kind of play that permits your being seated, for that is dead waste of time.

Vary the muscular activity with the mental forms of employment, and you will find yourself growing strong in heart all the time. In this way you will soon make yourself believed in.

FOURTH RADIAL LAW

Sex Magnetism demands an active mind.

There are two kinds of mental activity. One is the drift of thought, and the other is the working power of thought. When the mind drifts it takes with it, under the principle of leakage, its vitality as fast as it is generated, and only a minimum amount is generated in the process. When there is a working of the mind, as in hard and useful thought, a special degree of energy is created. It is only by hard thinking that the mind grows beyond its ordinary strength.

The mind is said to be drifting when it only satisfies its curiosity or desire for being entertained and pleased. Thus a person who reads light matter all the time, as the paper, or stories, novels, or simple facts, as in travel and history, is being entertained. A working mind is adding something to the individual power; is storing facts and knowledge away for future use, as the bee lays aside its honey for winter feeding. No man or woman need be mistaken about what the mind is doing; whether it is drifting or adding to its value.

The use of the brain for the latter purpose is denoted physically by the loss of phosphorus from the body. After a hard mental effort the defecta show conclusively that more than the usual proportion of this electrical substance has been thrown off, and there is a desire in the appetite for an excess of this kind of food. Facts of this kind have been overworked in the attempts to build up brain foods. These are impossible. Nature organizes its phosphorus in certain of its products, and man will never be able to make a substitute by compounding them. They must come direct from animal or vegetable life. There can then be no such thing as a brain food, and all claims in advertisements are tricks on the unthinking classes.

But the appetite craves food containing phosphorus in proportion as there is a hard use of the mind; and this chemical substance is thrown off in the act of so using the brain. If there is not enough of it in the blood, the loss will cause a headache of a neuralgic kind; for neuralgia is a signal or warning from nature that the foods are not of the right kind to support vitality, or that the energy of life is being wasted, as in excesses of some sort.

The main fact in this connection is the creation of magnetism in the act of hard thinking.

This working of the mind must take place in the same way as the proper working of the muscles, which will also generate magnetism of the muscular kind.

Thus we find two processes that generate two kinds of magnetism.

As has been stated, a man or woman is very unwise who works in any way to get tired. Nature takes care of exhausted people by demanding periods of rest for them; but she at the same time shows that it is not her desire that people make themselves tired in her cause. All work is natural, but hard and wearying work is abnormal, and has no excuse for being tolerated.

The same is true of the mind.

In order to understand what is meant by conservation of the magnetism that results from muscular labor, read what has been said in the last few pages. The same laws apply to the mind, the only difference being that the latter creates a different kind of magnetism. But this must be conserved also. There should be a daily margin between the created energy of the mind and the use made of it.

What straining of the muscles is to unnecessary hard work, so straining, fussing and worrying in the use of the mind make all it does too hard for the purposes of nature. The cure is not to stop the work, but to change the methods employed. Take mental study easy, by not taking one kind too long. When a problem cannot be solved in five or ten minutes, pass on to Latin or other study, and let the brain get its rest in that way.

You may think that a man who has worked hard all day is played out, but if he starts to do some more hard work that uses the same muscles in an entirely different manner, he will be surprised to know that he is not tired at all. As a test of what is meant, try the following experiment:

Stand on one foot a half minute, then stand on the other foot a half minute.

Stand now on the foot a whole minute, then stand on the other foot a whole minute.

Stand on the first foot two minutes, then on the other foot two minutes.

Stand on the first foot three minutes, then on the second foot three minutes.

Stand on the first foot four minutes, then on the other foot four minutes.

Stand on the first foot five minutes, then on the other foot five minutes.

The peculiar facts are that the first foot will become so

weary that exhaustion of the muscular powers will be felt; yet, after transferring the work to the other foot, the former will be not only free from all weariness, but will be stronger because of the way it was worked. If you keep up this practice for a month, devoting just thirty-one minutes a day to it, you will find the feet and legs have acquired wonderful strength, and you will never after that complain of being unable to walk many miles a day. Prolonged periods of rest will, of course, throw the strength away.

The facts are so remarkable that every man and woman should make the experiment. If it is conducted after eating a nourishing meal, it will be found that the food from the stomach, after about half an hour or so, will have been specially drawn to the legs and feet, in order to give them the extra strength required. This test is an old one, but is worth while. It has been used many times to destroy that tired feeling that people complain of when they try to walk ten or twenty miles in a day. One mile is generally the limit, and soreness and lameness follow as a rule.

The mind may be taught to conserve its forces and to increase them in the same way. Remember that this method actually increases the power of the faculty employed.

If you desire to be useful in the processes of thinking, get a line of studies that will lay aside for you a future hive of practical wisdom and knowledge. If you have no choice, let us suggest that the studies named in the fourth department of this book be first put in the list. Then add a work of landscape gardening, a book on floriculture, a book on greenhouse methods, a book on architecture, and any other useful acquisition that may occur to you. These books may be taken from some library, and thus avoid expense.

As the study of foreign languages, alive or dead, compels a person to find out more about his own language, they are always of the highest use in enriching the mind. People often ask what is the use of studying foreign tongues that will probably never be spoken by those who study them? Did you ever stop to think that a foreign tongue is not capable of being studied, except by being translated into the words of your own tongue? A weak mind is weak in the number of words it can use freely. It is not how many words you know the definition of, but how many you actually use and absorb from time to time in your own mental activities that makes your mind greater or weaker as an instrument of intelligence. The strongest of all mental giants have had large vocabularies. No person has been a success in life on a few words. What a man uses in speech is not his vocabulary but what he has in his system, and can employ in any way.

Such a tongue as Latin cannot be studied without studying English at the same time, for Latin is known only through its English synonyms. A word of a foreign language that had no synonym in Enlish would be like a tool that had nothing it could be used for. Then it would be really dead. Any one of hundreds of Latin words may give you a better insight into scores of English words. Take the word *duco* as an example. From it are derived our words duke, ducal, duchess, duchy, ductile, induce, conduce, reduce, adduce, introduce, and many others with their derivatives, until a small vocabulary is already acquired through that one term. A man or woman who has a usable vocabulary of five hundred words, outside of the street talk, is already learned; and here is a chance to acquire thousands of words.

We are not intending to insist that you study Latin. Our purpose is merely to suggest some form of mental activity that will store away value against the future. The greatest of all facts is this: You cannot improve yourself without making a new level, and to this new level you and your fortunes will rise in the course of time.

Because the continual use of the mind will generate mental magnetism, and the conserving of its powers will give an excess of magnetism, you should practice some habit of mental action, resting from it when necessary to participate in these forms of physical activity that do not require thought in their performance.

You will say that your time will be fully occupied, and that you will have no opportunity for doing anything else; but you will, for that something else is activity. It is only a choice between useful and useless activity. You will not elect to be inactive, for that will not harmonize with your character in going so far in the present book as you have. A lazy mind would not have got this far.

Any study, or studious reading, is mental activity.

To read and to re-read this work is mental activity. If you grasp its thoughts you will be benefited in the highest degree; so that, while you are perusing these very pages you are engaged in the most useful of all labors of the mind. Every time you review the various departments herein you will catch new ideas, for they come thick and fast, and seem to crop up in new crowds on each reading. They are the collected experiences and workings of well-established and old-time laws of life; and our only connection with them is to state them in their proper order. As all these laws are nature's, they have not been brought into being by any effort of man; and what is nature's laws must take high rank in any form of education. The same is true of all the courses in the Magnetism Club. Any man or woman who seeks a long period of mind work should undertake all those studies.

But there are many others that may be suggested. Latin was mentioned, not to advise it, but to suggest it as one of many. It is the best of all foreign tongues, if only one is to be selected. Next in educational value is French, if two are to be chosen.

What kind of special design was at work in the life of the young man who had grown up in the service of the government, and who was paid a salary of twelve hundred dollars a year, all of which he spent as fast as he earned it? He read written lessons in this line of training many years ago. Acting on this very suggestion of mental activity, he bought somewhere at a second-hand bookstore two old works, one on landscape gardening, and the other on greenhouse work. He knew nothing about flowers. Botany had been included in his early schooling, but had not helped him in any way, and he was satisfied that he could not derive any benefit from it now. But the practical side of floriculture appealed to him more by chance than by design on his part. He made himself familiar with the theory of greenhouse management and of landscape gardening. At the start, and often during the three years that he dabbled in this apparently useless mental labor, his wife would say to him: "What on earth are you doing with such things as raising flowers in your mind and laying out grounds on paper? It is a waste of time, but it keeps you out of mischief, and cannot do any harm. But it cannot do any good.''

A wife is disloyal to her home if she discourages her husband in any activity of the mind or body that is useful, even if there seems to be no practical opportunity for its employment. All that imparts knowledge is useful. A new level is sooner or later created.

In this man's life there came the fixed desire to visit greenhouses, and see for himself how they did things. Sundays found him doing this pleasant task, and here his wife took joint pleasure, for all women who have normal hearts love flowers and the beauties of nature. He had thirty days' vacation every summer, and these weeks he spent in practicing some of the rules he had studied in the books. Then he got more works, and they were up to date. From then he became scholarly in floriculture, and could talk with experts.

Still we ask what special design impelled him to do these things?

All at once came a cataclysm in the government offices. Hundreds of clerks were discharged, and he was among those whose time had come. Then there was wailing and gnashing of teeth. Families who had spent all the money they earned as fast as it came in were thrown out into the cold world, and it is a fact that not one man in fifty could obtain lucrative employment. This man, himself being more than fifty years of age, knew nothing but government work, which means that he was useless in every line of business and trade. He had no profession, could not tend a store, was too old to start learning something new, and altogether was helpless. But his fellow-clerks were in still worse plight. They averaged more than sixty years of age, and had no show to secure work in anything, not even as office boys at three dollars a week. Employers want new blood, not old.

Our friend had been taking a floral magazine for some years, and now he noticed advertisements for gardeners who could give proof of being strictly temperate and of good habits in every way. He replied, and moved into the country close to a great city. His house rent was included in his wages, and this saved him four hundred dollars a year, which was a large item. The remuneration of sixty dollars a month was seven hundred and twenty dollars a year, or nearly five hundred dollars less than his salary as a government clerk. But he received perquisites that helped him, and there were fewer expenses, so that he saved money for the first time in his life. He really had success as a gardener, and his employer liked him hugely, as he said he was the first gardener who did not get drunk. Then he grew more and more expert in raising flowers, and had another advantage over the ordinary gardeners—he was up to date. Men who have worked at this profession for ten or twenty years have not done any recent reading, and, as a rule, are too ignorant to read much in any event. Here was a scholarly gardener, a kind that is needed today, and that cannot be found. Here was a temperate gardener, a kind that is hard to find in this era; for gardeners that are good are so few in numbers that they are independent, and break all rules they wish to break.

In the second year this man received wages of twelve hundred dollars, and saved nine hundred of them. He had learned a lesson. Yet, in the city working for the government at the same salary, his expenses ate up all his income.

The next salary was fifteen hundred dollars a year, and later on he got as high as two thousand dollars a year, There are head gardeners today who receive five thousand dollars annual salaries. What clerk in the employ of the government is paid that much? The Supreme Court Judges sometimes get less and sometimes more.

Gardeners are very scarce, and of every hundred there is not more than one who is really learned in his work, while eighty per cent. of the good ones are drunkards. The gardeners who are worth having around are provided with rent free, and perquisites that reduce the cost of living to about twenty per cent. of their salaries, the other eighty per cent. being clear gain. There is no limit to the rise that is possible in salary, as we know of gardeners who receive five thousand dollars a year, and landscape gardeners who have been paid as high as twenty-five thousand dollars a year. Any person desirous of knowing something of the high salaries paid to landscape gardeners can find out by writing to some large estate, such as Duke's

Park, Somerville, New Jersey, which is but one of many thousands in this country.

One strong fact in gardening is that a man is never too old for his profession. It is the oldest profession in the world, as Adam himself was the first gardener. A man wears out in the ministry, and in the legal profession. In surgery he is old at fifty, and in medicine he is old at sixty. In the business world, if he has been brought up in it, he may be good until he is seventy or more; but woe to the man who loses his position of employment at any time after he is forty or fifty. No other employer wants him. But the expert gardener goes on forever, or until he dies. We have seen them lively and skilled at eighty-five. If he loses his place he can get another.

This kind of work tends to prolong life.

It is filled with beauty, and beautiful experiences.

The fault with most gardeners, outside of their drinking habits, is an unwillingness to keep abreast of the times; so there is a double chance to succeed by keeping sober and mentally active.

Any man who does not know what he is going to do when he gets too old to work at his profession or trade, or who fears he may lose his position of employment in case his employer should die or fail, will do nothing better than to equip himself as a gardener, fitted for greenhouse work and outdoor gardening, and all other branches of land culture, including landscape effects, orchards and truck raising. If he should have some money saved up, it will not require much land to enable him to carry on a place of his own, and very little expenditure will keep him alive and his family supported on what he may be able to raise if he does not care to work for another.

All the young men who can get away from the farms are going to the cities. There they suffer in poverty, and in time many of them join the bread line, and are fed by charity. In the meantime the farms and gardens, not having enough men and boys to conduct them, are compelled to go without attention. The result is that there are more people all the time in the cities, and fewer all the time raising food for them; and the cry is made that the cost of living is going up. It will continue to go up, obeying the most common of all natural laws. Ten years from now there will not be half as many people on the farms as now, and, of course, the farms will not produce half the foods needed for the cities. Ten years from now there will be twice as many people in the cities as now, and not half as many in the country to feed them. Food prices will rise, rise, rise, and the public will not even guess the cause. Poverty in the cities will increase, the bread lines will grow longer, and charity will do its part toward furthering this abnormal and unhealthy national condition.

Nature, in her laws, before man came to be civilized, took things in her own hands, and made those suffer who were responsible for this defiance of her plans. She did not stop at charity, but cut off the cities' excess by sheer famine and pestilence. Today charity fights the famine and quarantines the pestilence. But the next generation, being asked to pay four times more for food than it is able to earn, will hear the voice of nature speaking in tones that even charity can not avoid. You cannot feed seventy millions of people with the food that is intended for only ten millions.

But the wise man and the wise woman will build well and plan deeply.

The fortunates who own land in the country, who dwell there, who are versed in the latest and greatest of all laws of culture, who can raise what they need to eat, and who can advise those that have the money to pay for their knowledge and help, will hold the whip-hand when food prices soar beyond the reach of the great middle classes, as they already have beyond the reach of poverty.

Here is the greatest profession of the next two hundred years; and, if people only were awake to the fact, it is the greatest profession at this very minute. It affords mental opportunity and physical activity for those who seek employment for their faculties; but, more than this, it is the avenue for safety when disaster comes. When the waves of poverty and panic sweep the land, following the universal defiance of the laws of nature, those men and women who are prepared to look after themselves will be those alone who can get their living from the soil. Everything that is eaten, everything that is worn, everything that enters in the house or into its construction, is furnished by nature from the soil, and the products of the soil; and let him who runs read.

What is the use of wasting time in perusing newspapers or indulging in other forms of gossip and frothy mental effort, or in loafing about the house or down town nights, when there are so many useful ways of employing mind and body?

If, among those men and women who are wretchedly poor, there had ever been the disposition to improve a few minutes each day, a different story would now be told; for there is not an individual who has given honest attention to those little golden fragments of time who is poor today.

There are countless things that may be studied and practiced that will keep the body and mind busy. Many of them combine both sets of faculties, for there are some things that require the union of thought and muscle. These are sometimes best, and then the mental faculties need special and separate activity, as in the study of great principles.

The desire to be well opens up a fruitful field of investigation, and the public needs this line of instruction, perhaps, more than any other.

The wish to be prepared for a change of employment and of work should keep the active mind busy in fitting itself for such a contingency, even if it shall never arise. No one can tell what the morrow may bring forth. He who is ready for the unexpected is the most capable in life's battle.

This is a genius.

The mind that has been enriched by the studies of language and other courses and branches suggested in this book, will carry the body up to a higher plane than the mind that is cultivated in the plainer things only. Then the absorption of knowledge of health, or the arts, of philosophy and the better ethics, will be sure to bear its fruit. You cannot build a temple that will outrank all the hovels surrounding it without inviting a better tenant. That mysterious power called improvement will draw you up to its level.

But there are endless ways in which the mind can make itself active. No one book can cover all the ground in such a field.

The most important fact is the generating of magnetism by any kind of activity that is conserved and not wasted.

Keep the body active, and conserve the muscular effort, if you wish to store away a vast fund of muscular magnetism.

Keep the mind active and conserve the mental effort, if you wish to store away a vast fund of mental magnetism.

These are the laws that prove themselves day by day in the lives of men and women who are getting on in the world.

The wife should engage in both kinds of activity. It is true that she has many duties in her home, but she does more useless work than need be, and does not know how to conserve her muscular strength. She does not overtax her mind; for, if she did, there would be better food selection and better cooking in her house. She simply knows the way her mother has been cooking for years, and knows too little of that or any other method, and is content to learn nothing more. In fact she would be offended if you were to tell her that she did not know how to cook potatoes, or any vegetable in the list; nor could she make bread, cook rice, or eggs, or make soup as it ought to be made, or roast meats, or do the simplest things in the right way. Sure, she knows how her mother did these things, but she has yet to learn the right way of doing them. To prove to you that she has not been giving her brain enough to do, tell her these facts, and see how angry she will be, and how quickly she drops you from her visiting list; for, if she really knows, she will be glad you challenged her ability, and it will be a pleasure to her to show you.

All that man may busy his mind with, the wife may use for the same purpose.

There are hours in every twenty-four, if the household is conducted in an intelligent manner, that husband and wife can take advantage of for these forms of activity of body and mind. You cannot extract something from nothing, and get anything; and you certainly cannot subtract nothing from nothing, and find a remainder. Success is addition, not subtraction. You must take what you are, and add something to it if you wish to be more than what you are. No healthy minds or normal hearts are content to be what they are. If nature adopted such a doctrine we would not be here, you and others; for there would still be only shellfish, and possibly not even they would have been reached in the march of progress. Nature

has done remarkably well to take mud and separate it into
air and earth, sea and land, and to bring the animal kingdom
up out of the mud of the beach, and man out of the lower
forms of life. She has done remarkably well to take the kind
of people that dwelt on the sands of Asia, and out of those
naked savages raise up the civilization of the twentieth century. She is progressive, because she employs the rules of addition, adding something to something, and getting something
more.

This is her work.

Progress is addition.

If you are not in harmony with nature you will be weak,
unhappy, unprogressive and without goal or future. If you
wish to have all the forces of nature helping you on like the
great army of a nation fighting to place you on a throne, determine to learn the rule of progress. Take what you are,
and add something to that. The result will never be failure.
Never mind what you add. Add something. Anything that
will make the mind richer in thought, and the body more useful in its work, or healthier in its life. The trouble is that
most men and women spend all their time, if they have any
interest at all in progress, in hunting for what they will add
to their minds and their usefulness; like the modern woman
when shopping. She is weighted down with the fear that some
store a mile away may have a bargain that is a cent better
than any of the ten stores she has visited, and so she keeps
hunting for something better, until she decides that it is too
late in the day to get anything, and the next bargain day is
reserved for the next hunt. The spirit of the olden times, of the
hare and the hounds, is yet alive in this generation.

But if you will start with anything that is useful, and stick
to it, you will add something to what you are, either mentally
or physically.

Make a beginning.

Husband and wife can find these waiting hours, and can
put them into employment at home. At first let the physical
activity take possession of you. Do some of the duties that
are dragging in the home. Then do some real work in making the house more attractive. Do not be afraid of dirt, and
show what nature has done for you in your muscular depart-

ment. It is a pleasant sight to see husband and wife working together. What the nation needs is to see more of them working together, and in longer hours as well.

Do not be afraid of muscular work, or of mental activity of the hard and taxing kind. Nature will bless you and take care of you.

FIFTH RADIAL LAW

Sex Magnetism demands that the commonplaces be decreased.

This is so important a law that a full department will be devoted to its consideration.

In summing up the present part of the work, let the reader remember that no person is magnetic, either naturally or by training, unless he is constantly active, both in mind and body.

To the non-magnetic, languid person this may seem an overdrawn statement; but the facts are abundant that prove the correctness of the assertion. A magnetic person succeeds in proportion as he applies to his power the intelligence taught in the course, Mental Magnetism, and the interpretation of temperament taught in the other course, Advanced Magnetism. These are large, long and extensive schooling systems of training, but they are necessary to the attainment of the highest success in life.

But laying aside the ambition to mount high, and being content to reap a fair reward, this work as it stands alone will win much, and prove an abiding friend all through the years that are to come, if its instruction is given careful attention.

THIRD TESTS OF TEMPERAMENTAL UNFITNESS.

Referring to pages 198, 199, 200 and 201 of this department it will be seen that all persons possess certain prevailing emotions. Out of a list of nearly four score of these moods, of which some are bright and helpful, while others are dark and repugnant, a certain number will be found coming into prominence by habit or impulse in every person.

A man who is thinking of asking a woman to become his wife should ascertain what emotions prevail in her character; and with what readiness they spring into activity. This is not difficult.

A woman who is thinking of accepting an offer of marriage should take steps to ascertain what emotions prevail in the character of the man who seeks her; and what causes instigate their activity.

Let us take up a few of the emotions on the better side, such as respect, affection, generosity, serenity as in a peaceful disposition, mercy, sympathy, sacrifice, trust, hope, optimism, dignity, courage, reverence and the like; and some of the darker emotions such as worry, vexation, petulance, indifference, flippancy, immoderation, recklessness, melancholy, fear, hate, cruelty, revengefulness, arrogance, jealousy, envy, superstition, flattery, deceit, selfishness, craftiness and the like. These are typical of some character.

Assuming that you possess no other work but this on the subject of magnetism, you ought to have enough keenness of judgment to learn in a few months the prevailing emotions and moods of your would-be mate. But if you are unable to read human nature, then the study of Mental Magnetism, and of emotional powers which are taught in Advanced Magnetism will give you the ability to take account of stock at once of your own moods and emotions and those of the other party.

The rest is easy. If there are the better or brighter moods prevailing in both of you, all is well; and if any of them are alike, the harmony is perfect to that extent. If, on the other hand, there are dark moods that are alike in both of you, never think of marrying. All the magnetism in the world will not prevent you living lives of quarrels and unlimited hatred of each other; except when such feelings are held in abeyance by most careful watching under the power of Sex Magnetism.

Yet it is true that where one or two only of the dark moods prevail, a cure is possible by ordinary magnetism. But where the general moods are of the darker side, it is better not to invite wedlock or encourage it.

COMMONPLACES

OF the five laws of radial influence, the last and greatest is that which says that it is necessary to decrease the commonplaces, in order to build up the power of Sex Magnetism. By using the term decrease, it may be seen that the commonplace cannot be wholly got rid of. A commonplace is something ordinary. The word means various things in limited usage, but the public understands a thing to be commonplace when it is trivial, ordinary or common.

In its full scope it includes a wide range of matters, and these are all brought under the definition as employed here. The word vulgar originally meant nothing more than common; but the latter takes in what is vulgar and what is plain, ordinary and trivial, showing some shading in its ideas and uses.

The distinction should be kept in mind.

The marriage of today in civilization is the dumping ground of all the commonplaces. In some other lands this is not so. At one time in civilization it was not as much the case as it is at the present day. When a young lady sees her father and her brothers in the freedom of home life, and is afterwards the object of attentions from a well-dressed and careful-mannered young man, the change is so refreshing that wedlock is an allurement. It is a fact that every young man appears at his best when he is courting his sweetheart. She likewise appears at her best during that one period of life. Why, after the ceremony, she should be compelled to receive commonplaces far beneath those to which she has been subjected at her own home with her brothers and father is hard to understand.

It is argued that the relations of marriage are closer and necessarily more familiar than those in the home with her father and brothers; but, admitting that fact, all other relations should not be lower, or even as low, when there is no reason for such a condition of things. The hope of every girl is that one day she will be elevated to a higher plane of existence, not to one farther down in the scale.

She builds her castles in the air, and dreams of a happy future, of pretty surroundings and a half fairyland realm, in which she is to dwell when her cavalier comes to take her hence. She pictures him in her mind as gentleman in dress, in manners, in speech, and in his treatment of her. She believes that he is to court her after marriage as well as before, and that he will treat her as a little queen who is entitled to homage and devotion.

It is refreshing today to note the air of expectancy in the mind of a girl who will confide her hopes in her friend. She speaks of her lover as so nice, so gallant, so refined and such a gentleman. To what degree or extent does he surpass her own brother? Does not some other girl think that brother just as much of a cavalier?

Sex Magnetism requires the decreasing of all commonplaces that may be lessened, so that as much as possible of the hopes of both parties may be realized.

The commonplaces are numerous, and a few of them will be discussed herein for the purpose of lighting the way to all others that may arise in married life.

Speech.—When a young man is first introduced to a young lady of whom he has then and there a high opinion, he is vary careful how he addresses her. His words are carefully weighed and delivered. She is likewise very cautious not to leave in his mind the impression that she is flip, silly, shallow or ignorant. If she knows little of the refining elements in conversation, she will not long deceive him, unless both are of the same calibre.

Speech consists in matter and manner. Matter is what is said, and manner is how it is said. The material of the thought that is embodied in the talk will soon take the level of the intelligence of the mind behind it. You can for a few minutes hold back the awful secret that you have only commonplace material at hand for delivery. If the other party is of the same grade, it may or may not be well for you. Let us assume for a moment that you are a man, and that you are

now in the presence of a woman who is making an impression
on you, and you are desirous of making an impression on her.
If you and she are of the same mental calibre, she may or may
not mind that; although it is true that all women who are worth
winning desire some mental force greater than their own, or,
at least, greater than they are led to think is ordinary. A girl
is always hoping that some other girl's brother is a much nicer
man than her own brother. Most boys and girls that grow up
in the same neighborhood, and see each other from childhood up
to the years of marriageable age, lose the desire to wed among
each other, on the ground that they know too much about their
playmates, and have seen them in all their commonplace ways.
The glamour is not there. Romance is missing. They have
been wishing for something better than they have known.

If, therefore, some other man who can talk of better subjects
and give better material in thought to the same woman, although
she is no stronger in material than you are, she will much
prefer the better man. "I was so much entertained with what
he said" is the frequent remark of a woman after her first
meeting with a man. "He talked on such interesting subjects,
and his thoughts were so grand" is one of the comments made
by the woman.

The man who speaks of his dog, of his tailor, of his chums,
of his game of pool, of his tramp on the railroad track, and
similar themes, would not impress even the small mind of a
woman; while the same female would be charmed with another
man who spoke of the flowers he had picked in the woods, of
the fine lecture he heard the other evening, of the pictures he
had seen, and other matters of the same style. This would be
about the limit of the woman referred to. She would be out-
classed at that, yet would prefer the second man to the first,
because the something above the ordinary is alluring and
winning.

The second man with the superior themes might come in competition with a third man in calling upon a woman of a higher
mental grade than the one of whom we have just been speaking.
She would be, ordinarily, pleased with his account of his experiences, but the third man might speak eloquently of matters
that would include her ambitions, if she had any; or her fancy
and admiration might be aroused by less of the speaker's affairs

than of others who towered above him and what he had known.
The old story told to Pauline is a never-failing air-castle;
unreal as it is in the material world, it is full of that fascination
that the female mind feeds on. It may be told in a thousand
variations, and given a thousand different localities and change
of details to suit, yet the man who can tell something like it, and
be believed in at the same time, could win a princess out of her
kingdom, and take her to his humble cottage for life, or until
the charm had been fractured.

Here is what Claude Melnotte said to Pauline:

"A palace lifting to eternal summer its marble walls, from
out the glossy bower of coolest foliage musical with birds, whose
songs should syllable thy name! At noon we'd sit beneath the
arching vines and wonder why Earth could be unhappy, while
the Heavens still left us youth and love! We'd have no friends
that were not lovers; no ambitions save to excel them all in
love. We'd read no books that were not tales of love—that
we might smile to think how poorly eloquence of words trans-
lates the poetry of hearts like ours! and when night came,
amidst the breathless Heavens, we'd guess what star should be
our home when love becomes immortal; while the profound light
stole through the mists of alabaster lamps; and every air was
heavy with the sighs of orange groves and music from sweet
lutes, and murmur of low fountains that gush forth in the
midst of roses!"

It is in this spirit, if not in its promises, that the heart is
quickened. Magnetism is necessary to conceive such thoughts,
and a magnetic manner of delivery is still more essential. The
body of fact may be unreal, but the soul of desire for such
a life is there in every normal woman. We live in our emotions, and see with them. To know that a man has in his
nature the wish for something above the routine drudgery of
daily existence is pleasing to a girl. It may never be realized, but she does not think of that, and she has her dream
and its enjoyment while it lasts.

But some of this spirit can be made to last forever.

Most of it is beyond human possibility as a basis of fact,
yet the life that is suggested is worth hoping for.

In what is said, and how it is said, is many a heart touched
and won. The speech may never in real life be as gorgeous as

that made by Melnotte, but there is no reason why it should drop at any time down to the vocabulary of the street, the shop or the kitchen. It is, perhaps, better to have something within reach of possibility of realization as the material in what is said; and that something would only embody an ambition yet to be fulfilled.

Anything that is above the common themes, and that has the ring of sincerity and of genuineness, will help brighten the hopes of the woman. The material is important, and the manner of speech is also to be elevated.

There is no reason why marriage should be the dumping ground of all the cheap phrases and terms that dwell in the human mind. Some of them are low and common enough for the father and brothers of a refined girl; but there are others, always called Anglo-Saxon roots and original terms, that are a little too vulgar for the brothers and father to use in the presence of the girl who has got half way through her teens, that the husband feels at liberty to thrust into her hearing because she is his wife.

We do not propose to smirch this book with the usual number of them, for half a dozen will suffice as well as five hundred. Take the case of a young man of refined instincts who had met a very beautiful and apparently cultured young woman in a conservatory of a friend, amid flowers whose fragrance still lingered in his memory as he made a visit one evening to her home. She herself had an aroma of scented powder on her that gave him hope of finding her all he had anticipated, although his mind had not had a doubt or a thought in that direction until he caught a word from the adjoining room coming from the lips of a brother. He was not sure he heard aright, and the matter slipped his attention. But later on, when this beautiful young woman stepped back to the next room to speak to her brother, the visitor heard her say: "It stinks; throw it in the swill." When she returned to the parlor the young man studied in vain to find the beauty in her face that he had noted before. Instead he saw her as she was. The thin veiling of skin could not hide the woman that would be developed in the next few years, and, as he never called again, he did not meet her for a long time, but did, in fact, know her by sight when she had married six years later. Her husband was a different type from himself, and she was then what was behind her face as a maiden—coarse and all commonplace.

We live in our emotions and see with them; and they are the truth.

In such a word as "stink" there is nothing bad or wrong; but it is commonplace. There are other words that will convey the meaning better and shade it to a nicety. On moral grounds it can be defended, and perhaps on ethical grounds, but not in Sex Magnetism. A man who will tell his wife that she stinks will not long have her regard, unless both are below the grade of individuals who can be benefited by this study. A woman who tells her husband that he stinks is of the same degree of elegance as the word she uses. All words are reflections of the mind itself.

Here is an illustration of the fact that both the material and the manner are commonplace. The kinds of words used to convey the matter make the manner. But the material in the thought is commonplace. If husband or wife may be found guilty of the allegation, it is the subject of the third department in this book, not of this. The cause of the charge needs remedying; and this may be done in the first place by calling attention to the third department. If then the guilty party does not reform, have that part of the book re-read. It will in time remove the odor.

If, however, there is anything wrong that gives rise to it, let some other material be employed. Do not say "stink," and do not think "stink." Have some other shading of the meaning in your mind. Try to be elegant in the formulation of ideas, and your language will accordingly be elegant. If you reverse this and think more than you say, or worse than you speak, there will come times when the tongue will slip up, as the saying goes, and your mind will leak through. Then a new level will be found, and it will not be a higher one.

You cannot long think in one channel and talk in another, if you are married. The need is to think above the commonplaces. In the days of courtship both parties try to appear at their best; they have their better clothes on, their better manners on, and their better thoughts in the ascendency. If courtship could be prolonged for years, and the lovers see each other often, they would serve as foils to elevate each

other to that higher ground that they make appear in their
meetings.

Pretences develop habits in time.

The word "swill" is not elegant, nor is the thought. The
modern substitute of garbage is better as a word, but the
material is not elegant. The beautiful woman who entertains
her lover with an account of her garbage system, her garbage
can and its contents, and a similar trend of thought, is at a
far distance from the subject that he would be most pleased to
hear discussed, although she may be pouring out her mind to
him. Hunt as you may for synonyms for garbage, and clothe
them in the best garb they can wear, you are still wrong in
material. One woman who was a widow, and who had set her
cap for a man of some refinement, had been plunged into a fit
of anger by the manner in which the city collectors failed to
carry away three times a week the garbage from her yard. She
told her suitor of the fine cans she had purchased, and of the
tight-fitting covers which concealed the odor, and then to have
the cans remain uncollected for three days at a time was more
than her dainty heart and nostrils could endure. The man was
so impressed with her wrongs and suffering that he thought he
could smell garbage in the very room where they sat, so great
was his sympathy for her misfortune. When she shook hands
with him in saying good evening later on, he thought he had
carried off the smell of garbage on his fingers. At home he
took out of his desk her letters, and he thought they, too, had
the odor of garbage underneath the sachet perfume; so he tore
them up and threw them out. He soon came to regard her as
the garbage widow, and now after years of marriage with another
he thinks occasionally of all the smells he has escaped.

We smell with our emotions more strongly than with our
noses.

Odors are impressions in the brain, and the finest perfumes
are interpretations of the gray cells, whether they are stimulated by the nerves of the nose or of the emotions. In such
courses as Advanced Magnetism and Universal Magnetism,
which are included in this Club, there are abundant methods
for cultivating the brain impressions of all the senses. Let an
odor come to the nose, and the nerves there carry it to the
brain, where it is interpreted. Let an emotion become magnetic,

and the same brain centers will be impressed in the same way. No sense is interpreted in the sense itself. A nose without a brain could not create or convey an odor or perfume. An ear without a brain could not carry a sound. An eye without a brain could not transmit sight. It all depends on the final interpretation within the brain, where there is no presence of the senses, but merely their reports from outward impressions.

What wonder, then, that such high studies as Advanced Magnetism and Universal Magnetism should bring the interpretations into life without the aid of any senses, or through the sixth sense, which includes all five and intensifies them? There are cases where the smell of flowers has been passed all around a room, and, in fact, all through the house, by the magnetism of a person who has brought them into his or her own mind. A magnetic man has been able by thinking of any flower to transmit the fragrance of it to a woman. This experiment has been performed thousands of times, and is within the power of any individual of high magnetic quality, such as is taught in the two higher works just referred to. The experiments have gone so far as to include the varieties of flowers such as American Beauty roses, Enchantress carnations and numerous other kinds. A man who had, on various occasions, brought six different varieties of roses to his sweetheart, all of which she loved equally well, told her one evening that he had brought into the adjoining room a very large bouquet of one particular kind, of which she was very fond. These were Paul Neyrons, which she had not seen for months, and which she supposed were out of season. He did not tell her their names, but made it a magnetic creation according to the higher laws of this power. She had not thought of this variety, but knew it quite well from previous familiarity with it, although he had never brought her any of the kind. Now, to deceive her in words, while he fastened the magnetic creation in her mind, he declared that the roses were the Perle de Jardins. She at once exclaimed: "You will pardon me for saying that you have made a mistake. The roses that I smell are Paul Neyrons, but they are out of season now. Where did you get them?"

The experiment was most perfect.

When a man brings American Beauty roses to his sweetheart, he creates in her mind an exalted idea of himself and of the friendship that has begun between them. Thus flowers serve to refine and to elevate the mind and heart. Courtship in many homes proceeds amid flowers of the most delicious perfume, and the foliage is an aid to the mind through the sense of sight. It takes years for a man to rid himself wholly from these finer impressions, or for the woman to make herself believe that the man is commonplace, and, therefore, mere clay. The city professor who found a sweet maiden of sixteen, with fair, smooth, velvety complexion and large, shining blue eyes gathering marigolds by the roadside, learned to love the smell of the rank flower because he always associated it with the fair beauty of the girl he had met. His heart turned over several times in his conversation with her, and the seemingly dainty and rich nature she owned was most convincing; but she slipped out of his life as suddenly as she came in, and only the odor of the marigolds abided. From that time ever after he loved the flowers, and had them on his desk as often as he could get them.

People live in their emotions.

The rule is two-sided, as all rules ought to be. The first impression of a woman's face or smile or voice, if it could stop there, would set all men on edge under certain circumstances. Some men have learned to love the most unlovable things because of the first impressions that have never been erased. Then they are prone to hate what they admired. But the unlovable things are never commonplace. They may be incongruities or faults of the unusual sort; while a commonplace would destroy the whole romance at one fell blow. A lisp is not of the latter class. If there is a pretty face behind or around the lisp, and the man falls in love or is impressed deeply, he will be inclined to lean tenderly towards all girls that lisp. Let once the glamour of the first impression be broken, as by a slang term coming through the lisp, and he will despise all girls who lisp, if he has a refined nature.

It is not the bunch of beautiful roses that most pleases the maiden who sits in their midst as attractive as they. It is the contrast with the commonplaces with which her life is filled, and which she hopes to mount above. It is not the sight of flowers and their perfume, nor the taste of the delicately-boxed and adorned candies, nor the ribbons on them that most please. Her brother Jack has given her a dirty candy from his jacket pocket, from which she has extricated the debris in which they have fallen; and these are commonplace, to which she must return when the lover and the American Beauty roses and the dollar-a-pound candy in violet ribbons have melted into the disheveled locks of the grunty husband who tosses his wife a handful of tobacco-perfumed, cheap seven-cent gum-drops a few months after the marriage.

The most philosophical girl we have ever met was sixteen at the time we first knew her. She was beautiful, and her parents were of the middle classes, with a home that had been made attractive by the care and interest of both husband and wife. She was refined and well educated for a maiden of her age. She took part in the care and beautifying of the home, and never failed to be a companion to her mother, both in the house and when she went out. Thus she escaped the name of flirt. Owing to her beauty and special good name and finer reputation than most girls enjoyed because of her home habits, she had admirers among all the desirable men; and all others failed utterly to obtain permission to call. From the time she was sixteen until she was thirty years of age she met at her home, in the presence of her parents, many gentle-men, some of them of wealth, who vied with each other to make themselves most attractive to her. They dressed at their best, talked their best, and acted as well as gentlemen know how when there is a worthy and desirable girl at stake.

She thus unconsciously became a great influence for the good of these men. Some of them married other girls, and ceased to pay honors to her; some came once a month, others once in two weeks, but there were no regular visits from any of them in all those years. She joined with other young ladies in giving functions at which the men were invited, and these occasions were long remembered for their refining effect on both sexes.

In her home she was the recipient of many beautiful and most costly flowers from the men of wealth; but she prized even more the native bouquet which an ambitious young lawyer was wont to go out into the fields and pick, because his means were limited. Without his knowing it, and without her parents having any suspicion of the fact, she would take her gift to her room, and there study it in her quiet moments.

In those fourteen or fifteen years she lived above the commonplaces. The confectionery, the expensive fruits and the glorious flowers, aided by the better material of conversation and the influence of music, which she loved, surrounded by attractions in her home life, and enhanced by the elevated atmosphere in which she and her friends seemed to dwell, made her a woman of exceptional richness of character and elegance, free from artifice or pretence. She flirted with no man, and led none to believe that she cared for him.

At length she married the poor lawyer, who has since become a power in his community. Her girl friends have not made happy marriages, as there are not many such unions in a hundred. But any young woman who is of a philosophical turn of mind may make for herself a life above the commonplaces.

Learn to wait.

Take years in which to learn to wait, and years more in waiting.

In those years keep all men at a distance. Make them give you all they know, and they can learn, of the attentions that are above the commonplaces.

That higher realm is the domain of Sex Magnetism. It is not a dream, for it has been in the hopes of women for centuries, and in the hearts of noble men even longer. It has been practiced more million times in courtship than you can count all day long, making your figures as fast as you please. It is the one first effort of the two sexes to make impressions on each other. It is lost when the maiden is won or the man is caught, and then it evaporates little by little until the honeymoon is over. Being founded on thin air instead of solid magnetic habits, it does not linger any longer than its usefulness in deceiving the opposite sex is necessary.

We have shown the effect beautiful roses, sweet music and fine language have on girls, and the kindred effect their dainty words and ways have on men. Both learn to expect better influences than marriage brings. Now, the office of Sex Magnetism is to maintain the better condition that is above the commonplaces.

Two of the plain words have been cited to show what is meant by vulgar terms. There are others, many of them, and they need not be listed here; but we would advise every man and woman to make a private statement of them for reference and memorizing. Affectation on the other hand, should be carefully avoided. Some women assume a prudish nature that have none of it, in fact, in their make-up. They will not say leg, but prefer limb, during the first stage of courtship; and after marriage they toss out Anglo-Saxon words in profusion. The word "nasty" and the word "disgust" are vulgar, and are not often used, except when some mood is to be described by a writer. In the refinements of marriage they should not be heard. Anything that is "nasty" is not good material for the brain; and anything that is "disgusting" is just as vulgar matter. The word "rot" is never employed except by a mind that carries sewerage, and sewerage is not as nice as garbage. It is several degrees more vulgar. Yet today the sweetest lips speak of things and of acts, and of occurrences, and events, and efforts, endeavors, remarks, and most everything else as "rotten," and fair women of the theatrical profession, as well as leading men, Romeos, Juliets, Hamlets, Paulines, Claude Melnottes, Portias, and the whole tribe from the stars down to the star-dust and planet-dust, have but one adjective with which to express their lack of appreciation of anything; and it is "tommyrot."

The reason for this habit that is lower than garbage is that the mind of the actor or actress is a copying mind, as far as anything beautiful and noble is contained in it. The speech of Claude Melnotte is at the very height of elegance and richness of thought, and the man who can parrot it effectively may live for the moment in the grandest moods of a mind of which he really knows nothing. He is a parrot, and no more. In his private room, and on the street, and behind the scenes, he comes down to his natural level, given him by nature, and his one word is "tommyrot." That is his garbage mind.

Very few, indeed, are the actors who do not daily use the word "rot" a hundred times; and the word "tommyrot" as the comparative degree of rot. Very few, indeed, are the actresses who do not daily do the same thing. It is their nature.

In cheap newspapers there are editorials in which this same

word occurs. The reporters, as a rule, are made up of the mental slums of life; and they have "rot" on their tongues' end all day long, and ejaculate it in their sleep. In every city men who have suddenly become millionaires, and who give big dinners to the monkeys of society, use and hear the word "rot" a hundred times during the dinner; and in the smoking-room afterwards, and in the drawing-room also this word is passed from one to another by the shuttlecock minds of the hosts and guests.

The garbage is "rot."

The contents of the cesspool are "rot."

The water-closet contains "rot."

The foul sewer carries "rot."

And, by the law of addition, the human mind that, when opened to permit an idea to escape, sends forth "rot" as a word, is proving its contents to be garbage, cesspool, water-closet and sewer.

The word originated in the theatrical profession; and no wonder that marriages there are loose beyond all description. What well-known actor today is living with his wife? What well-known actress today is living with her husband? The whole nauseating history is one long line of mental and moral unfitness that may be summed up in the words that profession creates as its medium of outpouring its thoughts.

If you seek to find marriage, you must look for it in other directions, and if it is worth while at all it is worth making reasonably refined. The smartness that emits cheap and slangy terms is only an apology for ability. The rule is a natural one; that where the mind is weak in resources its words will be correspondingly vapid and smart. This is the balance of energy.

On the same principle the habit of cussing is evidence of a cheap and weak mind. It shows irritation and inability to control it; for, following along the same line, the more irritated the mind is the more freely it will employ oaths and profanity. The climax of irritation is insanity. This fact is well known to every physician and expert in nervous disorders. Many a doctor has said to a patient: "If you allow your irritability to get the better of you, the result is sure to be insanity." Partial irritability is partial insanity; and

all forms of this erratic action of the nerves are steps toward
mental breakdown. The history of such cases is well known.

In this way we have absolute proof of the assertion that
the weaker the mind the greater is the disposition to swear, become profane and use slang; for slang is only a very commonplace manner of swearing.

Many men before they are married refrain from profanity
in the presence of their mothers and sisters, and generally
keep from it when their fathers and brothers are present or
within hearing distance. But as soon as they are married and
the new has worn off they let loose and compel their wives
to submit to the profanity and nastiness that these cheap fellows are too cowardly to use in their parents' homes. There
is no accounting for the beast and brute in man. What a
woman is to expect can only be surmised. For this reason it
is well that she take time to decide whether or not she will
get married, and that she ascertain what kind of a husband
she is to marry. His outside appearance will not furnish the
truth, for he makes himself appear better than he is, as that
is the office of courtship.

No man should ever use any word that is not refined enough
for the most elegant occasions. If a word is out of place in
church or in the presence of the highest magistrate, or before
a queen, it is out of place in the home. The woman who has
been led to expect a gentleman as a husband, should not be
disappointed. There is much he cannot provide her with, and
there is such a let down from what she has been hoping for
in him when at his best that he ought not to add to her suffering.
In time she will become hardened and settle down to the dungeon feeling, where a palace was dreamed of.

If you are a married man, let these words come home to you.

That wife may have settled down years ago to the crown
of commonplaces that you have thrust upon her. If so, say
nothing about it. Just make up your mind that you will
not attract her attention by turning over a new leaf; but make
yourself more refined in speech at the rate of one word a day.
If she, too, has learned slang and cheap words, do not mention it to her, for she will in time adopt your improvement.
If you have been saying coarse, unrefined, vulgar or profane
words, omit one a day, and she will not see any direct change

in your style of addressing her and others, but she will instinctively feel that there is a better atmosphere. It will pay to do this.

Try it for a week.

Nothing pays better in marriage than the omission of all commonplaces in speech. There is every grade of slang, from the most imbecile to the upper forms; but they indicate a weak mind, and a mud mind. If there is an opportunity to learn in advance of marriage whether or not your sweetheart has this fault, it is better to first try to cure it by setting a good example; and, if that fails, look for another sweetheart who is not addicted to the debasing habit. When wedlock is stripped of all its better influences, there is no reason for the union. It is much better that there be no marriage between such minds and such bodies. The children of such people are not needed in the nation, for there is too much of the erratic mind at large at the present time. This is called by physicians an age of insanity and irritability, or neurasthenia and unbalanced temperament. Such an age naturally gives vent to slang, coarse epithets and profanity. Most of the slang of what is called good society is only a weak form of swearing. The manliness is wanting in it, and the purity of woman's heart, that which man hoped would be angelic in embryo at least, is wholly lost. This is the reverse of what courtship promised.

Actions.—There are many things that are done in marriage that are commonplace, and that destroy the magnetism that ought to exist between the two persons who are parties to the union. Many of these acts cannot be mentioned here, but may be surmised. There are others that can be referred to briefly.

Habits of the toilet should be done decently. The woman who combs her hair and leaves the combings lying around on the table or dresser is in need of reform. A wealthy young woman was very eager to marry a young man who also had great wealth. The sister of the young man invited the young lady to her house, as they had been friends for some years. This sister one morning, after the guest had gone down to the conservatory, had her brother look into the bedroom and witness a comb full of hair freshly taken from the visitor's head and left on the dresser. The color left no doubt as to who owned the hair. The sister said to her brother: "Is she the kind of woman you want for a wife?" The effect was complete. Not long after a coolness sprang up between the brother and the young woman he might have married.

The hair may be treated in a most slovenly manner, or may be handled with refinement, depending on the person. Stray hairs on the dress or coat are untidy, and often repugnant to those who see them. They indicate the character that permits them to be there. Dandruff should be cleaned out of the scalp, as can be done by using any tar soap once a week, but to see it fall like a snow storm over the clothes is unpleasant. It is not so much what it seems to be as it is the nature of the person that allows it to be carelessly manipulated. Some wives permit dandruff to fall constantly into the food they cook.

The nose is an organ that is fruitful in possibilities of offence. It is commonplace enough at its best, for which reason it should be given lessons in care and good manners. There are many ways of blowing it that are coarse and unnecessary; but the habit of using the lavatory or washbowl for a receptacle into which to blow the mucus from the nose is too commonplace. What say you of the feelings of a woman who supposed she was marrying a man gentlemanly as he seemed to her when they first met, and who after the marriage heard him discharging all the contents of both halves of his nose in the lavatory? He blew and cleaned, blew and dug, and blew and kept on cleaning and digging until the wife was sick at the stomach. What could she do? She thought that this was an exceptional instance, and that it would never occur again, so she took something to settle her stomach, and waited for further events. It turned out to be a daily affair, and she abandoned a man she despised, not for his moral shortcomings, for he was a consistent church member, but for a coarseness of habit that her previous life had never known.

Picking the nose is likewise an offence. If it must be done, let the curtain of secrecy be drawn over it, and not take it into the drawing-room or other place where the operation must be witnessed by the wife. Excavating the ears, picking at pimples on the face, scratching around the middle zone of the body, paring the corns, cutting the nails of any of the twenty digits and similar episodes are all commonplaces that are more or less vulgar. They should be done separate and apart from witnesses, and not as a social exercise.

Private refinements enrich the character.

It has been claimed that wedlock lets down all bars and makes everything allowable, because there are rights that are still more familiar and private to which no objection is ever made on the grounds stated. Such rights are not commonplace, but are peculiar to marriage. They are never vulgar, and carry with them no taint of coarseness or humiliating offense. On the other hand, they are by far the most refined and exalting of relations when legally sanctioned, and are the one atoning influence that helps to counterbalance the wrong done by the commonplaces and vulgarities that are crowded into some marriages. When properly surrounded by the higher conduct of the ordinary relations, they fit in place with all that Melnotte said to Pauline.

Yet most men believe that this familiarity lets in everything that is gross. It is not so. There is abundant proof that men and women after marriage have been as closely attentive to these rights as any couple could possibly be, and yet have never let down the bars to all the commonplaces and vulgarities that are usual in some unions.

The distinction is a wide one, and should never be lost sight of.

Commonplaces of dress should be avoided.

If it is necessary to remove the clothes that are worn in the presence of other members of the family, and remain for some length of time partly unrobed, there should be worn the usual gowns or undress robes that are made for such contingencies. There are also slippers or light shoes for the feet that are generally used by persons of nice habits. They are quite inexpensive, and there is no reason why they should not be in every family. If a snapshot could be taken by the camera of most wives and husbands as they go about and sit around in the intervals between wearing and not wearing clothes, and if these views could be published, with the names of the men and women of whom they are photographs, the result would be wholesome.

Some of these offences come within the teachings of the third department of this book relating to the senses, and others merely show the commonplace character of the husband or wife, and thus lessen all opportunity for the cultivation of Sex Magnetism, which is based on sex attraction.

Cheap conversation should be avoided.

Thinking should precede speaking.

The husband likes to hear his wife talk sense, not rattle along like a shallow brook over a bed of stones. Wives like to believe in the good taste of their husbands, and this is evinced largely in the style and manner of their many talks from day to day. A noisy cart is an empty one, for the full wagon moves steadily, while the empty one rattles along over the rough street. The gabbing wife is too much in evidence. Talk, talk, talk is tiring. Let it be reduced a little every day, and the wife will survive the restriction which is thus voluntarily adopted. The quiet woman is a jewel if she is quiet by nature, and not because she is pouting. The silent woman is not a pleasing one; but it is a fact that all men like the kind of women who talk no more than is necessary for the purpose of marriage. The happy medium is the best. In woman the habit of quiet speech and of limited conversation is close to magnetism. Such a woman holds quite a sway over her husband.

The man who blows and brags and tells everybody about himself, and repeats the story again and again, and has a volume to say on every subject, is merely showing a feminine mind of the gossipy kind; for there are female minds in male bodies, and male minds in female bodies. Such a man is a nuisance, and his talk is just the opposite of magnetic. His wife may or may not dare to tell him what she thinks of it; but she either verbally or mentally asks him to "shut up," and this calls forth a familiar commonplace. Couples live like cats and dogs when they engage in these experiences. Of course, there is nothing attractive in the parties themselves or in their marriage.

Too much talk is commonplace.

There is seldom too much silence. When it is a habit and is good-natured, then it is more or less magnetic. There is a mystery about a man or woman who has not an opinion on everything that occurs, and who is not frothy and exuberent in words. If a person knows but little, silence covers the ignorance. If he knows it all, it is better to be asked an opinion than to make it cheap by offering it unsolicited.

The flip man or woman is commonplace.

There is a lack of seriousness and of weight in all that is done and said. Smart remarks, conceited remarks, silly criticisms, a jocose nature and a monkey mind are sometimes seen in and out of what is called society. They are commonplace, and tend to make husband and wife lose confidence in each other where they prevail. No person can believe in a flip character.

An exalted mind is magnetic.

The habit of telling anecdotes that are heard by men in clubrooms, in saloons and in brothels, is far from setting a standard that will add to the appreciation that a woman should have of her husband. These anecdotes, or stories, are brought home by married men, repeated to their wives, by the latter carried to the wives of other men, and thus reach the ears of husbands who have never been in clubrooms, brothels or saloons. No matter how witty they may be they are worse than vulgar, for they carry the swine of nature of the slums into refined homes. A woman makes the following statement to show how easy it is to drop from one level to another:

"I was brought up as a girl under the best influences, having the most careful of parents, and the best schools and religious training. Nothing in all my life had come to me that was vulgar or unclean in thought. I married a man who was my equal in these matters. I had a girl friend who married a man of great wealth, who belonged to a leading social club. Her husband brought home to her many stories that were unfit to be told, but what could I do? I did not feel that I could rebuke her, so I listened and did not laugh, or show any interest in them. I even tried several times to turn the conversation, but she persisted. I must have heard a dozen or more unclean stories. One evening when there were several of us present at her home she, in the hearing of my husband and of her own, referred to the climax of what was known as a 'smutty' story, and the men both looked at me, as if I knew what was meant. From this episode came the still bolder attempt of this friend's husband to tell me a 'new one,' as he termed it. I could not endure the matter any longer, and cut their acquaintance. My husband sustained me in my decision. I then told him that this woman had been telling me these stories for months, but that I respected him too much to repeat them to him. He was glad that I had retained by self-respect and my good opinion of him by doing so. It can be seen how easily the women of different families may mix with the husbands of each other until there is the side glance, the word of temptation, and the ruin of some pure heart who is frail.''

It is true that vulgar stories pave the way to the fall of wives when the couples attempt to make clubs of themselves for the purpose of serving up this kind of mental filth. There is always a greater attraction in the face of another man's wife than in the face of your own, and that woman's husband thinks your wife more attractive than she seems to you. If the law and the voice of society permitted it, men and women would exchange consorts in a most eager manner for the sake of variety. Bargains of that kind have been made in the past, and many of them have been arranged without severing the legal union of the participants. Owing to the explosive moral nature of humanity under the least temptation, it is not wise to aid it by influences of the kind suggested. The purity of the wife is of greater importance than the purity of the husband; and he owes it to himself, to her and to the world at large that she be kept free from all acts and thoughts that will contaminate her.

The husband will have a more loyal wife if he sets her the example himself of the standard he expects from her. He should be above all appearances of evil in mind and act. His associations and conversation with other women, whether in the presence of his wife or not, should be free from all familiarity or good-fellowship. The reserve and dignity that a gentleman owes to any person for whom he has the highest respect should be maintained towards all women at all times.

Commonplaces about the house are to be decreased. Some men and women make good-fellows of their help, servants and employes. This is not best. The husband whose wife has female servants or attaches owes it to her that he be not familiar or common with them. If there are male employes in the house, the wife should hold a distance of manner towards them. Nor is it wise for the wife to be common with her female attaches as she is with her daughters; nor for the husband to make his male attaches as familiar as he would his sons. Dignity is always a sign of the higher nature in man and woman, and there is a severe drop in that quality when one class mixes too freely with the other. Every person in his or her place is a good rule.

Criticisms are commonplaces.

They generally can be avoided, for a magnetic person knows how better to convey the correction sought without the use of a critical remark than with it. Diplomacy is a name for evading giving offence or hurting one's feelings. There are a dozen ways to avert such unpleasantness if there is mental magnetism to find them. Some men make fierce attacks on wife and employes when anything goes wrong. That is not magnetism. The business man who once scolds his clerk or helper is ever after that of weaker influence. The rough methods are physical, whether they proceed from the body or the mind. The cheap and weak-headed man will always be found cursing and yelling at his men when they are stupid or amiss; just as though stupidity could be cured by a storm, or inability be mended by noise. To offend a workman by verbal chastisement merely clouds his mind, and nothing clear can come out of a clouded brain. If there is wilful dishonesty, the treatment is a discharge where there is no hope of improvement. Most men do not need the assistance of dishonest employes; they are better out of the way.

But stupidity is an inherited fault, and while it may not be eradicated, it may be lessened if the employer has the patience and desire to make the effort. Mistakes are the result of carelessness or inability of some kind. The servant makes them, and the wife makes them. So does the husband. A man about the office who storms at his help is a noise-bag. He has everything to learn about human nature. Some men who do not dare to lift their voices at their shops or offices are veritable one-inch guns at home; they see everything that goes wrong, and set about yelling at those who are at fault. That is cowardly, as well as lacking in magnetism. No wife likes to hear her husband scold anyone, servant or clerk. But she is his target just as often. It would be a most uninviting home for a woman to remain in where the husband could not be cured of this fault.

But when he assails her, either by scolding or by quiet criticism, in the presence of employes or servants, he becomes a very low kind of individual; and he is still more despicable when he makes her his target even of slight criticism in the presence of company or visitors. He has not left in him one particle of the quality that belongs to a gentleman. The rule of personal magnetism is very plain, and is clearly stated as follows:

No magnetic man or woman corrects errors, mistakes or stupidity by scolding or by offensive criticism.

All scolding is evidence of a low cast of mind. No criticism is ever needed, if by that term is meant the use of words that cause mental pain or sensitiveness; and scolding is a much more offensive assault than criticism. It is a battery of words discharged from an empty head at the air in general hitting no mark, although apparently aimed at some unfortunate individual. In women it is a mental disease, as nearly incurable as any constitutional malady of the nervous type. There have been no cases on record of a scolding woman being cured. In her brain there is a section that is abnormally constructed, and she must scold or die. No liquor habit was ever more firmly fixed. It is not only commonplace, but senseless, and without one particle of excuse; for, if a husband is debased and worthless, his wife has made him so. The best men would be rendered brutes by scolding wives.

As magnetism is powerless to put a stop to the operations of the brain that impels the scolding, owing to the lack of tissue there is on which to base improvement, it would be useless for a scolding woman to undertake this study.

But there are some who are only partly under control of this defect, who may check their bad habits by this and kindred studies. Mental magnetism shows the power of ideas. Thus a man who wants to call attention to a fault uses a third person in a very round-about way, and brings the matter home to the party at whom he aims. Take the case of a young man who was otherwise capable, but who had a bad habit of spitting everywhere. The employer did not care to offend him directly, and so dictated a letter to an applicant in the presence of the young man, and inquired what his personal habits were, including that of spitting. The following words were used: "Many young men who are well qualified to rise in their positions keep themselves back by this habit, which grows upon them without their knowledge." The effect was complete.

In another case a man spoke directly to his employe of a bad habit by telling him he once had a young man in his employ who had a certain fault that many have, and that he let him go on that account. There seemed to be no suspicion aimed at this employe, but he possessed sense enough to act upon it and overcome the fault.

There are thousands of cases where wives have adroitly corrected husbands of bad faults by telling them they (the husbands) were free from such habits. "I am so glad you are not like some men; you never pick your teeth in the presence of others. Some men even pick their teeth at the dining table, and there are others who pick their teeth after they have left the table. I saw a man doing this on his front-door step while waiting for a carriage. He showed ill breeding. I have never seen you do such a thing, and I know you would not do it." Statements of this kind may be made where husbands have the reputation of being addicted to such habits, although the wife, who may suspect, has not really seen the fault.

There was a woman who ran through the whole category of evil ways possessed by her husband by apparently fighting some other woman's husband, referring to him as guilty of each fault, until her own husband had ended the bad habit in his own practice. "I do not like to have Mrs. H. bring her husband to my house," said a wife, "because he is all the time working at his collar with his long finger down his neck, and it makes me nervous to see him do it." As a matter of fact, Mr. H. never did such a thing, but the husband did not stop to think of that. He was never told that he had that fault, yet he found himself at it quite often. "I do think what you said about H. has set me doing the same thing," said he; "and I am going to stop it before I get as bad as H."

There are many instances where maids in the house, servants in employ as domestics and otherwise, and laborers have been corrected by this round-about method. A cook who had the habit of getting roasts and other dishes done a long time before a meal, and who was so very sensitive that she would have left had she been criticized, was told by the woman who employed her: ''I am so glad you know just what time to cook meats so as to have them done in plenty of time before dinner. The cook that my friend, Mrs. J. has, gets things too much the other way. She cannot tell time, and has everything done and cold or dried up an hour before dinner.'' Here was a double working of the mind under Mental Magnetism. The cook was, if at all suspicious, looking for criticism on having things done too soon; but she was taken off her guard by hearing the woman speak of her being too late, a fault which she knew she did not have; then, after the suspicion was out of the way, the opposite fault was touched upon by charging it to another cook.

A suspecting mind is thrown off its guard by a hint about something exactly opposite to what is to be discussed.

Every man or woman who is disposed to find fault must remember that no one is perfect; that to err is human, and to be absolutely right in every detail, large and small, would detract from growth. It is only by mistakes and wrongs that improvement is made possible. There should be a disposition to overlook every thing that occurs, if there is no wickedness in it, no matter how wrong it may be otherwise. Just ask yourself, What difference will it make a hundred years from now? As a general rule, magnetism does not look at anything at close range. Everything is seen in the light of a broad vision and distant effect.

This habit of the mind results in a straighter course through life. It is like steering an automobile. The best experts at the wheel take in the whole road, keeping in view the farthest part ahead, with an occasional glance of what is close by; but the mind and gaze concur on the full length of the road in front. The result is that the machine is kept in a straight line when so managed. But there are men at the wheel who are not experts who watch only the part of the road that is right in front of the car. The automobile is constantly veering, bobbing from right to left a few inches only, but enough to make it uneven in its course, and leaving a track that is crooked. The effect of the mind on distance is so strong that this habit of steering has been the subject of many experiments to determine if an expert could avoid the veering motion in case he kept his gaze on the close part of the road. It has been found that the expert does not keep his gaze close to the machine, but far away most of the time, although cognizant always of what is near, yet not studying that part of his way as he does the longer portion. The non-expert sees only what is very near in front of the car. When the expert forces himself out of his habit to observe only the near part of the road, he soon loses the control of the wheel that keeps it in a very straight line of travel.

While this seems a very trivial illustration, it embodies a law of life both physical and mental. It is a double law. It shows what has been shown in many other ways—that the muscles obey the mind in an unconscious way, known as a psychic influence. What the muscles do, on the other hand, the mind will adopt unconsciously. Thus life is shaped by habits.

So in the faults and mistakes that fill the existence of every person day in and day out the same law prevails. Those who are associated with you may not be all you would like to have them. A wife may be careless or stupid. A husband may be weak in his methods and full of blunders. There is a way of reducing all faults, except where the brain itself is lacking in constructive tissue. This reduction may be extended to yourself and to other persons. You may lessen your own defects, as well as those of your associates.

At the same time that this lessening process is going on, it is wise to adopt the long-range view of life. If you see people at close range, which means in their commonplaces, you will steer the craft of life in a wobbling manner. But if you overlook the smallnesses of others, which means to look over them, you will see beyond them. If you take the close-range view, it will be magnified like everything else that is at close range; faults will look larger than they are, and people will seem disagreeable to you. When you seek trouble you look at the little things about you, never at the great ones. It is, of course, an old saying that you can find what you look for; but it is also where you look that determines what you see. And it is how close you look.

Do you know that at close range your dearest friends are unattractive to you under certain circumstances?

Do you know that at close range the little things, the small ways, the trivial character of a person will be revealed; whereas at long range nothing would be seen of them?

Many a woman, having known her lover only in his larger character, has been filled with endless disappointments because, after marriage, she has insisted on knowing all the trivial characteristics that he possesses, and has tried to get rid of them by the scouring process?

Do you know that that brother of yours, whom you once loved and of whom you knew nothing wrong, has smallnesses and disagreeable ways that now make him different from the olden days?

Do you know that your sister is less attractive than she once was because you see her with eyes focused on trivial faults?

Here is a daughter who has married a man of wealth and has moved into a mansion, is surrounded by luxuries and seeks the stamp of approval from a social set that makes its estimate of her largely from the side she displays to public view. Her old mother, living at the homestead in the quiet of life's evening, is plain but lovable, sweet but of homely ways, and always tender of her daughter in thought and deed. This old lady was once a young mother, and when her only daughter lay at the point of death through long days of illness, there was the ceaseless watch and the endless care, the touch of a hand that eased the pain and brought comforts to the bedside; but that mother, now grown aged, is allowed to call on her daughter at stated intervals only and then she must enter at the back door for fear some of the social set may see her.

In the light of new circumstances, the daughter sees her mother at short range and her many crudities are magnified until she is no longer a fit person for the social set.

When days of adversity come, as they may, and the daughter is again in want of love and tender care, she will view life at long range once more, and the faults of the mother will have become invisible. Back to youth when the little girl sat at the knee of the most perfect woman on earth, as it seemed to her then, will memories revert and the old scenes be lived over again; all too sweet to be real in the revival of recollections in after years.

Our homely ways, our old-fashioned temperament, our plain

and simple methods stand out as ugly blotches on the face of the false conditions which are called society. So wicked are these new conditions that they would impel that daughter, in her home of luxury, to deny its plainest room to her mother's body when death came, for nothing shabby could be brought into its precincts.

How many rich women today are not ashamed of father and mother who live on the farm and have not learned the nicer ways of using a fork at the table?

To these social newcomers the crudities and uncouth habits, while not vulgar, are commonplaces, and prove offensive in the presence of their guests. It is not our purpose to settle the question of etiquette here as having a bearing on the peace of mind of children who have grown up into better circumstances than their parents enjoyed. The only fact of importance is the change of feeling toward a person with the change of range in the view.

This feeling acts both ways.

When you begin to observe a person at short range, all the small faults come into sight and are magnified; whereas at long range they would not be seen at all. When things go wrong, and there is very little prospect of a remedy being at hand, it is well to take a very long range, as by asking yourself the question, What difference will it make a hundred years from now?

But this view is not justified when a remedy can be applied.

Therefore, if you have little faults, call them in one at a time, or lessen them; while, on the other hand, paying very little attention to the small faults of other persons. If your consort can be induced to lessen his or her trivial errors and unpleasant habits, that result may be obtained by setting this book where it may be read by such persons; for it will have its effect.

But do not scold.

Do not criticize.

Do not nag.

These are meannesses that take out of married life all the beauty it possesses, and all the hope it was founded upon when the contract was entered into.

In an article just from the press in a magazine is a reference to the personal magnetism of Robert Louis Stevenson; and the following extract will give a light upon what marriage can be made to mean where the commonplaces are lost to view. The writer, after speaking of the characteristics of Stevenson, said: "I saw him in his home, and found a lofty love present there in the simplest forms. I knew him under many varying circumstances, and in his many flights from poverty, undertaken over and over again. * * * Last of all I pried into that period of simple human happiness at Samoa which was the crown and culmination of his life—and as I read, all of a sudden the intense magnetism of the man came upon me also, and I, too, bowed down and worshiped. Why question it, after all? Who can ever explain the attraction of one temperament for another, or the influence of one mind over another? As well one might try to explain the still sadness of a summer night; or the terrific effect of organ music on any sensitive, nervous organization; or any of the other influences, personal or impersonal, which are in a small way psychic phenomena and, therefore, inexplicable. Like all those who have, to a very developed degree, the power of inspiring friendship, Stevenson had felt one or two deeply romantic friendships in his own life, among which might almost be included his attachment to his wife. This lasted from the first days that he knew her as an unhappy woman to the time when she followed him to the South Sea Island, in that earthly paradise to spend the late honeymoon of a profound love. There also Stevenson, who had so often and so gallantly defied death, met it face to face at last, with the pluck which was always his predominant characteristic—asking only that he might pass out of the beauty about him with his mental faculties unimpaired, and 'in his heart some late lark singing.' "

It is wedlock such as this that brings the world nearer to heaven in its attractiveness.

The question may be asked, why destroy the spell that was thrown over the hope of the woman when first she found a lover and felt the thrill of her response to his devotion?

Look at that word, *devotion*. It has a pleasing force as it is written. It holds a power that might lift all humanity up into a better realm. During the days of courtship, it is said that the two lovers are devoted to each other; but how often is that term used of married couples? The suitor says: "I offer you the devotion of a true heart.'' After marriage, if he is shown the letter that contains the statement, he laughs at it and says it must have been written when he was daffy. In that one denial, villainous and baleful, is contained the low dregs of the human heart, outpoured on the altar of marriage.

There is hardly any need of special vision with which to look into the home of which he is ostensibly at the head. 'It is full of commonplaces, and there is nothing else there. It is cheap, flip, dreary, unwholesome in every part, and a constant shifting from one mood to another, all of the darker sorts. The wife has no future in this world with that man if he cannot bring magnetism into his life, or she does not succeed in bringing it to him by her own powers, such as will be described in later parts of this work.

The husband is generally at fault when the commonplaces appear in marriage, but not always. The kind of wife that has been referred to many times herein is fully as culpable as the husband. But, as a rule, the husband, being coarser-grained in his ethical nature, is the one that drives out of the union those better sentiments that give it a place above the common drift of life.

There are all sorts of ways of living.

Some folks eat, sleep and let everything else take care of itself. Some do not care what they eat, so that they get enough. Some do not care where they sleep, so that they are allowed to sleep somewhere. The tramp that selects the barn loft, or the empty freight car, or the trench by the stye, is contented with his lot. Anything better would jar on his nerves. This same principle, slightly raised in point of convenience, prevails in most marriages. It is eating, sleeping and working. Once in a while there comes the opportunity for diversion, which is enjoyed more in the anticipation than in the reality.

Both parties ate before they were married, and, therefore, the union was not necessary for that service.

They both wore clothing, were housed, and went through with the duties of life in some form or other, so that wedlock did not bring them something new in these things. In fact, there was nothing that of itself depended on matrimony for its having; so that the inducement must have been some hope that had lingered for a long time in the hearts of both.

In the form of that hope marriage held a charm that was strong enough to lure them on. The thought itself was magnetic, and the perpetual enjoyment of a higher relationship that either had ever known was a possibility up to the time than commonplaces began to creep in.

The remedy for those who are now married, and who have settled down to a prosaic existence, is to drive out, one by one, the commonplaces of each day, until there is a different atmosphere about them. Hunt for these little things that take the edge off the finer sensibilities. Make a list of them. See how many commonplaces you will be able to include in that list. Learn what a commonplace is. If you have one, or ten, or a hundred, get acquainted with them, and so recognize them, in order that they may be avoided.

A woman some years ago, whose married life was so dull and uninteresting that she wanted to fly from it all, no matter how she got away, was told to list all her commonplaces, not paying any attention to her husband's. At first she did not think she had any; in a week she had found ten, a month later she had found twenty-eight, and in three months she was sure of fifty. She made herself familiar with the impulses and habits that brought them into activity, and she carried on a campaign, as she called it, against them, one at a time.

The first commonplace that she conquered, according to her report, was carelessness in her attire. She found herself wearing torn dresses and clothing with some buttons lacking. In a week she had all her dresses and other clothing mended. Her husband did not notice the difference, but she felt better over the fact. Then she had been in the habit of wearing soiled clothing, some of her outer garments being dirty, and others in need of cleaning. This fault was remedied. As a third commonplace she was of the opinion that she talked too much in a vein that did not impress him as the height of good sense. She did not do, as some women have done, become silent all at once, and have him ask her what was the matter, she was so still; but she lessened her chatter ten per cent. at least, and took themes that were of better quality. Still he did not seem to notice any change.

It was very gradual.

She had been slangy. So had he. She dropped slang terms,

one by one. He was less inclined to be slangy, but he hardly realized that her care of her words was having an influence on him. It was an instinctive change; such a care in the choice of words that a person will take in the presence of some individual who is respected. If you command respect by your methods you will generally get it from others.

On mornings, evenings, Sundays and holidays when there had been no occasion for fixing up, she had paid no attention to looking her best for him. Little by little she adopted a new plan, and began to look better. This seemed to make her more attractive to him, and she went still further, until she was always neat and well appearing in his presence when they were up and dressed. She even became more tidy in her undress habits. A woman can be slack or neat at all times. It costs very little extra effort to be at one's best.

At the dining table she had not always been as ladylike as she could have been, and so she adopted the rule as follows: When at the table think that there are many persons near by at other tables who can see everything that is done, and behave so that there can be no criticism of any act.

She found that there are several degrees of conduct that may be employed in eating and serving at the table. She set as her mark the imagined fact that she was dining with some very great personage, before whom she wished to appear a well-bred lady. How would she eat if her husband were her lover, and this was their first meal together? These thoughts had an effect upon her, for day by day she became a better-bred woman, and the transition was so gradual that he never knew fully what was going on. But he felt that greater care was being exercised, and at last, in a burst of wonderment, he said: "Bess, I have been feeling for some time as if I was dining out."

She did not become active and bring him his slippers, get his evening gown, and do the things that a wife, shortly before Christmas, might do; but she began to note that there were little matters in his own clothing, and in other things that might add to his comfort that she could remedy as well as not; and these, one at a time, were made right. He did not know how it came about; perhaps he thought it happened so by some law of nature; but he was pleased by the change.

Her tastes in a literary and musical line were next to receive attention. She had been exceedingly devoid of ambition to improve her mind or her love for the beautiful side of life; and now she thought she could do so with some advantage to him and to herself; for a wife draws her husband to her by these influences. Better books were secured from the library. Novels were laid aside. She had a piano, and a higher class of music took some of her attention. A few of the classical pieces that she had mastered when she was in her period of betrothal were reviewed and brought out with fine effect.

Her husband did not seem to care for them. But, as all that is classical in music grows on one's attention by repetition until it is appreciated, he soon found a real desire to hear these selections. Had she given up after a dozen repetitions of them, she might have thought that he no longer cared for high-class music. She used to sing, but the commonplaces of marriage had caused her to drop that line of entertainment from her life. Now she came back to some of the songs that he liked; and one evening he asked her to repeat certain songs for him. Another evening he said: "Bess, if you are going to sing and play this evening, I think I will not go to the Club, as I would rather hear you than the men." A tear stood in her eye and her voice choked, but she went bravely on, and he had a royal time alone with his wife. It was different from that other occasion years before, when, for the first time, he put on his hat and coat, and told her he was going out to see some friends, as he was tired of being housed so much. A tear then stood in her eye, for it was the first time that he had made known the fact that he was tired of her whose society he had so longed for when their courtship was yet very new.

One morning when she sat alone and pondered on the way she had been treating her husband in the years that had been so dull and prosey, she came to the conclusion that she had not been as gracious in her manner to him as she formerly was in the first years of wedlock. She knew it would not do to make a display of a change, for she despised pretence and sudden resolutions to do better that might flash in the pan and soon be cold again. She much preferred to let things drift along in easy gradations, so that he would not suspect and charge her with some kind of reform, for this would humiliate her. She did not know why, but she dreaded it.

So she became more gracious.

The smile that women assume she could not adopt. She was too sincere; but she did make herself quietly agreeable and pleasant in her manner, and in all she said and did. She looked upon life at long range.

They sat alone in the twilight, and once he talked about their future, about their prospect for being better off, about a better home, and about themes that lured on to a more satisfying existence. She had never heard him talk like that before; nor had he felt sure of an audience had he tried. But now they seemed to be coming closer together in life's firm purpose to rise in the world, and he wanted to formulate an ambition to such an end.

As the twilight deepened, and as the coals from the fire sent shadows across the room, a prayer went up from her heart that he might learn to know her better; that she might make him worthy of the best wife in the world, and that she might be that wife to him.

The commonplaces were dropping out of that home.

Her birthday came. There had been several of them since they were married. Before the wedding, and during the first months of the courtship, he had brought her beautiful flowers and dainties that she loved. Once after the marriage he had given her a very plain bouquet, but that was all; and after that she never knew whether he was aware of the return of her birthdays or not, and she was too proud to mention them to him. But now, wholly unsolicited and without reminder from her, he did remember, and he brought to her the biggest bunch of the grandest roses that could be had in the city. And he had other presents. And he had a surprise dinner for her, arranged all without her knowledge. She seemed to expect this attention, for she was not moved in the least by it. He wondered why she did not make a great demonstration of the gratification in return for the revival of the olden regard. But she was nonchalant. This annoyed him.

At length when the day was ended and they were alone she went to him as he sat with his face buried in his hands, and she said:

"I did not thank you before the others, and I did not let on that I was surprised, for I wanted them to think all these attentions were regular occurrences in our married life." She placed one little hand in his, and they sat there in silence. At length he drew her to him and he took her in his arms, as he said: "Bess, I love you more than I ever did before in all my life. I do not know what has been coming over me of late, but I know that I love you, and that I am intensely happy with you."

The foregoing case is absolutely true in every detail, and has been repeated in other homes more than once.

It is useless to say there is no magnetism in decreasing the commonplaces of life.

When such decrease will gradually take you back to the first days of courtship, it means that there is a power behind it that is capable of changing human nature. What was it that made you forget your wife's birthday? What was it, after the reply that gave her to you as your affianced wife, long before the marriage had taken place, that made her less and less desirable to you, and that took off the fine edge of your devotion to her, even before the wedding day was agreed upon?

What was it that made matrimony seem dull and wearying after the first weeks of novelty had passed?

It was a simple law.

It was the law of retrograding back into the tiresome sameness of existence, and it was brought about by the appearance of one commonplace after another. As they came into your life and her life, the beautiful devotion fled, and she was a very common piece of clay, not by any means as charming as the wife of your neighbor, of whom you know nothing in a common way.

Every man and woman possesses personal magnetism, but they do not retain it. About one in a thousand hold some degree of this power, and all others let it slip through their nerves. They are like men with high wages and higher expenses; they have all they can do to keep alive, whereas, if they were to save one per cent. of what they earned as a sinking fund against future use, they would soon be independent.

True personal magnetism is founded on two influences:

1. The prevention of physical and nervous leakages.

2. The attainment of an inexplainable charm.

That which charms us is something out of the ordinary. The

people who have lived in lands where there are royal families and nobility rarely ever desire to get rid of them, for they are parting with a kind of worship that must exist in the human heart or it will die of famine. In the times and movements of democratic feeling, when caste is leveled to the ranks of the hodcarrier, there rises up the love for something that appeals to the fancy. In the simplest forms of religious worship among the peoples of earliest Caucasian civilization, there was the outer temple, and the inner temple, and the holy of holies. To-day in the Christian church that touches the lowest and simplest forms of civilization, there are ceremonies proportioned to the dearth of other means of attracting the imagination; and these rites rise higher as the people fall lower in their social rank. An army of invisible saints hover over the earth, with new ones being canonized every year.

Thus the love of a charm that is inexplainable in its character and power dwells in human life and draws it up out of the dregs of toil and suffering, planting beauty where roughness and shadowy forms of gloom would otherwise rule all the world.

If there were 365 days in the year all alike, and all on the same level, people would go mad with the commonplaces. Discontent follows a crowd of commonplaces. Men in the severity of unvarying toil lose their minds, and women who are kept in one line of duties go insane or break down both nervously and mentally. If you keep a child in a dull monotony of existence it will become weak in its brain, no matter how much power of muscle it may acquire. There are men today who have no charm before them to lure them on; they fall into ugly tempers and are bad citizens. One kind of work, and one thing or one line of things to think about all the time, makes the mind both stupid and irritable, and from sameness come the breakdown and desire to end it all as quickly as possible. Women seem as if they would like to fly out of themselves because of the awful monotony of the same flood of duties, with no hope ahead for something different.

If there were all week days in the year, the world would never endure a half century. The injection of the seventh day of rest is an inspiration coming from a power that is higher than human invention. The duty of all men and women then is to make Sunday different from the six days of the week; different in every way; different in the meals, and in the arrangement of them, different in the appearance of the house and the clothing that is worn, different in thought, duty, work, diversion and everything the ear hears, the eye sees, and the body comes in contact with. It pays to have some attraction in the house, and some attraction out of doors that is in harmony with the best ethical sense; not the games that are suited to working days and their holiday releases, nor the things that can be had on week days.

We are not appealing to men and women to attend church if they do not desire to do so; but we do ask them to dress as well as if they were going to church and to be in their best dress all day long; to have something beautiful and attractive, although quiet and in accord with the sweet idea of peace in their minds and customs on this one day in the week. Let the change be complete. That is all that is asked. It should be a radical and thorough change on account of the relief it will bring to the mind and to the nerves. Of itself, if there can be a "wholly different" day on Sunday, fifty-two times every year, it will do more to make the mind normal and the nerves controllable than any other single influence.

That day should be freed from the commonplaces, and lifted in an ethical sense to a higher plane. If the public as a whole cannot and will not do it, then the husband and wife should do it. The Sunday paper should not be read until after the last hours of a true Sunday have been spent in something better; for there is nothing that will so quickly cause the mind and the body to drop to a low level than the Sunday paper, with its sensational murders, gossips, scandal, racetrack gambling, sporting news and inane comic sheets, the most imbecile offerings of the human mind, or what remains of it after a few years of dabbling in such sewerage. These influences are the most degrading in modern civilization. That man or woman who wishes to be thought endowed with personal magnetism can make no better test than to refuse to admit a Sunday paper in the house. Have you enough magnetism to set your will up against your lower tastes? Which is stronger in you, the depraved desires for the garbage of human life as it is served

in some newspapers, or your personal magnetism in its effort
to keep such filth out of your mind?

Try it, and let us know which is master.

Also, when the rubbish and sickly sensations, the diabolical
crimes, the scandal and the suicides, the gambling that is
daily encouraged by the papers, the silly cartoons that most
men and some women have come to regard as witty, when they
are only inane, the flingers of mud against every public and
prominent person of the nation, the ridicule of all good customs, the pretended charity sought to deceive the public, and
the smearing of everything that is beautiful and sacred with
the ink of the press, all tend to destroy the charm of life and
fill it with commonplaces and much that is worse. Some day
there will be a daily press that will publish the news as a
line of current history, retaining only such facts as would be
worthy of remembering ten years hence. Here and here alone
is the test, outside of the weather and official statements.

The Sunday papers have well nigh destroyed the day of
rest. They have almost wholly taken away the charm that
the day is capable of bringing into the home, and in the place
of all that once was beautiful they have brought crime, suicide, gambling and scandal. How many of our students will
go on record as having enough magnetism to keep Sunday
papers out of their homes? How many others can such students add to the list who will do the same thing? Civilization
demands the rising up of an army of brave men and women
to accomplish the return to the era of respect and beauty,
of charm and sweet influences on the one day of the week
that can lift the mind out of its slough of deadening commonplaces.

One day in every seven should be devoted to an extraction
from the dreaded monotony of cheap existence. It's trend
is in an ethical direction.

But there are other days, and they are to be welcomed, the
more the better, when the habits of the working days can be
laid aside and life be lifted up into something beautiful. They
are holidays. Thanks to the hustling and eager enjoyment
of them, the daily paper is cast aside unread, and the day will
not begin with the cutting of throats, the blowing out of
brains, nauseating divorces, attacks on the great men of the

nation, gambling from the racetracks, and the mass of degrading filth that makes up the daily news.

Therefore, on holidays, throw it away unread. Enjoy the period of change. A holiday is supposedly a day in which to get rid of the commonplaces that take the charm out of life. Let is be so in as many ways as possible. If the public are not with you in your efforts to make the times better, you can make your influence felt in your home. Be sure that you try. One home lifted out of the commonplaces is one unit saved in a great nation, and enough units to become a force for good is invincible. It is not numbers, but influences that sway the world. It has often happened that one man has led the way to revolution. There is only one right way, and thousands of wrong ways; and a small band in the right can outgeneral the scattered forces of error. This has always been the movements of history in the past, and must always be the method of civilization in the future. God and one man make a majority.

Be of good heart.

Do not lose courage.

You can become a power in this world if you choose.

What you may be unable to accomplish in changing the public purpose you may win in the realm of your own home. There let all holidays witness the disappearance of commonplaces. Anticipation is the soul of happiness. Prepare in advance, and some days or weeks in advance, some program for each coming holiday. The longer ahead it is discussed the more it will be enjoyed. If you have no family except a wife, let her know that you are thinking of what can be done on the next holiday. If she has been saturated by commonplaces; she will say something that will discourage you, like this: "What is the use? All days are alike to me. It is time enough to see what we will do when the day comes. It is too far off now." These remarks are natural, for they tell you how she has been thinking in the past. The charm of life for her died long ago. Never mind. Go ahead, and refer to it in an off-hand manner once in a while, and let her see that you have been doing a little something for that day. After a few of them have come and been made different from the other days, she, too, will begin to take interest in them.

Skill and good judgment are required to bring about these results. The husband who was ridiculed by his wife for wanting to make a holiday different from any other day, and who desisted with the remark that he was through trying to make home happier, was unlike the other husband who said nothing after that, but showed his purpose in doing something which was better. The greatest of all mistakes is for husband and wife to seek enjoyment in different ways. The man who wants to get happiness in a selfish way will find out some day that it does not pay. All his Sundays and all his holidays belong to his wife, whether he or she so wills or not; and his spare evenings are hers also. If he is in the way at home then, or at any time, it is because she has no faith in his generous impulses to make her happier. The man whose wife is happier in his absence is pretty near beyond salvation, and the fault is generally with him. There was a time when he was wanted or she would not have married him. No woman, except one of depraved tastes, wants tobacco odors and tobacco smoke filling her nostrils and lungs for hours every evening, and on Sundays and holidays. She knows full well that her lungs need pure air, not smoke. There are many homes, millions of them, in fact, that have no air except that which is tainted with smoke from tobacco; and this in times when the lungs are being destroyed by tuberculosis because of want of pure air. No wonder that the wife wants her husband to spend his evenings out. He is gross and selfish who will smoke in the house, and all because he was born with his mouth open hunting for something to wrap his lips around.

It is claimed that smoking is a gentlemanly habit.

This is not true, for it is not allowed on street cars, and on railroads all smokers are herded in the cattle car, known as the smoker. Smoking is not allowed in churches, nor in schools, nor in colleges at instruction, nor in any bank by the clerks, nor in any business conducted by a gentleman. Therefore, the claim that it is a gentleman's habit is not sustained. It is ostracized, despite the fact that it is a numerously pursued habit. Of the Christian Church, Christ is the example for all men to follow, and there has been no portrait of the Saviour showing this so-called gentlemanly habit.

It is merely a sucking and drawing habit, due to the first

action of the lips of the new-born babe. It is not due to the hold that tobacco has on the lips; for in the absence of that weed men and boys suck at and draw dried leaves and even grapevine stems, so fixed is the sucking and drawing habit with which human infants are endowed as the one great automatic habit at birth.

It is a test of personal magnetism to be able to lay aside this commonplace. Wives who pretend to like it do so because that pretence has been schooled in them by the selfishness of their husbands. It is their lower natures that like the habit. Deep down in their hearts their native refinement, now dormant, hates smoking and kindred faults. A man who wants to show his love or respect for his wife should make this test of his personal magnetism.

Drive away all commonplaces on Sundays, on evenings, on holidays, and on all special occasions. Know the date of birth of every member of your family and celebrate it in some way. The poor woman who paid five cents for an artificial holly wreath for her window a few days before Christmas, and kept it hanging there until after New Year's day, and then laid it aside until the next year, when it would serve the same purpose, filled with joy the hearts of her children. It was a departure from the commonplaces, and those children, afterward grown up and able to have homes of their own, held in sacred reverence this simple custom, enlarging it as the years sped, and bringing other homes to adopt the same habit.

In proportion as you make Christmas, and New Year's day, and Easter, and all the better holidays more esteemed, in the same proportion will you add a charm to life by decreasing the commonplaces.

And that birthday. Do not forget it. Get flowers, get a little present, no matter what, even if it costs less than a dime; it is a reminder. Let something better be brought into the house. Do something to celebrate the birthday of each child and each relative. Not much is needed. One carnation or one rose at the side of the breakfast plate will help, for it decreases to that slight extent one commonplace at least; and it matters not so much how fast you are going as it does in what direction you are traveling. When once you have started on the road to lessen the commonplaces, you are moving in the right way.

An endless account of these wonderful little influences might be written here. But enough has been said.

Seek to bring back the charm that hallowed the first weeks of your courtship, when the roses were brought to her because you thought she was worthy of them.

Every woman who was worth asking to become your wife has in her make-up somewhere, perhaps hidden and lost almost hopelessly, but it is there nevertheless, a beauty of heart that you once thought you had detected. That loveliness is still in her. It will not come out now under the power of an invitation. The smile that she once looked for would seem ridiculous now, and the kiss that you thought yourself lucky to get years ago would now be perfunctory, cold and leathery. All is changed. You and she eat, sleep, dress, go through the work of the day and the monotony of the evening, and that is all. Life that began on the edge of Charmland is sunken in the dregs of more commonplaces than you think you will ever be able to drive away.

If you do, in fact, get rid of one commonplace, in its stead will come Sex Magnetism.

When two commonplaces are driven away, then double the power of Sex Magnetism will come in to take their room. This is the method by which life can be elevated little by little to a higher place. It is a fight against the commonplaces that are dumped into marriage. No other kind of magnetism has this to contend with. The orator has his audience, his distance, his auditorium, and the better conditions that attend careful preparation. In the pulpit are many influences that help the preacher. In the courtroom the jurymen are mostly strangers to the advocate, and he has his time of getting all things ready for the plea in behalf of his client. Every profession has its helps to the men and women whose magnetism must fight its way to victory.

But marriage drifts to nothing but commonplaces. In that familiar relationship it is possible to dump every bad habit, every foul custom, every littleness, every bit of bickering, every neglect, every aptitude for laziness and slackness, and every fit of irritability. The wonder is that wedlock stands up as well as it does under this fearful strain; and the coming freedom of women everywhere will open the door to their egress from this nasty and bestial life. They are not called upon to endure it, and there is no power on earth that will compel them to do so. Even the mother love of children will not in the near future be strong enough to force them to remain in the home with the average man as he is now constructed in his habits. There was never a time when women took the reins in their own hands in this regard as they are doing today. Ten years ago the separations, legal and otherwise, were less than one-third what they are today. This year they are thirty per cent. more than they were last year. Next year they will be larger, and so it will go on until there is an awakening. Homes are being rapidly broken up.

Some generations ago women were extricated from the bondage of slavery in the home. Then she was non compos mentis in law. She has been legally free for some time, but has not realized the meaning of the new condition. The desire for support is now the one impelling reason for marriage, except with the rare few who believe that there is a charm yet in the union of hearts and minds.

Education is fitting women for self-support. Then only the poorer classes will adopt marriage; and, as their temperaments are identical in most instances, they will take up the burden of reproducing the race. What the outcome will be can be surmised.

Many of the marriages that took place years ago are being broken apart, but the severance is occurring in largest numbers in those unions that are most recent. It seems that the newest entrants are the least stable.

In every woman who is worth having, and there are millions, there is somewhere a charm, and a divine beauty that needs a different kind of man to give life and nurture to it; not the man of today, but the man that has once lived; noble in spirit, generous in nature, gallant in conduct, and devotional in his appreciation of the fairer and better sex. It is such a man that is invited to come with us into Charmland.

There are women waiting in great numbers for, such men, and they are worth winning.

Both sexes must possess qualities that are attractive. The finery of clothes and the assumed habits of an evening soon wear away their charm when the eternal grind of daily life begins. You look your best, you act your best and you dress when you know that "your best" is absolutely necessary to win the regard of the opposite sex. But how soon after marriage is "your best" cast aside? Here are two pictures for your contemplation: one is that first evening when you sought to make a deep impression; and the other is the last Sunday morning as you were half-dressed, impatient, fretted, untidy and curt in your remarks.

The secret is here:

Every man has an inner nature that can be made charming if he will only cultivate it into a permanent habit; and every woman has a similar nature. But it must be natural, and not a veneer. It must be drawn out and not skimmed on as a coated surface. There is but one natural way of building a native condition of attractiveness and that is to fight down the commonplaces until they are removed. Then what comes to the character will be natural; otherwise it will be an assumption that cannot withstand the wear and tear of marriage.

The best method is that which was taught many years ago. It consisted in making a list of all the commonplaces that occurred during the day, and keeping up this practice until there were at least one hundred of them. If you try to think of all you possess at once, you will find very few; but if you have the skill of observation you will find scores of them. You surely have at least a hundred commonplaces. See if you can find them. Then charge yourself with them; and, as one after another may be driven out of your life, credit yourself with the gain; and so proceed until you are charming in manner and in heart.

MAGNETIC MARGINS

AINS are made by making margins. By this term no reference to stock margins is intended, as they belong to the field of gambling. There is a margin along the edge of a book, and a margin between the edge of the precipice and the road over which the carriage passes. These are protections to the page and the road. Between the earning capacity of any individual and his expenditures the margin is what is saved. The greater the difference between the two, the greater will be the savings.

It has been stated in the early part of this book that a man who spends all he earns saves nothing; but the man who lives within his income is making gains. If he earns ten dollars a week and spends nine, the margin is one dollar a week, or fifty-two dollars a year. If he makes nine dollars and spends eight dollars and fifty cents, the margin is half a dollar a week, or twenty-six dollars a year. If he earns seven dollars a week and spends five, the margin is two dollars a week, or one hundred and four dollars a year. Thus a married couple who work in the home of their employer, and receive each forty dollars a month, and spend only one hundred and sixty dollars a year, would have a margin of eight hundred dollars a year, or eight thousand dollars in ten years, as is actually the case with a large number of such couples, while a high-priced mechanic who earned fifty dollars a week and spent fifty dollars a week would have nothing at the end of ten years, as is the case with many such men.

The boy who began his clerkship at seven dollars a week and spent five dollars and fifty cents, saved money because he had a margin. In the second year he received ten dollars a week and spent seven making a still greater margin. In the third year he received thirteen dollars a week and spent nine, making a better showing still. In the fourth year he received seventeen dollars a week and spent eleven. In the fifth year, when he was twenty years old, he received twenty-one dollars a week and spent fourteen. The next year he earned eighteen dollars a week and spent seven. When he was twenty-six years old he owned a house surrounded by a large piece of land, and he then married an old maid who was ten years older than he was. The marriage occurred twenty-two years ago, and it has been filled with happiness and blessed with five children, all in perfect health today. The wife looks as young as the husband, and they both seem younger than their years because they have had nothing to worry about. Such a marriage is secure in nine hundred and ninety-nine times out of a thousand, because it is well founded.

Another man who from the time he was twenty years old had earned twenty dollars a week, saving only two dollars a week for a period of forty years, was, as he said, "rich all the time," because he earned more than he spent. The few thousand dollars he had when he was sixty seemed a large fortune to him. But he spoke of himself as coming all along the years ahead of his expenses; independent, and full of that confidence that is born of the margin on the right side.

A margin that is on the right side is known as a magnetic margin. The reason for so terming it is that it is magnetic. Confidence is power, and it is the father of power. Anything that is a margin on the right side gives confidence. It is when there is no margin that the blues come, and a person with the blues has no magnetism. Only optimism begets this power. One cannot be optimistic with the margin on the wrong side. As will power and the use of the principles set forth in the second department of this work will surely bring a magnetic margin, it is useless for a person to find fault with his luck or his goddess of fortune.

There is in the air, in the head, in the heart, and in the blood a drawing power that magnetism works upon and makes active. Just the moment that you set in motion any kind of magnetism it becomes a force that will draw what is called good luck. Some persons are said to have luck in everything they undertake, and others to have failure in everything. "Why is it," asks a friend today with whom we have been talking, "that my brother is worth a million dollars and I cannot get income enough to keep my bills paid?'' That brother seems to have luck in everything. We know him. And we know the one who complains. The former has magnetism, and that draws something to him all the time. The latter has not one bit of magnetism and is a most unattractive man in all his ways and methods, and he repels good fortune.

It is said that money makes money; that if a man once gets a start he will keep on making. This is true if he gets magnetism with his start, otherwise his money will come and go.

But there is a mysterious power, such as is described in the final work of this club, known as Universal Magnetism, that when once it is acquired draws and keeps on drawing other power, and then it is that everything seems to bring luck; everything that is started turns out well; and nothing fails.

All margins are steps toward that mysterious power, if they are on the right side. It makes no difference what they are, all that is necessary is that they be on the right side. The man who spends more than he earns is on the wrong side, and he will be going away from his good fortune because he has no drawing magnetic power.

The feeling of confidence is most helpful. The feeling of satisfaction is founded on something substantial. The feeling of gain as the result of day-by-day work is an inherent energy that keeps the heart strong and the purpose set towards a steadfast goal. These are powers because they are margins.

Any habit that can produce a magnetic margin becomes a power, and each such margin makes the acquisition of others easier and more to be desired. In the first department of this book there are uses of Sex Magnetism that admit of margins. In the second and third departments all the references are on the darker side of the habits that drive the sexes away from each other. Every one of those deleterious habits that you can lessen begins to result in making a magnetic margin. We will not refer to them here, as they have been amply discussed there; but you should know them all. Do not miss one of them. They all stand in the way of success, and no one of them can remain if you wish to win where you now lose. Make a list of them. If you think you are wholly free from them all you are mistaken; and if you think there are some of those faults that you are wholly free from, you should make a deeper study of their meaning, so that you will not be in error.

Begin to build up magnetic margins out of those departments.

Then, in the use of the senses themselves in an affirmative way, there are many opportunities to create margins and gains, all of which will increase your ability to win control over others.

The real gains begin in great strength under the teachings of the fourth department, where the attractive force is like the earnings that are made from week to week; all that is added over and above what is lost is a magnetic margin. This may be explained by saying that a person may have a certain attractive power that counts much in the opinion of others, and that this power may be balanced by faults that detract seriously from the gains. The difference is always in favor of the bad side, and this should not be forgotten. While the principle is the same as in dollars and cents, the amount of difference is figured in another way. One little meanness outweighs a big goodness. If you are brave, and at the risk of your life should save another person from death, that would be an act that ought to always count greater in your favor than all the wrongs you could possibly be guilty of; but human nature, whether of the wife, or the husband, or the general public, is built in another mood.

What could be braver and more heroic, as well as more useful to the nation than the campaign of Admiral Dewey, especially his entrance into Manila Bay over the sunken mines of the enemy, as it was supposed, and into the firing range of the Spanish battleships, carrying war up to them when victory was necessary to avoid his own destruction? He was on the other side of the world, with no aid at hand, no base to fall back upon, and no supplies except what he had on his own boats. The venture was daring, the attack most skillful, and the result will pass down into history as the one great naval battle of the age. Yet, after he had brought all this glory to his nation, and had been given a reception the like of which has had no parallel in modern history, one little act of indiscretion lost him his prestige, and he became the butt of ridicule.

What was his indiscretion? Friends and admirers presented him with a home absolutely his, and free from all conditions; and, to guard against the financial reverses, such as overwhelmed General Grant under like circumstances, he had the title placed in other hands. For this indiscretion, which was entitled to a bad mark of one-tenth of one per cent., he lost his margin of 999 good marks. Margins of conduct, therefore, must be carefully protected from losses of good will. Wellington, the hero of Waterloo, who did what all Europe had been trying in vain to do for many years—end the career of Napoleon—won as high a percentage on the right side, and received the greatest honors ever paid to mortal being; only to be scoffed and to suffer a revulsion of popularity by so simple a thing as a vote on taking beer.

Take the case of the husband who had been kind to his family for all his married life, who had provided well for them in every way, and who sacrificed himself to make them happy, yet who, in a moment of indiscretion, kissed the cook on her birthday. His wife left the home, never more to return. Perhaps she was too hasty, but he had no right to kiss the cook. Balances of conduct are not made by weighing the grade of offence and comparing its gravity with the quality of all the good a man has done. One margin cannot be deducted from another and the difference be allowed to stand, either on one side or the other. The dark act is taken as the measure of the whole man, with the assumption that his better side is largely pretence.

On the same principle right conduct does not attract attention, while one bad act will be heralded far and wide. "Another good man gone wrong" was a saying many years ago to explain the sudden wickedness of a famous divine. In a court trial it is allowable, under certain circumstances, to show by evidence the reputation and long period of honorable life of an accused individual to counteract one act of wrong, and by so doing the law seems directly opposite to human nature, but as a matter of fact it requires many good acts to overcome the effect of one bad one, even in law. If a man has forged a note, and there is doubt as to the testimony, the jury may consider a long life of good behavior, showing the difference in the quantity of the margins. But there seems no other way.

It becomes a question of probabilities.

But this unevenness is not as bad as it would appear on first face. The test is the nature of the offence. Right living is always normal living, and wrong acts are always abnormal. If the latter gives evidence of perfidy or moral turpitude, then it discloses character that must be behind all the outward display, just as treason is inexcusable even after a long life of loyalty. Circumstances sometimes combine in a freakish way to make a husband or wife appear perfidious when there is absolutely no guilt at all. The error made is to put the burden of proof on the accused party. A true husband or wife will go slow in accepting so damaging a mass of evidence as may be at hand even when there seems no alternative; for there are cases well established of innocence after the guilt seemed established beyond all controverting.

Personal conduct varies in its kind.

It may be moral or immoral; ethical or coarse; refined or boorish; and attractive in beauty or ugly.

A pretty maiden, handsomely dressed, with hair and adornments at their best, and charms abundant, whose conversation is pleasing and manners seemingly good, would drop suddenly in the estimation of her admirers if she were to be seen chewing gum, sucking her teeth, or cleaning her nostrils out with her finger, as some pretty girls are in the habit of doing when they think no man is watching them.

In such a case there is a large margin on the right side and a small one on the wrong side, but the later is intensive, while the former is extensive. The smaller margin outweighs the larger one.

Selfish and dishonest margins are not magnetic. Thus the girl who was heiress to a large estate, and who could not correctly spell ordinary words in her letters to gentlemen, was desired as a wife nevertheless. It was a dishonest margin; money outweighing a serious fault. An educated man would have very little liking for an ignorant girl; and the desire to marry her for her money is but a willingness to earn it.

With an understanding that perfidy or treason to wedlock is generally unpardonable, all other offenses may be put in the scales against the good side of a person, and the margin will be considered in the light of both views. A woman who has been well treated by her husband will let that balance his boorish ways, but there will be no magnetism, and nothing but tolerance, which is unpleasant.

All persons are earnestly advised to master the teachings of the fourth department, for thereby the attractive force is acquired, and the errors and failings that detract from them are reduced to a minimum. All margins made therein are magnetic.

In the fifth department the sex influences become the basis for further margins; and then comes the sixth department with some guiding principles that add still more gain to the progress already underway. The next step is to cultivate the heart interests of the seventh department and add more margins. In the next two departments great care has been bestowed upon the five magnetic laws that apply particularly to this study. We come now to

THE GREAT LAW OF SEX MARGIN.

The expenditures of vitality must be less than the income.

By taking the earnings of money and the uses made of it as the simile, it will be found that the principles remain the same. There should be a greater income of vitality than expenditure, just as there should be a greater income of earnings than expenses of living. In other words, a person should live within his income. Earn more than you spend. We find ourselves face to face with the question of physical and nervous vitality. Countless examples may be gathered all along the line.

There is no better illustration of a margin in vitality than that seen in the uses of the appetite. A person who is hungry has that much advantage over one who has no keen desire for something to eat and will digest and assimilate the food that much better. If you sit down at the table hungry you will draw into your system the nutrition from the food; whereas, if you are not hungry, the food will be of less value as nourishment. Then, starting hungry and keeping hungry all through the meal, you will have the same advantage; the margin being helpful to you all the time. As appetite and magnetism go together, it is important that you learn to come to a meal hungry, remain hungry all through the time of eating, and then arise from the table hungry. By this is not meant that you are not to eat all you need; but you must not destroy the entire hunger at the table.

If you are starving, your hunger is placed at one hundred per cent.

If you are very hungry, your margin may be placed at fifty per cent.

But suppose it is a case of great hunger, but not enough to bring on neuralgic headache, which is evidence of too long a period of not eating, or else an insufficient breakfast, or loss of vitality in some way which should be avoided; suppose you are hungry enough to be ranked forty per cent., and that this is the case at the beginning of every meal; then, as you eat on half through the meal, you will have reduced the margin to twenty per cent. When you are nearly through, the hunger is only fifteen per cent.; and as you are done, you arise from the table ten per cent. hungry. This means that nine-tenths of all your demands have been complied with, and one-tenth left open. You will go away still a little hungry.

This is a magnetic margin.

Why?

Because you have not surfeited, nor even filled up.

A filled up person is never at the highest vital point, for the body has no working margin.

Take the case of the steam boiler; fill it full of water and set it to boiling; how much power will be generated? None, for there is no margin left in the boiler in which the steam may be formed. If you have too little water you will have too much margin and the power will be excessive. It is in such excess that boilers blow up. But in human beings the greater the resistance that accompanies the margin, the more vitality may be created.

As fuel in the body is the physical cause of all life and vitality within it, so the surfeiting or over-feeding of fuel will make it impossible to generate the proper degree of energy. A person arising from a meal is taking away with him the source of his vital powers. He may be in one of three conditions:

1. Just filled, which means that he has fully met the desires of his appetite.

2. Surfeited or stuffed, which means that he has over-eaten.

3. Underfilled, which means that he has eaten less than his appetite demanded, and that he has a margin of hunger as the basis for the next meal.

There has never been a magnetic person who ever lived, or who lives today, and there will never be one who will live in the future, who has been, or will be, addicted to the habit of stuffing; for gluttony does not permit of magnetism. It is constantly lowering the health and vitality of the body.

Some degree of magnetism may be generated in those who fill themselves to the capacity of their appetites; but experiment and tests in countless numbers show that the man or woman who cultivates magnetism is the one who has a margin of hunger at the end of every meal. This means that you ought to get up from the table hungry. It is not necessary to be very hungry, but to have a slight desire for something more. Yet how many thousands are full long before they stop eating, and still keep on after they have again added what they did not need; and then there is some extra dish to be taken at the end.

Try the better way.

It is very easy to study this margin, for it will soon be realized. Persons who try to analyze themselves soon are able to fix some percentage to their hunger, both before sitting down and on getting up. So small a margin as one per cent. serves a good purpose in keeping the vitality high. It is attended by the development of some magnetism.

A man at the switchboard does not have to run out in the track yard and take hold of the great levers and throw the switches; that would be hard work, and would keep him on the run much of the time. All he needs to do is to stay where he is, make a slight move here, another there, and so control the movements of giant engines and massive trains as they rush on.

It has been supposed that personal magnetism was cultivated by physical exercises only. While there are some nerve exercises in the foundation book, they are but a part of the whole training; and, after that work has been taken, the methods of further developing magnetism are those of habits. You touch this key, and there are results that are quite different from what they would be had the other track been taken. Life may be switched to any one of a hundred or more tracks. Your mind and will power will be at the switchboard, and your conduct will obey your fixed determination to do one thing or another.

One habit destroys magnetism, while another habit develops it. One course of conduct is unfavorable, and another is highly favorable. It depends on how you shift the switches. But you need not go out into the yards and there work with muscles to effect the change. It is done at the switchboard of the will power.

Before there ever were any training courses in the cultivation of personal magnetism there had been for centuries and centuries, and thousands of years, men and women who were naturally gifted with this power; not because they had themselves studied it, but because they had by chance fallen into those habits that tend to develop the gift.

At length such people were separated by observers from all other people, and the difference in their habits were noted. This difference was supposed to be the explanation of the problem why some persons exercise great magnetic control over others, and some people are swayed at will, seemingly having no resistance.

It was found unmistakably to be due to their personal habits.

As one of these habits, it was known that men and women who were gifted with personal magnetism were not gluttons; nor did they overeat. On the contrary, they seemed to limit their meals, to eat up to a certain point, and then to stop. This habit became fixed in their lives. To prove that there was a margin, they were sometimes induced to add something extra after they were through, and they continued eating more food, as where some special dish had been prepared, and the host pretended that there would be offence given by not partaking of it. No discomfort was experienced after this added course. In one case a man formed the habit of eating more than he had been accustomed to, and he fell back in his magnetism perceptibly. Many experiments were made during a period of years to test the genuineness of the theory that habit made magnetism, and that it was due to nothing else but habits, when it was naturally possessed.

The mind will not work well on a crowded stomach, because

it has not the nervous surplus of vitality needed to give it power. Magnetism is largely nervous vitality, and follows the same rule.

Just try this plan of eating. Rise from each meal not quite satisfied. The stomach will make greater use of the food it has taken than it otherwise would, and more of it will be turned into nutrition on that account.

The avoidance of causing pain to the stomach and digestive membrane by eating indigestible food will be necessary; but when this is accomplished then the diminished quantity of food taken at each meal will aid digestion, and tend to bring on a state of remarkable health both of the nerves and the brain, as well as the organic structure of the body, from which all forms of vitality proceed. It is worth the experiment. You will feel better than you have ever felt before in all your life. The difference will be so great that you will wonder why it has escaped your attention before to adopt this habit. If to this you add the still grander habit of ingestion, then there is nothing more to be sought in the health line except food selection and the new era of cooking, both of which have been fully discussed in this work.

It has always been known as a principle of personal magnetism that this power is associated with the energy of the nerves and the general use of the mind and body. It has always been known that every normal man and woman generates personal magnetism in greater or less amount every day.

It is now known that what comes in goes right out in most cases. When the expenditure is greater than the income, life begins to droop, there is nervous prostration and loss of vitality and energy. That this is due to the extra expenditure over the income has been proved by the cultivation of personal magnetism as a cure for neurasthenia, or nervous prostration. When trips abroad have failed, when the baths have failed, when change of scenery and all sorts of influences have been brought to bear on the health of the invalid, after medicines and treatments of every kind have proved powerless, the developing course, as taught in the foundation book in the cultivation of personal magnetism, has brought about a speedy and permanent cure; not once or twice, but in thousands of cases, during the past twenty-five years. One doctor, a great expert in nervous disorders and diseases, said he was sure that this course would never fail to effect a cure, as he had watched its results in many of his own cases.

Thus the close relation between vitality and personal magnetism may be seen. It develops a great fund of vital energy. It supplies that which has been lost. It adds to what is on hand. And, strangest of all facts, it depends on the margins for doing its work in certain lines of progress.

Take the case of the runner who desires to win the race. He has a certain percentage of vitality on hand to begin with. If he runs that all out, as most runners do who are inexperienced, he will not be able to endure the strain of a long race. Even in sprints for short distances the runners hold back some vitality. But in the long contest it is necessary to let out all that can be spared, while keeping in stock a sufficient proportion to feed the body, so that it may continue to generate more. It is a double law. If there is none left, there is no basis for creating what will be needed. A margin of fire is required to keep alive the energy, and to give rise to more.

In all contests this law remains true.

There is the exercise of power in muscle, nerve and mind, and the tendency to let it all out is a common one. The child is not given power enough to overdo, and its over-zeal is never great enough to tax its strength, although its muscles become weary after a while. But it has, in most cases, a much greater vital fund than it has ability to employ the same to the limit. This is due to the intention of nature to keep the child growing until it has built a mature frame. After that its excess of vitality is gradually lessened until, at the approach of old age, it is not enough to sustain any great effort without danger to the heart.

Thus, in a healthy growing body of a child, nature makes her own margin, and sustains it for years after that period. Could the young man and young woman in the twenties be taught then to take up the excess of vitality where nature let it slip out of her control, a different fate would await the race.

But it is only the normal young man and young woman that is given this excess of vitality. When the child has come up out of the vicissitudes of infancy, and the first ten years following it has lost much of its physical and nervous vigor because of a bad diet in the home, the methods of living are far from right there. But nature has been making heroic efforts to pull it through, although one-half, or five hundred thousand children out of every million, never grow up. Death is the reward of an ignorant diet and errors of living. Parents charge this fearful percentage of deaths to the will of a higher power, when it is due always and wholly to their stupidity in the first place, no matter how hard they try to save the sick offspring. They never tried to prevent its illness.

But, assuming that the boy has begun to grow into young manhood, and the girl is on the threshold of young womanhood, then arises the question of natural vitality and normal conditions in all respects. If the vitality then is below the normal, the future is bound to be doubtful, as far as magnetism is concerned. It will rarely come as a gift. But it may almost always be acquired, and when acquired is more useful than if it were a gift, for it is given intelligent direction at all times.

In this work there is no space that can be devoted to the consideration of the general rules of health, or the moral conduct of the boy and the girl. The important point is that which attends the generation and expenditure of that quality which is the distinguishing feature of sex life. It begins with puberty, and endures for many years, being male and female. In the remaining pages of this department it will be called ''quality'' in quotations when that word means the sex nature of one or the other of the sexes.

This peculiar power is not vitality, but is created, in part, by the vitality of the body and nerves, and reduces that vitality as it is itself used. It rises with the energy of the nervous system, and falls as that is decreased. It buoys up that energy, and it also takes it down. It is thus a two-sided power, being dependent on the very life that it saps and that supports it.

Before it appears in any individual it is preceded by the vitality it requires for its own existence, but is not a part of that vitality, except as the energy of the plant is a part of the sunlight on which it thrives. After it has had its day and its life has run down, human existence pales and begins to fade with it, but may continue for decades after it has gone, and that is second childhood. Thus there is truth in the name, for the first childhood preceded the dawn of this power, while the second childhood never appears until it has departed. It seems that without it the mind is of the childish timber.

What is known as "quality" never comes into life, either male or female, until puberty is well established; but it need never go out of life even to make way for second childhood. The coming of the latter condition is, therefore, the result of the waste of "quality" during its years of existence.

This brings us to the threshold of a new and greater law than any we have yet undertaken to explain in this work.

Before it is brought directly before the student it is necessary to have the relation of natural processes made clear in the development of all forms of magnetism; because the claim is often made by ignorant persons, or those who have not probed deep enough into the subject, that magnetism when taught is dependent on exercises.

The fact is that magnetism is an inherent power, and all that any exercises can do is to call it into activity or release it. The small ball of snow at the top of the hill may not be able to start itself, but a very little hand may set it going, and it will then proceed of its own energy, aided by the gravity that is in it and that is in the earth, to gather size and weight until it becomes a mass to be feared.

If a person is known to be magnetic, as all persons are, and is losing the fund of power that gathers daily, and this loss is due to faults of living that may be driven out by attention to them; that is not exercise, but a natural aid to the inherent force born and grown up in every man and woman. But if there are leakages in all persons' vitality that make the accumulation of magnetism impossible, then if those leakages can be stopped by exercises and in no other way, it is the duty of all persons who wish to become acquainted with their own powers, to check the losses in any effectual manner that will accomplish such end; just as the water system of a great city cannot do its best work when there are thousands of weak pipes leaking water in all parts of the system. The man who has the most intelligence is the one who will see the necessity of ending losses.

This rule applies to life in all forms.

It is a rule of business, of health, of government and of war as well as peace. If all persons saved what they lost they would have very little worry about being rich. The first thing to do in the management of home, of the expenses of the table, of the conduct of the office, of every branch of work, business or government, is to look for leakages, and the stopping of them is the beginning of a new era of prosperity.

Then if it is possible to store away personal magnetism by direct exercises that are in accord with the laws of nature, this should be done. All these things constitute the foundation work of this Club, as taught in the first book, which is known as the developing course.

When the fact is discovered in magnetic studies that all persons are subject to the feeling on the one hand of seventy-six emotions, and may learn on the other hand to express them through certain exercises in practicing their increased use, so that in time any person may, by the law of sensitiveness, receive at once from any other person far or near the exact mood that person may be in; then deception becomes impossible and the pretender must go. Assumed feelings, or acted emotions, have no power to conceal what is within the heart. Politeness, fair promises, nice language, and all the methods by which men and women try to make themselves appear more friendly than they are, will be useless covers for their genuine feelings. The world would then, if this culture were universal, find it impossible to cheat, to pretend, to deceive, to mislead, to cajole, to win falsely, to tempt, to subdue, to take any advantage, or otherwise harm or defraud another; and every man and woman who goes into such study will reap the gains that the general public may not secure. Some day, however, it is predicted, the use of emotional magnetism will be generally taught and practiced, which would mean the end of crime and of wrong-doing.

All these things are taught in Advanced Magnetism; but the only exercises are those that develop the power to feel, to receive and to express the moods and emotions that make up human life. All else is the natural unfolding of the methods of near control and distant control, which are inborn in every person, but are lost in the leakage of life through certain habits of carelessness and lack of knowledge.

In a similar way the very different course of magnetic training, Mental Magnetism, proceeds. It deals with the multitudinous uses of thought instead of feeling, and proceeds to the greatest possible results, the benefits of which are so great that no person can fail to gain vastly by the instruction.

But the present work on Sex Magnetism does not build its results on exercises any more than the works just referred to, all of which make up an interwoven system of educational training along magnetic lines.

The summing up of this study may be made as follows:

1. All leakages and losses must be stopped.

2. All power held in check must be released without losses or waste of expenditure.

3. The various forms of leakages must be ascertained, and each in its natural use must be turned into a fund of supply.

4. Artificial power cannot in any way be employed, any more than a substitute can be found for the sunshine's nurture of plants, or the current of electricity's energy can be duplicated in the power-house.

5. Man today in his development of personal magnetism stands where he does in his development of electricity for commercial and mechanical uses; the energy is nature's, but man is finding out how to use it and to become its master. Two generations ago the world would have laughed at the idea of a trolley car, an electric light, a telephone, and the wonderful accumulation of inventions that have accrued to civilization because more knowledge of electricity has been acquired since that time. And what electricity is to the mechanical world personal magnetism is to the human heart, mind and body.

Life is most complex.

Yet it all comes from the sun in some form or other.

The purposes of life are not fully understood today, but magnetism is unfolding them little by little.

For each stage in human existence there is a condition and a power suited to the life as it is unfolded, ever shifting as some new stage is entered upon. These sections of the span of existence are as follows:

1. First childhood.

2. The end of childhood as the impulses of the young man and the young woman make themselves felt in the body.

3. The development of "quality."

4. The impulse of parentage.

5. The weakening of "quality."
6. The appearance of second childhood.
7. The period of waiting for the end.

One of the saddest of contemplations is the too oft-expressed belief that humanity is created solely or principally to reproduce its kind, and that each generation is merely a link in a chain, the end of which is too remote for our enjoyment of its achievements. In almost, if not all, other species the perpetuity of the kind seems to be the only reason why any one of them exists. Parents are continually giving birth to children, and the children are in turn becoming parents, proceeding from one link to another blindly and without any other visible motive.

Centuries, thousands of years, if not millions, may elapse before the goal is reached, and it may be as different from what is now expected as the present age is different from that of the prehistoric man.

This view is not even philosophical.

It is true that every individual in any species, if normal, is but a link in the chain of reproduction. But it does not follow that this is all that such individual is created for. Of course, there must be wants supplied, as food, clothing, shelter and comforts, as well as enjoyment, but these are supposed to be merely incidents of the main purpose of reproduction. It has been argued that if life is made too dull or too uncomfortable, people as they become civilized will take matters in their own hands and give up the battle. The moment you satisfy an intelligent person that there is nothing to life but playing a tool in the hands of nature, and that after this is over nothing follows, then that person is pretty sure to become a bad citizen, and to seek existence only so long as it can be enjoyed, after which the end will be brought about.

But the reply to this claim is that a normal mind is satisfied that there is another life after this, and that immortality awaits all who wish it, while annihilation is the fate of all who do not desire immortality by their decision made in this world.

This is the test of a thoroughly sane mind. Any other view indicates present or inherent mental defect. No normal person will ever think of self-destruction. It is not the weight of woes and disappointments that break down the desire to live; for in the darkest ages millions of men and women suffered torture, lived in underground passages and were subjected to all the agonies that superior force could inflict on them, and this for many centuries in the name of Christianity, during which period there were practically no suicides among them. Today, in the light of modern comforts, what poverty suffers now would have been regarded as palatial luxury by those former people; yet today suicides are increasing at a fearful rate.

Civilization has grown faster than the vitality of the mind that participates in it. We stand in this era at the very door of a new earth, and the progress that has been going on for countless ages is not far from its culmination today. A recent article presents the following account as upheld by the most learned men of today:

"The total of the geologic periods of the earth is calculated by such an eminent authority as Professor Ward, of Brown University, to be about 72,000,000 years. Man, however, has existed, according to the best evidence, for about 250,000 years, but has only been of a sufficiently high order of intelligence and really alive mentally to his opportunities for about 5,000 years. His work, however, has been largely done within the last 3,000 years, and so it is plain that comparatively he has just commenced his existence. His growth has been rapid, and within the past 500 years great strides in intellectual achievement have been made. The secrets of nature and science have been fearlessly attacked and ruthlessly solved, and yet man is only on the threshold of his career. Saint Simon, the eminent French writer, said 'man's golden age is before him, not behind him,' and what man will achieve in the future no one can predict. The mystic forces of air, electricity, steam and flying mechanism are being utilized, and as the door of invention opens to revealed secrets it but shows other doors further down the pathway of research, awaiting the crowbar or the key of the coming scientist. What the years have in store for us no one can tell, but that the past, brimful of achievement as it has been, has exhausted the possibilities of invention and discovery no one will believe. And so facing greater revelations of scientific knowledge and greater insight into the world of mystery that surrounds us, we can well await with interest and, indeed, with a measure of awe, further investigations into the wonders yet unknown to us, but which are destined to become a part of our cosmic knowledge.''

Here, then, are two views of the place of humanity in the range of progress that extends from the dim past into the present hopes of the immediate future.

One makes man an animal.

The other makes him the climax of earth.

If he is no more than an animal, his part in the progressive march of life on this globe is only to be one of millions of connecting links, and his chief office is to do his share in reproducing the race so that it will not die out and end that progress.

Of all the species that have been created, the human is the only one that possesses what is called in this department as ''quality.'' In all else it is merely impulse, which, being used, ends itself, until a new impulse comes to take its place. There is no magnetism present.

Taking the optimistic view of life, we find that the purpose of everything is advancement. Earth is advancing because the human race is going forward, and this era is one of climax. The human race cannot go forward except as its individual members improve themselves, and this is done by the energy shown in sex attraction. In the first departments of the present work this attraction has been fully explained. By analysis it resolves itself down to a simple focus which is herein termed ''quality.''

As long as ''quality'' can be maintained, then there will remain the attractive force that impels one sex to so respect the other that the best side of existence is always turned toward each other. This means that the conditions of marriage and of home life will be improving all the time, and that the advancement of the world is only the sum total of its individual progress.

Marriage as it exists today in great part is but the dumping ground of animalism. Where it has been elevated to something better there has gone forth from it an influence that has been felt through its radial magnetism far and wide. The animalism of marriage follows the loss of ''quality.'' It was not present in the better days of courtship, when the maiden was worthy of the American Beauty roses, the perfumed candy, and the delicious attentions that were upheld because there was ''quality" urging them on to a display of their better natures. Then the girl was at her best, and the man was at his best. If all the world could remain as this couple once was, what a change would come over the human heart!

There are seven ages to the two sexes.

They have been stated in a previous page. The first is childhood. Here the boy and the girl should be raised as differently as their opposite natures demand. The boy should not be surrounded with the same influences as the girl. His toys, his plays, his interests should be of the boy's kind, and should be made distinct all the time he is passing through the years between infancy and young manhood. There are exercises for him that are called forth in a natural manner by his methods of play and the kind of tools and toys that are given him. He should be made to think as a boy and of some day being a man. He may be controlled for a lifetime by the teachings his mother or father gives him in these years of plastic youth.

The girl should be given her separate toys and work, her mental, heart and physical interests, all different from the lad. As she grows she should not be made weak and delicate in the supposition that it is feminine to be so; but her body should receive full growth in all its parts and be developed for strength and endurance in those functions that will some day appear; the foundation of which should be built years before that era. Diet, fresh air and activity of as varied a kind as possible should receive attention. Many little girls are sickly because their food is not balanced; they are allowed to eat one line to the exclusion of other kinds. This brings on thin blood, deranged nervous system, and weak heads. They are unfit for the vocation of wife. In fact, there are not three girls in a hundred who are in their teens today that are really qualified to enter wedlock, if we seek them among the middle and higher classes.

Surface conditions are not enough.

The greater the mental variety in the first years of any child's life the sounder the mind will be made. Erratic natures and temperaments may be thus avoided. The three rules that make the well-developed young man and young woman are:

1. The interests that excite and absorb the mental attention should be of the widest variety suited to the infant's and young child's life.

2. There should be every variation of physical activity, and as much of it as possible should occur in the fresh air.

3. The diet should be balanced so as to provide an all-round support to the body and all its operations and bring into perfect condition every part and every organ. Lack of a balanced diet results in the misfortunes and maladies that are peculiar to youth and the years that follow.

It requires but little study and but little attention to these matters to change the whole course of a child's life.

The second stage of sex growth is that period between the premonition of coming puberty and the development of "quality." In the first years of that period it may or may not be possible for the boy or girl to enter parentage; but, if so, there will be none of the "quality" that makes Sex Magnetism. This second stage may begin on an average about the tenth or eleventh year; sometimes before, and oftener later than that time. It generally ends in the fifteenth or sixteenth year, when "quality" is established. The fitness for parentage is merely a physical condition. A girl who is deeply in love before she is fifteen is a rare exception; but sixteen marks the birth of what is called the first fancy, and it is a very severe disappointment if its object fails to respond to it. The boy has about the same experience and at about the same time in his career.

It has been shown in the physiology of both sexes that a girl or a boy may become a parent two or more years before there is any feeling such as is called love. Thus there are instances of a girl becoming a mother as young as nine years of age; and in the Southern States it is not a very rare case for a girl eleven to thirteen to become a mother. Yet in all such occurrences love has never been felt, and what is called "quality" is wholly absent. Boys have been married as young as twelve, and some have become fathers when they were not yet thirteen years of age; but love, so-called, has been wholly apart from their minds or hearts.

This, then, is the second stage of sex life; coming between the first premonitions of puberty and the development of "quality."

The third stage includes the many years, more or less extended, when "quality" is present as a potent force in the life of a man or woman. This will be discussed in the present department.

The fourth stage is included in the third. It is that in which the impulse of parentage is present. Most men in their younger years do not like children, and young husbands desire to avoid having them born. Even after they have come as unwelcome guests, the father-love is not then like the mother-love, nor like the father-love as it develops when the man is out of his teens or out of his twenties. It is when the contemplation of loneliness in old age brings the desire for a new generation growing up to take the place of others who have passed before or who will eventually, in the averages of nature, be out of the arena of existence, that the man feels the impulse of parentage. At first he rejects the idea through his own selfishness, and then he is swayed by the longing for companionship in the later years of life.

But nature helps him out of his dilemma, as she has an abundance of tricks by which children are given him whether he wants them or not. Some come too early and others too late for his full enjoyment of their social characteristics. It is a peculiar phase of man's disposition that he is not only willing, but is even eager, to have the unborn babe destroyed; and he does this under the pretence that his wife's health demands it. When he is in his teens or twenties this disposition is the strongest; but it gradually weakens as he advances towards the forties, often becoming just as strong in the opposite direction, for at the later period of his mature life he feels the longing for children. This characteristic should argue in favor of late marriages for men, or in favor of women delaying wedlock with men who are not eager for children.

When the child is unwelcome by both father and mother its life is morbid, and the world is full of people who, when it was known that they were in prospect, caused bitterness of feeling and often quarrels between their parents. For the benefit of the race and in the interests of healthful minds in true men and women for the next generation, marriage should be founded upon a mutual desire for offspring; and should be delayed until such desire is apparent. All other marriages are extra-natural; they need not take place. There is not one reason why they should be encouraged. If one or the other of the couple is unable for physical reasons to become a parent, then both should understand that fact and, if they are already wed, they should resolve to be true to their vows as long as they live. But if they are not yet married, and have knowledge of their condition, the unction should be avoided.

Yet the marrying of such persons is of less importance than the choking off of children for selfish reasons. The unborn child should be wanted; not merely tolerated, but really and earnestly desired, and for months before its coming. In order to bring about this blessed welcome, several things should occur:

1.   There should be ability on the part of both parties to maintain the state of matrimony, not only for a few years, but for a long period of existence in health and happiness.

2.   There should be a home in which the child is to be born and reared; not a tenement, nor a flat, nor a boarding-house, nor a hotel; but a real home where the family may dwell for many years.

3.   There should be an affirmative eagerness on the part of the mother for the coming of a child.

4.   The father should want offspring and should act deliberately in the matter.

5.   The child, wanted and hoped for by two parents who are happy with each other, and in a home where the institutions of domestic life and of child life may be firmly established and maintained for an indefinite period, should be the central influence around which all that part of the world revolves.

6.   In these combinations there will be a new earth.

The young woman in her teens rarely ever wants to become a mother. Some are willing, and once in a while there may be one who is eager; but it is not the usual experience, especially today. In the early twenties the desire of motherhood becomes a half negative; that is, the wife does not care much either way; but in the late twenties and early thirties the normal woman wants to bear children. Then the impulse of parentage is keenest. It is generally true that a woman who is past thirty when she gets married will want to begin at once to raise a family, and the lack of it will be the non-desire of the husband.

There is every reason why parentage should be delayed until the parents, or one of them, shall have passed thirty years of age. In the younger years the children will be neglected because of the immature judgment of the parents; they will not thrive as well, and death will mow them down in greater numbers. Of all the deaths of babes, and children, numbering half a million in every million, it appears from statistics that ninety-two per cent. of the fatalities of this kind come to the offspring of parents who were under thirty years of age when parentage began; and most of them under twenty-five years of age. Less than eight per cent. occurred among the children of parents who were over thirty years of age when they were born.

This fact shows that young parents either do not know how to take care of human life, or that they do not have the same eager desire to do so. Mothers who were in their teens when their babes died have not shown the grief that is present when mothers are in the twenties and lose children; but the most intense suffering comes when the mothers are in the thirties at the time their first-born come into the world and afterwards die. This proves that mother-love is coincident with the impulse of parentage. If child-bearing can be delayed until one parent at least is past thirty, then the children will be more loved, will be welcomed with greater zeal, will be protected in health to a much greater extent, and will have the influence of mature minds to look after them in their infancy and as they grow up. They will not be left at any time to look after themselves. There will be no more of them than the home can maintain and everybody will be the better for this increase of safety to child and wholesomeness to the home.

The world will always be divided into two classes:

1. The served.
2. The servers.

The served will be found eventually among those who deal with the marriage problem as it must needs be dealt with, so that permanence of the union may be guaranteed, and the best care given to the bearing and the rearing of children. They will of necessity be the served class. They will be masters of themselves and, therefore, will be entitled by nature to be masters of mankind.

The servers will be found among all others. They have no control of themselves, cannot control marriage, or parentage, or the raising of their children; and the most they do is to take things as they come, find fault with their ill fortune, let matters shape themselves as they will, getting what low grade pleasure they can out of life, and being willing to work for hire to others who are their superiors. Their children will come at all ages and die at all ages.

The test of superiority is a simple one: Whoever is able to control himself is the greater person when compared with one who is controlled by circumstances. Entering wedlock in the teens or in the twenties is not self-control, unless a good reason can be shown for marrying at that time. Raising children when the parents are in the teens or twenties, and when they are not best prepared for their coming, is not control, but is being swayed by circumstances.

The age of parental impulse is the late twenties down to the early forties; and it is in this age that children should be brought into the world, and marriage should take place. Reasons count up fast when both sides are examined, and all the reasons favoring marriage and parentage concur in the period stated; while there is every reason why an earlier period should be avoided.

All these matters are part of home life, of marriage and of Sex Magnetism. They cannot be separated from each other.

The fifth stage of sex life is that which is known as the weakening of "quality." It will be discussed a few pages later on.

The sixth stage, or the appearance of second childhood, in which all "quality" is lost, is the natural reversion of nature to the conditions that existed before puberty dawned. It shows that parentage is the purpose of earthly life, but it does not show that it is alone the goal.

In the seventh stage of sex life the old wife and the old husband are merely waiting to die. That is the whole fact, the truth as they know it and feel it. The fact is not a pleasant one, and the only power that saves them from agonizing suffering is the hope that is held out by religion. Nothing exists for nothing. There is a reason for every wish that ever entered the human heart, and the desire to live only for making better preparations for another life is born of the uselessness that seems to loom up like a dark mountain in this life. When the mind is healthy there is hope leaping from hope all through the years that follow youth down to the last hour of earth.

The pith of life is in the third stage, or that which witnesses the existence of "quality," beginning when puberty has been under way for a few years, and lasting until it weakens prior to the appearance of second childhood.

This is not only the pith of life, but it is that part which, above all other years, is most worth living. It is that part which carries in itself all the possibilities for that exalted state of happiness that crowns the fondest yearnings of heart or mind. All that precedes it is a blind following of events; and all that succeeds it is the settling down of nature prior to the payment back to mother earth of the clay that was borrowed in order that one frame might exist for its brief span.

Long months before this "quality" entered the life of the young man or woman, then a boy or girl, it gave some idea of what it was like. It made the boy stop and think. He knew not what was taking place within him, but he felt a delicious sense of something that was in store for him in the distant future. He had "day dreams," and young as he was, there were periods of "brown study" when in the creeping hours of evening and oft in the twilight he communed with the mystery of that future to try to catch a glimpse of its meaning.

To him a woman's form was a thing of wonder. It made no difference who the woman was, or how she looked; as a generic being she was most marvelous. No girl attracted him, but the female sex astonished him. Then came the finer sensations of sweet friendship, apart from physical association. Many men of after-lives of sensuality have said, as did one of their number when this part of their youth was brought up for analysis: "I have seen the world and have been as bad as a club man is expected to be. When I was eighteen years of age I joined what I was told was a literary society of young men; but it was only a band of fellows bent on hunting women for immoral purposes. We let young girls alone; but found women in plenty. In fact, they were thrown at us, and as one of us said, they were literally handed out to us, giving the club a reason for calling itself a literary association. What I want to say is something different. I was in love with a girl when I was seventeen, and she was about a year younger. For a year I courted her and wrote her love letters in floods. I did love her to distraction, and she loved me. As I was well fixed, her mother wanted me to marry her. I was allowed to go anywhere with her and to sit up with her until midnight any night I chose. Well, the point is this: In all that time, and with all those chances for getting at her, I never even kissed her once. Never held her hand, and never had my arm around her waist. I sat with her for hours and talked and blushed and she talked and blushed, and I am now glad that I had not the slightest desire to wrong her. Had I waited a year later things would have been different; but we parted, I to go to the bad and she to find a husband ten years afterwards, and a happy home. I believe she was just as good a girl then as when I knew her.''

It is true that what is called "quality" does not appear with puberty. The latter is the power of parentage, and is wholly physical; while "quality" is sex respect accompanied by Sex Magnetism.

A triangular condition of human nature thus is made to appear. There may be parentage before there is the feeling of love; and there may be the feeling of love before there is the birth of sensualism.

It seems that the power of propagation in both sexes comes first; then after that is born, there comes "quality"; and the animal nature, which is sensual, is the third to develop. Except where a young man or woman is a monstrosity, there is no case on record where the sensual nature has been coextensive with the dawn of puberty, or the power of propagation. The strong fact is that the physical power precedes "quality," and this comes between the physical and the sensual, if the latter is to appear at all.

From what has been said thus far, it might be inferred that "quality" and love were identical. They are not; but the first fancy and "quality" come together, showing that they are separable from the power of propagation and the sensual nature. The lower species, as the horse, the cow, the dog, the cat, and others below man, have only the first of these three natures: the power of propagation. They have none of the sensual, and "quality" is unknown to their kind.

It is likewise absent in certain human grades.

In logical order, it is true that "quality" must be founded on the power to propagate, and that the sensual must be founded on "quality." The last two are not born together, as the sensual is the final of the three natures. It is a perverted mood, such as would be dealt with in such a training course as Advanced Magnetism.

Every bright mood has its dark mood. Every bright emotion has its dark emotion. There is summer balanced by winter. There is day balanced by night. There is light and darkness. There is love opposed by hate. There is warmth opposed by cold. There is fire opposed by ice. There is comedy opposed by tragedy. There is hope opposed by despair; and everything that is beautiful has its ugly enemy. Life is made up of wickedness and honesty, of crime and right dealings, and it is no surprise to find the respect of the opposite sex tainted by a misuse of its offerings.

"Quality" is seen now as the middle ground between the birth of a power and the misuse of that power. It is the offspring of the power itself, and runs away with itself when it is misused. In proportion as it is abused, it takes away all that is sacred and beautiful in this world and substitutes nothing in its place. Yet it is the oldest of all sins. It began when human nature was lifted up out of the animal realm and placed on the highest pedestal in life. Since then it was the dominating influence in civilization. Among savages it is not a leading trait. Among beasts it disappears altogether, serving only the needs of reproduction. But as the brain and heart are given wider scope in existence, and freedom prevails, there comes this awful tide of wickedness to stain all that is noble in the breast of man.

It is the one chief sin of the Old Testament. It was the high crime of Greece and Rome; and if you will enter the private museum which contains the pictures taken from the ruins of Pompeii, you will see that it was the prevailing spirit of that once mighty city. All men and women worshipped at the same shrine. In every country on the globe today where there is freedom and civilization combined, this sin outbalances all others. A physician said recently in a scientific meeting, in which this trait of human nature was being discussed: "I am not overdrawing the truth when I say that there are at this very moment while I am addressing you no less than one million persons committing this deed as a criminal act, outside of matrimony and beyond the pale of honor."

If there were one million people so sinning at that moment,

how many in the world were guilty in every twenty-four hours?
This wrong destroys "quality."

As long as it is satisfying itself, so long will there be no
"quality" remaining in the marriage relationship. It is the
same kind of a law at work that was described in the early
pages of this department with reference to magnetic margins
as seen in the habits of eating. If you come from the table
hungry, you will have a margin of appetite that will digest the
food that has been eaten; but if you just evenly fill the desire
for food, there is no margin, but a lessened ability to digest the
food; while, still further, if you crowd the system with surfeiting, you will actually go to the other extreme and cause distress. Here is seen the opposing forces of a magnetic margin,
and the dark side which contains the ill effects of abuse which
rapidly lessens whatever magnetism may have been in store.

In this department we are dealing only with normal persons, not with monstrosities in morals or in body, nor with
defectives who wholly lack interest in the opposite sex. There
are men who are bachelors by nature, having no liking for
women. They do not care for their mothers or their sisters,
or the women whom they meet in business or social ways.
They have never entered the stage of possible parentage. Some
such men marry, but they have other motives for so doing.
It may be for a home, for a cook, for money, or for some gain
otherwise. Many instances have been investigated, and selfishness is behind the union. These men are disappointments to
their wives, and the latter almost invariably are untrue to
their husbands; so that it is not a help to the world on the
moral side for men of this sort to get married.

They should remain single.

Women, on the other hand, may be undeveloped in the same
way, and not know it. A man could easily ascertain his own
condition, but women have not the same means. Men hit upon
it by accident or in the inevitable course of events in their lives;
their apparent indifference to the other sex being the result
of physical conditions. Women are often diffident in their
estimation of men, and some are very cold by nature, who
possess the power of parentage; while others are affectionate
and fond of attentions who are devoid of this power. Their
husbands, if they get married, are, as a rule, untrue to them;

and thus such marriages do not tend to help the world morally. Any thoughtful reader admits this fact.

Normal persons may be wicked in their habits or imperfect in their development. A person who is incapable of parentage is normal.

One who is capable of parentage, but lacks "quality" will never pass into the sensuous. It is necessary to go beyond the first steps in order to pass into the third. The steps are: Parentage, "Quality" and the Sensuous. They succeed each other. Without the first there could be no second or third. Without the second there could be no third.

The lack of the first is an abnormal condition, such as has been described. The possession of the first only marks the lower grades of the human species, and is exactly on the level of the lower forms of life. It is a condition known to the horse, the cat, the dog and others below mankind.

While the second is necessary to the third, there are classes of men and women who use it only as a stepping-stone to the latter. It is only a transition from one condition to the other. It is not a part of their lives. In fact, most sensuous men and women are lacking in a margin of "quality," which alone makes Sex Magnetism possible in its high degree. When there is a possibility of being sensuous, there is always a presence of "quality" which, if cultivated until it reached a margin, would bring the most potent charm into married lives.

Those who have only the first nature, that of the possibility of parentage, are never interesting to each other. No tie binds them to each other. They are true to their marriage vows in this respect, for the reason that they have no reason to be otherwise. But there is nothing to live for except to eat, to sleep and to remain animals all their lives. Hundreds of thousands of such men and women exist in this country today.

Those who have the third nature never possess any margin in the second nature. They are unable to appreciate the good in their consorts. They are seeking change, new attractions and other affiliations.

Husbands of this third nature never were true to their sweethearts, and are incapable of experiencing fidelity to any woman. As lovers they sought the ruin of other girls or women, and even did not hesitate to take advantage of their own betrothed. They are the men who, under the promise of marriage, will lead any girl astray. There are not many women above twenty-five years of age, and, in fact, not a large number above twenty, who would believe the promises made by such men, as they would instinctively shrink from them, and, if misled, they would prefer to be so used rather than lose the attentions of men. From this class come the roues and the libertines of the world. Every woman they see, whether married or not, they look upon with eyes of conquest. Every girl of marriageable age they feast their gaze on, but without seeking them in wedlock. It is such men that form clubs and make up the town fellows who pride themselves on being called "the boys" and the "men-about-town." It is such men that attend the theatres and sit in the front rows when there are girl shows on the stage, as in the "follies" and revues of to day. It is such men who are untrue to their wives, being the respondents in divorce cases based on statutory grounds.

Disappointing as the fact is, these men number millions, and make it possible for the houses of cities and towns to exist where girls and women pursue their profession. The number of such men may be estimated when it is stated that in New York City alone there are over two hundred thousand professional females plying their trade with men. Were there no men who were false enough to themselves and to their homes, there would be no such women. But how many men are required to make this profession profitable for the two hundred thousand women and the backers of such enterprises?

"All men are bad," said the philosopher.

If one woman was visited by one man only on each night in every month she would have thirty different men; but if she had the same man once a week, she would have about four different men. As a matter of fact, each female averages two men each night, or fully eight different males all the time; and the sum total would be more than a million men who are supporting these women in the houses of ill fame in New York City. Its population, counting the outlying cities, is about five millions, and the extent of the wickedness prevailing there may be seen at a glance. It is true that visitors, traveling men from other parts of the country, and the transient public furnish a large number of the million or more men who are false to themselves and their homes. Next in total census, but more vicious and more virulent as a social ulcer, is the city of Chicago, whose political gang maintains a veritable Sodom of bestial crimes.

It has been estimated that when one man is induced to abandon his patronage of such business, he becomes a factor towards the downfall of the politics that set up the profession of the prostitutes; and this always means that whatever political party is in power is to blame for it. There is always a strong denial and protest coming from the party in power, a pretence of virtue, and then a cry that a wave of moral hysterics is sweeping over the land; for these felons love nothing better than to set going some term of ridicule against honesty.

When two men have been induced to abandon their support of such houses, then a still further gain is made in the right direction. We mean the men who consort with bad women, not the men who are behind them in the business itself. The latter are city politicians. But the men who go to such houses as patrons are the ones who can reduce the number of such women, and take away a large part of the income of such politicians.

If you who read this book will work to induce some man to stop his patronage of that profession, by telling him that he is making such profession possible, and is also paying his money into the hands of the politicians who are a pest to the town or city where he resides, you will be doing the best work of the present century. It is worth your while. In a town of twenty-four thousand inhabitants, which was cursed by a political system that kept eighteen houses of ill-fame in the floodtide of prosperity, a group of men banded themselves together on the principle of good citizenship and loyalty to their town, and made efforts to find out what patrons went to the houses. In a few weeks they had the names and addresses of practically all of them. More than seventy per cent. of them were married men; twelve per cent. were members of churches in active participation in religious services, and a large proportion of the married men had wives and children, who did not know or suspect what was going on. These married men would go out for an evening, telling their wives they had important engagements which might be to their financial benefit, and they would come back to bright homes and smiling faces of trusting wives and children yearning for parental attention.

What a travesty on manhood!

As many of these patrons were otherwise decent men, they were easily persuaded to abandon the houses in question. The result was that the whole business was broken up, and there were better homes and more money for legitimate uses.

This same method has been adopted elsewhere, and can be used in any city or town. It is important that men should understand that most of the money wasted in such places goes to corrupt politicians and to breweries that back them. The politicians are after the profits, and they, with the breweries, reap rich rewards, the latter furnishing beer, which is sold at exorbitant rates to baudy houses. Then a large number of votes are controlled, compelling the decent public to accept rulership by the most despicable of all human beings. In other words, the honest classes are controlled by the interests that force houses of ill-fame on the public. Let partisanship be laid aside, and all good men combine for their own good and that of their homes and country.

This third nature, the sensuous, is the inward impulse that drives women astray. It is a paramount evil in some females. It is almost a disease in many lives. Girls after they are sixteen, but rarely before, unless they are monstrosities, follow the bent of their blood, and go quickly into this fearful abyss of crime that has chained their sex since first they felt the dawn of civilization. If they do not fall between the ages of sixteen and twenty-five, there is not one chance in a hundred of their taking the first steps after that period. It is when parentage is not advisable, in the years of immature formation of character, that they are overwhelmed by temptation. Eighty per cent. of all bad girls become bad when they are sixteen and seventeen years of age; and beyond the later age they gradually become strong year by year. The time to save them is in the two or three years of severest temptation.

It is, however, an accepted fact among physicians and others who are in a position to know accurately, that about ninety per cent. of all girls who marry go to wedlock impure, especially in this country and in France. In England there is a greater percentage of chastity, owing to the better system of chaperonage, by which girls are not left alone with their lovers. In America the philosophy of the parents is: "My daughter is able to look after herself, and it would be an insult to her to provide a chaperone to remind her constantly that she is not able to protect herself." The result is that nine in every ten girls here fall before marriage. This is not guesswork; it is a well-established fact. A man who marries a girl who has had a previous lover, stands only one chance in ten of getting a virgin wife. She may be adroit enough to deceive him, but the fact remains the same.

One of the frequent causes of separation after marriage is the confession of the wife that she had been doing wrong with some previous lover. Lawyers, physicians, husbands, and sometimes priests, secure such statements in the course of their professional and marital duties.

It can be seen at a glance that a chaperone is needed; and, in her place, the avoidance of privacy to lovers in their teens, or when the girl is young. It is much more to the credit of the girl and the young woman that she be not alone even with her accepted lover; no matter how close their marriage may be. There are many courtships where the man is perfectly willing to remain in the same room with other members of the family, not asking to be alone with her; and in one town it was agreed by the men themselves that they would not permit girls or women to whom they were paying attention to be alone with them. Thus the good name of the girl was protected and the intentions of the man were made clear. When he found it advisable to propose, he first secured the consent of the mother and then that of the young woman. It does not require long guessing to catch the answer that is coming; for there are many ways by which she may make her feelings known even in a crowd. To pure men there is no need of privacy before marriage. It is foolish and weak to put in long evenings fondling, embracing, holding and kissing girls. Instead of setting aside a few months for that before marriage, it is better to arrange about forty years of it after wedlock has been commenced.

Many men who go wrong are not wrong at heart, but only because they do what most husbands do—let the edge of "quality" be cut off by the sharp desire of sensuousness. Like the appetite at the table, a control can be exercised, and then the mind will wake up to the enormity of the offense, and it will cease. Many women are not bad at heart, but are tempted either by being neglected by their husbands or by a course of abuse that can have but one outlet. Yet there are women who can never be honorable. They are morally diseased in this line, but gentle and even religious in all other respects. Some abnormal nerve growth is responsible for their going astray. They cannot be cured. Some of these wives who are untrue have the best of husbands, who remain with them all their spare time and give them constant attention and the deepest respect and affection. One case is typical of many thousands. A girl who was seventeen when she was married, and who had been astray a year before, and had associated with six different men by her own subsequent confession, married a wealthy man nine years older than she was, who had been attracted by her wonderful beauty. He gave her all his time, as he was free to go and come as he pleased. He consulted her wishes and tastes in everything and surrounded her with luxuries in full measure. But despite the fact that he was in or about the home at all times when she was there, she managed to slip out under the pretence of making social calls, and to meet men at houses where she committed wrong most wantonly. Nothing could hold her in check. In dances she actually made brazen assaults on men, even those who were strangers to her. There was no trace of insanity. Her only excuse was that she could not resist her feelings. Another woman who married a man whose income was seven million dollars a year committed adultery within sixty minutes after the ceremony by pre-arrangement with a former lover; and she was divorced by the husband.

These types stand for two classes of women in society and in all ranks of life in America.

They are beyond cure. It would be useless to waste the time and effort on them. The only way a man can protect himself from them is to know all about their habits and propensities before marriage is promised.

On the other hand, there are cases where girls have been tricked into leading immoral lives and, after years of such existence in which they were immobile clay, they have gone out into the world, taken new names without asking aid of the courts, and settled in two places; one in which by labor they have earned a year or two of good repute and church influence; then they have moved to the second place thousands of miles away, perhaps, and there have been able to refer to many people in the first town and have been able to conceal their wicked past, on the principle that it is not easy to see through a double veil. We know of scores of such girls who have married well and have been true to their vows after wedlock, some of them today being at the head of palatial homes.

The women who cannot control their habits and nature pass directly through their period of "quality" to that of the sensuous. They have no margin of safety or repression.

Those who, having been led into immoral lives, have come back, are types of savable women. They may have never gone beyond the first nature; or, if they have entered the second, have gone over to the third, and have been able to get back again; whereas the unsavable woman is the one who cannot get out of the sensuous. She is stained with it as with an incurable disease.

This study is for the following classes of men and women:

1. Those who have never passed beyond the first nature.

2. Those who are easily capable of passing into the second nature.

3. Those who, in the present possession of the second nature, leave no margin, but pass constantly into the third.

4. Those who, having become slaves to the third nature, are savable by being brought into the second.

All these things, being translated, read as follows:

Men and women who are married, and who have no nature beyond that of animal habits, should develop the second nature known as "quality."

Men and women who are sensuous, either as a habit, or at times, should fall back into the second nature and develop a margin which will establish "quality."

Or, in other words, learn the power of affectionate respect for the one who is your consort, if you are of a cold and animal nature; or, in the event of being sensuous, acquire control of your nature and resolve it back to affectionate respect.

In either case the focus is the same. It is either coming up to the standard of affectionate respect or else coming down to it. The man who grovels in the mire should rise to his feet; and he who is in the air should get down to solid ground, as taught in this book.

Affectionate respect is exactly that regard for a wife that the lover had for his sweetheart in those days when he thought she was the most attractive woman in the world; or the regard that a woman had for her lover in those days of courtship when she thought he was a gallant gentleman, a cavalier, and of noble character; all in the blur of a dimly-seen landscape.

A courtship in which the man acts the part of a beefy, stolid, phlegmatic fellow is coarse, and can have no place in our study. Let the women have character enough to let him alone, even if he has millions. He is an animal. The girl who is dumpish, stupid, dull and uninteresting should likewise be unloaded long before there is any thought of marriage. She will make only an animal wife. Here is such a wife in the very locality where this work is being written. She was married when she was thirty years of age; fat, slow, dull, heavy, and selfish in the extreme, yet worth a million in her bank account, but not in her character. The man who married her is handsome, large, strong and attractive; but he was after money, and had boasted that he would never marry one who was poor. Now he is miserable in the fact that he has so many pounds of pork, and she has the money, not he; nor is he able to move any of it in his direction.

In all such cases Sex Magnetism is impossible.

These are types of the physical or animal nature, where there can be no happiness, because there is no "quality."

But it has been proved that many husbands and wives who seem to have developed only the first nature have been afterwards able to acquire "quality" by ascertaining more of their own natures. If they were needed in the world for no other purpose than to breed, they would fulfill that mission, though, perhaps, in a limited extent; but when they are able to extricate themselves from this animal nature, they are often happier than those who pass over to the third nature.

Thousands of men have complained that they have married women who are cold and dull; no display of affection will awaken them; and they are without sympathy and community of temperament. Under such a course of training as that which is contained in the several works of the Magnetism Club, such women have been melted, and have become attractive wives. We cannot give the details of such conversion, but the pith of the process is in setting up an appreciation of "quality" in the dull and chilling wife, following a thorough course of training in personal magnetism. Some women do not wish to be different, others are willing to try, and still others are anxious to merit their husband's attentions.

If a husband cares enough for his wife's affectionate respect to assist her in developing it, he can do so by himself first becoming magnetic, starting with the first book, which contains the developing course, and following especially through Advanced Magnetism, and, above all else, taking Universal Magnetism, where such results are absolute certainties when there is a faithful practice of the habits that are taught. Such a development is not a matter of guesswork, as it has been attained by thousands of students who have persisted to the end in the adoption of the teachings included in those courses. Nor is it a difficult matter. For thirty years these methods have been tested and put into practice, and the results are already exactly proportioned with the efforts made to secure them.

For this reason we state as an absolute fact that any man who seeks to change the nature of his wife can do so by his own exercise of "quality," based upon his own developed magnetism.

To show how simple the process is, let us state the whole plan:

1. He should do what more than six hundred thousand persons have done in the past quarter of a century, study and adopt the plain teachings of the foundation book, which is known as the developing course in the cultivation of personal magnetism. This is so plainly taught that no person has ever been unable to study and adopt it in his or her own way. Other help is not needed.

2. Then, above everything else, the training system known as Advanced Magnetism should be pursued, as that develops the emotional powers or feelings, which are directly involved in marriage relations. Thus far the student has acquired personal magnetism as a power or energy, and has been placed in full control of his own feelings and those of all other persons.

3. Before the final course, Universal Magnetism, is taken the present work is necessary, or else they should be studied together.

4. In the present work which, in many men, will be found sufficient without any of the other works, if personal magnetism is present in a natural way, each department should be mastered in turn. These departments are eminently practical, and unfold the actual experiences that men and women must encounter when they become husbands and wives.

If you have read each department, and then re-read it several times, you must have ascertained the fact that this entire work is directly human, not artificial. It brings home to you life as it is. It makes clear to you the facts of real life in wedlock. It is not a book of theory, or advice, or high-flown idealism, but a plain, simple, effective course of instruction that brings you in contact with inside facts that seem so plain that they really do not appear as teachings, but as reflections of the mirror of nature. You recognize these truths, and then you think that they have always been known to you. This is the best way of teaching.

You should live in these teachings.

Think of them, read them again, ponder over them, try to find them present about you, and absorb all they would instill into your life. Every thought that takes hold of you will do its work. It is sure to.

As there have been men who have prized their wives, despite the coldness of the latter, and who have, by these very processes, melted the natures of those wives, so you who may desire to repeat their successes may do so in the same way. It is done by magnetism. As a climax of all studies in this power, learn to secure a margin in "quality." This will be presently explained.

Look back to some of the similar cases mentioned in the first part of this portion of the present work.

If you eat less than your hunger desires, you save a margin of appetite, which means that you will digest your food more readily and get out of it a greater proportion of nutrition, because when there is no margin left the vitality required for digestion is gone. The process will be merely that of disposing of a stuffed stomach and its contents by mechanical change leading to fermentation and later diseases.

If you run a race and let all your power enter into it, you will not be able to finish it creditably.

If you try to lift a great weight and permit all your energy to participate in the effort, you will be tired out when you get through, if not before.

If you perform any work and do not conserve some of your vitality in doing it, you will be exhausted.

Any man or woman who lets out all the stored vitality in any effort will break down in time; but one who saves some and is never at the limit will grow stronger. This rule is seen at work in gymnasiums where men and women are in search of more muscular power. Atrophy is the penalty of full exertions. It is a fact that premature deaths occur among athletes in far greater proportions than in any other class in life. Consumption, following a career of a few years of supremacy in some line of sport, is the usual fate. We have a list of over eight thousand young men who were athletes in their teens and twenties, but who died when they were in their thirties.

The reason is plain.

They never saved a margin of vitality.

If you let out all the energy you have, you lack muscular magnetism and can never build any power of any kind above that.

Now there is a middle between two extremes. The middle is always the realm of magnetism, let it be where you choose to put it.

1. In mental work the middle is between non-use on the one hand and the loss of margin on the other.

2. In muscular use, the middle is between non-use on the one hand and loss of margin in the other direction.

3. In emotional life, which contains all the happiness in the world, as shown in Advanced Magnetism, the middle is between that dullness and slow, stolid character on the one hand, and the escape of all emotional power on the other hand, leaving no margin.

4. In sex nature, the middle is between non-use on the one hand and the lack of a margin on the other, which results in "quality."

The mind that is not employed, and given a large share of work to do, will be weak; or if it is fed on literary sugar all the time it will soften. An unused brain is nearly smooth; but one that has been given much to do of a taxing nature is deeply built with convolutions that show intelligence. But if that brain is allowed to run in one rut of work or thought, it soon exhausts all the vitality that feeds that part, and the margin is lost. Then danger sets in.

You cannot afford to deprive your mind of its margin of vitality.

What is called sugar food for the brain is novel reading, newspaper reading, light magazine reading and all forms of entertainment that hold the attention and make a man or woman hate to do anything solid. Mathematics, which has had more to do to cure softening of the brain when it has threatened to take the mind away, in its incipient stages, is hated by the novel reader. Ask any woman. Mathematics that has had more to do than any other agency to build up a strong, manly and virile mind is hated by the lover of newspaper sensations. Ask any man who must have his daily paper for an hour a day. If he desires to build a good brain, let him read the headlines of the legitimate news and throw the paper at once into the waste basket. By so doing he will get all the current history and none of the sewerage.

All sensible men do this.

Whatever is undertaken by the muscles should be in the middle ground of use. If you do not exercise at all, you will have soft, flabby flesh and muscles, and your bones will get dry. The same force in a fall that would be only enough to break the arm and leg of a sedentary man or woman would not do any harm to one who exercised constantly. There is nothing so injurious to man, woman or child as lack of physical action. There should be work in variety and activities in every conceivable way to give to the whole body each day a full share of tax, all in the middle ground. Never get tired out. Never go to the extreme that means exhaustion. If you adopt this middle stage you will have wonderful health of body, just as you will get wonderful health of mind by taxing the brain in severe tasks, without producing weariness.

It is all in the secret of maintaining a margin in everything.

But in the emotional realm, in the midst of the seventy-six moods that make up human feeling, and out of which one gets all the happiness in life, it is necessary to avoid either extreme. Until the work of Advanced Magnetism was published a few years ago, there was never any training course for the emotions.

It has been abundantly proved in centuries of experience that the use of the mind was necessary to develop it, and to make it a power in the world; while worrying, or any excessive thinking on one thing, or undue work along one line of thought, would break down the brain by taking away the margin of vitality.

It has also been abundantly proved that it is necessary to use the muscles in order to give strength and health to the body. The man that carried his arm in a sling for three months, although he was otherwise attentive to all the demands of health, was surprised to find the arm withered, thin, emaciated and useless until it was given activity again. The law is one that cannot be challenged.

It is the same with the emotions, but whoever gave them a thought?

Of the seventy-six emotions, as described in Advanced Magnetism, and there grouped according to their value or harmfulness, it is shown that development by scientific practice will bring a new realm into the existence of every man and woman. That individual who never smiles is morbid, and the nervous system is deranged; but, on the other hand, the person who is frivolous, flip, silly or given to excess of pleasure saves no margin, and magnetism in that emotion is lost, where it should be most useful in the world. One who weeps, or mourns, or is melancholy, or grieves constantly, or is subject to fits of depression, is in an extreme of another emotion, the proper normal character of which is seriousness and earnestness; and it has been found that Advanced Magnetism will train all such morbid natures out of every man or woman who suffers from them.

These are but two of the many emotions therein dealt with.

But as they carry in themselves all the pleasures and all the happiness, as well as all the sorrow and suffering of life, no work is so important as that.

The best of us, without training, have but two or three emotional powers, as they are not well controlled; all the others are vagaries that run wild when the vicissitudes of life call them into being.

In sex nature there is the tendency to go to one extreme or

the other; and as nature seeks to impress on humanity the necessity of reproducing the race, the third condition, that of the sensuous, is the more common extreme. When a man or woman is not given over to that state, there is generally a dullness of interest, and the limited use of the power of parentage.

When such power is given use and a margin of vitality is maintained it is called "quality."

When "quality" is passed over quickly and without saving the margin as a constant habit, the result is sensuousness.

In the period intended for use the lack of it is a serious blunder in married life, especially after thirty years of age. It should then be extended into the very latest years of life, even to the age of ninety or a hundred; and this will be possible only where there has been a conservation of the margin, with its consequent result in magnetism.

Men who are more than ninety years of age have retained such powers through the principle of magnetic margins; and women have also, in the late nineties, been able to participate.

Such powers come from the training found in this present course converging with the training of Advanced Magnetism.

The most foolish custom prevailing in wedlock is to use up the margin of vitality in this respect. The rule adopted by the good doctor who studies the features of his patients is the appearance of the face. If the lines under the eyes are visible, then the margin has been used, and surfeiting, as in eating, has brought on the negative condition, or the other side of the dividing line of magnetic margins, with the struggle to get back to a flat basis of energy.

Look for a moment at the result of this condition.

In the first place, the man wants the woman, not merely for such companionship, but because her presence to him is an attractive force; but after the magnetic margin of vitality is gone, even for a few hours only, he does not want her. He does not care to see her. Her touch to him is a source of irritation. This fact has been testified to by many persons who have been honest with themselves, and by physicians who understand the reason of it. One man who represents the best of his class of frank and conservative men of perfect health, says: "It is the plan of nature that the two sexes should meet, and then ignore each other for a time. I know that I do not want to see or to hear my wife for several hours, and I am greatly bothered when she speaks to me. She says I am at one time a very affectionate man, and then am cross as a bear. This is nature.''

To avoid this loss of magnetic margin in vitality means that men and women take a constant interest in each other, and have a drawing power each for the other. It is affirmative magnetism as long as this margin is preserved; otherwise it is negative and repellant. Surely nature made the negative part of electricity, and of magnetism as well.

The most disagreeable person in the world is the one who has used up this magnetic margin of vitality. The brain suffers, and cannot do its best work, as is seen in the lives and present-day careers of sensuous men and women. Who expects anything of the roue, or of the prostitute? No mental achievement, no position of trust, no work of any value to the world can come from such sources. Even the geniuses who have astonished the world for a few years have died very young, because this extreme burned up their powers all at once. But the great law of averages proves that nothing comes from a sensuous nature that can have value.

Not only is the attractive force gone, but the mental and physical powers are reduced to almost nothing, and there is a stopping of the progress that gave hope of a successful career. Men make a mistake in marrying under thirty, if they are unable to control this habit. But at any time they should, for the sake of holding their powers of attracting their wives, keep a magnetic margin. The difference is most marked. Take the case of the young man who had won the affections of a very beautiful and talented woman of wealth. She was not yet thirty, and was capable of becoming an ideal wife. The man was about her age, and seemed much younger, because he had conserved his powers all his life. He had wealth and a good profession. The public looked upon the coming marriage as the most suited to the contracting parties of any that had taken place in that city.

When the time was not more that two months away for the ceremony this young man was unanimously elected a member of a new club of wealthy men and by them initiated into habits that he had never before indulged in. He had been accustomed to reach the home of his affianced soon after eight in the evening that he called on her; but now, although he was just as prompt, he left his home an hour earlier than usual and spent the extra time in a certain house. He then proceeded to call upon his sweetheart. On the night of the very first visit he paid her after he began his career of wrong she said to her mother, "Charles seems to me to be different this evening. He has not been as entertaining and as magnetic as before." After the next call following such misdeed she told him that he was not pleasing to her. He took the hint and behaved himself for a week, then repeated the wrong and called on her the same evening. In the week he made six visits to her in seven evenings, and the last four were in his old self, and she was again gracious to him; but after that week was up, and he thought it was merely imagination, he again repeated the offence for three successive evenings, and she wrote him the following letter the next day after the last call: "I have discovered that I no longer love you, and I cannot for your sake enter into a loveless marriage."

This experience is not of one man, but of many hundreds and thousands of men. It is occurring, in one form or another, in all walks of life and in all parts of the world. Men who patronize the bawdy houses are coming home late in the evening to their wives, and despite the extra efforts they make to please their wives by their manners, there is lacking the magnetism that tells something the women cannot put in words; but their feelings translate it.

A man who has no magnetic margin of the kind called "quality" cannot substitute pleasing ways and kind words for that which he has thrown away, whether he has parted with it away from home or in his own legitimate marriage.

The mother who loves her child may speak to it in tones that are not very pleasant, but the child will love that mother better than it will the stranger who talks to it in the sweetest and kindest tones known to the human voice.

Why?

Because the mother love is in the voice, be it cross or kind, and it is translated to the child by the mysterious channel of communication which nature has created for that purpose. But kindness without mother-love is not so felt and translated.

The husband who has a magnetic margin in his vitality has

that "quality" that makes his wife want him, and makes him want her if she really wants him. This law is fixed and never changes.

It works both ways.

There is a woman whose husband loves her and tries to make her happy at all times. But she has been left alone too much evenings by this same husband who intends to do right. He merely goes down town. So she has been visiting the house of a woman friend, and there has met two men, and wrong has followed. She is at her home before her husband gets back, and he never suspects her; but he finds that he does not have that peculiar liking for her that he did. In some way she no longer fascinates him. For merely animal uses she is perhaps as much of a wife as ever, but even these are growing less all the while.

There are in the city of New York, in the city of Boston, in the city of Chicago, and in almost every great life center of this land, women who live in homes of wealth and luxury, surrounded by every comfort that riches can buy, who, nevertheless, tiring of the club interests of their husbands and the unending neglect to which they are subjected, go to high-priced houses of ill-fame, not for the money paid there, but because they require attentions that they cannot receive at their own homes. They are society women. Some of them are beautiful, and in their ranks are the noted beauties of a few years ago. Many of them are young. A society man making the rounds of the high-toned houses, as he calls them, found the wives of six of his own club associates, and more than once has a wife, hiding behind a veil, seen her own husband in such a place.

She reasons in this way: "I am neglected at home. My husband goes ostensibly to his club and I am told to make myself as comfortable as I can. He goes astray repeatedly. He is in these houses. By using my veil I can escape his gaze, and he will never know. From these houses he goes to his club and I to my home, so I am in bed and asleep long before he comes in, and I am not likely ever to be discovered."

But is she happy?

Never. There is not a moment when her heart is not wrung by the agony of it all. No wonder many a society woman has put the revolver to her temple, or turned on the gas. The man, used by nature and instinct to adultery, has no pangs of conscience.

The remedy is in the union of man and wife at home, evenings and holidays and Sundays together in sight of each other. It may be a dull life for a while compared with his escapades, but it is sure to bring solid happiness which he can never get from prostitutes.

No man can do wrong outside and come home with the magnetism that belongs to his nature. No woman can live in sin and attract the man. Bad women have very little magnetism; it is sensual attraction which flares up and leaves only disgust and hatred.

But assuming that both husband and wife intend to be true to each other as some are; and that they are in fact faithful to their marriage vows; there comes into play the law of exhaustion, the loss of the magnetic margin that is most attractive. One woman said to another woman: "Do you never tire of your husband? Do you never want attention from some more magnetic and attractive man?" And the reply was, "My husband is magnetic and attractive. I do not know where I could find a man that I would prefer to him." "But," said the first woman, "if all men and women were released from matrimony and it was made right to select any man in all the world you wanted, what one would be your choice?" "My husband," was the reply.

The reason for this answer was that the man whom she had married was careful to keep his vitality always on edge, as he called it. He has many times given an account of his habits, and he never loses the magnetic margin of vitality. He has plenty to spare. He makes himself attractive and magnetic to his wife at all times. He does not neglect her, and they are happily of one temperament. But even if a couple may be of the same temperament, it is possible to become wearying to each other by repeatedly losing the margin of vitality. Let both become tired in a nervous way, and they will want to see little and hear little of each other. It is the law of nature: meet and then ignore one another.

"Quality" may be maintained by the use of good judgment and careful planning. It will not regulate itself. Nor is it sensible to live apart, for this is not intended by nature.

There are other uses of the sex attractions than to merely produce offspring.

What a superb man is he who combines all the good traits of the first departments of this work with all those better powers that are discussed in the later departments, and secures his climax in a large margin of "quality." Non-use deadens and weakens any power. Do not be guilty of that extreme. But excess is still worse. Avoid that extreme. Always secure a margin.

Such a man is attractive. He is not ugly in feature. If his face is mis-shapen, he possesses the force of manliness, of nobility, of affection and of the best powers of his sex. They all stand forth as marks of the man. He is a KING.

Such a woman is attractive. She can never be ugly. She is of the sweetest disposition. She has a loveliness that wins all who approach her, and she is reserved for one alone—her husband. She is beautiful to look upon. For a year or so in the life of a girl or a woman who is sensuous there is beauty, if she is so cast in her creation. But the reason why some such females are beautiful is that they have passed from "quality" into the lower estate, and have taken the brightness and fascination of that middle nature with them, but not to retain it. Time very soon brings out the ill that is seething within their frames.

Time is the great arbitrator of all things.

But the woman of "quality" is really most fascinating. She fascinates her husband. She could fascinate any man who was manly. She is a power among women. She has ways that are in the middle ground, going to neither extreme of callous coldness or excessive warmth.

Such a couple will never separate.

There are some few men, and, perhaps, more than a few women who are either abnormal or cold in nature by habit or temperament, who still insist that the personal relations of marriage are disagreeable. Their place in the world is in singleness. Let them stay out of marriage if they know more than nature and nature's God.

Do not go about the house all tired out.

Exhaustion gives indigestion, for it uses up all the nervous vitality, and leaves very little for the stomach to employ in its work. Some of the worst cases of gastritis and chronic dyspepsia have been cured by accumulating the power of "quality." As day follows day in the practice, the tone of the stomach grows better and better, until all is well again. Recently a woman who, after the most careful dieting, was too weak to digest her food, simple as it was, and who got no better with treatment and medicine, was told by her physician to spend a month with her sister. She did this, and her husband followed, and the cure was not forthcoming. So she chided her doctor. Then he told the husband to go home, and stay home for a month, which he did, and the indigestion disappeared entirely. Then she went home a well woman, and had the same trouble again.

In the voluminous reports made by members of the Ralston Health Club to that organization, it appears that its natural methods of treatment fail among married people who are of the third nature. They try to live up to the true standards of health, and then report that they fail. Medicines will not help them; nor will change of climate or treatment of any kind. They sometimes die before they find out the real trouble. Now, the Ralston Health Club cannot go about telling people who are married to use moderation, for the Club is not able to include the reasons why in its teachings. The reasons are magnetic ones, and are led up to by long discussions and explanations before they will be satisfying. Then there must be magnetism on which to found the basis of will power to practice moderation in anything. Many men have died while finding out the truth. Not long ago we warned a man not over forty-seven years of age against what was too apparent in his face, a loss of "quality." He was in his third nature, sensuous, but true to his wife. She was of strong vitality, and was slowly taking his energy from him.

The usual result of the loss of vitality of this kind is the weakness of the stomach. Doctors have said millions of times: "If this man or this woman will live alone for a month, the stomach will get its tone and strength back again, and find digestion easy and normal," or words of similar inport. The man whom we warned could have been saved, but his stomach had no life, his nerves were depleted of all their vitality, and he died at the home of his brother after eating a meal that he had no power to digest.

When you have lost the margin of "quality" let the stomach rest for ten to fifteen hours. It needs vitality, and you have none to offer it.

Neuralgia is another result of the loss of the magnetic margin. There is no more common experience than the wife arising in the morning with a sick headache, due to loss of vitality. Of course, loss of sleep will bring similar pain in the head; and indigestion, as of some one thing that hurts the system, like chocolate, pastry, cake, ice cream, or fried food of any kind, will set up a severe neuralgic pain in the back of the neck, or in the head near the neck, or at the top of the head. This is because the food cannot be digested readily, and the vitality is overtaxed in trying to dispose of it; although sometimes the lack of easy digestion sets up poisons that cause pains to lodge in, or within a few inches, of the heart, and in the lungs, liver or head.

Such poisons produce death without warning.

Married men and women have ninety-three per cent. of all the neuralgia in the world, and seventy-nine per cent of all the indigestion.

When "quality" is in its widest margin, which means when it is used and not allowed to run to the sensuous, then the following advantages are secured.

1. The brain power is at its best, for men and women accomplish more with their minds then than under any other conditions.

2. The health of the nerves is at its best, for then the nervous system seems absolutely perfect.

3. The organic condition of the body is in its best tone.

4. The eyes are brighter and the face more attractive; in fact, the features themselves are decidedly different.

5. There is greater inherent possibility of happiness.

6. Out of this nature called "quality" arises the constitutional power that sets up the strong hold on life; for statistics show that married persons live longer on the average than those who are not married, and this better nature promotes longevity.

Certain families have for the past thirty years practiced

the regime in marriage that is taught here. Out of several hundred thousand pupils, it is not surprising that many would be found who would give heed to these rules; and they have been amply rewarded for it. The regime is not at all difficult when once it is understood.

Keep your mind bright. Do not have periods of weakness and depressed vitality. Keep your face bright. Do not let it show the drag of excesses. Keep your eyes full of life and light, for they will show dull with the general weariness of the body or the nerves.

No person should run to the end of the margin in anything. Do not spend more money than you earn, and do not let your bank account get empty. Have something always saved ahead.

Freshness of health and spirits will have the opposite effect on the home and family from that which follows neuralgic headaches, exhausted nerves and irritated minds. Yet it is a fact that most marriages are dull on the one hand, or a fight for recuperation on the other. The wise man or woman is the one who can display self-control in this relationship.

Practice delay. Be exceedingly careful in all uses of all powers of mind and body, of faculties and energies, and thus save loss and weakness.

As a result of many years of experiments, carried on by several thousand families, it has been found true that when a man or woman is able to accumulate a margin of "quality," the mutual interest is "on edge," as the saying goes. This is the most to be desired of all conditions in matrimony. Then the husband likes to be in the room where his wife is working or reading. Then he wants to hear her voice, and see her in actual presence. Then he is glad of the little attentions that she longs to bestow upon him; sometimes a look, sometimes a word of kindness, sometimes a touch of the hand, and often a closely-held conversation together. If she is "on edge" in her interest in him, then she wants to be where he is, listen to what he says, receive any caress he cares to bestow, if only a pat on the shoulder or a grasp of the hand, and there is the same exhilaration of heart when they are thus affiliated as in that first period when they met and talked together years ago.

This change has been brought about thousands of times.

It is a most remarkable rejuvenation of life.

How much better it is than the usual methods now in vogue, even in families where men and women are faithful to their marriage vows! Even where men stay at home nights and give their wives all the attention they crave in the home, in helping in duties, in pleasures, in observing holidays, and in all the many things that make the wife believe that her husband still cares for her, this extra interest, born of a high state of vitality, adds charm to her existence, and he finds it paying him in return; for all men of the highest sense are willing to be taken back to that spirit that prevailed in the early days of their courtship.

This is really what it is.

It is going back to that same spirit. People who see married life only as a routine of drudgery and the dumping ground of commonplaces, have come to find the old spirit of the days of courtship born again, and solely through this influence. And they have been thankful for the light that has shown them the way to return to that sweeter era.

While the use of any faculty or power increases its energy and prolongs its time of existence, this can be true only when that use is within magnetic margins. To leave no margin means wearing out. This rule applies to life itself. It applies to everything. If you want to make the body grow old, never save any margin of energy, but work up to your full limit of endurance. Never let your strength be conserved, but do all you can each day. On the other hand, if you want to have power of muscle, you must use your body and keep within some margin, avoiding weariness. He who works and saves no margin of strength will wear out fast. He who runs the mind to its limit of endurance will break it down or bring on age fast. But he who does not use the muscles will be weak, and he who does not tax the mind will have no mental powers.

The same rules apply to the period during which "quality" may be kept alive; and this means the time of extending the faculties into the farthest limit of old age. No man or woman should court second childhood.

It is supposed that this era, known as second childhood, is the result of all the faculties breaking down. But it comes solely from the inability to save margin in "quality." This question has been the subject of the most careful inquiry for many years, and it is now well settled that the childishness of mind and body is due to the return to the same conditions that prevailed prior to the dawn of puberty, and so the keenness of sight and of hearing follow the same influence.

The eyes follow the stomach very largely, although there are exceptions to this statement; but in the long run the sight will be weak when indigestion is impaired by nervous weakness, such as attends losses in marriage.

In cases where those losses have been checked and perfect digestion has been attained, bad eyesight has passed away. The vision clears in good health. There are thousands of children wearing glasses today as the result of a wretched diet, owing to the ignorance and indifference of their parents on the subject of food selection. They all grow old before they are ten years of age.

Second childhood, therefore, is not the result of aging because of loss of the ordinary faculties; but the return to the conditions that prevailed before puberty. Yet, closely allied with it is the better health of all the body and the better powers of the faculties, when the margin of "quality" enhances the vitality that prevents the coming on of second childhood.

The roue ends his energy twenty years sooner than the healthy man of conservative habits.

The professional women die twenty to thirty years sooner than the average woman of good health; some of the former ending their lives when they are in the thirties, some in the forties, and very few ever reach the fifties. A small per cent. live longer, but the death rate is very much greater in the ranks of that class than among other women, when the health is the same to start with in both classes. The wife who may be honorable, but whose vitality has been lessened during marriage, is subject to maladies that women would escape who conserve their energy. Those who survive disease with weakened vitality pass early into their second childhood, although there are occasionally exceptions to this rule. Some constitutions can endure much loss.

But regardless of these exceptions, and following the proofs that have been secured in a large range of investigations, it is a fact well established that the habits of saving magnetic margins is the grandest of all habits in life.

It makes no difference where that habit is applied, it brings power, and the power is natural. It is nature's conservation. This principle may be seen at work any day in many ways; in the public where men and women are engaged in the whirl of life's activities, and where they are breaking down by the thousands, ending useful careers prematurely; and in the home where worry, quarrels, wrong habits and the misuse of the vital powers are mowing down both sexes with startling regularity.

That man or woman who learns how to save any margin in any way is laying aside a fund as useful as the surplus earnings spoken of in the early part of this book, in the second department. Like the rule of never spending as much as you earn, the other rule of never using your vitality up to the limit of its generation is bound to bring you a fund of power that will add to your happiness in many ways.

Thus it will be seen that the same natural law runs through the whole study; beginning with the suggestion that all persons should save a margin of their earnings, and ending with the conservation of a margin of vitality in marriage that shall give to the owners of the home built by the earnings the opportunity for the highest enjoyment of the blessings that accrue there. If you save enough money by years of economy to buy you a home, it does not follow that you will be perfectly happy there if you are weak and sickly. Something more than a home is necessary. The laws of the second department reach over this whole work and join hands with the laws of this department.

Write it down in your mind and never forget it:

A successful life is founded on margins that bring magnetism; and they are margins in money, margins in muscular power, margins in nervous energy, margins in mind, and margins in vitality.

Never get tired in brain, in vitality, in muscle, or in any of the uses of the body.

Be active. Use what you have been endowed with. Lay no talents away. Keep them going. Non-use destroys life in anything. But do not go to the limit.

All margins on the right side are magnetic.

Many, many times, we have been asked, how can this practice be undertaken, and how much time is needed each day to bring about the required results? The answer is that no time is needed for practice, for it is all a matter of habit. When you see a man or woman who is naturally endowed with personal magnetism, you say at once that such person has been born with a gift. But the facts are just the opposite. Habits make or destroy the gift. If there is any inherent power at all, it is wholly due to the desire and willingness to pursue a certain line of habits.

If you are lazy, it does not follow that this fault was born in you. If you are active, it does not follow that activity is a born gift. And that is all there is to most of the power of personal magnetism in the making. Active persons, having become rich, have also been dragged down into a life of laziness; and lazy persons, having been aroused by some stirring appeal, have turned their lives into the greatest possible activity with results that have astonished their friends. It all comes down to the question of habit.

We teach the making of lists.

In a preceding department we have advised the listing of all your commonplaces. This is an easy way to acquire a wonderful degree of magnetism. If you are willing to make these lists you will show surprising progress from the very day you so start. With a hundred commonplaces before you, your attention will soon drive them out of your life; a thing that is not possible without lists.

The same is true of the study of margins, which is the grandest of all phases in the study of Sex Magnetism.

Make a list of all possible ways in which you may begin to save margins in your daily life. It will take a little time to begin with; but, once done, you will have it for reference. Adopt a system. Have your lists where you can see them and think of them, especially during the last few minutes before falling asleep at night. They will enter your mind and nervous system and soon become a part of yourself.

From this list you must cultivate, not by practice but by attention, the habit of saving margins in everything. People who are naturally magnetic do this without plan or thought; they simply feel that it gives them unusual power.

Of all the men and women in this world who rule others with a royal sceptre, there are none who can equal those who possess this habit of saving margins. The power is conscious, and is felt wherever the persons go. Opportunities arise every minute of the day for the practice of this remarkable custom.

In the Foundation Course the student is taught to avoid leakage of nervous vitality. Here we teach the avoidance of leakage in the higher uses of the faculties of mind and heart, of body and influence. There is one rule that can be given in closing this series of lessons:

"Never allow free rein."

CHARMLAND

ROM the hour when two persons first took an interest in each other until that later hour when they awoke from the day dreams in which they had indulged, they were under the spell of nature's charm. This was an intentional spell. It was no accident. It has been at work in every generation since the human race made any pretence of being better than the lower animal. Poets call it love. The world calls it love, and this word is as convenient as any that may be found in the dictionary.

The peculiar fact is that this charm never comes into a life that has not been endowed with the physical conditions that attend the development of young manhood and young womanhood. When anything abnormal checks that development, no matter how young or old the individual may be, there is nothing but the dull, animal interests. But when these conditions do arise properly there are sometimes temperaments that are so cold that they go through the perfunctory animal habits with neither mind nor heart warmed. To them one sex is the same as another in all respects but one, and this never is anticipated or thought much about.

Such people never enter Charmland.

But the wholly normal, natural and perfectly developed young man or young woman is sure to be ushered into the outer portals of this wonderful realm, and there be given a taste of its inner possibilities, as revealed by the true temperament. It is almost always a matter that is regulated by temperament. The young man who saw the sunset sky in the heart of the mountain, and who, on being asked to express his opinion, said that it reminded him of a ham he had seen in Chicago, a streak of fat and a streak of lean (pictured by the intervals and bars of crimson and pearl, as seen by the eyes of a friend who was able to appreciate the delights of nature), was the type of man who never enters Charmland. If the hues that hover about the western sky in the hour of sunset have no response in his nature, there can be no love in his heart. He is ham-fed, and his brain is ham-nurtured, while his blood is warmed by leaf-lard. There are too many such men in the world.

They may marry, and undoubtedly will; so do animals. These men will never have a caress for their wives after the honeymoon is over, for their temperament forbids it. They see nothing worth while in it. One of them, when asked if he kissed his wife good-by mornings when he left for his office, and again in the evenings on his return, said he did not; he once did for a few times, then stopped the practice, for he thought it useless. "What good does it do her or do me? I support her, buy her clothes, feed her well, and give her a comfortable home; but what is the use of palavering over her?" He is a distinct type of man. He has his place in nature, but not in Charmland.

In that beautiful country called Charmland there is no room for men and women who are ham-fed, whose minds are matured with ham nutrition, and whose blood is warmed with leaf-lard. They would not know what was the use of Charmland.

Let us escape from them and come to that larger class of normal men and women who are built upon natural lines, whose hearts have good, red blood flowing hotly through them, and whose minds love something more than a streak of fat and a streak of lean ham.

It is true that nature is tricky.

She brings the two sexes together by opening for them the outer gates of Charmland, lets them take a look within, and then leaves them to themselves to enter further or to linger there at the portals, and then recede to their old haunts and habits. Most men and a large number of women do recede, and are lost to the great happiness of the world. The part that nature plays is to show them what is possible. In so doing she purposely charms them. At that time the young woman is sweeter in the eyes of the young man than ever mortal being was before, or ever can be since. To her he is all that her fancy has painted—the ideal lover from the first dream of her dawn.

Then they come together.

They may be engaged, or marry, and there nature leaves them for a while. But as the race must be kept alive, it is necessary that the two sexes get acquainted; and so they are made to appear not only at their best, but in the spell of a charm that is woven about their brains and through their hearts until the dirty kid of five years ago is the dainty and delicious maiden of today, and the nasty-nosed boy has been made into the mold of a chevalier.

This is nature's trick, and, no doubt, she smiles at the way it works, for, in fact, it works like a charm.

Then the crafty husband and the selfish wife both agree that they will never have children; or he may not want them, while she pleads with him to allow at least one when she is forty; but, bless you, nature gives them five before she is thirty. Nature is more selfish than the woman, and far craftier than the husband; for all the children that are born in the world, ninety per cent. come before they are affirmatively sought, as surprises. One in ten may be deliberately planned for, but the other nine are nature's gifts. So in two ways she is designing. She brings unattractive sexes together in courtship by throwing a charm over them and making love blind; and later on she takes them off their guard by delivering offspring without receiving orders to that effect.

So the world wags on.

These things have been happening since five thousand years ago.

The study of the ways of nature has led investigators to inquire what depth of sincerity she intends in her fascinating schemes by which the sexes are blinded to the faults of each other. Is there any real charm, or is it merely her attempt to bring the people together for the purpose of saving the race?

No question is more worthy of debate than this. Not if there is such thing as true love, but is the charm, which is admitted by all who know life at all to be a fact, a real endowment intended to endure, or is it a makeshift used for the sole purpose of bringing about the union of the two sexes? From time immemorial men and women have debated the question, Is there such a thing as love? And, when they have replied that there is something that is so-called, they have passed on to the further inquiry, Is there such a thing as true love? They have decided that there are different phases of the regard that springs up between the two sexes, the first a fancy, and the last a deep-seated attachment; but that there is a real, true, genuine first love possible all through life they have doubted.

One thing has been unanimously agreed to by all normal and intelligent men and women who have given the subject a full analysis and test of many years' duration; and it is this: There is a charm that nature throws about two persons when they first begin to take an interest in each other, and this charm is not surpassed or equaled by any other pleasure in human life. This much is agreed to, and is known as a proved fact.

Nor is it doubted by any person who knows anything of the matter at all. It is universally accepted. But men who do not think there is such a thing as love, whether true or transitory, look upon the period of charm as the time of being fooled. "That was the one time of my life when I was a silly fool," has been said in substance more than one hundred thousand times in every generation. The most exquisite language of poetry tells nothing half so sweet and glorious as the feelings of the young man whose whole thought has suddenly been centered in a young woman whom he wants to marry. There is nothing half so sweet in life as love, is an older saying that any recorded axiom of this world.

Leaving out of our own account therein the word love and substituting in its place the word charm, which is nearer the fact, we will proceed to make a search for the truth. Of course, we must use the word love when we quote from others, and when the experience of others is made public; but our own word is charm. In employing this term we make no mistake, for it is a conceded fact that the charm has been proven, while love takes shelter under many varying conditions, changing as the years alter the associations. Thus the maiden, sweet, pretty, demure, dainty, and all else that is said of her, who fell in love with a grand man, a great man, in fact, a Senator in a mighty nation, was charmed at his magnificent bearings, his lordly manner, and his fine personality. The two looked together like grandfather and granddaughter. They were a pair in contrasts. Yet he cared for her and she adored him. He wanted her with him at all times, and she wanted to be near him. He could not attend to his common duties without her love, and she even aided him in everything. It was a charm that a great man held for a pretty girl, and she for a great man. Such a feeling could not exist between two persons of the same sex. It required the difference to make it possible.

How did they become acquainted?

He was overworked, bluff, stern, unyielding and unattractive except in his public appearances. In his boarding-house he was known as a cross bear. He had many private secretaries, and could not keep them on account of his bluntness and outspoken manner. They feared him and he would not relax for the sake of policy and harmony. One morning, when he was vexed by some delays, he roared to his secretary to do this and do that and the other thing until the young man slipped out and ran off, while the Senator still supposed him to be in the room behind him at the table. But the little lady, a demure maiden of seventeen, who had called to see her brother, the secretary, stood in the latter's place trembling. With a final, gigantic roar, the Senator wheeled around in his chair and beheld her. She was of flushed face, excited eyes, and vibrating lips. He ceased to roar. He looked at her and his nature softened at once. She started to withdraw, but he asked her to be seated and to tell her name. She stood at the door and informed him that she was the sister of the young man who had just ran away.

"What did he run away for?" asked the Senator.

"Because he was afraid of you, for you roared at him like a lion."

"Well, I will not roar any more, at least not at your brother. Go and see if you can find him."

The girl did as she was told and soon returned with the scared secretary. From that day ever afterwards the Senator addressed the young man as gently as one tender human being can address another. It made no difference how much he was tormented by things going wrong, he gave only the kindest of treatment and the gentlest of words to the secretary. A whole year passed before the girl and the Senator were in love with each other, and in those twelve months the brother was the object of the deepest solicitation from the great man. The latter must have been under the charm from the moment when their eyes first met, for that was the dividing line between his rough, masculine ways and his better nature. The secretary, always discreet, never told his sister much about the man, and once remarked in a casual way that the Senator had been as gentle as a lamb ever since she caught him in a tantrum. She realized that he had been influenced by her coming in; but how could that one visit have held him down to such good behavior all these months? Then the truth came into her heart.

The union was a happy one, and still endures.

But there was no trick of nature to bring them together in the same mood that the two young lovers are brought under the charm. It was the delightful opposing of two sexes, one created for sweetness and beauty, and the other for manliness. Here are the potent factors of all charms in the sex relations.

Just as long as a girl or woman realizes the fact that nature made her to be beautiful, if not in face, at least in manners, and also to be sweet and lovable, just so long will she have her place in the world, and her true place; but when she no longer tries to be beautiful, or sweet, or lovable, then she will fall back into the charmless period of humanity.

Just as long as a man realizes the fact that nature made him to be manly, virile, honest and attractive in his manner and conduct, just so long will he have his place in the world. But the fellow, be he rough or smooth, be he a countryman or a city-bred gentleman, who ceases to be manly is no longer an attractive force in sex relationships. If he is not the soul of honesty and of honor, then he is not a true man. And his manners must be, as the word indicates, of the true man.

We have traveled much. We have lived in the city many, many years, and in the country many, many years, and we have studied human nature in all places and under all conditions. In the country there is now and then a manly fellow, perhaps rough in his etiquette, but well built, of native intelligence, without much book learning, and honest to the core. There are young men, rare, but nevertheless in existence, in whose blood never a drop of dishonest compound has entered; honorable and virile. They bear on their foreheads the stamp of the kingly power. They may stay in the country, but if they do they will be the best product of the soil. Many drift to the city, and there in time tower over their fellow-beings.

There is no mistaking them. We picked out a hundred or more
of them in years past in widely separated localities, and all
these hundred have risen to the level that was given them by
the training of their younger years.

There are in the country smart, bright, naturally intelligent young women with pleasing ways, gentle manners and
kind hearts full of sympathy and generous impulses. It can
be seen at a glance that these two sexes belong to each other.
The trouble is that love, being blind, the good judgment of the
young man will not be allowed to have its rightful opportunity. If he remains in the country to grow up a king, he
may never meet that particular kind of young woman that
should be his queen. If he goes to the city he may be captured by some frail, sickly, indigestible shell of a girl, who
has nothing for him but complaints and doctors' bills; or,
if she feeds well, she may be a bridge-player and loafer at
home; and so his life is deprived of the happiness that a
better knowledge would give him.

To that kind of a man, whether he is raised in country,
town or city, this training course should come in time to
save him. Let him discover the temperament and fitness of
the woman before he weds her, or even promises to marry
her. If he adheres to the rules laid down in this book, he
cannot make a mistake.

To that kind of a young woman, whether she is raised in
the country or in the city or town, it is to be hoped that this
study will come in time to guide her to her true mate.

It is most pitiable that the kingly man should be shackled
to the empty woman; or that the queenly woman should be
bonded to the boor or the roue. Let like find like, and it
will do so if time and deliberation are allowed. It is haste
that makes waste in wedlock and in love.

But while these seem excellent as bits of advice, nature is
still laying her traps to catch the unwary. Nature does not
want you to wait. If you have a flower garden, nature will
not take care of it for you. With smiles and with jokes she
will run in foul weeds to see what you think of them. She
furnishes the impulses, and you must do the rest. You must
act. In marriage she gives that wonderful impulse that is
known as a charm, and she gives it early in life, so as not to

waste any time, and you are then given a head, inside of which are brains, and she tells you how to get your brains in working order and well poised, and then she steps aside to see what you will do. The charm is potent, and the brains are slow. When the charm is at its strongest then the brains are almost stopped; like the case of the Judge of a State Supreme Court who fell in love, and for five months could not see anything to the cases before him except the bright, sweet side of human nature, and he acted accordingly. Or, as Whittier says in one of his poems, the Judge whistled an old love tune in court after he had met a maiden that turned his heart over for him.

No matter what the strength of the charm may be, the brains must not be allowed to stop their work. Nature is tricky enough to have them cease; but nature must be controlled. Do not forget this fact. She would ruin your garden for you by letting weeds grow where beautiful flowers are more effective; and she will let marriages run to weeds if you are not as much in command of the charm-period as of the garden. Remember these truths. Life's greatest ruins are built on the charms that never grew into facts, but remained only a far-off mirage turned upside down in the sky.

The brain is crafty. Nature is tricky. She takes the noblest minds and works havoc with them at her own sweet will, if she can but get a hold. Look at the history of great bankers, great merchants, great statesmen, and the solidest characters in the business and professional world, who have been giants in their mental work, and yet who have lost their poise of mind when a dainty skirt comes in view. As long as the true red blood courses through the avenues of the heart, so long will nature throw her charm over the strong man.

What kingly gentleman can withstand the glance of a woman's eye when leveled full upon him from out the misty vale of fascinating interest? "I wish that woman had not come here," said a merchant one day, after he had been visited in his office by a lady who sought contributions for a charity. She was not married, he felt, for a married woman has a look out of which the charm had gone years before; and it takes widowhood to bring it back. If there still remains any charm whatever, it is for her husband, and even then it is not his unless he wins and deserves it after marriage. The battle is not in courtship, nor in the honeymoon, but in the hard, practical days of married life shorn of its false pretences and allurements that have no fact in them. Few married women can charm a man. It is almost a contradiction on its face to say they can; for they have none of that virgin sweetness left in them since once the veil was lifted from the hopes of married life.

There are three kinds of charms:

1. The attractions of a convenient marriage is the first kind.
2. The love-charm is the second kind.
3. The sensual charm is the third kind.

Let us look at the first for a moment. If a man and woman are in good health, and he can give her a home and she can take care of his house for him, that is the first or animal match. But the same kind of union based on different motives takes place when the man of title seeks and wins the woman of wealth. It is the match of one commodity with another. None can be happy. Some remain intact, but most fall to pieces by the law of gravity lacking natural cohesion.

Royal marriages are spoken of, one time in ten or so, as love matches; and the union of Queen Victoria with Albert was of the true, but rare kind. In all that period of wedlock the charm remained unbroken; just as strong at the end as when they first met as young maiden and young man. That union will stand for all time as the ideal type of love-charms.

But royal marriages are for the most part unions of convenience born in a national desire to keep the peace of the world.

Before looking into the second class of charms, let us dispose of the lowest of all, the third class. It is built upon mere physical desire; not passion, for that is noble, but a sensuous propensity, which is an excess of the most common kind both in and out of wedlock. Most women act on the defensive in this matter, while in love of a pure kind they are rarely ever on the defensive. Those who are evil disposed are in a class by themselves and ply their trade in all sorts of ways; some by pretence of goodness they possess not, and others by brazen attempts to influence men.

But there is a better class of women who have attractions and yet who do not feel true love, but who are always tempting men by their treatment of them; not one of whom can be said to be of inherently evil heart. Some of them succeed in winning proposals of marriage from the best men; in which case they are temperamentally mismated. Others draw to themselves their own kind in this matter, but in all others they are mismatched, and they lead lives of cats and dogs. It is hardly possible for a happy marriage to come out of mismating.

History is too full of the opposite results.

A woman who wishes a heart union should be careful not to wed a man who is moved by these impulses; for, if she can move him, then one of two things must be true:

1. Either he does not deeply respect her; for, if he did, he would never respond to certain quiet hints that she gives him to test him.

2. Or, if he does care for her in the right way, he will be just as easily led to another woman after marriage as he now is led to her.

There are hundreds of little ways, all apparently accidental, that can awaken a man's nature; and it is true that clever women have not hesitated to use them in order to find out what kind of a character was seeking her hand in marriage.

Leaving now the extremes and coming to the middle ground, we find the love-charm in all its glory awaiting discussion and analysis. As has been said, it is known beyond all doubt to be a fact as a charm, but the genuineness of its love nature is and always will be the subject of conjecture. It is enough that it exists as a fact.

We live in our emotions if we live humanly.

The charm that nature throws over the mind and the heart when love knocks for admission into one's life is most blissful while it lasts. It is not confined to any one class, so that it has manliness and honesty in the man, and sweetness and lovableness in the woman to found its power upon; and, having these, it builds giant castles of the most superb architecture and entrancing beauty.

It is the poetry of existence.

Nowhere else in literature should we look to find it. True, there is love in most novels; and the modern playwright can not hope for success if he omits love from his drama. It everywhere demands attention and in all ages and under all conditions takes temporary possession of every healthy man and woman. But the poet tells the story just as it exists in the belief and experience of those who are held in its spell.

Our language is as nothing compared with the true pictures of the heart when this charm falls upon it. Some lines are reproduced here from an anonymous writer; and they take the mind out into the plainest form of life, where it would be supposed that only the hardships were to be found amid an excess of commonplaces; but the charm goes there if it has the true heart to touch:

Early on a sunny morning, while the lark was singing sweet,
Came, beyond the ancient farmhouse, sounds of lightly-trip-
    ping feet.
'Twas a lowly cottage maiden going—why, let young hearts
    tell—
With her homely pitcher laden, fetching water from the well.

Pleasant, surely, were her musings, for the nodding leaves in
    vain
Sought to press their brightening image on her ever-busy brain.
Leaves and joyous birds flew by her, like a dim, half-waking
    dream;
And her soul was only conscious of life's gladdest summer
    gleam.

At the old lane's shady turning lay a well of water bright,
Singing, soft, its hallelujah to the gracious morning light.
Fern leaves, broad and green, bent o'er it where its silvery
    droplets fell,
And the fairies dwelt beside it in the spotted foxglove bell.

Back she bent the shading fern leaves, dipped the pitcher in
    the tide—
Drew it, with the dripping waters flowing o'er its glazed side.
But before her arm could place it on her head of wavy hair,
By her side a youth was standing! Love rejoiced to see the
    pair!

Tones of tremulous emotion trembled on the morning breeze,
Gentle words of heart devotion whispered 'neath the ancient
    trees;

But the blessed, holy secrets, it becomes me not to tell;
Life had met another meaning, fetching water from the well.
Down the rural lane they sauntered—he the burdened pitcher
    bore;
She with dewy eyes, now dropping, grew more beauteous than
    before!
When they neared the silent homestead, up he raised the pitcher
    light;
Like a fitting crown he placed it on her hair of wavelets
    bright:

Emblems of the coming burdens that for love of him she'd bear,
Calling every burden blessed, if his love but lighted there.
Then, still waving benedictions, farther, farther off he drew,
While his shadow seemed a glory that across the pathway
    grew.

Now about her household duties silently the maiden went,
And an ever-radiant halo o'er her daily life was blent.
Little knew the maiden's mother, as the feet like music fell,
What abundant treasure found she, fetching water from the
    well.

In the foregoing picture of country love-charm several truths
are told. It is a fact that such experiences have come
to maidens; they are not denied the happiness of those who
live more sumptuously. Indeed, it is more than likely that
the simplest girls and women have the deepest yearnings.
The city girl thinks of the soda water, the candies, the theatres, the drives, the furnishings of the house, the many dresses
needed to clothe her, and all the things that she must be provided with, or she will be miserable if her friends know what
a cheap husband she married. He is not able to keep up with
her wants, and they must soon part, he to go to some distant
locality where he can escape the courts, and she back to her
mother.

But the country girl has a home. Her lover has a home.
And they together will sometime have a third home, all theirs.
There is life all about them, plenty to eat and to wear, and
comforts of all kinds, with no hothouse expenses such as rise

up like spectres in the city; no soda water to buy; no two-dollar-a-pound candies to buy; no theatre tickets at four dollars apiece to buy; nothing of elegance for the home furnishings to be bought; no series of half a dozen new dresses to get every six months; and nothing to bring on worry and insanity in the fevered brain of the man or the broken heart of the woman. So in the country maiden there is a larger share of the real charm-love than in the city lady.

The poet tells us that this girl's musings were pleasant; she expected to meet him. Then we are told that gentle words of heart devotion trembled on the morning breeze; but the great fact of all is this:

"Life had met another meaning."

This fact overtops all others in value. Life, before running in narrow grooves, now opened out, and a new meaning came into it. Her dewy eyes drooping grew more beauteous than before. How tenderly he handed her the little burden, having carried it as far as he could! The rest was hers to do; symbols of life's history!

He left her side. Away he went, slowly, always turning and waving adieus to her as she watched him; and then a glory was over all the land.

She went in and took up her duties once more. They were a pleasure to her. Work served to give her thoughts free play. Days came and went, and an ever-radiant halo surrounded them. Her feet, stepping from room to room, and in the crowd of little duties that fell to her lot, made music as she went about them; while the old mother, unobserving and not anxious to know that her child might divide her love, was oblivious to the episode.

This is nature's law.

Light up the fires of your imagination and bring these facts vividly before the mind. There is nothing overdrawn. The charm is there, and it is simply portrayed; told as naturally and in as plain language as it might have been described to the young lovers themselves.

She felt the charm. He felt it.

It was real. She may not have been as beauteous to others as she seemed to him; for life is lived in emotions, not in the senses. But there would not have been another girl in all the world for him at that time. She was thoroughly under the spell of the charm.

It is the old story.

Now what we are interested in is to know how long it lasted, and what became of it. When they met a second time, or the next time after that episode, was she as beautiful and he as attractive as before, or had the charm lessened? Just as soon as they had come to some understanding the power of the halo would be decreased. But if they found it hard to meet, or were not allowed to see each other often, or there was rivalry, then "love that grows best with most pruning" would have been sustained under the spell of the intense charm. Otherwise it would have drooped some; not much at a time; but some, and then more after that.

Such is the history of the world.

If men and women could build up the magnetic power of mental sight such as is taught in Universal Magnetism, and increase this power to its full magnetic size, they would have eyes in their emotions, and not depend on the fading memories to bring them joys.

Animals, even the best of them, and the animal grade of humanity, live in their senses. But there is a grade better than this and it has a higher realm in which to dwell. It is not concurrent always, but often coincides with the all-round mind of the man or woman who loves shadings of colors, and blendings of musical harmonies. The more animal the mind is, the less variety of color-effects it can see; not the mechanical matching of goods in a store; but the softened union of two natures in the light, symbolic of human love. Animals do not know shades of color, and few know more than three different basic colors. To an animal-man, such as a butcher or pork mind, the color of red or blue is beautiful; but to a refined mind nothing is rich but the union and sensitive blending of opposing shades.

The woman was right who said: "If I were to pick a husband I would select one who was with me and a group of others at the coming on of twilight in the summer sky, following the descent of the glowing ball of fire amid a bed of clouds. I saw a dozen or more young men the other evening, and as many young women, sitting on a hotel piazza when a wonderful scene was transpiring in the western sky. I could have picked couples then and there who were adapted for each other. Most of the young men were smart. They saw nothing of the glory that God was painting in ever-changing colors in the clouds and on the vapors there. One young man saw all that was being enacted; and far from him, not even known to him, sat a young lady who was also enraptured. There were the two who would have been happy together for life."

She spoke truly.

The smart young men, flip and silly, shallow of ideas and of sense, saw nothing. Had their attention been called to the scene they would have thought "rot," even if they did not dare to say it. Yet they were well dressed, versed in society manners and believed in their own ability to win whatever women they sought; so great and common was their conceit. They are like the great tide of men that surge over the world; smart in talk, low in ideas, and flip in mind.

The young man who saw God in the heavens, who watched the wavering streams of light gleaming through the clouds, who noted the ever-shifting hand of the painter sending his colors here and there to adorn the vapors and make them breathe with beauty, who felt that a sea was engulfing the world and out of it a new city was rising to bring back the kingdom of heaven to men, was rich in mind. He was capable of living as he felt, and of appreciating the charm of love as it comes to him from a pure heart.

At some distance from him sat the young woman whom he did not know. Her eyes were fixed on the unspeakable glory of the burning sky, in which she saw many colors and infinite shadings. Her heart was full of thankfulness that earth could be so beautiful.

It may be that this young man was already engaged to marry some flighty maid who could not see in such a sky anything more than something that would match her shirt waist. It may be that the young lady was already engaged to some man who had a pork-brain, and to whom music and harmony of colors would be no more than the streakings of a slice of ham. If such mating was made, it would mean the loss of a lifetime of happiness to both.

For they belonged to each other.

There were two temperaments that were bound to harmonize. Assuming that she could pass through the refinements of the various departments of this study, and that he could do the same, they would come to each other in the purity of a natural charm that, with careful watching, could be made to endure for a lifetime. Here is one of the many tests of temperamental fitness that are contained in this work.

It is the same with musical shadings. The tune that catches the slang ear, like ragtime, is not a blending of musical shadings such as are found in classical harmonies. The latter are not understood by the untrained ear at first; but there was never a fine-grained man who did not in time learn to prefer these better airs to the footbeat tunes of the commoner grade.

Then it is the same with flowers.

They are efforts of God to talk to humanity. They are the kindnesses of heaven speaking to the heart of men and women and to the souls of little children. What is more enjoyed by the boy or girl than a holiday ramble into the fields and woods to gather these little messengers; and yet how few fathers will take the time away from their selfishness to form so intimate an acquaintance with their little ones? How the heart of that wife and mother aches and yearns for the companionship of the man who once was charmed by her beauty, and who now takes his holiday off with coarse men, to smoke and talk in the vocabulary of their class; all different from the language that he used when he told her that she was more to him than all the world besides. He cares nothing for flowers, and the last bunch he bought her on her first birthday after they were married he threw in at the door and went off to have a smoke; and never saw them again.

In Charmland there are beautiful colors, rich in art and flush with nature; and there are beautiful harmonies told in music that inspires; and there are flowers that speak more eloquently than language of the human tongue. Once a man who tried to tell the woman how much he cared for her found the words choking in his throat, and he took a rose from its fellows and laid it in her hand. Then she took one and kissed it, and this he grasped eagerly for his own. Thus the flowers talked, for they bloom in all sweethearts for sweethearts. Tenny-

son, writing of Charmland for lovers, speaks in the vocabulary
of many flowers:

> I am here at the gate alone;
>   And the woodbine spices are wafted abroad;
> And the musk of the roses blown.
>
> For the breeze of morning moves,
>   And the planet of Love is on high,
> Beginning to faint in the light that she loves,
>   On a bed of daffodil sky.
>
> All night have the roses heard,
>   All night has the casement jessamine stirred.
> I said to the lily, "There is but one
>   With whom she has heart to be gay."
>
> I said to the rose, "The brief night goes,"
>   And the soul of the rose went into my blood
> From the meadow your walks have left so sweet
>   That, whene'er a March wind sigh,
>
> He sets the jewel-prints of your feet
>   In violets blue as your eyes,
> To the woody hollows in which we meet,
>   And the valleys of Paradise.
>
> The slender acacia would not shake
>   One long milk-bloom on the tree;
> The white lake blossom fell into the lake,
>   As the pimpernel dozed on the lea;
>
> But the rose was awake all night for your sake,
>   Knowing your promise to me;
> The lilies and roses were all awake,
>   They sighed for the dawn and thee.
>
> Queen rose of the rosebud garden of girls,
>   Come hither—the dances are done;
> In gloss of satin and glimmer of pearls,
>   Queen lily and rose in one;
> Shine out, little head, sunning over with curls,
>   To the flowers and be their sun.

There has fallen a splendid tear
  From the passion-flower at the gate.
She is coming, my love, my dear,
  She is coming, my life, my fate!

The red rose cries, "She is near, she is near;"
  And the white rose weeps, "She is late."
The larkspur listens, "I hear, I hear,"
  And the lily whispers, "I wait."

She is coming, my own, my sweet!
  Were it ever so airy a tread,
My heart would hear her and beat,
  Were it earth in an earthly bed:

My dust would hear her and beat,
  Had I lain for a century dead;
Would start and tremble under her feet,
  And blossom in purple and red.

Despite the fullness of poetic fancy depicted in these verses, they tell of the real charm that a girl weaves over a man's life. She may be false to him, as is indicated in these lines just quoted from the great English poet; but she is the focus of nature's fire in the heart of man. What is written in this warm poem has been written millions of times in the inner soul of lovers who have waited for the grace that came too slowly to satisfy them.

How much real control can a woman create in her own nature and use to secure the mastery over a man?

Her power is almost unlimited.

In the first place, she should create in her character a new level, and this must be done as taught in the fourth and fifth departments of this book. Having laid this secure foundation, she must next rise to the standard set in the ninth department.

The magnetic margins belong to marriage, as far as this control is concerned, and they need not be considered at this time. But it is certain that if she has put into practice the doctrines taught in the departments named, then she has grown more beautiful and more lovable. There are three ideas she must keep in her mind at all times, night and day, during her waking hours. They are these:

To be beautiful in demeanor. To be sweet in disposition. To be lovable in character.

If you who read these lines are a woman, read them again and still again, and say to yourself that:

YOU must be beautiful in demeanor. If you have adopted the teachings of the fourth, fifth and ninth departments herein, then your face will show quite differently from what it did before you began the study. These lessons have been taught in private for more than a quarter of a century, and photographs have been taken to show the remarkable change that comes over the features under their influence. Try it. Have your likeness taken just as you begin this training; then, at the end of a year of earnest following of the instruction; and if you have been sincere in your adoption of these teachings, you will see a great difference in your own face. Beauty is the reflection of something real. That which passes for beauty is an empty face, is merely shape and color; they both pass away with the first change, and they never come again.

Look to the character.

YOU must be sweet in disposition. This means that you must not be cross, irritable, acid, sharp, critical, severe, sarcastic or mean. Be generous, and be patient. Never say what is hasty and illconsidered, and never think what you cannot say or should not utter aloud. The face is a mirror of the mind and heart.

YOU must be lovable in character. You can make yourself so if you are so resolved. It all depends on what you decide to do. But there must be substance as the foundation of any character building, and the only solid ground on which to set your house is found in the fourth, fifth and ninth departments of this work. Master them. Then come to your own will power and exercise it in real earnest.

Beautiful. Sweet. Lovable.

These are the three traits of woman.

Are you beautiful? How do you know one way or the other? Do you think you can make yourself beautiful with face rouge, and pencil, with bella donna in the eyes, with waves on the hair that came from the store, and with a baby stare on the countenance? You may deceive a worthless man by such things, but never a real man. He will find you out. You may hurry a worthless fellow into a hasty marriage, thinking that once you have crossed the line of wedlock with him you have him tight and sound; but he may leave you at a time when you cannot afford to be left, and your last condition will be worse than the first. Such pretences of beauty fade away. No art can take the place of the mind and the soul in the face; and if you have an unlovable mind and a cheap soul you cannot cover them up by face powder.

The more you depend on the artifices of color and smoothness to hide the blotches of character in your features, the less successful you will be. The man of the next few years is not to be deceived by any subterfuge. He is going to know what he is getting, and he will not take what he does not want. Tears, smiles, sadness, ingeniousness and all the shifts of women are known now to men. They want a real woman who is

Beautiful; but not in color or skin necessarily.

Sweet; but not assumed and dramatic ballet-girl smiles.

Lovable; but with the character of her mind and her heart stamped in her face to stay there.

Now, if you who read these lines are a man, read them again, and still again, and say to yourself that:

You must be noble, virile, manly and attractive.

Here are four traits that belong, not to woman, but to man. The second and third are nearly the same, and may be regarded as one.

Say at all times to yourself:

YOU must be noble. The woman must be beautiful; that you will admire in her. You must be noble; that she will admire in you. The handsome woman is womanish. The noble man is masculine. The woman who thinks a man most noble often mixes her adjectives and calls him handsome by mistake.

To be noble, you must be above all petty feelings, all petty habits and all the errors mentioned in the third department of this book. Then you must make yourself master of the fourth, fifth and ninth departments of this work. They will help you, just as they have helped the woman and just as their teachings have helped hundreds of men in the past to rise out of their smallnesses and be true to themselves and to the sex of which they are members.

YOU must be manly. This means that you must have strength of mind, strength of will, strength of purpose, strength of body, strength of character, and all the traits that separate a mean man from one that is of high stature. Women like manly men. You like a woman when she is sweet; she likes you when you are virile, which is the moral side of manliness; honest, fair, generous, true to the best principles of the human race.

YOU must be attractive. You like the woman who is lovable; she likes the man who is attractive. What is the use of being noble and manly, and not clean, nor kind, nor of good habits in personal matters? Her love is pleasing to you and is magnetic; and your attractiveness is just the same to her. You can make yourself more and more attractive every day if you will get down to the resolution to do so, and then live to it through thick and thin. Women want men who are:

Noble; but not in birth of title so much as in birth of blood.

Manly; not in sports and games, but in nature, disposition and honor.

Attractive; but not alone in dress, nor in artificial manners and the forms of society, so much as in personal habits and genuine worth. True men are wanted; men who deserve the best love of the best woman that lives on earth today. Get her; she is yours. Let her have in exchange the best fellow that draws the breath of life in this wide world.

You, men, can be getting better all the time. It is not hard work if you are in earnest. Remember those departments, the fourth, fifth and ninth. Master them. Take them along with you in thought, and write a short synopsis of them for ready reference wherever you may be. They may be glanced at when you are in the car, the carriage, walking, or in the intervals between the duties of the day. There are hundreds of little moments when they can be read and their truths brought closer to you as a means of help and inspiration.

You women can be getting sweeter and more lovable all the time. Do not think or believe otherwise. Whatever you make up your mind to do, you will do successfully and completely. Do not falter.

Charmland has been yours in the past; perhaps for a day, and more likely for a week or more. It was yours until that fatal answer when you made the conquest certain, when the promises were exchanged, and then all you had to do was to sit and look at each other and wonder what to do next. The lover wanted Maud to come into the garden, that he might tell her that he loved her. She was an attractive country girl, nothing more; perhaps vain, and not too deep in sincerity. He loved her the more because she cared for the men of higher rank. She was at the all-night ball, where he was not desired, as he had not the manners of the better social classes. He was worthy of a good girl. She was flattered by the attentions of the immoral fellows of social rank, who cared nothing for her except what was wrong. She could float around the ballroom in their arms, but she could not be received in their parents' mansions. The country fellow who talked with the flowers when he was there at the gate alone stood in Charmland in hope only; when Venus rose in the east above the coming sun he was still conversing with the flowers, and still his girl was dancing with men he did not want to embrace her. She had been willing to walk with him through the meadow, and the March winds, cold and bleak, had set violets in the jewel-prints of her feet, every step of which led them towards Paradise. They had been happy together, or he would not have recounted these experiences. Then the passion flower at the gate drops a splendid tear, and the rose that is red gives hope, the rose that is white gives fear, and the larkspur and lily add their surmises; but she comes at last.

Symbolic of human yearnings as these lines are, they tell the story of that Charmland towards which every man and every woman of good, red blood has once trod in eager steps to see what lies beyond. Few have gone over the portals. They stop short of bliss because they have not the character and the value in their nature to receive welcome within.

One thing is true—no woman can ever enter Charmland alone. No man can ever enter Charmland alone. Two women cannot enter Charmland together. It is for one man and for one woman; and they must be together, rightfully together, heart in heart, mind in mind, and soul in soul. They must be man and wife, married according to the laws of the land in which they live; and they must be true to each other; true to the letter and the spirit of the wedding vows; true to their home and true to their God.

Then they can enter Charmland, if they will make themselves what they must be in order to draw and to hold, each the other, for life and forever; the man must be noble, manly and attractive in all his nature; and the woman must be beautiful, sweet and lovable.

They now will enter Charmland.

Sometimes circumstances mold the character of two persons into one final form that can never separate. Fate takes the place of training, but gives just the qualities that training imparts. To illustrate this natural drift of life, the following authentic histories are repeated here:

One case is that which has had its duplicates many times, except in one essential. The man entered the hospital poor, and during his illness became the heir of a large property, of which he and all others there knew nothing. There was no chance for information to reach anyone connected with the institution. The man had been stricken with typhoid, and was removed to the hospital by the advice of a local physician. In the ward where he was placed there was a young woman who nursed him. She was there by reason of her desire to learn how to care for the sick. She owned in her own name a large property that yielded an income, which she spent in doing good for others.

Thus the usual conditions were reversed.

In most instances it is the rich man and the poor girl who nurses him; but it was the poor man and the rich nurse in this history.

In his delirium, such as attends this kind of fever, he became wild, and threatened to run away from the place. She was not strong, but she resisted him, and was badly hurt in the struggle, so much so that her life was despaired of. When he became conscious and was convalescent he asked for her, and was at a later time told the facts. He got well at last, and had her brought to the home of his mother. At that time he had received word of his good fortune under a will; but she had no knowledge of it. She remained ill for many months, and then it was announced that she would recover. She had been living at a hotel in the city before she became a nurse. Now she wished to return, but the man's mother prevailed upon her to stay. The home was humble in the extreme, and the nurse desired to pay liberally for the attention she had been receiving. The best medical care had been bestowed upon her, and there was nothing left undone that could be done for her benefit in order to hasten her recovery.

She noticed that the man had no employment, for he stayed in the house much of the time, and was at her bedside constantly. Flowers that were inexpensive, but attractive, were brought in fresh every day. The man had not allowed his mother to know of the wealth that had fallen to him for fear she would tell the invalid. The period of convalescence was long and tedious; but the man still spent much of his time in the little home.

To the sick woman, on her pressing inquiry, the mother confessed that her son was rather poor, but that he had been a hard student and was sure to rise in the world. The invalid said, "I have plenty of money and will see that he has a good position as soon as I get well."

To him she said, "You were not to blame for what happened in the hospital, and I fear that you believe you are. You are not under any indebtedness to me because of that. It is one of those chances that all nurses must take everywhere."

Still he said nothing to indicate that he cared for her.

When she got well she offered him a position, which he declined with thanks and in full sincerity of gratitude for her kindness. He said that he had made plans that would interfere with his acceptance of such an honor from her. Here the mystery began. She instituted an investigation of this man and found that he had never been anything more than a poor fellow who was somewhat of a dreamer, and yet well educated and a gentleman by nature. His clothes were plain and inexpensive, the home was most humble, but neat and very comfortable, and he was always in attractive condition, despite evidences of a struggle to keep up appearances. He owed no bills, as he had drawn from his new fortune, and had paid in full all the debts that he had incurred by reason of his long illness and rest. His mother still knew nothing of the wealth that had fallen to him, and this lady nurse was unaware of it. While he could draw all the money he needed, he purposely kept up the appearance of being poor, but out of debt.

She was in wonderment at what it all indicated.

Surely, she thought, he had some means laid away from which he could obtain a frugal allowance; but she could not find out where it was or the source of income that seemed to supply him with funds. As a friend of his mother, she not only called at the humble home, but made it her place of constant visits, until she seemed a part of the household. This friendship lasted for months, and in all that time she could not induce him to allow her to even share part of her own cost of living there. Then she threatened to never come again except on a social call, at which he smiled. This aggravated the situation. "Now I am in earnest," she said. "I need an educated man to assist me in some of my financial plans, and you can have the position at a salary to be named by you." She had never, since her illness, returned to nursing, and was free to carry on other work of a charitable and helpful kind. He accepted the position and named a salary of twenty dollars a week. To this she demurred, as she could not employ a man who was not worth at least fifty dollars a week. But she was held to her offer, and he received the twenty dollars every week, every cent of which he spent in beautiful flowers for his mother and the young woman who employed him.

"How can you live if you spend all you earn?" she asked, somewhat vexed.

"I am not a good financier. But if you will tell me how I earn twenty dollars a week doing work that requires less than an hour a day, I will tell you how I live when I spend all I earn."

"You are a man of mystery," she replied. "Will you not confide in me? I want to help you, and I am able to do so; but I cannot understand you. Is there some person who is supplying you with funds, or have you in the past lived humbly in order that you may save money, and are now using it? Will it soon be gone? Please tell me."

He took from his pocket a roll of ten-dollar bills and said to her:

"See, I have money. Would you believe that I am a gambler,

if I told you so, and that I make money in that way, assuming
by day the appearance of a poor man of leisure?''

She said she would not believe it. ''As I look into your face,
and as I know you and have known you for months, I feel and
am sure that you are the best man I have ever met. I know it
surely. Nothing you could tell me of ill would be accepted by
me as anything more than jest. I do not know how you get
money, but I will say from the depths of my heart that you
receive it honestly.''

''It is true, I receive it honestly. I have earned much in the
past and have not spent it all as fast as I have earned it,'' he
replied; and he spoke the truth.

''But you will soon exhaust the fund you may have laid away
from past earnings, and then your mother will suffer.''

''No, she will never suffer from lack of money as long as I live,
or afterwards, if she survives me,'' he replied.

''Still I do not understand,'' said the young woman, ''What
I want is your full confidence. Can I help you in any way?''

''I am trying to find out two things. In the first place, I want
to know if I really care for you as much as I believe I do, and
have believed for months. Then I want to know if you care for
me at all.''

''I will not tell you until you have learned the answer to your
first inquiry. When you know for sure that you care for me
then I will tell you if I care for you.''

''Do you know?''

''Assuredly I know.''

''What do you know?''

''I know the answer to both your questions, and have known
for months better than you know.''

''Would you accept a poor man as a husband and be willing
to support him in idleness all his life?'' he asked.

''I will accept a man like you and take my chances of having
a worthy husband who will work when he has work to do. I
know something of the law of temperaments and we both have
the same dispositions in this regard. We will not have occasion
to disagree. I want only one promise, and it is this: There has
been a charm in my life ever since I came to love you, and I
know that you have felt the same influence. To me it seems
divine. Whatever it is, I wish our marriage to be delayed until

we can analyze it and grasp its meaning and its nature. I wish to have that same feeling of supreme happiness follow all through our lives. Let us study it, and find out what it is, and how we can keep it with us forever.''

They came to a complete understanding and were married. Years have passed since that event, and they still dwell in Charmland, simply because they made up their minds to do so.

Most people are willing to live in such a realm if they can find somebody to push them there and to hold them there; but they are not willing to make the effort to get there. They drift. It is easier to drift than it is to row against the stream. Life is made up of rowing up stream or drifting; fish swim against the current, for they know that in such direction only is there safety for them.

Nothing is ever gained by drifting.

How many men and women are there in the world who are down. Dead fish let the current take them along; all live willing to make the effort? In one thousand you may find, perhaps, ten who care to take the trouble; the others let the trouble take them. Eternal vigilance is the price of liberty, and eternal effort is the price of happiness. Here is a couple that is provided with all the good things of life, except the disposition to be on guard against the little enemies of Charmland. What are these little enemies?

1. They are, in the first place, the offences to the senses that are described in the third department of this book. They work havoc in the feelings of respect and appreciation that the wife should, and wants, to have for her husband, and that he should have for her. As most married people drift along in these matters, they soon become dead fish floating down stream. It takes manliness to row against the tide. It takes womanliness to be alert and watchful of these little faults. Like the rolling mass of snow, beginning at first in a tiny ball, they gather force and danger as they proceed along by the law of gravity.

2. Another group of offences is found in the erratic dispositions of men and women. As described in the tenth department, there comes a constant weariness and loss of vitality that take away the bright "fine edge" of a person's good nature, and it is then so easy to let drop a remark or

to do some small thing, trifling in itself, that annoys and frets another. This shows that a pleasant disposition, no matter how deeply rooted it may be in one's life, is not as deep as the fundamental character; for, when things go wrong and efface the good nature, the rock basis is always a cross word or a cuss word.

Good nature is not a veneer in some lives.

It is assumed in many cases, as when the woman who is tired out, as nearly all women are, has nothing but ugly looks and sharp words for her family, will change in a flash when a visitor enters. Then the face puts on a smile, the manners are gentle and the words kind. That is veneer, because it is not natural; it is not a habit; it is not the fundamental character. When the woman is again alone with her family she shows herself as she is.

It is this veneer that rubs off so quickly in marriage.

The man knows what he is at all times when no one is around to whom he must appear to advantage. He knows how he treats his parents, his brothers and sisters, and the children, servants and others day by day, and yet when he calls upon his girl he assumes politeness, good nature, careful words, and all that is calculated to please and impress.

That is veneer.

It is as sure to rub off as is the surface gloss on cheap wood.

The man who is thus constituted must know, if he thinks at all, that his wife will very soon see him as he is under the veneer. In other words, you cannot be one kind of a person ninety per cent. of the time, and another kind of a person ten per cent. of the time, and drift into the latter kind when you relax your severe vigilance. In all stresses of weather you will fall back to the level that is most usual in your habits. Before you are married, stop and look at yourself. How have you been in your hours of loneliness, in your hours of work, in the family associations, and among the servants, children and common classes whom you meet?

You say that when you are married you will be careful. But you cannot be careful then, as there are more things to tax your patience and fret you than when you are responsible only to yourself; and your true level will be struck so soon that you will be dazed, and will bring the shock of an awaken-

ing to your wife. This has occurred millions of times in every
year, and will never cease as long as people think they can
be one thing most of the time, and the other thing when they
please.

The groundwork of a better self is built in the hours when
there is no reason for putting on. If it is a veneer, then so
be it; but remember that veneers deepen with each new layer,
and each period of self-presence when no one is watching you,
or when your mother, your father, your sisters and brothers,
and the children and servants are all the objects to behold you,
then put on veneer, and keep on doing so until ninety per
cent. of your life is veneer and the other ten per cent. is cross
words and cuss words, and then you will have a level to which
you will rise on each rebound from your poise in marriage, and
such rebounds come thick and fast at times, but grow less and
vanish when the new veneer is deep enough.

This experience has been tried and found practicable.

It makes a man manly.

The woman has the same struggle ahead of her if she is
to be lovable, and all good women wish to be sweet and attractive.

Some wives imagine that their beauty is the continual feast
on which their husbands will find delight. Beautiful women and
handsome men, read your fate in these lines. If you have
nothing to offer each other but beauty and handsome looks,
you will find that an empty mind and an empty heart will not
long satisfy the double demands made upon them; for they are
double if you and your consort both must depend on them for
sustenance of interest.

To them there is no Charmland.

It is the height of human emotions to seek something better
than life's commonplaces. Let the feeling be what it will, the
one end sought by true heart and full mind is a different gar-
nishing of existence. One man has wisely said that if men and
women could live in the atmosphere which is created by the
first impressions of two lovers ere they had come to an understanding, a happiness would overspread all the earth that would
give it a touch of heaven.

It is thought by most people that money secures life's supreme
enjoyment; but it has very little to do with it. What would you

do to make your wife happy if she were just now at the thresh-hold of your wooing? You would make every promise that would please her. But how many of them would you fulfill? If you had the power, you say, you would give her just the home she would like. And what is that? Pictures of the mind flow into words and you build a cottage or a mansion, surrounded with fairy scenes; but she might be afraid to live so far away from the rest of the world. The palace might bring the burdens of great cares which she would be crushed under; and the cottage might be too lonely for her. The gardens might bring insects, and fountains might be damp. It all depends on what is in the heart and in the mind rather than what is around one's life.

Infinite patience, infinite care, infinite watchfulness, infinite self-restraint bring the joys of Charmland.

Remember that your good-nature is an outer crust resting on the unattractive ground beneath it in your make-up; and when anything happens to break that outer crust and your good-nature is fractured, the underground is revealed, and it is always ugly and repellant. The best disposition in the world has this basis of ill-nature; all you have to do is to crack the veneer and there it shows itself. Guard your words and your manner in order that you will not display to your consort the character that underlies your life. On the other hand, build a deeper and stronger veneer all the time and make it so vital that it will endure the severest shocks of irritability and worry, of annoyance and mishap. Be patient all the time. Be careful all the time. Be watchful all the time. Be self-restrained all the time. Pull against the stream. Never drift. Try to be something better than you are.

Then put into practice the methods of the coming depart-ment, by which you can build a new power in your own person-ality that shall eventually bring Charmland into that blessed relationship—marriage.

SHADOWS IN BONDAGE

HUMAN life is made up of facts and feelings. Facts bring nothing of themselves. All we enjoy and all we dislike must be found in feelings. Facts are the things and transactions of existence. Work is a fact. Dollars and cents and bank accounts are facts, if they can be had. The lack of them in most persons leads to the feelings of disappointment and sufferings. The ground is a fact; grass, trees, shrubs, fruits and flowers are facts; and so are bricks, stones, wood, tools, furnishings for the house, clothes, and whatever else can be seen, heard, handled, tasted, smelt or known. Deeds, bonds, securities, income, profit and loss are facts.

It is a rule of human life that a fact brings of itself no reward, but it may become the agent of feelings that are pleasing or repellant. Thus there was a time, and there were people in that time, who saw no happiness in the possession of money; today all persons who have an earning capacity are fond of money. But the money in itself, and of itself, cannot bring help or harm. It is the root of all evil, if it prompts crime, avarice, wrong-doing, worship of false ideas and a narrow existence. It is the source of much good if it checks crime, brings health, insures comfort, and sets up homes where love may prevail. The evil that money does is in its getting. A miserly disposition may hold to it after it is secured; but many a wicked heart plots for its getting; and, when it is obtained in abundance and over-abundance, then the opposite impulses may prompt its distribution.

In winning a hoard there are hours and days of unscrupulous effort to secure the wealth, little or great, that is seemingly wanted for the doubtful years ahead. It is in this wrong seeking that homes are often wrecked, and husband and wife are brought to a lasting hatred of each other. Here is a woman sixty years of age, with a husband some years older. By scraping hard, living in a mean spirit all their married lives, using each other as horses are used, for what benefit can be taken in money value out of the labor of each and by earning a name among neighbors for closeness and grasping that will outlive them by a decade or more, they have plodded along in the one desire to lay away a few more dollars every week. The woman goes to bed at night counting the dollars in prospect; and she can tell to a cent all the thousands she has in bank, and what interest it is making each day. She is saturated all night long with counting and figuring up of dollars in the bank, in chickens, in the little store with its seventeen dollars' worth of stock, and in the coming days of grasping avarice.

Her face is a sight that would blast an honest heart to look upon; it is livid with the yearning for more dollars; pinched with the fear of want, although she has thirty thousand dollars bearing interest and bringing an income three times more than she can spend or ever need in the sorest straits that may be ahead of her; her husband is working like a horse, sometimes lazy, sometimes alert, but responding to this eternal fever of the soul for more dollars, being animal in his appetites, animal in his looks, animal in his enjoyment of the feed and shelter the meanness of life accords him and she is flitting from home to chickens, and from chickens to the cheap, tawdry store, opening the till to count the money she counted a half hour before, and smiling as some stray patron parts with another nickle that is to go into the same till.

The home is in keeping with the characters that dominate it. Every piece of furniture in it is counted each day, and its first cost and present value known, and there it rests sacred from use except in narrow lines which must be trod on tiptoe for fear of wearing off a shred or two. The people all around laugh in their sleeves, sneer to each other, smile to the faces of this despicable and despised couple, pass a word of good cheer as though they cared for them, and as soon as they are out of sight again they have their low-toned jeers and furtive glances for the wonders of money-mad meanness. Not a man, woman or child can be found in a large city that has a good word to speak of them, although they speak pleasantly to them. There is talk, talk, talk all the time about their habits, and the generosity they displayed when they gave ten cents to charity in one year, and called on their acquaintances for three years afterwards to keep the fact alive.

This couple is typical of many others; the amounts may be slightly inaccurate, but the facts are known to be true, and the principle stands the same everywhere. It makes no difference how much or how little the accumulations may be, the soul that strives on to add to it when there is nothing at stake is bringing the curse of money into marriage, where some little sunshine should have been expected.

There are women today who are using their husbands as horses are used to save where they need not to save. They know nothing of happiness, and care only for the time when, as widows, they will still have the money that their parsimony squeezed out of the toil of their husbands. There are husbands who care nothing for their wives, except the housework they can extract from their muscles, who bring never a word of cheer to them, nor care for their happiness. If these men and women must squeeze animal value from each other, why not add now and then a moment of hope for something better, if it can be done without costing anything?

Take as examples the couple in question. There is an income of about fifteen hundred dollars a year. They spend less than five hundred dollars a year. On the law of averages, he will live less than three years more, and she less than five. But in their belief, he will live twenty years longer, and she as long. Suppose both were to lose their earning capacity and must employ servants; even then they would never spend their income. Under the most lurid extravagance, in which they would throw out money like water in Niagara, as it would seem to them, they could not possibly spend their income. When they die they have no one to inherit their accumulations; he is cursed with relatives who despise him and he could not allow them to receive a cent; and she has been sized up so accurately by her relatives for years that she would not allow them to receive a cent of her money; and it will all go to freak bequests.

With an income far greater than she could spend, she was offered a river trip costing nine dollars one day; and was eager for it, for herself and her husband, as they "both needed a change so much,'' but she declined with emphasis when she found that other people were not to pay her expenses. Never has there been a breath of fresh air get into their lungs from country, or river, or ocean, or drive, if somebody else did not pay the expense. Fifty cents or fifty dollars is all the same to them; it is too much; and, when they die, more than thirty thousand dollars will go to no one they ever knew or cared for.

People talk about them; eye them; sneer at them; are pleasant to their faces, and sarcastic behind their backs, as people always are when they live in a community with meanness. There is no cordiality of intercourse between this family and others. There is nothing that takes their attention away from the sordid lust when Sundays come, or when holidays bring their invitations of happiness. Christmas is a dull day to them, all the hallowed memories and tender thoughts being jammed down under the hat of greed and lust for dollars. On one Sunday they went to church, and as a nickel was the smallest change they had with them, they were compelled to part with it, but the experience made such a deep impression on their minds that they never walked again on a street where there was a church if they could avoid it without wearing out too much sole leather. And for years they told time by the date of this occurrence; as when they would say, "It happened three weeks after that Sunday when we put five cents in the contribution box," or words to that effect.

Money is a fact. Earning money is a fact. Saving money is a fact. Lay ten dollars on the table and let it stay there, and see what it will do. It will not turn itself into shoes, nor into food, nor into clothing, nor into a river trip for enjoyment of the world that God has made for the pleasure of human beings. As long as that money remains there on the table, it will be lifeless and useless. Putting it in the pocketbook is a fact. Putting it into the bank is a fact. Allowing it to remain in the bank is a fact. It cannot do good as long as it is carried in the purse or left in the bank. Not until it turns itself into something that is more than a fact will it bring pleasure or comfort or ease or value.

The same is true of labor.

There are two great ends in all work. One is the power it makes to bring something more than fact; for toil is a fact.

The other end sought by nature is life in the body. The muscles, bones, tendons, cords, nerves and all parts tell the one great fact that activity is life, and life is activity. Not in rest is there pleasure. Not in idleness is there life. The sunlight is absolute blackness until it strikes the atmosphere which envelopes this earth. Out in space, where there are no shadows, you would expect to find a dazzling light from the sun and stars; and you imagine that because Venus and Mercury are so near to the great central orb, they must be unendurably hot; but out in space there is no heat. Everything is colder than our own North Pole. Light is activity, and heat is activity. This earth would have no heat and no light from the sun if it did not possess an atmosphere to be made active. Where there is nothing to be given activity, there can be neither heat, nor light, nor life. Our world would be black, cold and dead.

It is, therefore, our wonderful enveloping atmosphere that is aroused to respond to the action of the light, so-called, that comes from the sun. The fact is that it is not light until it gets here; but is merely a powerful waving movement of the fine ether, or inner air, that connects the sun with the earth. These ether-waves are most intense. They move on in blackness through the sky and in ice-fields of cold so severe that words cannot paint the fact. But as soon as they touch the envelope of air that wraps this world in its folds, that air is given vibration, and this is called heat; the same air with the ether in its inner self becomes active in a different way, and light is produced; and the air, ether, light and heat coinciding, set up life.

It is the air that becomes charged with these three powers, the trinity of earthly existence. The lessons taught are that activity is always associated with life, and that both are born out in the open air. Nothing ever came into being in the plant world except by the conjunction of the three powers of this trinity; and, as the human body is made up of plant existence, and thrives best when treated as an outdoor plant, it depends on the same laws.

In providing enough of any power for human good, nature has been compelled to give bounteously. She is then of necessity excessive in her gifts and seeks to tone them down by a balance that swings to an opposite extreme. Playing between enough and too much on the one hand, she gives too little on the other hand. Excesses are facts and must be dealt with as such. Says nature, "I will give all the heat that man can use, but it is not possible to give an exact quota to each person, so I will give more than enough." Then the sun is too hot in summer, in order to provide enough to balance the extreme cold of winter. Nature swings from one extreme to the other, and the wonderful fact is that she will never burn a careful person to death with too much heat, nor freeze a careful person to death with too little heat. The citizens of the Arctic lands, with the thermometer fifty degrees below zero, survive the frigid winters. By a little lack of care on the part of nature, all humanity might be frozen to death in any winter, or burned to death in any summer. That there is the adjustment as we find it speaks volumes in proof of the presence of a power that watches our every need.

The earth yields food in excess for some and in scarcity for others. Between these extremes there is a middle ground that would bring enough for all. As food is required to keep the body alive, and as happiness and enjoyment would be impossible without sustenance sufficient to maintain good health, it is the first great problem to be settled.

But people forget that food is the product of the air; or light, heat and life, as interpreted by our atmosphere in its response to the waves of ether, sent here from the sun. Traveling in blackness and in cold unspeakably intense, they awaken to life and warmth of life when they touch the air. Just at the surface of the ground, where this warmth has penetrated a few inches, and this light has called up the sleeping particles of soil, life is enacted, and the world of food supply is created.

The human body is built of four elements in the main, and to supply these is the work of solving the food problem. There must be nitrogen, oxygen, hydrogen and carbon. The first three are found in air and water, as such; and the carbon is contained in fruits, vegetables and grains. There was a time when perfect health and perfect happiness were found in these sources of sustenance.

It has been ascertained in several hundred thousand lives in experiments of years of duration, conducted by the Ralston Health Club, that the body retains its health for scores of years when fed properly on fruits, vegetables and grains, pure air

and pure water. The only air that contains life is out of doors.
You can live in indoor air, but not on it. The only water that
contains life is rain water, free from taint of taste or color,
such as can be collected in sand fields from rains, and drained
through the sand to receptacles, where it is then conducted to
iced vaults. In a few years the world will learn to get its
pure water in that way, as nature has been giving this hint for
centuries.

The trend of city influences is to draw country people away
from their semi-civilization on farms to the city to starve,
and send out intelligent people a generation hence to re-make
the farms into homes where perfect health can be secured from
pure air, pure water, fruits, vegetables and grains. The cost
of living is higher now than ever before, and will rise year by
year until the break comes. It will be a revolution.

There is no other end in view for humanity; at least, not in
the next fifty years.

Some wise men and women are today anticipating this revolution, and are seeking pure air, pure water, fruits, vegetables
and grains in small country estates, where it is possible to
raise more than is needed to eat, and to have an excess. The
barons of the future are those who today make preparations
for that day, when the prices of food will be so great and the
supply so small that starvation will run into a long famine,
the end of which cannot now be predicted; but when the blow
falls it will descend without warning.

Then the rich will suffer.

There are mean men and women grinding out their lives
in narrow lines, struggling for one more dollar day by day
to lay aside against a year of distress, and it is this awful
struggle that turns married life into nothing but facts. There
is no magnetism in the sexes then; it's nothing but two horses
hitched to shafts and pulling for money.

In the early days of young manhood and young womanhood
such efforts to win a home are praiseworthy; but when the home
is won and the span of life is far spent, it is reprehensible to
become the couple that is pointed out by neighbors as the
"meanest folks in town;" to be pinched in the face and in soul,
warped in brain and heart, contemptible in all the qualities

that make life worth living, and to die mourned by no one, and remembered only for a despicable nature.

In New England it is estimated that there are more than one hundred thousand couples who are over fifty years of age, and who have saved away in banks or elsewhere a wealth in excess of ten thousand dollars, some several times this amount, and who live the lives of groveling serfs in spirit and in fact, mean in everything they do, and small in everything they think; still scraping to add to a capital, the income of which they will never be able to spend. They are buried alive in the horrors of a dungeon, on all sides of which is stamped the words, "Sordid souls dwell here."

Take the case of a couple, both of whom died in Vermont recently, leaving some bank accounts that paid an annual income of over five hundred dollars. Never in any year had they spent as much as four hundred dollars, and rarely half this amount. They had become so pinched in face with the love of money that they had the look of rats; and pictures taken of them six years prior showed the rat-look in every feature. Now, had they spent ninety per cent. of their income, and laid aside ten per cent. for the rats to follow them, they could have had fresh air, comforts, pleasures in abundance and some real life, all of which they, like the other thousands, never knew, and never can know. In the State of Pennsylvania it is said there are two hundred thousand people or more who live in one or two rooms, although they have more rooms to spare, and who never spend more than half their income, even after they are very old; grinding out their lives in the same New England fashion—mean, close and despicable. Somehow these people manage to live together, but in storms and quarrels, ill nature and criticisms, suffering and pain, letting chronic maladies eat out their vitality and peace of mind in order to save what they can never spend. In practically all such cases they die with the still increasing income. Said a husband: "Had I known my wife would have died so soon, I would have looked after her health. She was a terrible sufferer for twenty years." He was seventy-six, and she was seventy-four when the end came, after twenty years of suffering. Yet they had not in that twenty years spent half of their income in any one year, and when he soon afterwards died the income was going on. In a letter to a minister just before he died he wrote: "My wife suffered for more than twenty years. She was sorrowful and broken down in spirit, and the world was dark to her. She was shut in. Had I known what I do now, I could have spared her all her misery." But the income went on after he died.

Grasping, penurious people save money in abundance before they die, and when man and wife get the same spirit, as many do, they stick together for fear to separate, lest one shall be the gainer over the other. But it is better not to live at all, married or single, if the soul must be sacrificed to the love of dollars. Lives of that kind are cursed. If there is discrimination after death in punishment and reward, the sordid soul could not be allowed entrance to heaven, for she would criticize the waste of precious stones and luxury of gold and silver everywhere abundant. This female of whom we first spoke had a dream one night that she had seen a glimpse of a world of glory, and she awoke in a night sweat, talking to herself, asking what things cost that she saw in her dream. Her one desire was to turn them into cash and put the money in the bank.

Living in two rooms, denying the body its food and care, and taking all the beauty out of life, is the fate of almost ninety per cent. of the married couples that learn to save their money. Those who do not save are usually separated by death, the woman surviving; and she goes to some public home for the aged, such as used to be called the poorhouse. If the husband survives, he finds a similar place in which to end his days. Thus the extremes hover about the lives of the aged. Too much accumulation on the one hand, and too little on the other.

As has been said in the tenth department, magnetism is always between extremes, never in either of them. It does not show itself in that unlucky drift of life that falls prey to poverty, for nature never allows a magnetic man or woman to long remain poor. It does not show itself in grasping, penurious, sordid souls. There never was a mean man or a mean woman who was both mean and magnetic. One or the other must give way. The individual who has no more adjustment of mind and sense than to let an income accumulate needlessly can never know the power or the blessings that magnetism brings.

In the mind the middle ground where magnetism dwells is

sense. Lack of mental acumen is the cause of poverty, and magnetism has nothing to do with that defect. Over-sharp mental acumen is greed, and nature hates greed as we hate poison. Freed from both these extremes, under the law of the tenth department, magnetism enters the mind and lives in the realm of good sense. This power develops its consort, and the two grow by each other's aid.

Magnetism is the maid, and sense is the man.

They make the union that lifts humanity out of its vaulted dungeon.

Good sense compels the mind to turn to the sources of life, and there find them in air and nature, in outdoor exercise and companionship with the vital power of the universe as it is expressed everywhere about us.

There is no magnetism in extremes. In the crowds of city life, with the ill-health, the sickly air, the dirt and odors, the manure-laden dust that rises from the streets and floats into the houses upon the food and through all the clothing, the artificial cost of food and shelter, and the awful struggle to keep body and soul together, we see one extreme; and it is devoid of magnetism. In the country home, located against a fifty-ton bank of manure, with manure on everything indoors and out, and brought by flies and insects to stain the food and the body, with a semi-civilized routine of work that is the veriest slavery and the warping of mind and of heart by the hardships that torment men and women to desperation, and often to suicide and insanity, we find the other extreme—the turning of God's land into dirt and drudgery. In such existence there is no magnetism.

Sense is the middle ground of the mind between lack of mental acumen and its sharp greed; and in this sense is to be found the solution of the problem.

The more one's sense becomes free to assert itself the more loudly it proclaims the law:

Facts bring no happiness of themselves; in what we feel must be found the secret of true living.

This law was recognized centuries ago, and has brought to some men and some women their full measure of joy in life. But they have been few indeed. People, seeing the falseness in living solely for facts, have sought a remedy by some other extreme. Some have shut themselves up in religious houses, there to be deprived of the blessings of earth and the fullness of a well-spent life. That was an extreme that failed to please the God it sought to serve. Life is activity, and it is magnetic in the open, not in the closed vault. True life seeks the air and the wide wealth of nature; not the dungeon nor the walled home, no matter how great the devotional habits may be.

Nature never enters the house.

Others have gone to a different extreme, denying themselves everything that gave pleasure. They sought to prove that whatever we liked most did us the greatest harm. There was a long array of facts to show that the things we drift to when left to the choice of our desires were hurtful either to mind, body or to soul. This feeling some people today entertain. There are thousands of men and women who are generous in all ways, and who are good folks, too, who nevertheless believe and show some evidence to prove that we must not indulge in anything we like. They assert that nature wants us to reproduce the race; then get off the scene of action as soon as possible. They cite the fact that, in some grades of the animal kingdom, the males die in the one duty of parentage, and that humanity ought not to survive the raising of a family.

It is to get rid of people, they assert, that the things we like tend to bring on our deaths. Here are some of the facts they have tabulated for consideration:

1. They say that foods are divided into three classes: First, the kinds that are best for the health; second, the kinds that are hurtful to the health, and third, the kinds that are direct enemies of the health. It has taken more than a hundred thousand years to find out this last fact.

2. The foods that are worst for the body are those that child and man will first eat if no restraint is offered. Thus the child, answering the call of its instinctive nature, will eat candies and pastry to the total exclusion of plain food. Ice cream tastes better than milk, and sweet cakes taste better than bread.

3. Admit any thousand of men and women to a banquet hall where two lines of tables are set. Let these men and women be in perfect health, as the phrase goes. Have on one side of the hall the foods that will better the body, add to its

nutrition and increase its vitality; and on the other side the usual rich courses of the banquets and dinners given by society. Let these men and women have free choice without hint or suggestion, and they will drift over to the rich foods, and there eat until the blood has been charged with the poisons of a sickly combination, wholly barbarous in its inception, and reflecting the lowest state of civilized life in this country.

4. The things that make crime and disease are most preferred. The power of alcohol will never be broken. It kills like a two-edged sword, slaying the victims and their victims. Tea, coffee, stimulants, tobacco, opium, cocaine and drugs of various kinds entice at first, then embrace the will and bring voluntary slavery; while water, the only drink that can help the body, is set aside as too plain. There was a river of champagne flowing through America every year that cost one thousand million dollars, and that made mind and body weaker by its use. Yet that man or woman who would tell society these facts was most brave.

5. Set a thousand healthy men loose in a strange city, and ask them to make themselves as happy as they know how, giving them freedom to choose for themselves, and all but ten of them will make tracks for certain houses as a start-off; then they will hunt the saloons, but not in so great numbers, and after that they will breathe smoke-laden air from their cigars for a few hours. All this is pleasure.

6. It is claimed that one of the cleverest ruses of nature to hurry men and women off the scene of action, and to make room for each new generation, is witnessed in the death-dealing combinations that result from wholesome foods when not eaten in their plain forms. Sugar is wholesome, flour is wholesome, eggs are wholesome, butter is wholesome, and so are many other things when eaten in proper form. But nature makes them taste better in certain combinations, as when butter and sugar come together, a fearful ferment of a poisonous character is let loose in the body, and the heart, the lungs, the liver and the kidneys are hurt. So sugar and eggs, as in cold sauce, icings, cakes and other uses, produce a still more virulent irritation and poison. Yet everybody likes the taste of these combinations much better than to take butter on bread, butter on eggs, and sugar in different ways. Plain loaf sugar,

or any plain form of sugar by itself is a food, and gives strength to the mind, the blood and the tissue.

7. Nearly all the good food produced by a bountiful nature is ruined for nutritive purposes by the manner in which it is cooked. Thus the frying of any food makes it a slow or quick process towards death. You may not feel the results of eating fried potatoes, fried pork and fried meats and foods, but every mouthful you take reduces your life.

8. There are two million women in this country who are leading professional lives that are ending all chances of longevity, as such crime cuts their span in halves. Go to them and look into their faces, even at the age when they are least unattractive, and you will see less than ten years of life left there. Forgotten graves will be their fate very soon. Among both women and men there is a steadily marching disease that blots out lives every year by the thousands. Yet such conditions are tempting, and yield great pleasure when people stand on the threshold of bad influences. If there were no legal and moral codes to deter some, all the race would be given up to debauchery, as was the case just at the time when the old religion fell to pieces, and Christ came upon the arena of earth. Pleasure then had run riot, and virtue was mocked at.

9. The simple forms of life, free from nervous excitement and attended by peace and gentleness, promote longevity, and contain the greatest degree of health and safety to mind and body; but such methods are made the butt of ridicule by the vast majority of people, especially those who are money-spenders in extravagance. This disposition proves that nature hurries men and women to their graves; but does she do this to get them out of the way, and thus make room for those who are to follow? If progress is the watchword of the ages, and if the improvement of the races requires many generations, how can the world hold all the people who would be here at one time if health were easy to maintain?

All Asia and Europe and Africa are crowded, and the American continent is able to feed twice as many people as now live on it; but the care of the health would so prolong the lives of the masses that there would soon be five times the number of people that are now on earth, and it would be impossible to support them.

This fact being true, it must follow that the majority of humanity must step lively and get out of the way to make room for the coming generations, and the gradual advancement of civilization.

In carrying out this arrangement nature kills off half a million children in every million. Then she destroys a large number of adults in their younger years. There are more diseases than there are bookshelves to contain their records. When the doctors begin to understand how to check one kind of sickness, another kind comes into being. Then there is a profound disinclination to heed the warnings of death, for it takes something more than the fatalities that pile up every year in any one line of sickness to awaken an interest in suppressing the cause. Typhoid fever has millions of victims in the ground. But these millions of deaths, all unnecessary, do not serve as a warning to those who survive. In one town of two thousand people ninety-four died in five years of typhoid, and still the people there would not, after being told of the danger, fill up the wells that caused the tragedies. As each new victim was told that he or she must die, the words would come faintly: "I should have taken warning from the deaths of others ahead of me, but it is now too late." Still the survivors would not check the cause. This is human nature everywhere.

It is not often curable.

Causes are at work in many ways to cut off the lives of the people so as to prevent the crowding of the world.

But does this law of nature make us believe that we should lay down our lives on the altar of indifference? If nine out of ten persons are indifferent, and will so remain despite all efforts to move them, does this fact convince us that we ought to be indifferent also?

Progress is the watchword of nature.

She does not want her followers to join the ranks of those who are scoffers at her laws. The latter are not permitted to care for their health, either of body or mind; and nature places a revolver in many a hand, shows the way to poisons all about them, lays open the floodgates of disease and disaster, and says: "Here, you folks who are of no use to me get out of this world. You think only of yourselves. You are given the sacred temple of the body with which to clothe a soul that might have been immortal, but you have been selfish, arrogant, grumblers, grovellers, useless in mind and heart, and have looked to me for all your needs and comforts. I have held open the grandest opportunities that have ever been offered any people, and you have shut your eyes and sought sordid pleasures that reduce you to the rank of beasts and vegetation, as far as being of value to my plan of progress. But the age is now at its climax. There are men and women alive today who may live, if they desire, to see the present earth revealed to them in a new glory that shall be consummated by the power of civilization working under my commands. I have a life that is multiform, and I can walk with any or all of my followers, helping them in their struggles from day to day. I have power to do all they wish. I work through special design. Any person who is willing to help make the world better physically and morally will receive my aid day and night through a long life. I want them to live in happiness and in the enjoyment of their faculties as long as they wish to be on earth. But all others must go. They are in my way. I teach them how to neglect their health, how to ruin mind and body through temptations they cannot resist; how to make the world hate them and want them in the ground, and I throw through them all the diseases that mow down life in wide swaths every year. Choose ye.''

It is a question of choice.

The people who fail in their earthly existence and die abjectly useless to the world, believe they have been prevented by ill-luck or fate from making successes of themselves. But life is complex, and the reasons are to be sought in one fountain of power, and that is the human *will*. What you are able to make up your mind to do you will accomplish, and what your *will* lacks you will fail in. It all comes down to the power to cultivate a *will* that shall be invincible, and that is the work of the climacteric course of this Club, known as Universal Magnetism.

Nature needs more recruits.

All she is waiting for before bringing glory to earth is the increase of her followers to such numbers that they can sway her laws into new conditions. Then death will be far away, and youth and vital life will walk with all her devotees.

Progress such as she desires can be made only in the true

home, and under the sway of marriage that is holy, sweet, pure and noble.

Such homes must be built where life can be had in the open air, except when shelter is required. Thousands of such homes have been established in the past few years, and they will grow in numbers all over the land. In the pure air of outdoor exercise there is found the trinity of light, warmth and life; the direct gifts of the sun. God put the sun in this part of the sky, and commanded it to send to earth this trinity. He also gave it the powers of magnetism, which carry in their bosom all the joys and bliss of heaven, and these come to earth to enter the lives of those who choose to seek them.

The purpose of producing many generations is to bring up a people that shall elect to accept these sublime opportunities.

When one generation arises to receive them, then the ultimate end of race production is in sight. It is only in the ranks of the classes that are mere links in the chain of progress that children crowd into the world. As each grade of humanity rises higher in the scale, the rate of child-bearing decreases by instinct. There is no point in bringing children into the world for them to die in childhood to the extent of fifty per cent., as is now the case; or to become victims of crime and disease, and thus hurry out of the world. Nature has a purpose in everything, and her only object in cutting off ninety in every hundred before they are old is to get rid of the crowds that are of no use to her, as they take no interest in the bettering of the human race.

She demands people of progress.

But magnetism is now being understood simultaneously with the uses of electricity; and there will be given to the better minds and the better personalities of the race a power of the HUMAN WILL capable of deciding what course to pursue; the result being that recruits will flock to the standard of nature and become members of the army of progress. They will rise in their might and will fight for pure home life, for pure marriage ties and for a new earth. Nature will sustain them and aid them day and night through the law of special design.

These people will carry the banner of a new civilization.

They will be deliberate in marrying, delaying the union as long as possible, except where it is now consummated. They will fall in line with the instinctive law that children coming of late marriages will naturally be fewer in number; and, coming of pure home life and nobler unions, will naturally be superior in character. Thus quality will supplant quantity, and the world will not be crowded.

Nothing can be more wantonly absurd and cruel than the doctrine that a family should bear children in great numbers rather than in few numbers and of better quality.

It is by far the best to delay bringing children into the world until the parents are advanced in years far enough to be able to properly care for their offspring and give them the attention mentally and physically that the best children are entitled to. One of the parents should be in the thirties at least and, if older, it will be better. Two children are all that nature requires, and one will suffice if there is better opportunity for its complete care. In one town we counted eighteen families having seven or more children in each, and not one of this crowd of children would ever be of use to themselves or to the world. They would join the masses that come and go and are taught indifference to the laws of health so as to become easy victims to disease.

These are the facts of life.

They are the ugly facts that stand in the way of human progress.

They are the repellant facts that make nature discard them and leave them to get through the world as best they can, unaided by any of the impulses of happiness or enjoyment.

In this era the most obtrusive fact is the love of money, that agency that has always been thought the root of all evil. The fact of greed, leading to dishonesty and fraud, stands forth like a mighty shadow over the world. Greed makes the merchant wicked, the food manufacturer a murderer of thousands, the banker crafty, the speculator bloodless in his thefts, the monopolist savage in his selfishness, and the schemer heartless in his quest of marriage. There are at this moment more than a million women biding their time when they can enmesh men of wealth in promises of wedlock, and millions of men seeking the consent of women of wealth to marriages that have no other basis than desire for money.

The parsimony that has been described in the early pages of

this department in the old folks who narrow their lives, cut off all happiness and entomb themselves in unhealthy rooms in order that they may live on less than half their incomes, is in the blood of this generation.

It is this greed that is making unfit marriages. It is this greed that is laying traps for rich women by unprincipled men, and for rich men by soulless women, all for the gain of dollars. Meanness is the enemy of home life and pure matrimony. Some men fail to win the consent to marriage until they assert their wealth, and then the answer comes in the affirmative. Girls who are in doubt between two or more offers find it easy to select the man who says he is wealthy. In many cases the claim is false and the union stands on weak ground. Short-sighted men and women, falling into traps, do not hold their bonds tightly, and in the present state of feeling, there is no sentiment that keeps most married people together.

There must be the bond that is strong in other ways.

There must be worth in the man, and worth in the woman.

There must be magnetism in the place of greed. If you have greed in your heart, and would marry to gratify it, stop and think that you will not be the gainer. A better union can be founded on personal worth instead of money value. Kill all greed out of your heart. Strangle it in your life. Rise above it, for it is mean and despicable. It will warp your soul and chill your better life. The claim that penurious men and women who are married to each other live together all their lives is true, because each is trying to beat the other. Separation means loss of the share of the savings, and of all the accumulations in case of the earlier death of the other party. It is a cat and dog life, filled top full of misery and horrible meanness.

Kill greed.

Let each married man be a noble, manly and attractive husband.

Let each wife be beautiful, sweet and lovable.

Then think how can a man be noble if he is greedy for mere dollars? How can he be attractive and be shut in from the companionship of nature, which alone makes life worth living?

How can a stingy, penurious, dollar-hunting woman be beautiful?

She is hideous, and has the eyes and face of a rat.

How can she be sweet and lovable, when she is imprisoned in the shut-up rooms of her miserly home, thinking only of her savings and the interest they earn each night while she dreams of dollars and pennies?

Beauty can never outlive manners.

In the fresh air of outdoors will be found light, warmth and life, and it is only out of doors that the magnetism sent from heaven through the portals of the sun can reach the human heart.

Throw greed away.

Open the narrow home to the blessed sun, and make it a jewel set in the crown of lawns, gardens and beautiful flowers. God does not talk to mankind today in words, but in influences. Every plant could have been created to bear itself and to reproduce itself with no other aid than its own seed-pods and roots. But those apparently unnecessary things called flowers, rich in their varied colors of petals and wonderful fragrance of perfume, are the smiles of the great God talking in kindness to the people who will look and listen.

Throw greed away.

Open the home to outdoor influences and join hands with nature. There alone comes the magnetism that holds the hearts closer and more firmly together than any other power. If you are not yet married, wait until you can have a home set in lawns and gardens, to be made by you and your consort, and then live all you can in the open. There alone is true life.

If you are not yet married, you have the whip-hand of your fate. Take time to look the situation in the face. Do not be in a hurry. There is plenty of time. Ascertain your own temperament, and that of the party who would join hands with you. Then you two go over this book together from beginning to end, and if the other party does not like what it says, there should be the turning point in your lives.

Time will bring about your wishes, no matter what they are, if you make yourself worthy.

The home such as we have described is a magnet.

Other forms of life are not.

Make up your mind that all humanity is divided into two classes, of which one is great and numerous in bulk only; and the other is small, but growing. The bulky class is composed of the people whom nature asks to step along, to be indifferent to their health, and careless of all the graces and sweetness of life, to fall sick and die and make room for others. The second class is composed of people who are sincerely desirous of being worthy of a better world on earth, and who want to do what they can to make it better. That second class is composed of:

1. Men who want to be manly, noble and virile.

2. Women who want to be beautiful in heart, sweet in mind, and lovable in their nature.

Decide that you will join the class that, while it is small in numbers, is yet the potent factor in a greater civilization. Belong to that class. Then find for yourself a consort in the same class.

MAGNETIC CONSORTS

ACTS and feelings make up human life. In the twelfth department facts were discussed, and some of them were most ugly and uninviting. In the present department the feelings will hold attention. As has been repeatedly stated, the work of the Magnetism Club is interwoven, each part with each other. Sex Magnetism is helped at every stage of the way in the other courses. It is wholly a study and development of the feelings, and these are unfolded and given great magnetic power in the work entitled Advanced Magnetism. In that course the feelings rule. Then the power of self-impression, and also the power of mental vision, are taught in Universal Magnetism, the climacteric course of the Club. Owing to the intricacies of the gifts bestowed by nature on humanity, it is not possible to place these auxiliary helps in any one work, or to repeat them in all, as they would break abruptly in upon the instruction without being amply understood out of their proper associations.

Having in the twelfth department gone through the unpleasant duty of dealing with the salient facts that surround marriage, we now come to the better realm of the feelings. As has been said, life is made up of facts and feelings. Facts are the things that exist, and the deeds that are done. Feelings are the reasons why deeds are done. A fact alone is fearfully tiresome. It is a drag to life. When it is clothed with feeling it has less or more value. Thus the duties of the day are facts, and cannot be interesting unless they inspire the feelings. Suppose those feelings are of hatred for the work, a belief that the labor is useless, or that it is unnecessary, or that it is imposed upon you, then you will do your work in bitterness and reproach.

On the other hand, suppose the work seems to be a step towards something else that will bring comfort to you or others, or that it is work necessary to the happiness of yourself or others, or that it will give you opportunity to keep the body active and, therefore, healthy, the feeling will enable you to do it better and with content.

Still further, suppose you have no ill-nature towards those duties, and that, while you are performing them you are thinking of other scenes, of other faces, of coming events, of pleasures yet to be, and that all this time you are happy and contented, your work will be supplanted by feelings that will cause the fact to disappear. A man was willing to bring up a scuttle of coal for his wife, or for anyone else, when he was sure it would give him healthful exercise. All persons need more muscular activity in variety. Some get too much of one kind. The hard toil of the day may employ a limited number of muscles which are relieved by taxing other muscles. No physical work should be regarded as drudgery as long as some part of the power is conserved, and it is all done gracefully.

Thus the feelings may be brought to the aid of all kinds of toil, and may either uplift them or supplant them.

The woman who sings while she works has something more than the fact of labor in her mind and heart. The same is true of the man who whistles while doing something useful. The woman who thinks and feels that her toil will bring her certain reward some day, or in the immediate future, will not mind the work so much as one who sees and feels nothing ahead but the thing she is doing. If, after she has been paid for the work, she will have nothing left of the remuneration except the exchange of the money she earns for the bare necessities of life, and will take but little interest in what she does. But often a surplus, with which she can buy a better dress or take a day of vacation, will inspire her to toil on. The love of children, and the hope that some day they will grow and be able to care for her, urges on to hard labor.

Feeling of some kind is necessary, or life will be a blank to most toilers. It is on this ground that any relaxation or any indulgence at the coming night, or half-holiday, or Sunday, or in the days ahead, will make the burdens easier to bear. It is on this principle that men carouse at night in drink or other temptations, and women follow their footsteps. They think ahead during the day, and feel the coming relief from drudgery.

The substitution of a better ambition than to drink and carouse is sure to lessen the dangers of such evil temptations. The experiment has been tried, and has worked wherever properly made. New ambitions of a wholesome sort will ease the work, and give the feelings due play in the mind and heart. But it is agreed that the facts of hard toil must be veneered with the hopes inspired by feelings of some kind, either good or bad.

Thousands upon thousands of instances could be cited of the operation of this law in human life, but it is so common in all experiences that space need not be taken here for example.

But the chief interest for the student of this course of training is in the bond of feelings that will serve to make the two sexes attractive to each other, and add to the tightening of the ties that hold them to their home life.

Some great goal in life which is alluring to both husband and wife must be set up and never lost sight of. Then there must be the daily hope and prospect that will come into the close range of their vision. These are the far-off hope and the nearby anticipation. There is nothing in the human heart so great as the feeling of anticipation. It has more possibilities of magnetism than all other pleasures and all other experiences combined. It is the most powerful magnet ever set in the mind or heart. The skillful use of the agency of anticipation in the hands of a person who can control the belief or the confidence or the loyalty of another, is capable of accomplishing all the work of a better civilization. All progress rests on this feeling. All happiness rests on it. Heaven itself is not alluring except for this feeling. The rejection of religion will always be easy as long as there is not the double force of hope and anticipation bringing men and women into its power.

To the people who are about to die religion holds out the hope of a better world beyond; and this is eagerly accepted, because then all hope in this world is gone. But younger persons do not care to take up the life of religion, which cuts off so much opportunity here for happiness on the far-away prospect of a better era after this life is ended. Before religion can have a natural bearing on the hearts of men and women it must give them something in this life in return for the self-denials that are required. No religion is natural, or founded on the laws of heaven, that makes earth nothing and heaven everything. "Peace on earth, good will to men" is for this world, not the next. Each has its place in the true heart, and each must witness its joys. Every pleasure in this life that is substantial and not vicious is in harmony with the promises of immortal existence.

So plainly are the laws of nature stamped on every epoch that he who runs may read. She has but one goal, and that is perfect humanity. For this she has striven through countless centuries, and she is still working out the fate of the race. The goal of eternity is immortality, and that is taught by true religion. The goal of earthly existence is a better life here, and this is possible only through better homes and better marriages. The marriage gives the right to produce the next generation; the home gives the place of nurture and care, and the better living is the fruit of the best marriages, combined with the best home conditions.

Here is the real stepping-stone to heaven.

These are the true goals of the noblest people of this age.

But there must be the daily anticipation. The husband is away from his home for some hours each day; and what is there in the home that lures him back? Is it the wife? If so, why should she attract him? There must be something worth while, for no man can long come back to an unattractive woman. Then she alone is never enough. Life is complex, and the personality is not enough to fill it. The meals are not enough to make a magnet. The old saying that the road to a man's heart is through his stomach, is true only when the stomach is not the cause of heart failure. More wholesome cooking and an interest in food selection will help make some attraction; but life is complex.

The attractive wife and the health-giving meal will make up two parts of this intricate existence.

But there must be more.

Attractiveness includes the many better conditions of the mind and the heart that have been described in the several departments of this work; they are powerful magnets; but all the neatness and all the refinement in the world will not make home and wife the greatest magnet. Something more is needed. There should be in every woman that drawing influence that will make a man dislike to leave her presence in the morning; and that will make his thoughts turn to her all day long in those little intervals that creep into the busiest brain.

In his office, in his employment, in his duties of earning and winning the means of taking care of her, there should be the face and the form of that wife always near at hand, seemingly to look in his eyes and there read his desire for her, and to look into his heart and hear the beating throbs of love for her and her alone. This yearning for her presence should never fade from his life; whether she is eighteen or eighty.

To put into practical test the wish to see and be with her, he should plan a campaign of anticipations. Surprises are not one per cent. as anticipations; and the way to make them effective is to make them habitual, so they may be expected. "My husband is always surprising me, and I never know what to expect next." This waiting to be surprised furnishes the magnetism of anticipation, and takes its place. There is something pleasant to look forward to.

Then there should be something worth while planned for the evening at the end of each day. When the week ends something else should be in waiting. Every Sunday should be sought with eagerness, not because of secular enjoyment, but for the companionship of husband and wife all day long amid variations of pleasure such as may be in harmony with the day. There may be flowers, visits to or from relatives, walks, and other means of making the day attractive. A little study, some ingenuity, and a real desire to be the source of new thoughts and new ways of bringing a charm into life, is necessary.

It is all wrapped up in the one law of anticipation.

Your wife should have something each day to look forward to; something each week greater than that of each day; and something each year; in addition to which there should be a life purpose. All these things have been discussed in earlier departments.

If you are a wife, remember that your husband should be eager to return to you at the end of every day of absence; and the magnet is not yourself exclusively, but some form of attraction that you engage in for him and with him. It is not a magnet to meet him with a kiss; for he needs more than that. Nor is it a magnet to have his slippers ready for him to slip into. Nor to have the armchair placed where he can connect

with it most conveniently. He is better able than you to attend
to those matters, and you should let him get his own slippers,
if he wears those articles about the house; and to grope for
the armchair himself.

What he really wants is not something to eat, although he
may be very hungry, and would appreciate a wholesome meal
that would not leave him in distress. Eating is one of those
commonplace facts that must enter into all lives, and every
good wife should not depend on the meals as the chief power
to keep her husband in love with her.

He want you, but not you exclusively.

With you he wants a bright mind and a refined body. In
you he wants to find a sweet, lovable and beautiful woman.
He wants a sensible and a smart woman. But these things are
you. More than that, he wants some method of making the
evenings pleasant and profitable to mind and heart. No man
can be expected to court and make love after he is married.
He may be willing to hold your hand during a portion of each
evening when you are engaged; but after marriage he needs
larger game. He knows, or should know, that life is real and
life is earnest, and there are interests that are paramount to
the little things of the day. Find something worth living for,
and let him know that you have found it. This cannot be
done in a week; it takes time; but keep your mind on the wish
to make your life and his something above the drift of existence.

The facts of marriage are tiresome after the newness has
worn off. They do not hold a charm for man or woman, and
then there will come the spirit of unrest and yearning for a
different condition. This yearning is natural to both parties and
must be satisfied. The man or woman who can discover the
means of satisfying it develops genius, and this is magnetism.

It may be said that Charmland is an unreal land.

Some persons may regard it as only a veil thrown over the
mind and heart to make things seem fairer than they are.
If this much is accomplished, it is enough. If love is blind,
it should remain blind. What that young man can see in that
young woman is a mystery to his friends and to hers; but to
him it is as real as anything in the world. Time may show
him his mistake, and then he will know that his love was blind;

but until he learns the error he will be happy in his short-sightedness.

The real mistake was in waking up.

There are many men who go through married life love-blind. They have an exalted regard for their wives that may not be reciprocated, but that gives happiness. They devote themselves to making every day as pleasant as possible for their consorts. But the disadvantage of this regard is that it is generally one-sided. There are some wives who are love-blind towards their husbands, and this feeling is often of years' duration; yet generally it is not mutual. Yet there are many cases of men and women great enough to carry till death the same exalted feeling for each other; notably in lives such as those of Gladstone and his wife, Browning and his wife, and others where genius is of the grandest type. The lower the standard the less likely are people to become love-blind.

What name can be given to that condition of mind and heart that is in control of lovers during the happiest period of their courtship, when both are in doubt, and yet both are supremely hopeful each of the other? It is as near to Charm-land as they can then get; and yet it is a living in their feelings, not in facts. They come to the facts all too soon, and then the bliss disappears.

From evidence in great abundance it is apparent that the state of feeling of the lover makes him see in his mind, and experience in his heart, a being almost divine. During the weeks that elapse while the agitated ocean of happiness is settling, he sees a person that is different from all others, in that she is far more entrancing to look upon and to listen to than any woman he has ever known. Many a time a man has been in love with a face that has been denied to him by fate; and he has tried to surfeit his gaze upon her portrait; yet, after he had married another, he has found that the former's face was actually ugly. "How could I ever have fallen in love with that?" is his inquiry. One of the closest friends we have ever had fell in love with a woman who rejected him after an acquaintance of two years, during which time she said she was trying to make up her mind. She married another man, and he married another woman. Several years afterwards he discovered that the face he had adored was misshapen and ill-favored in feature, eyes, nose, lips and look. "Is she just the same now in looks as she was then?" he asked. On being assured that she had not depreciated, he was surprised to think that he saw anything beautiful in that countenance.

We live in our feelings, not in our senses.

Those who live in facts do not want to live. They have no hope in life and there seems nothing ahead for them. They fall prey most easily to disease, or make way with themselves; for health, vigor and a strong hold on existence must have a cord of hope binding them to earth. Let this cord slip away and life fails.

When the feelings are strong enough they summon up beings at will that are better or worse than the facts warrant. A man who has been hurt in some way by another man, or who has been cheated or wronged by him, will entertain feelings towards him that will make the enemy a monster. He will magnify every fault and see nothing good in him. So it is with a man whose wife has done him wrong. If he cannot forgive her, he will entertain for her feelings that will picture her in a character far beneath her actual merits. To her relatives who love her she will be a good woman and sweet in her ways; while to him she will be ugly or venomous.

There are many instances where women have been looked upon as termagants by their husbands who have aroused in them a feeling of dislike and been scratched by feminine claws; yet these same women, after being divorced, have been wed to men who looked upon them as most beautiful, sweet and lovable. There are many women today who are hated by their husbands and who have lovers desirous of marrying them because they believe them to be attractive and fascinating. One man at a club said, "I have a wife who is the most disagreeable woman in the world in my opinion." A clubman to whom he made this statement said in reply, "I have danced and talked with her many times and I think she is really divine. I wish she were my wife." "By Jove, I wish she was." Events brought about a legal separation and the second man married that woman, and he resigned from the club to please her. He devoted himself to her, made her happy, and they are today the most congenial of couples. The former husband simply had incurred her ill-feeling and his own regard had changed to an opposite view, making her in his eyes an ill-natured female. As a matter of fact, she is a very pretty woman. "We have dined at their house many times and have always found her bright, vivacious, home-loving, sympathetic and refined in the highest degree," said some friends recently. Her husband said to them, "She is that way always with me. I would do anything to please her. I hate to go from home in the morning, and long to get back again so that I may be where she is." The peculiar fact is that the former husband has married another woman, with whom he lives happily.

It is all in the feelings.

Strong inclinations build strong feelings, and the result is a new condition to everything that comes within range of this influence.

One of the results of continuing the study of magnetism to its highest course is the building up of the power of self-impression; that is, gift of voluntarily creating the same feelings that come from outward causes. When a man is love-blind and cannot see the glaring faults of the woman whom he adores, his feelings have been given mastery without his own act. They have come about as the natural result of falling in love. The practice of self-impression permits him to voluntarily acquire the same condition without having an irresistible cause.

There are two of these ultra-high powers of magnetism:

1. Self-impression.
2. Outward feeling.

Self-impression is wholly an inward influence that acts on the feelings between self as a cause and self as an effect.

Outward feelings are assumed relations with other persons.

The stronger one's magnetism grows as the study proceeds from one course to another the more vivid become the self-impressions, and the easier it is to build outward feelings.

The result is that the magnetic person lives in a world of his own creation, and can invite and compel others to come with him into that same world whenever and as long as he wishes. The action is double.

Over thirty years ago the effect of creating self-impressions and outward feelings was discussed, with a view of giving to humanity, through the higher realms of magnetism, the same exalted experiences that nature affords those whom she wishes

to lure into wedlock. If she is able to make one person blind
to the real face and character of another through what is called
love, the same result can be obtained through magnetism, with
the double advantage of raising the character of both parties
to new levels all the while.

It is because of the substitution of new feelings of exhilaration that men become addicted to alcoholic drinks. To secure
release from the terrible facts of living, men have for centuries
had recourse to the aid of drugs, such as opium and others
that build, for a limited period, new sensations of joy and bliss.
It is the one desire to get away from the realities of life that
prompts these bad habits; for if existence could furnish a state
of mind one-half as agreeable, men would never look to false
stimulants for such aid.

There are but two natural influences that bring men and
women to these higher feelings of enjoyment; one is temporary,
and is known as the power of love; the other is a succession
of more or less permanent influences known as anticipation.
While nature compels men and women to reproduce the race,
that is not her whole aim; for she tries to bring on a state of
earthly happiness in conjunction with love. She is not to be
thwarted. If all humanity were to resolve to remain single, and
never bring another child into the world, nature would rise
above that agreement and throw reason aside for the feelings.
Love is so powerful at certain times in life that there can be
no deliberate action of the mind against it. The love of man
for woman, or woman for man, and of the mother for the child,
can never be argued out of existence or legislated down. They
are born in feelings altogether too strong to even be lived down
until they are satisfied in part, if not in whole. When minds
become able to fight down the feelings of nature's creation, something snaps and the asylum doors open.

Such is the intense energy of nature.

It is not pretended that magnetism is stronger than nature
and can defeat her. The most that can be said is that magnetism makes use of the better impulses of nature, and employs
them in a natural way. Such better impulses are self-impressions and outward feelings.

They have been experimented with most successfully for
more than thirty years, and have been found perfect substi-

tutes for the exhilaration that comes from drugs and the heated imagination that attends love-making. And, in proportion as magnetism is increased by years of development along higher lines, in the same proportion will these superior feelings become more intense, realistic and natural.

The principle is this:

Men and women are seeking at all times to get away from the facts of life. They resort to anything to do this. It is better to avoid the injurious agencies of taking the dullness out of the harsh facts, and to adopt those that are wholly natural and beneficial. For this reason the stimulation of magnetism in its higher degree is better than drugs, such as opium and cocaine, or alcoholic habits. Magnetism is always strengthening the will power and adding to the god-like qualities of men and women, while drugs are always making beasts of them.

Nature uses the love charms that she throws over the minds of young men and women to bring about a hasty union. Gertrude Atherton, in discussing this fact said: "Very young men are not conscious of the demands that will be made on them by marriage, and very young women do not meet them. For they are urged to marry by the call of the race, the insistent demand of Nature to continue herself. But if a man survive this period of youth without marrying, he will seek an intelligent companion as a wife, not merely the first pretty girl he happens to meet. If a woman wants to make anything of her life, she must resist this call during extreme youth. She must before marrying, have definite interest and occupation in life. I have a niece whom I am educating with this idea. A great deal of the unhappiness of American marriages is due to the wife's lack of interests and occupations. She is either a pretty drudge or a society idler. Every woman has an embryonic talent for something, but most of them do not try to find out what it is. Something should be done to arouse that interest and set them to hunting within themselves for the better work of life. Occupations that make the home more attractive to all who enter it are first in importance, but this does not require that a woman be a toiler, and nothing more. There are many ways of doing the same kind of hard work, and some women have the faculty of making drudgery seem delightful. But the homes of today are not the homes of the past. Formerly a woman had an entire house and a little garden to care for, and there were many more children to a family than there are today. But now the average woman lives in a flat. She has a servant to relieve her of the housework.

"Her days are dedicated to idleness, then to strange cults and isms, or to morphine or cocaine. Why is it that so many wives have nervous prostration? Simply lack of interest in life, lack of occupation.

"How many wives do you know who are really happy? They say they are happy, of course, but if you get to know them well enough for them to tell you the truth, you hear a different story. Haven't you often heard the most devoted wife say when her husband went away: 'Thank heaven, he's gone! Now I can have a few days to myself!' And this for no graver reason than because she would be free for a while from growling about the meals, or, perhaps, from suffering from his lack of the little refinements for which men care so little and women so much."

Here we find that the strange cults and isms are adding their power to the influences of morphine, cocaine and alcohol as stimulants to relieve men and women of the burdens of facts. The cults that invite them are sure to have a following in proportion as the mind begins to sag under the weight of facts unrelieved by the better trend of the feelings. Take the belief in reincarnation—it could not secure attention in a mind that had healthy employment. It will appeal to the woman who loafs much and finds the day a drag, who wants to be kept nervously tensed all the time, or she will almost fly out of herself.

The mind when it follows the healthy course of earthly existence, is satisfied with very little law of any kind beyond the teachings of nature, which embody the best sense founded on the best judgment, and the attainment of the worthiest ends in living. The best brain of man seeks the highest civilization with the least wear and tear on the physical and moral nature. The shortest distance between any two points is in a straight line; and the only straight line in life is perfect honesty. It must be honesty to the body, to the mind, to the moral nature, to the soul and to the Creator. Cults and isms, and the stimulation of drugs and drinks, are dishonest substitutes, because they deviate from the straight line set by nature for securing the ends aimed at. Everywhere nature has offered happiness in the world, and what of misery exists is the fruit of man's substitution of false stimulation for the true. The drowning of tedious living in strong drink is as old as man himself. Thousands of years ago the Bible said that wine is mocker and strong drink is raging. But men by millions still adhere to this slavery. In one county seat it has taken hold of the lives of every man and young man, and almost every lad; because there is a sentiment there in favor of personal liberty, which means the right to let baser cravings rule the mind and soul. On the same principle the sensational and yellow newspapers excuse their diabolical work by saying they cater to the demands of their public, which means that public teachers, such as newspapers are sure to be, are first to be allowed to teach wickedness and evil desires, and then cater to their own creations, because they have them educated into their patrons. In the past ten years the theatres have been teaching profanity and obscenity without restriction, until today there is hardly any objection to exposing almost entire female bodies, from the toes to the bosoms; nor does the clientele of the theatres any longer object to hearing men and women curse and swear in plays, because the plays are true to life, and carry the profanity and vulgarity from the drawing-room to the stage. Thus the theatre, which, with the press, is one of the greatest public teachers, has educated the masses to believe that obscenity and profanity are nature's mirror, instead of being the bestial depravity of evil minds. In the outer edge of the new literature following the dark ages, nothing was humorous or worth laughing at and enjoyed unless it was obscene; and the faces of men and women were like swine, just as the faces of penurious and greedy men and women are like rats.

We all seek something.

Life that has nothing at all in it that allures is sure to break down the mind, and end quickly in suicide. The false glare of modern civilization is bringing the minds of men and women to see double; in one direction they see the senseless, useless slavery to habits of stimulated pleasure; and in the other direction they see the emptiness of their own nature to build the right kind of existence for themselves and for others. In the seething mass of humanity that is thus moved there are millions who declare that the world owes them a living, and they will ask for it without earning it. They are tramps when poor, and are the idle rich when affluent. They add nothing day by day to the world's storehouse of treasure, mentally or physically. They take and do not pay. They are nothing more than clay, and are the same to nature whether dead or alive; if dead their bodies have direct fertilizing power, and if alive they furnish some of the fertilizing change needed to make this old planet productive. But outside of this compost profession, they are nothing to the world or to nature; they are merely tramps when poor and idlers when affluent.

The comedy of the lives of the compost profession is that the rich idlers, stung at last by conscience as they realize that they cannot wrest from the world a living after they are dead, the idle rich give of their abundance to the idle poor; thus joining hands in life and dwelling in the lap of earth for the purpose of fertilization when dead.

The lure of idle pleasure that fills the home and social existence of the rich does not take away from them their natural rank and their coat-of-arms as high-degree members of the compost profession. These idle rich give dances, give dinners, give hunting parties, give golf parties, give coaching parties, have week-end parties, give receptions, and thus pass from one excitement to another, catering to the stomach through the eagerness of the mouth to be the most active faculty of their lives, and in it all, from sunrise to sunrise, from Monday to Monday, from year to year, they do not one useful thing, and have not one useful moment; they make not one genuine stroke of work, nor think one honest stroke of thought, merely shining to outshine their neighbors, and dining to outdine their neighbors, hoping to be called sumptuous hosts and lordly spendthrifts. They have one good physical habit—they stuff their already overloaded stomachs, and thus increase their usefulness as fertilizers; and they, in after days of remorse, give of their bounty to the idlers of the slums, and thus help them add their fertilization to nature. Beyond these assets they have not one iota of usefulness in the world.

It is the blundering charity of the rich that is making the great army of tramps and slum dwellers.

When a man who has to work for his money gives to charity he is careful and studious in the manner of its disposal.

As nature wishes useless people to hurry out of the world to make way for those who are willing to help raise the standard of civilization, she is imposed upon by the charity of the rich. She demands that every man and woman regard the temple of the body as sacred to the cause of health and longevity; that every faculty of mind and heart be kept in normal power; and that these powers be used constantly and never allowed, like useless talents, to remain hidden or obscured. If the denunciation of Christ means anything, it means that it is a sin and a crime against nature and God to hide talents. Talents are faculties, powers and uses of which the mind and body are capable; and to allow them to remain idle is the first chief sin of humanity. They should be used, and used usefully. Golf and other games have their place in a part of each life; but to make them the only physical activity of the body is but changing the form of idleness.

The most powerful of all magnets in life, and especially in matrimony, is useful activity of mind and body. There must be no idleness. There must be no waste of energy in health-defeating functions like dinners that stuff the body and serve only to increase the fertilization of nature. Here is a wealthy woman who says, ''I have been so busy that I have not had time for any other work than to give receptions and dinners. Why, do you know that I have given eleven dinners this past season, and I tell you it is all I can stand to keep up after so much hard work.'' Hard work! Is stuffing the over-loaded stomachs of her select set hard work? Not one of them but would have been better off to have gone home before each dinner and have given the stomach a needed rest, instead of adding to the activities of the drug business, the medical profession and the fertilization of the earth! Yet so many women are posing as martyrs to gigantic tasks who do these very things and then add some blundering contributions to charity in order that their fellow-members of the compost fraternity, the tramps and slums, may do their share likewise.

There is only the difference of dollars between the two extremes of society.

There is no difference in usefulness, brains, brawn or morality.

Therefore, you who think that your era of a happy married

life must wait till you have an abundance of dollars are making the gravest of all mistakes.

It is when you and your consort are planning to rise to new levels of power as taught in the third and fourth departments of this work that you will be most happy. Then there will be the magnetism of a life anticipation in securing the higher levels to which to rise, and this magnetism will bind husband and wife close to each other. This method has been in use for many years in many of our families who study magnetism, and it has proved powerful enough to maintain a constant interest and holds husbands and wives to each other in the happiest unions.

In summing up this part of our present work we find that there are two divisions of allurements:

1. The false.
2. The true.

The false allurements are those influences that men and women fly to in their first efforts to get away from the awful burden of facts, and they may be summed up in the following list. It must be remembered that people cannot endure mere facts, as the human mind and heart are built of the intelligence and emotions that rise above facts. For this reason they MUST have allurements; and if they will not find them naturally, they will make them artificially. The false allurements or drowning influences that bury up the tediousness of facts are:

1. Alcohol.
2. Morphine.
3. Cocaine.
4. Drugs that deaden the mind; including opium and nicotine; as cigar, pipe and cigarette smoking plays some portion of this influence, and are easily given up when there is a true allurement to urge on the habits to other lines of attraction.
5. Idle pleasures, as when the rich indulge in games of golf, cards, gambling, horse-races, coaching, auto-riding, theatres, dinners, week-ends, dances, novels, sensations, and other diversions, to the total exclusion of the plainer duties of domestic life and partnership with nature. One unending round of pleasure leaves the mind hungry for what it cannot have, and the heart a wreck; so that, added to these diversions, there always comes the ruin of the body through stimulants

and the ruin of mind and heart through the softening effect
of luxury, just as the brain is softened into paresis by sexual
excesses. Such a mode of living is sure to bring the most
abject misery on earth. A chain that cannot be broken except
by poverty binds the rich to this kind of unending folly. They
cannot get out of its meshes and are compelled to defend it
the best they can.

6. The wild chase after excessive wealth is an allurement
that always has one end; sorrow and failure in the goal of
existence. People who are burdened by the weight of facts
in drudgery and routine toil say they will be supremely happy
if they can find the way to get wealth. When they succeed,
as many do, they run either to the extreme of miserly penury,
cutting themselves off from the happiness of life; or they run
to the other extreme of being idly rich, and thus joining the
compost profession, which has been fully described herein, the
chief value of the latter being to furnish fertilization to the
earth both during their existence and after they die.

.7. The allurement of resting is one of the most potent of
the evil influences of life. It makes the tramp, the lazy man
and woman in middle ranks, and the idle rich. They all belong to the fertilizer-class. The good book says that if a man
will not work he shall not eat; but he does eat, and still he
has his value in the world; for, without him, there would be
a scarcity of nutriment with which to carry on the processes
of growth in the earth. The lazy class have no hope of heaven;
for there cannot be a greater contradiction of religion and
nature than the existence of any person who, being able, will
not do useful work; or, being given a body fit to work with,
so eats and luxuriates, or loafs and deteriorates, that useful
work is impossible. Some day disease will be made a crime;
for the world is awaking to the fact that it is always the
fault of somebody.

8. Then there is the false allurement of appetite. Some
persons live from meal to meal, and their anticipations of
pleasure are limited to what enjoyment they can get for the
stomach. The only right way to eat is to make food subservient
to the demands of a healthy body and mind; all else being
gluttony.

On the side opposite these allurements that are false can

be found those that are true and that, in fact, bring genuine happiness; not in theory, but in the proved histories of many families who have adopted them in the past thirty years or more:

1. The first true allurement is the love of useful domestic and wage-earning work.

2. The second true allurement is the margin above what is earned and what is spent until there is a home free from all debt as the reward of toil.

3. The third allurement is forming a partnership with nature; for this brings on the most powerful of all influences in human life. This is taught in the several courses of the Ralston Health Club, and into this important work you should enter. But for the purposes of this present course in magnetism, it can be said that a partnership with nature is joining forces with her forces in outdoor life, and making her impulses yours in garden and lawn, in orchard and field, and in all her beauties and offerings everywhere. The man who puts on his walls the great paintings of natural scenes may die from lack of life; but he who becomes a part of those scenes will live because of the fullness of life. That is magnetism, and it invites the support of nature. The promise of heaven is built on language taken from the best gifts of earth. There is not a word about heaven's glory that is not a picture of the beauties and grandeur found in this world. If heaven is no greater than the magnificence of its description, then it is no greater than the best things of this globe, for the description merely likens heaven to those things that are found here. One long, unending train of happy experiences attends a partnership with nature, as has been attested by thousands of devotees to these teachings; and, above all, nature stands night and day by the side of every person who is her partner. No harm, no disease, no misfortune, no failure, no unhappiness can come to such devotee, as is amply proved. A special design is created for the watchful care and helpful maintenance of every one who is helping nature make the earth more like heaven, and the home a veritable heaven, as its own name implies. Here are allurements that make the eight false influences seem shameful.

They are noble attractions.

4. When an excess of wealth has been acquired, which means when the assured income, under proper economy, is greater than the expenditure, then this excess must not be allowed to make the mind and heart penurious and mean, nor the face rat-shaped; but it must be employed right out in the lap of nature, extending the partnership that has been begun. It is wrong to allow an inch of land to go uncultivated or running to weeds. Cottages should be built on estates, and little gardens should surround the cottages, and families of worthy and industrious laborers should be given homes and work to do, so that they may support themselves and lay aside a margin against old age. It is your duty to know where the money goes that you give to charity and in the employment of labor of every kind. Many persons of wealth have followed these doctrines with the result that they have reformed men of drinking habits. Finding work for men who live in cities, and who will not go into the country, is wrong; and nature resents such charity. There are more than one million people in this country who are worth hundreds of thousands of dollars. They have an excess of what is a proper expenditure in their annual budget. Let them each build one cottage a year, and there place a family at living wages on condition that the man employed shall not drink any alcoholic beverage of any kind, and the result would be one million new homes where poverty would be impossible, and health and temperance would be assured if the employer looked after their interests as he should, since they are in his charge. As each family would average more than three persons, and probably four, these present-day wasters of wealth would be placing four million people out of the reach of poverty. The barons of riches must not forget the massing of idle men in the cities is making a new French Revolution possible in America, with a different date, and a different name, but the same bloodthirsty hate of the arrogant classes; and that, as in the French Revolution of more than a hundred years ago, the peasants were not involved, so in the approaching cataclysm of classes in this land, the safety of the barons of wealth is in a contented peasantry. This plan is the only method that is in harmony with nature. That it can be made to work is already known, for it has been tried for many years, and there are today in the employ of the rich classes more than a million

of people on estates such as we have described. But what is wanted is the building of cottages on estates at the rate of one million a year. The cost of living is too high, far too high. The government is powerless in the hands of monopoly. It took nine years to get a judgment against the ice trust and a fine of five thousand dollars, which will not be forced to settlement for another four years, owing to the incapacity of the courts to shorten trials, and this fine is not equal in fourteen years to one day's extortion of the trust; so that prosecutions against monopolies are a farce. The people are awake and really on fire, but the breaking forth of the storm against government for its incapacity, against the courts for their incapacity, and against monopolies for their greed, will come in a flash, and like a flash leave the rich in its wake dead and blood-red with murder. The remedy is in the methods stated, and in no other way. Here is the allurement for those who have an excess of income; as we had an allurement for those who lacked such an excess.

5. The fifth allurement is in the saving of magnetic margins under the teachings of the tenth department.

6. The sixth allurement is in the creation of a Charmland for yourself and your consort, as taught in the eleventh department of this course.

7. The seventh allurement is in the brief daily and weekly anticipation which you must establish for yourself and your consort, and for both to enjoy together. These anticipations must be realized. The mother who promises her child candy if he will stop crying, and who forgets to keep her promise, loses the confidence of the child. We have known little boys and girls who were actually suffering from thirst which the stupid mother did not know enough to relieve, and who were promised candy if they would keep quiet, to stop their demands and go on suffering, only to be treacherously deceived in the promise. The allurement in the form of anticipation must be honest, and no amount of excuse on the ground of forgetfulness on the part of the promiser can atone for the failure to do what has been agreed upon. It requires a mind that is a mind to furnish these anticipations. Cheap brains will give birth to almost nothing, and will find the duties too irksome when they attempt to hunt for something that is gen-

uinely worth having, as the means of brightening the lives of others. The first duty of a husband is to his wife; and of a wife is to her husband. After thinking out one thing that will be worth while, another will come to mind, for like breeds like, and the faculty of giving pleasure is a gift that grows with the using. Probably this means of making marriage happy is the most magnetic of all, for the little anticipations may all be realized in short time, while the big anticipations may never be fully worked out. Try them.

8. The eighth allurement is in the life goal. There should be something to live for that will include both parties. The husband may desire to become a great man in his line of work, but that does not help the wife, unless she can be brought to feel his ambition and to sympathize with it.

There are many notable cases where the husband has risen to the highest rank in political power, aided all along the way by his wife, and both have been happy together. There are also many cases in the professions where the wife has pushed the husband on to the achievement of fame and success, in which she has shared the fruits of victory. If the man can be wholly loyal to the woman in such matters as home attention and fidelity of marriage vows, he will merit her aid, and there is no better bond of magnetism than that for such persons. The greatest happiness, however, has come to those who are neither rich nor poor, neither famous nor infamous, who have struggled together from the first days of wedlock to the last hours of existence, hand in hand and heart to heart, true and tried, honorable and honored, but unknown to the great world. They have done their work better than all other classes.

9. Self-impressions make the ninth allurement.

10. Outward feelings make the tenth allurement.

These are always seen at work in a pair of magnetic powers, as one gives birth to the other.

The best example of a self-impression is a mental vision, such as genius will behold. It is the result of natural or acquired magnetism. The latter, being more scientific, secures greater accuracy, and becomes of higher value on that account. The grandest all-round genius the world has ever known is Michael Angelo—architect, poet, painter and prose writer. The grandest cathedral ever built on this globe is the fruit of his brain. In his mental eye he saw it finished before the first stone was set. Angelo performed nothing that he could not previously behold as a fact in his mental vision. His faces and forms were to him living existences as real as those things of substance are to other minds. It is said more than once of him that he could not distinguish readily between the picture of his mind and the picture of his canvas.

HOW CAME IMAGINATION?

QUESTION

"How came imagination to the brain,
Stirring the fibered cells till nerves alert
Sped messages of life to flesh inert,
And all the marvelous things of joy or pain
Filled mind and body? Came it by the main
Method and law old Nature must assert —
As the blue lotus or the ruby's stain —
Or, by sheer accident law failed t' avert?

ANSWER

Came it that love might fear and fearless die.
Came it that blood might steal Promethean fires.
Came it that thought might drain the fount of truth.
Came it that self, the spirit-lark, might fly
With the great sun, and sing as night expires.
Came it that soul might know and win immortal youth."

The architect of St. Peter's at Rome, this same Angelo, was the foremost painter of all time; and yet in all ways a normal man with a normal mind. His power of mental vision gave him his genius as a poet, architect and painter; and wherever this power is limitted the genius is less, but where the power is increased the genius is enhanced. Emerson, in his account of the visions that are living truths in the lives of great men, says:

Not from a vain or shallow thought
His awful Jove young Phidias brought;
Never from lips of cunning fell
The thrilling Delphic oracle;
Out from the heart of nature rolled
The burdens of the Bible old;
The litanies of the nations came,
Like the volcano's tongue of flame
Up from the burning core below—
The canticles of love and woe.

The hand that rounded Peter's dome,
And groined the aisles of Christian Rome,
Wrought in a sad sincerity;
Himself from God he could not free;
He builded better than he knew;
The conscious stone to beauty grew.
For out of Thought's interior sphere
These wonders rose to upper air.

The word unto the prophets spoken
Was writ on tablets yet unbroken;
The word by seers or sibyls told,
In groves of oak, or fanes of gold,
Still floats upon the morning wind,
Still whispers to the willing mind.

In analyzing the power that comes from mental vision, it will be found that self-impressions are built up by the interest the mind takes in the work to be done, while the outward feeling places the result in tangible form.

No man can become an architect, even for one building, who does not see the end at the start. He cannot make an intelligent plan unless he knows what he is to do before he starts to do it. A very commonplace architect, having worked in an office, might imitate the ideas he has become familiar with; but they lived in the minds of other people before he saw them. The creative genius does not copy, but gives birth to ideas. In such case his mental vision takes shape in self-impressions, and then in outward feelings, building and placing his work in actual form, complete in all details.

Herein is found the chief difference between the talker and the orator. The former has words and ideas, perhaps, in abundance, and may talk and talk endlessly; but the orator has mental vision. Facts turn to fancies before his gaze, and he lives in creations of his own. His hearers are borne upward to higher realms than they have occupied before; while the talker, be he ever so voluble or emphatic, soon wearies because he has facts only to deal with. The genius builds beautiful edifices on facts, and not facts on facts.

To become great in genius is to develop more and more the power of mental vision in all its uses, in art, in oratory, in the professions, in inventions, in thought, in private life and in the highest uses of anticipation, even lifting the soul up to its noblest ideals. Students often wonder why there is so complex a work as Universal Magnetism at the climacteric stage of the Club; but this one phase of that study alone shows the necessity for a grand system of training in this exalted power.

There have been many inquiries why the author of these systems has been a student of the dramatic instincts in men and women. The answer is that the child is a natural actor, and is then fresh from the hand of nature. In later life it has been found that the child who takes up the profession of the stage is either a genius or is not; most of the actors being in the "not" class. Once in a while a genius comes to the front, like the elder Booth, and also Edwin Booth, or Salvini, Bernhardt, Forrest, Keane, Siddons, Garrick and others whose fame will live for centuries yet.

It was a well-known trait of David Garrick that he saw his counterparts standing before him. "I can summon any of the cast at will," he said, "and I can see them in the flesh before me." His power as an actor was stimulated, not by the mediocre people with whom he played in the parts, but by the people as they ought to have been—fit foil for his art.

This ability has been present in the work of every genius in the drama; and it is the reason why one man or woman will be lacking in genius and some other will possess it. The commercialism must leave the work, and the only ambition must be to act up to the highest possible standards. A famous actress, now living, was once asked how she, so beautiful then, could play Juliet to the Romeo of a very unattractive man who was in the cast. She replied: "I do not see him, but the real Romeo, when I am on the stage." She has often referred to many instances where she has beheld characters in the flesh, but having the same positions and general movements of those who, in fact, are present. There are thousands of anecdotes told along the same line, and of every great man or woman who has been in the drama. In one case Booth, when his counterpart had left the stage, went on with the play with his mental vision of the character until the man again appeared, having missed his cue.

Edwin Booth was, perhaps, the best type of real genius the modern stage has known. He has said many times that he could at will construct on the air in front of him any personage with whom he was to act, and could see the face, form, play of features and stage movements in exact detail, just as vividly as any actor in the flesh could appear. But the actors he saw mentally were of far greater stamina than those that were in the flesh.

A well-known painter said: "I wanted a face, and could not find one that seemed right. I thought intensely on the face I desired, and one stood forth in the air in front of me so very lifelike that I started to touch it, but could not. Still I held it there in my mind until I had painted it. I am sure that artists have this power of summoning forms and faces to suit their needs."

It is also known that intense thinking, accompanied by a high degree of magnetism, will bring almost anything before the mind that is wanted, and, on the other hand, will keep the mind clear when visitations are not wanted. The visions are not those of spiritualism, but simply creations out of nothing but the mind. A man who desired to make a plan of a grand house better than anything he had ever known, or that had ever been known to him; not in size, but in variation of structure, thought of it until he had not the power to proceed, and he gave up the matter for a year. Happening by chance to come upon a course of training in magnetism, he mastered that study, and again by chance undertook the work of making the plan that he at first failed in. He now thought about it very intensely, and the building stood before him one afternoon in a nearby field. "That is the building, and someone has been at work on my ideas." On going into the field he found the building to be but the creation of his own brain. He was able to transfer it to his studio, and there to make drawings as he desired, there being many surprising details that were filled in without his aid or suggestion, as far as he knew; although his sub-conscious mind may have been at work while he slept.

Unseen powers surround humanity.

There have been many things in the experience of magnetic people that have come about unsolicited. Some persons imagine that magnetism brings on unwilling things, as hypnotism does; but the opposite is true. The magnetic person has only to make commands and their own will powers obey instantly. In such a study as Universal Magnetism, after its work has been completed faithfully, the graduate is able to make any command of the will power and it will obey. This has been tested in thousands of ways. People who are troubled with hallucinations may drive them off in a second. Men and women who have been fearful that they would develop some form of mental derangement have been able to put the mind into safe condition any moment of the day or night.

Magnetism, therefore, while it increases the will power, is master of it also. It is able to keep away the visions not wanted, and to bring on visions that are desired.

Magnetism works while the body sleeps as well as when it is awake.

It is one of the common phases of high magnetism that it will carry on during the unconscious state of the brain any operation given it just before, and while sleep is coming on. This is also one of the characteristics of a psychic process.

Thus far in this department we have reached the following laws:

1. The law of high magnetism which makes it possible to attract any power needed to aid human life.

2. The law of self-impressions, by which the mind, aided by high magnetism, is able to create anything and give it actual existence to the eye outwardly.

3. The law that magnetism works during sleep as well as in full wakefulness.

These three laws have been as amply explained as is possible in the present work. They are so extended and involve so much training that they are helped by every day's study of the higher grades of magnetism.

But, for the purpose of testing the work herein, they are sufficient with the help that this book alone affords. Enough can be gained in results to warrant making the following experiments.

Take any quotation you please and build the reality from it, making the form appear to your eyes that is described in the words:

1.

The following extract is taken from Pinckney's poem:

> "Of her bright face one glance will trace
> A picture on the brain,
> And of her voice in echoing hearts
> A sound must long remain;
> But memory, such as mine of her,
> So very much endears,
> When death is nigh, my latest sigh
> Will not be life's, but hers."

The test is made by repeating the words from this page until there seems to be built in the mind some form of woman of whom this may be said. The beginning will be vague for some time. There should be quiet and exclusion of all other matters, so that the mind may be wholly devoted to this test. It is not intended that the vision be actual at present, as stronger words and pictures will follow. But this step should not be neglected, as it leads the way to other tests.

2.

The next quotation is taken from the short poem of Dinah Mulock Craik:

"Yet is this girl I sing in naught uncommon,
    And very far from angel yet, I trow.
Her faults, her sweetnesses, are purely human;
Yet she's more lovable as simple woman
    Than any one diviner that I know."

The mental picture should present the following points in detail:

A young woman who is like common girls, with nothing grand or unusual in her appearance or manner, should be in mind.

No attempt must be made to imagine her an angel of a woman, as the saying goes.

She must seem to be human in her faults, and human in her attractions; and these may shine in her face.

Blended with the simplicity of her womanhood there should be the loftier sweetness of one who is rare and rich in lovable qualities.

These details must be repeated and then allowed to enter the mind until they are absorbed in its thoughts. By devoting a few minutes a day to the practice, if there is magnetism in the brain, the picture of the girl will stand faintly before the gaze.

3.

The next quotation is taken from the poem of Samuel Rogers, entitled "The Sleeping Beauty":

"Sleep on! and dream of heaven awhile!
    Though shut so close thy laughing eyes,
Thy rosy lips still wear a smile,
    And move, and breathe delicious sighs.

Ah! now soft blushes tinge her cheeks
    And mantle o'er her neck of snow;
Ah! now she murmurs, now she speaks,
    What most I wish, and fear, to know."

The picture to be brought before the mind is that of a very beautiful girl asleep. Her eyes are shut close, although they were laughing eyes, and full of happy mirth when open. Still, the face is wreathed in pleasant lines and the rosy lips wear a smile.

Slowly the cheeks change color, and the white shifts to soft pink-like blushes, and these creep gradually down to the snowy neck, which also changes in hue. The lips seem about to speak. A murmur comes from them.

These pictures are very easily impressed on the mind, and from the power of mental sight they can in time be transferred to the air. This test has been the easiest of all in this line of work during many years of private instruction, and no person has failed to make the visions perfect in the course of a few weeks.

4.

"Like to the clear in highest sphere,
　　Where all imperial glory shines,
Of selfsame color in her hair,
　　Whether unfolded, or in twines;
Her eyes are sapphires set in snow,
　　Resembling heaven by every wink;
The gods do fear them as they glow,
　　And I do tremble when I think.

Her cheeks are like the blushing cloud
　　That beautifies Aurora's face,
Or like the silver crimson shroud
　　That Phoebus' smiling looks doth grace:
Her lips are like two budded roses
　　Whom ranks of lilies neighbor nigh,
Within which bounds she balm encloses
　　Apt to entice a deity.

With orient pearl, with ruby red,
　　With marble white, with sapphire blue,
Her body every way is fed,
　　Yet soft in touch, and sweet in view;
Nature herself her shape admires;
　　The gods are wounded in her sight;
And love forsakes her heavenly fires
　　And at her eyes his brand doth light."

This very old and classical poem is filled with the high ideas of a woman of stately and queenly quality, and yet rich in the best gifts of nature and love. The successful use of the extract to bring mental pictures before the mind, and out into the air as though they were substance, requires an exalted magnetism, but is within the reach of every person who is willing to take the following steps:

1. The lines must be memorized until they become a part of the mind.

2. They must be repeated at night after retiring, and when there is no light in the room. The repetition is to be done silently. The words will seem to speak aloud to the brain, although no person could hear them but yourself, even if but a foot away.

3. When you have succeeded in making the words seem to be spoken aloud to the brain, while making no outward sound in fact, you may know that you have achieved the first and most important step in self-impression. This means that you possess magnetism of a high order. It is of the greatest advantage to reach this stage, although it may require months or only a few days to do it.

4. The first mental picture must come after the words sound aloud. This will give a mind-view of the "the clear in highest sphere, where all imperial glory shines."

5. The next picture is that of the hair, which is of a golden color; then the eyes are "sapphires set in snow." These must be made in the mind to pass from their jewel beauty to a natural blending of the human expression.

6. The further vision brings the face to view, and it is seen with cheeks "like the blushing cloud that beautifies Aurora's face." The lips are like two budded roses; and then the whole form of the maiden is summed up in the superb language of the last eight lines.

As the mind becomes intensified by its magnetic power it will behold the form of the young woman standing forth in the room. In the beginning, when it first makes itself visible, it will be like a floating veil, taking on human shape little by little. In some reports of these experiments there seems to be a great variation with the same person. A woman makes the following assertion, which is known to be true with many others: "When I felt in the humor for the practice, the vision would come very quickly, and seem very real. At other times it would not come at all, and then again it would be faint. I find that my own magnetism is not the same every day." The fact is that vitality varies, and with it magnetism changes.

There are cases where intense feeling, coming on very suddenly, will bring visions to the mind, especially if the latter is unstrung; but these are the unwilling visions. Let the nerve be expectant and the mind afraid or overwrought, and almost any kind of a vision may be expected. The man who has been inflaming his brain with liquor sees many ugly things. The woman who has been left alone after hearing some awful story that has frightened her, will possibly see ghosts. It is in the power of the mind to stamp visions on the air, willingly or unwillingly, that all the genius and all the supernatural effects are produced. Any person who doubts this law of nature may experiment for himself. Just in proportion as he acquires magnetism he will be able to bring these self-impressions under his command, and they will all come or go in obedience to his wishes and orders. They make him a genius, for this power he can apply to any profession or art, or in business or otherwise, to make him equal to the greater tasks of life. On the other hand, let a person be a natural subject of hypnotism, which means that he utterly lacks magnetism, and he will be the prey of unwilling things, from small startling visions up to every imagined ghost, and the forms will seem real to him while they last. The cure of hypnotic tendencies in a subject is to study magnetism. The cure of ghosts and bad visions and wicked dreams, hysteria and the like, is in mastering magnetism.

Having acquired the power to create at will any outward-feeling, the last moments of the waking period just prior to falling asleep should be devoted to making a mental picture of some person of the opposite sex who is exactly like the person to whom you are married, or engaged to wed, or one whom you would like to wed. While the mental picture is to be the same as that person, you are to do as the great actors do with their counterparts. If a man is playing the role of Romeo, and the Juliet is played by a woman who is not at all what an ideal Juliet should be, the actor always makes a mental picture of the ideal Juliet; that is, if the actor has genius. He then sees all through the play where these two characters come together the ideal Juliet in the attitudes and work of the real actress.

The vision is seemingly a fact.

If a woman is playing Juliet and the Romeo is not up to her standard, then, if she has genius, she will make a mental picture of the ideal Romeo, and to this picture will take the place of the actor who in fact plays the part.

This method has been in use for centuries and is taught by nature.

It embodies the old law of emotions being greater than facts. The facts are the two players, Romeo and Juliet in the flesh; the emotions are their ideals; and the latter are always better and grander in every way than the facts.

In so far as the emotions of the actor's genius are able to lift the character out of the individual of flesh who plays it, to that extent will the audience be lifted out of their dull appreciation of the commonplace fact and be made to enjoy the ideals.

The effect is twofold.

The actor whose mental visions are able to create ideals in place of facts will have before him a richer enjoyment of the conditions he is able to establish. But he will also add to the pleasure of those who are within range of his creations. He will find his power useful to himself and to others. The same is true of the artist; he will love his art through its ideals and through those only; never through the commonplaces of it; and he will give genuine pleasure to others who are capable of appreciating his art. There is no power in the world that can do either of these things except the power of mental pictures. The architect has much pleasure in his own creations, and he gives lasting pleasure to others by the results of his ability.

Thus the power of mental-picturing is always twofold.

A man is able to make himself what is called blind to the faults and defects of his wife by creating an ideal woman as near like her as circumstances will allow; and, in turn, he will lift her up to the standard that he creates.

It is the same law at work in this use as in art, and all forms of special power.

The steps are to be taken as already described and may be summed up as follows:

1.   There must be the power of magnetism as the basis.

2.   There must be practice in developing ideals by first using quotations to furnish the subject matter.

3.   Then there must be the making of your own ideal suited to some living person, and creating only such improvements as your wishes indicate.

4.   The absorption into your nervous system is the final step. This takes place under psychic law. In a general way these laws are stated as taking into one's mind and body through the nervous system any feeling or idea that is lodged in the mind just as it is leaving consciousness for unconsciousness.

In the waking hours the mind is in working condition. Sleep puts a stop to the work of the mind unless there is fever or irritation of some kind, in which case there may be delirium or dreams. A dream of the conscious mind occurs when it is unable to pass into sound sleep, or is coming out of it. No sound sleeper ever dreams when in full slumber. But the subconscious mind carries on much of the work of life in the absence of the working mind. It sometimes takes part during waking hours with the ordinary mental forces; but does its greatest work in what is called the reverie. Then the conscious mind also gets a grasp of the other mind; almost recognizes it; almost knows it by contact.

The reverie is the mind standing on one threshold while the other mind, that of extraordinary powers, is standing on the opposite threshold; neither in full possession of the individual. It is in the reverie that all the great geniuses of the world have achieved their victories over facts and commonplaces.

The exact conditions of the reverie are found at any time, night or day, when a person is just falling to sleep. The minds are in that half-entrance to the brain, and one is able to pick up from the other any order, wish or command. It is a rule of the other mind that it will obey implicitly any such order, wish or command of the working mind, if the latter can reach the former; and this contact is possible only in the genuine reverie, and in the stepping out of wakefulness into slumber. By countless experiments (the results are fully given and explained in our book, Other Mind) it has been proved beyond all doubt that a command, wish or order given by a magnetic person in the interval just preceding sleep will be taken up and executed by the controlling mind of the body.

This other mind obeys implicitly. It never assumes that it is to argue or discuss the command; but it simply puts it into execution. There is never any doubt about the results when the following conditions agree:

1. There must be magnetism to act as a carrying power to convey the orders from the conscious mind to the other mind.

2. The only time when the other mind can be reached with orders from the conscious mind is when there is some form of lapse, reverie or fading consciousness. Lapses and reveries come in full wakefulness and are taken advantage of by experts in magnetism, and by the world's great men and women; for it is this power that makes a person great. But the approach of sleep can always be used by every person; and the only advantage of magnetism is that it merely makes the results come sooner and in greater distinctness.

Wishes and mental-pictures which are made clear and strong during a lapse, reverie or fading wakefulness, conveyed by magnetism, become a part of the life of the person engaged in so employing them.

Assuming that you have magnetism, it can be said with certainty that every mental-picture that you are able to create will become a part of your own life through nervous absorption.

Any wish, hope, desire or command will likewise become a reality in the same way.

The reality will remain permanent. As we all live in our emotions and tire of facts very soon, the same realism is attained in this way that is secured by the young man or woman who is blinded in judgment by the impulse called love. In a few lives that impulse is never lost, but lives on through old age and is carried to the grave. But in a vast majority it is lost soon after the engagement is accepted by both parties, and is pretty sure to be obliterated entirely by marriage in nearly every individual.

But the control of the mind and the sway of the feelings, while love-blindness lasts, cannot be denied.

It resists all counter influences.

Here the first part of the present course converges and joins the last part of the training. Both ends meet and all that comes between is interwoven in this work. Every road that is ascending in its grade seeks the highest level; and all roads that ascend a mountain are sure to meet at the top.

Looking back to the first department, which should never be forgotten, the student will find the plan of nature explained. Marriage is intended in part as the means of saving the human race. In order to make this means sure, nature brings the two sexes together with much intensity of interest; and they are made to believe each other the highest ideal in existence. This is the blindness of love.

But reproduction is not the only purpose of blinding the sexes to the faults of each other. There is a period when these emotions hold such control over the mind and heart, and the ideal seems so grand, that each party seeks to become worthy of the other, and becomes more refined, more polished, more careful of what is said and done, and more desirous of seeming better than others, so that there is a distinct improvement of mind, body and morals.

As the law of the survival of the fittest has been in operation for countless thousands of years, and is made effective chiefly in the period when mates select each other, the best preferring the best, and as this law of the survival of the fittest is the cause of evolution and the agency by which evolution, and even civilization, have been made possible, and is the same law whereby humanity finds its way to rise step by step out of its lower conditions, it must be regarded as the most important principle in this world's existence.

Nature, therefore, is shrewd and keen, for she works a two-fold result in this law:

1. She makes lovers blind to each other's faults, and so brings them together with an intensity of interest.

2. 'She makes them, in their blindness, improve themselves in every possible way so as to add to their attractiveness, each to the other.

In this brief period, all too brief, we are sorry to say, the impulse is set in motion that makes the world better; slightly better, it is true, but nevertheless better. So important is that period to humanity that, if it were omitted, there would be absolutely nothing on which to build any improvement.

The foregoing is, in condensed form, the story told in the first department of this course.

In the present department we find that magnetism is able to restore permanently that same exalted regard that nature instituted for her special ends; that the man, even the husband of years, may come into a new feeling for his wife; and that she may come into a new feeling for him; the result being that both will seek to merit the better opinions thus secured.

The final step in this practice is the creation of magnetic consorts. A consort is a husband of a woman, or a wife of a man. The actual consort is the husband or wife in the flesh. The magnetic consort is the husband or the wife in mental-pictures.

When an author sets out to write a novel he is pretty sure to found it upon some kind of a love story. He seeks as his heroine a young lady of superior quality. She has a better form than any young woman he has ever seen; she has a prettier face, and finer ways than the best girl of his acquaintance. That is his ideal heroine. Many authors have had their lives sweetened by the influence of these imaginary women, but they miss the opportunity of making these characters magnetic consorts, by not having the power to absorb the personality of the ideal heroine into their own lives. It requires a high degree of magnetism to do this, and then the result is the same as if the author were married to such a woman and retained his love-blindness for her.

Assuming that a magnetic man has gone far enough in mental-picturing to produce an ideal woman, just as the author does in his mind before he begins to write his novel, he must complete the work by the following steps:

1. The ideal must be absorbed into his own nature.

2. She must be made the chief character in a plot or bit of human history, not complicated in its structure.

3. He must be the one person above all others who is desired by the ideal he has created.

Authors go some ways in their mental-picturing, but they come short of final success because they lack magnetism, and also because they are not in the plot themselves. The story is not directed to them in the second person, but all the characters are in the third person to the author. The latter should be the hero in developing magnetic consorts.

The only difference between an ideal heroine of a novel, as conceived by an author, and his magnetic consort is that he does not himself enter into the plot; and if he does, he probably is wanting in magnetic power.

It has been argued that the practice of creating magnetic consorts leads a man or woman into authorship, and stimulates their minds to take up that profession whether they will or not. In reply to this claim, it may be said that no man or woman who does not wish to take up the profession of authorship need do so. There is nothing that compels the avocation. Magnetism, as a rule shows the better vocations of life, and if the authorship is one of them, the call will be very clear. Magnetism has brought many ministers out of the pulpit because it has shown a fitness for other work; and it has brought some great preachers into the pulpit by showing them that their former vocations were wasted effort. The same rule would prevail in authorship.

But the ability to create a character and a plot is one of the most pleasing diversions ever engaged in for man or woman. In that plot you, if you are a husband, may find a wife that is perfect, and you may spend many happy hours, days and years with her. Gradually you will become more refined to your own wife, and will treat her as your magnetic consort must be treated, to be won and kept in a state of exaltation. In your plot you will be the hero, and will attract the heroine by your superior qualities. In that plot you will be constantly bettering yourself, and this improvement will be absorbed in your actual life.

It is going back to the conditions described in the first department of this work.

It is taking nature's lesson and enlarging it, and making the better state permanent, and thus building on nature; just as the fine varieties of roses, carnations and many flowers and fruits are built on nature's impulses and improved in every change.

When shall these plots be made?

In the last moments of wakefulness, just as you are falling asleep at night; for what then occurs will become a part of your life. By transferring the plot-making power to the other mind it will be made to create something better than you can evolve; and this is genius.

You will refine your own nature, and its influence will give delight to your wife, and you will draw her up to your new level of nobility.

If you are a wife, you may find in this practice a husband that is far superior to the one to whom you are married in the flesh; and you will in time blend him with your ideal. The result will be a double benefit, affecting both you and him. This has been done many times before, and can be done always if you so wish.

The making of these plots whereby magnetic consorts are produced takes no time away from any other duty. If you belong to the psychic society it will fall right in with the practice of that system, and thus save half of the time. A man who had looked at first with disfavor on the practice took it up and sent the following report: "I had been troubled for a long time with insomnia. I took up the work of plot-making as soon as I retired at night, and I found myself entering into the most refreshing sleep I ever had. Each plot required less than five minutes, and ended in sound sleep." A woman who had been very nervous, and who took up this practice said: "I had become so nervous that sleep was out of the question. As the plan of making plots was a pleasant diversion, I began the habit, and I found that I could invite sleep at will, and my trouble disappeared." Aside from its effects on the nerves as a matter of health, plot-making has had other results, which are embodied in two typical letters, one from a man reading as follows, in part: "The most telling effect of making plots with mental pictures has been the sweeter influence that has come into my life and my heart. I feared to tell my wife what I was doing, but after four weeks she said to me one day that I had become like my younger self, when she thought there was no one in the world as nice as I was. I dislike to quote her phrase, but you ask for exact statements, and here they are." A woman said: "I was not as gentle a wife as I ought to have been. My face had become sour and rather repulsive, even to my own gaze. I know of nothing that can so quickly bring a woman back to her better girl-hood nature as this practice of plot-making.''

Men and women have caught the idea of this practice, and have given it a more difficult interpretation, as may be seen in two letters from which we quote: ''It did not take me long to grasp the meaning behind the practice of plot-making. I saw that it was merely putting a new nature in a man and in a woman. I saw that it could be as effectively done in daily life as in the last moments of wakefulness. I began to see my wife in a new light; not as she was, but as she could have been had nothing detracted from her grace and sweetness. I began to make the plot in real life, with her as the heroine, and both came back to the days of our first fascination for love-making, which is better than plot-making.''

A woman has this to say: ''It is now three years since the private lessons in plot-making were received. I have used them with intense pleasure for a long time, and they bring a finer influence to bear on all my days and nights, on all I do and say, and in my feelings towards the man who was fast falling out of my heart. I have now made him the hero of a life-plot, in which we are the two characters. From the dream of happiness we have come into its real fruit.''

Thus the old law of nature, the improvement of the human race through the impulses that are given strength and progress in the first meeting of the two sexes in mutual admiration, can be made a permanent rule in marriage.

Two lovers who become love-blind through their emotions towards each other are furnished by nature for the time being with magnetism. This remains only so long as it serves the purpose of nature; then it fades out, and the facts come to the front and blindness is gone. By the reversing action of this law the acquisition of a never-failing magnetism will restore what was given naturally in that blissful period. It will come to stay, when it comes in this manner.

Thus nature joins hands with her own art.

Thus the cause that makes the effect is re-made by the effect itself.

It cannot be denied that there are men and women in this world whose lives are ineffably sweet and are kept in good poise all the time, no matter what clouds come over them. They seem inspired. We have hunted them for years and have always taken supreme delight in forming their acquaintance, for there is nothing so productive of genuine happiness as the presence of such persons.

It is possible that one man in ten thousand may be of this rare class, and that one woman in two thousand may be found in it. They are beautiful at any age from the first years of youth to the gray of winter. They are always magnetic; naturally so, if habits of living can be called nature. Now it is also true that many other men and women have acquired this sweetness and poise of heart, and from it has come the formation of habits that are exactly like those found in the lives of the rare few we have mentioned.

The secret is this:

All human character contains every possibility of good and bad; and what is drawn to the surface and stays there is the result of habits that are accidental or acquired. When they are accidental they are called natural; when they are acquired they are longer abiding because they are the fruits of the will power that created them and that can sustain and use them.

Magnetism draws up to the surface the best influences of the human heart and turns them into permanent habits. No person is hopeless. If you could only know the brutes whose lives have been softened and sweetened by this study, you would have a new faith in humanity. Coarse women have been refined into pure gold, and boorish men have been made gentle and noble; because there is in the depths of life the good and the bad, and the choice is a free one at all times.

The difficulty in the past has been in the lack of all power to bring forth so grand a progeny. Magnetism is will power, and creates it as well as uses it. Once this will power is set in motion, and the right habits are established, the fruit will be found in abundance. It is the wish of all who promulgate these doctrines that every man who reads them may become noble and kindly, and every woman may be made lovable and winning.

WRECKAGE

NOWLEDGE is power when it is absorbed into the nervous system, of which the brain is a part. To merely know and understand a thing is not true knowledge, for there must be a taking in, and using of, the thing before it can be of value. Use is the real test. There are many things men and women do not know about themselves that they ought to find out before marriage; or if that has not been done, then after marriage, and as soon as possible; but these things should be more than found out; they should be absorbed and utilized.

As has been taught in the preceding department, the time when a thing is absorbed, is in the last moments of wakefulness, just before sleep comes on at night. Any command or wish made then and transferred from the conscious mind to the other mind will, by the latter, be executed and become a part of life itself. The only difficulty is in reaching the other mind. Many repetitions at such time will bring results. There must never be discouragement because results are not speedy, or because they do not come, for they are sure to come if there is magnetism combined with the uses named.

It is on this principle that prayers made at the last moments of wakefulness bring answers. The right time to pray is just as the mind is relaxing its working power. In fact, a person prays best who falls asleep praying. All the energy of an intense wish, coupled with natural or acquired magnetism, thrown into a prayer at such a time, and then given consistent support in the way of living from day to day, is sure to bring results. The principle is a psychic one, as any person can easily understand who has taken up the practice of psychic laws in the society of that name.

This is not stating that prayer is not an agency of the divine power; nor is it placing prayer in the mere realm of science. All true psychic studies prove the existence of God and the certainty of immortality for those persons who take part in the upward movement of civilization towards perfect honesty and a better home life on earth; and the psychic laws teach that all others return to the earth to aid in fertilizing it for the next generations. For these reasons there is no more important study than those same psychic laws. But they are so great in their scope that time and space cannot be devoted to them herein.

As God makes use of human means for human help, so the psychic period at night is now, and has always been made use of as the direct and powerful channel by which prayers are answered.

It is in such periods that knowledge is absorbed into the mind and body. Great thinkers know this, and have employed that faculty for thousands of years. Great poets have always known their power rests solely in the three psychic periods of the day or night; in lapses by day, or reverie by day or night, or the relaxing of the working mind. Necessity of success has made them know these periods. They also know that their mightiest thoughts come to them in the quick jumps of the lapsing mind, passing from one to the other mentality; and so they have been ready to seize their thoughts and note them down in the very instant they have come. There has never been a great thinker, a great poet, a great artist, a great inventor, or other person who has possessed and developed genius, who has not had pencil and paper ready to take down the quick flashes of ideas that come when the mind lapses by day under psychic laws. People at large have come to believe that the psychic laws are occult affairs; but they are nothing more than the governing principles of two minds—one giving humanity for working purposes, and the other for reaching out after something worth while in existence.

All men and women have these two minds, but not one in a thousand makes use of the power that might be drawn from the inner mentality. All humanity, excepting now and then one person, plods along with the working mind, and never gets on in life in the true sense. It is the inner mind that brings earthly happiness, better conditions, hope, the fruition of desires, and the true promise of heaven.

Two sets of information are needed to give a person something worth living for on earth:

1. What can be done to bring perfect honesty and better home life to everybody so that existence will take an upper trend?

2. How can such knowledge be absorbed and made a part of life itself?

The latter question is answered in the preceding department, which teaches us to take advantage of the psychic periods for drawing into our minds and hearts the impulses for a nobler personality, both for ourselves and our consorts; or for those who, while not married to us, are nevertheless worthy of our esteem and influence.

Just as the actor learns his lines for a new part by taking them to bed with him at night and falling asleep in their study; just as the hardest problems in scientific work have been solved at such periods, and gigantic facts and principles of invention have come into birth then, so the man or woman who desires to make all the preceding departments of this work effective in actual life, and in all of life's battles, so they should be taken to bed at night, and be the last study of the waking hours, to be followed by the putting out of the lights, the closing of the eyes, and the making of mental plots with which to drop asleep, always using some one of the teachings of this course as a basis for a plot.

This is a practical use of the brain.

Most persons worry about something, and go to sleep worrying.

Which is better, to absorb into the system the habit of worrying, or to take into it the habit of improvement?

It is sure to be one thing or the other. No person who has any knowledge of the immense possibilities of using the psychic periods can long remain out of their friendship; for it is now predicted by the best educational experts of the world that the greatest training lines of the future will be in making use of the psychic periods, such as the lapses, reveries and relaxation of the working brain; all of which will be found through them.

To fall asleep at night thinking of the woes of the past and the fears of the future is the common experience of ninety-five persons out of every hundred of the ambitious classes. Much of their woes and fears are born in this practice. It is from such habits that life gets its toboggan, and loses its firm grip on the world. Something better is close by.

Let us see what it is.

For some weeks this book should be taken into one's sleeping-room, and some of its teachings should be gone over and reviewed in the mind. It is the purpose of the present department to state in condensed form some of the most important truths in this work, and to add suggestions that will be of help in making it a success. If you take the book to your bed at night, open it first to this department, and here get the stimulus to go back over the past pages for help and power. The great truths may be summed up as follows:

1. Man is not refined enough. His larger refinements are to his advantage in society; but the best cultured men as husbands are not in the habit of showing the many little refinements that a woman will most appreciate.

2. When a man gives way to his lack of little refinements he is sure to lose his wife's best regard, or to drive her to a lower level in her own habits.

3. Refinement without prudery, and modesty without repellent ways, are necessary to the retention of respect and love. There is something in the boor that is never lovable, whether this character is of men or women.

4. Most women are too talkative on matters that are trivial. A woman's opinion and judgment are not valuable unless they arrive at a conclusion that is based on good sense. It is true, as has been stated by other women who are writers of their own sex, that one woman will become the enemy of another when the latter copies her hat or gown, or for some similar reason or lack of reason. The bent of woman's mind is such that her old-time inheritance rules her, rather than the principles of civilization. Women that talk much are not good listeners and therefore absorb only what their emotions catch; nor are they good students. The first principle of the student habit is to be a good listener and let the tongue have a rest.

5. There are women in the world who succeed in business because of their judgment and good sense. They are always

quiet women. Imagine, if you will, a successful woman who is a voluble talker. It is a contradiction on its face.

6. There have been six thousand years, at least, of female slavery, in which period woman has been the abject serf of her husband, her father or her brother. In that time she has felt her wrongs; and nature, bursting forth in the expression of these wrongs, has developed in time a Darwinian section of her brain that finds its vent in the clatter of the scolding tongue.

7. This scolding habit has become a mental disease. It has never been cured, when once it is established. The ducking stool has been tried for centuries, but while the water may drown the voice, it has never drowned the disease, unless it has drowned the woman; and if such strenuous methods will not check scolding, what can a poor, meek husband do with such a woman. There are many ways of finding out the nature of a girl in this respect; for a long courtship will discover all the incurable faults of both sexes.

8. The curable faults are well covered in courtship; and if this state lasts long enough it will reform the faults. The incurable faults, such as scolding and the drink habit, when in the blood, may be concealed by the crafty man or woman; but not after the commonplaces begin to appear, as they are sure to do in a prolonged courtship. A mother says to her daughter: "Annie, if Jack does not marry you soon, he will find you out. You cannot keep up this appearance much longer." The appearance referred to was that of being quiet and gentle. This Annie had a tongue that was sharp and active, and she had claws concealed in her hands. But Jack was wise—he waited and found her out. Then he started another courtship, and found at last a woman who would make his home a heaven instead of the place that Annie would have made it.

9. Nine men out of ten who have married in a hurry, or after a short courtship, have secured wives that are making their lives unendurable, and the surprise is that men stand this eternal drag on their efforts to better themselves. The chief fault in such women is their scolding tongues.

10. One thing is known well enough, but not given heed; and it is the law of human nature that makes a man or woman what one will, if the other party proceeds right. A man is a

mixed devil and saint; a woman is a mixed she-devil and an angel. All persons have two parents, four grand-parents, eight great-grand-parents, and going back twenty-two generations, they have more than one million ancestors. Heredity governs all persons. If your parents were perfect, it is safe to say that your ancestors sometime back were hung as thieves or criminals. The children of a saint may be as bad as it is possible for children to be, and their grand-parents may control them in their blood. You can never tell what will break out in the next generation, or how far back the influence of heredity may run.

11. You can touch a certain spring in man-nature and open out the floodgates of a past power that is most infernal in its character; or you may touch another spring in the same man and open out another floodgate of gentleness and noble qualities. Every man has both influences locked up in his heredity.

This is seen in the boys and girls that play about the streets. Many of the boys are not born criminals, and will grow up to be good men if their good springs can be touched, or will grow up to be habit-criminals if their bad springs are touched. The born criminal boy and the born prostitute girl is incurable except by death. If nature could be consulted, the born criminal would be put to death for his own good and for the good of the world; and the born prostitute should be put to death for the same good reasons. Then there would be fewer born criminals. That class can never be cured, and the fact is known too well to be discussed. The habit-criminal and the habit-prostitute are curable. It is best to save them before the age of fourteen; next best before the age of fifteen; next best before the age of sixteen, and so on, each year of delay making the habit harder to shake off. Much as the world is given to sentiment through its weak and flabby women, there will come a time when nature will make humanity kill off all its incurable criminals or prostitutes, which may be done in one generation by segregation so they may not create offspring. One simple little lapse of time, known to us as a generation, and to nature as a second, will kill them all off, and not a life be taken. This seems easy, but the present public is too selfish to understand it.

12. In marriage the woman who once touches the devil-

spring in her husband may not let out the contents of that side of his character; but if she keeps on touching it, she will be sure to do so. No man is so angelic as to be a saint when you are touching nothing but his inherited evil nature. He is not to blame for having a devil side. He did not choose his parents, or his grand-parents, or his million ancestors; and when he is compelled to fight an army of a million bad men and women in his blood, and a termagant wife in the flesh, he is just human, and nothing more, when he spills his devil-character all over the house.

13. The greatest of all mistakes is that which places blame on a person for inherited tendencies. The born criminal and the born prostitute are not to blame. They were born as they are, and the world must take the consequences. The hope of civilization is not in curing the incurables, but in preventing and curing the habit-nature when it is wrong. The cat eats the canary bird, and the cat is whipped; but the feline sees no point in being whipped, for she says she was born a cat and not a rose, and as cats for thousands of years have eaten birds, what is there in the habit to be whipped? The tiger is a mean animal, and will kill human beings, but it is not to blame; it was born that way. The spider is venomous, and is hated; but why blame the spider, as it was born with venom in its blood. If every man and every woman has two natures, why blame them? If you pound a bad child, you will pound the bad into him, and not out of him. No wicked person, young or old, was ever reformed by being punished. The only sensible method of dealing with that class is to find him wise enough to discover the born criminal from the habit-criminals, and then segregate the former. Just as soon as you are sure you have a born criminal in your possession, never let him get away. He will be as certain to continue his crime, and possibly commit murder, rape and arson as he is sure to be alive, and no sentiment can save him. But civilization is not civilization as long as it cannot determine which are the born and incurable criminals, and which are the habit-made and curable ones; and, having advanced far enough to ascertain this fact, it will not be genuine civilization until it takes upon itself the power to segregate the born criminals, and thus end in one generation their evil tendencies.

14. When all the born criminals are in their graves, then there will be in the world the many curable criminals. The latter pass along to their posterity their class of habits, and the former pass along their class. Unless insanity comes in the brain, the habit-criminals will not give birth to incurable criminals. Thus the disposal of the latter will save the world.

15. Civilization itself, as it stands in this age, may be indicted on ten thousand grounds of incapacity and selfishness, of greed, wickedness and crime, all of which is growing faster than the good is developing in the world. Ministers say the world is getting better; and this is so in one direction only, for there is a better stand among the better classes for a higher morality. But their numbers are getting less, and the criminal classes are growing in much greater ratio. This is due to the fact that the latter give birth to three times as many children as the former. Those who understand how to multiply three times one, and to keep on doing this until you have three million times one million, and then thirty million times ten million, will see the next chaos and revolution of the world in the telescope of prediction. In fact, the most indictible offender of modern times is civiliation, which, after all its boasts of invention, has given noble America two million prostitutes, three million murderers in the past ten years, sixty million lawbreakers at this very moment, interwoven systems of corporation graft, theft and public felonies that are no more likely to be punished or checked than the sun is likely to be blotted out, and a universal system of political corruption that has so saturated the nation that grand juries indict with slowness, petit juries convict only when they do not dare to acquit, and trial judges throw such cases out of court in nine times out of ten, showing that the judiciary, the outcome of politics, is as dishonest as the public. It can be asserted that a thousand cases of ballot frauds can be committed with openness, and certainty of proof, that will never be brought to trial and conviction, so completely dipped in wickedness are the masses of the people. The dear people, as demagogues call them, are told that their enemies are the grafters and the corporations and the trusts, when, in fact, they (the people) are their own enemies. The toilers who are today being bled for twice the value of the food they eat blame someone higher up; but these same

toilers when asked to go to the polls to change the constitution that binds the courts to wicked technicalities, always stay at home and grumble at hard times. This same public will not, as grand juries, indict political criminals, or will not convict them when indicted. This same public is a wheedling, growling, complaining, fault-finder, and when the tools are given it for its own remedy, it will not sharpen them. Civilization, therefore, is indicted as a failure in its smart classes that, like the Japanese, are educated to believe that ability is given man to use in graft and robbery of the rights and property of the masses; and it is a failure in its weak classes—the toilers—because they, with the remedy close at hand, go on grumbling and refusing to amend the constitution and punish the political scoundrels who rule them and give their rights to the great corporations and trusts.

16. These things being true, the most expected traits that will crop out in man or wife are dishonesty and selfishness. This is an age now of universal selfishness and almost universal dishonesty. Even in the churches the preachers are dishonest, and they know it; for, if they were honest, they would know that they are not qualified for the work of saving the world. In church membership, no matter how steadfast men and women may be in their attendance at devotion, they are mostly dishonest. The outside lives of men in business and work, and the home lives of women, tell their great insincerity as members of the church, and they themselves know these things better than they want to. We are not called upon to prove these assertions, as the accused plead guilty. A woman has said in a report: "My husband and I are members of the church in our city. He says he cannot be honest in his business, and I know I am not honest in my private home life. But we are both desirous of becoming better. What can be done?" These two persons were both regarded as the very souls of honor, and their words were taken as always straightforward, and to be depended upon. But they simply know themselves. This trait of insincerity must be always kept in mind by the wife who studies her husband, and by the husband who studies the wife. Allowances must be made for heredity, for, if civiliation is under indictment today as a failure, it cannot produce men and women who are honest.

No husband can be perfectly honest with his wife who inherits the taint that is universal—the taint of graft and corruption. If he will not indict political scoundrels or convict
them when on trial, or if he will not take part in amending
the constitution which makes the courts mere barriers of technicalities through which the rich and powerful can slip with
perfect ease, he surely cannot come into his home and live
an honest life with his wife. She must, therefore, know that
he is not honest with her in all things, yet for policy sake he
may be sincere in things that she may find out.

17. For this reason the greatest demand on the wife is that
she plan her ways and life so as to keep her husband as near
to her at all times as possible. For his sake she should know
where he is always. This knowledge has kept many dishonest
men straight. When the wife does not know where he spends
his evenings or his spare time by day, she is remiss in her duty
to him and to herself, for, as habit-crimes are curable, so his
dishonesty may be cured. And as habit-crimes, when left to
themselves, run to worse conditions, so his freedom to go and
come at will is sure to lead to errors that may be great enough
to bar forgiveness.

18. On the same principle the woman who wants to spend
her evenings out with a dear lady friend should take her husband with her. The dear lady friend is too often a curable
prostitute, so cleverly heralded as to divert all suspicion. Two
women together evenings can hatch all sorts of mischief.

19. The husband makes a mistake to allow his wife to go
alone too much to her parents' home. Those parents are hers,
and he is not their son. He took her from them. They see
him, not through the eyes of the daughter who is his wife,
but through the eyes of the parents who have been deprived
of a supposedly lovely daughter. All persons are more or less
dishonest, and all are wholly selfish. Suspicions of others are
born in the inherited dishonesty that is in the blood; and it is
a sure thing that the least flaw in the habits or character of
the husband will arouse the suspicions of the wife's relatives.
This has been going on for sixty centuries in the world, and
you will not change it in your life. It is human and, therefore, fixed. The remedy is to call with your wife, and keep
her at home as much as possible. Confidences of mother and

daughter always poison the daughter's mind against her husband; sometimes not much, for the mothers are shrewd at times and breathe gently the vague hints they dare not face if made openly.

20. The same is true of the husband taking too much advice from his relatives as to the manner in which he should deal with his wife.

21. The best thing for the wife to do is to honor her parents in every way, and steel her mind and heart against their subtle influences. The best thing for the husband to do is to honor his parents in every way and cling to his wife.

22. Husband and wife belong to each other, and should be let alone. It is the beginning of the end when her parents, or one of them, will come to live as a part of the household; or his parents will do the same; for the contradiction of interest will be seen very soon, and the counter-influences will eat all the romance out of the young lives. Husband and wife belong to each other. They are human. They inherit both kinds of characters—the devil and the angel. They have much to discover in each other, and much to cause disappointment in their choices. They have a fearful struggle to endure each other, even under favoring conditions. To add to their heritage of bad tendencies when aroused, and to their bitter battles to keep the bond of marriage from snapping asunder—to add the presence and the failings of old folks—is more than poor human nature can stand; and, in this age of greater freedom, they WILL NOT STAND IT. It is not a question of supporting the parents, for, goodness knows, the husband has all he can do to keep body and soul together in his own family; but it is the question of cross-interests, of the wife's relatives touching the devil-spring in the husband's nature, and of his relatives touching the devil-spring in her nature, and then off they go. The saturated minds of the old folks see everything wrong in the other party, and nothing that is good. No modern marriage will long endure this torment.

23. Whatever else you do leave out the relatives from the home until the home has been built on a rock. Let them visit, and together visit them. Be cordial and keep up the best of feelings; but leave the relatives out of the struggling period of matrimony.

24. When the home is well established, as after fifteen years of married life, then husband and wife may take in such of their relatives as both are willing to have come, but the willingness must be voluntary and gracious, not niggardly and cool.

25. When relatives do come into the home life of a married couple the latter should have a frank, heart-to-heart talk, and should let it be understood that the little hints, subtle influences and brief suggestions of such relatives grind like sand against the feelings of one or the other, and lead to lack of confidence in each other. There have been husbands who have been true to their wives for half a lifetime, and who have been held in perfect confidence by them, whose reputations have been undermined by some suspicious relative of the wife who has come into the family to live; and there are wives whose neatness and good habits have been highly esteemed by their husbands, who have lost their reputations in the eyes of their husbands by discoveries made by his relatives who have come to their home to live. Old men and women are acute in their suspicions and faulty in their senses. Old women have many times reported remarks and occurrences to husbands or wife against the other party, when there was not the slightest ground for the statements. Each, rather than have trouble in the family, has borne the false belief in silence. Thus, when the mother of a wife told the latter that she had heard the husband say his "wife was not as good as she should be," the wife, offended to the quick, but not wanting to make trouble in the family, had her cry to herself day after day, and bore the accusation in patience, until she found out from the minister, to whom the husband had made the statement, that he had said his "life was not as good as it should be, for he let much of it go to waste in idle reading." Through the failing and faulty senses of old people they are continually getting things wrong; and this, added to their naturally acute suspicions, makes them very treacherous in the home of the younger people, although the old folks may really be good souls, and have not the slightest desire to make trouble. But they make it just the same, and it is as good doctrine now as when the Bible laid down the law that man and wife should leave parents and cling to each other.

26. If asked what is the greatest danger to the peace of

matrimony, the answer may always be this: The ease with which the wrong spring may be touched in the nature of the husband or the wife. Why?

Because:

a. A man is a mixed devil and saint.

b. A woman is a mixed she-devil and angel.

Any woman knows that unless she keeps her husband henpecked and hypnotized all the time she can touch the right spring, and get a good disposition in streams that are checked only by indigestion; or she can touch a wrong spring, and get the very old nick out of him. Policy may tempt him to suppress his nature, as where the whipping-post stares him in the face; but if he does suppress his evil disposition, the wife has gained nothing by touching that spring.

She knows, if she has any sense left, that she can get only torment and abuse, or neglect and suffering by touching that wrong spring. Yet she likes to do it. The love of scrapping is so strong in some women that they insist on getting their husbands going some, so they can hear and exchange opinions and vituperation. "When I want to know what Bill thinks of me I start him, and he gets mad right away. Then I let him know just how mean I think he is," says a woman, and she accomplishes all she starts out to do.

Any man knows, if he has any sense at all, that he can touch the wrong spring in his wife's nature, and get either tears and a headache, or set her to scolding in streams of eloquence.

27. What is the use? What difference will it make a hundred years from now? The man is not to blame for having the devil-nature, any more than the cat is to blame for eating the bird; nor is the woman to blame for her disposition. These are heredity. If they are incurable, find it out before marriage and drop the engagement. If you have money, it is cheaper to pay damages than the cost of after litigation and the penalty of a wrecked home. How many homes are safe today? Not five in a hundred, for freedom is growing fast, and the great public will soon redistribute itself through the divorce courts unless a remedy can be found, and that very soon.

28. Remember that the devil side of character is inherited, and cannot be blamed on the possessor of it. You have it, and we all have it. How you hate to be stirred up, or agitated by

the fretting remark of your consort! Then do not do it to her or him. Never touch that wrong spring. It leads to all the bad blood in wedlock. It has been said that it takes two to make a quarrel; but it is cowardly to fight with a person who will not fight back, and you ought to be ashamed to pick a quarrel with one who seeks a gentle life; peace on earth, good will to men.

29. It takes but one to touch the wrong spring. If your husband starts the day wrong, it is due to lack of digestion, or to the exhaustion of his vitality. He himself or his stomach has touched the wrong spring. Keep out of his way. Do not look pleasant, for he will think you are laughing at him. Just keep out of the way. It may irritate him to offer to find his collar button for him, as he will look upon you as a natural enemy until that indigestion has either gone off or killed him.

30. Study repression of your character. A husband does not like a gushing wife, nor one too free with her favors. Do not deny him, and do not throw them at him. Let him seek and find.

31. Study the science of food selection, and new ways of cooking. If you make things as mother used to make them, cut them off the diet, and start making things as mother would have made them had she been born with native sense and judgment sufficient to know that the health of the body and nervous system may be ruined by bad foods and bad cooking, and that ninety per cent. of the failures of marriage are due directly to indigestion, caused by the lack of wisdom on the part of the wife.

32. The husband should pay his wife constant attention. He does not care for her gushing, and he should simply be allowed to help himself to her as he may wish; but he, on the other hand, must remember that she wants his attentions, his kisses, if he does not smoke or chew tobacco; his embraces if he is neat and clean-smelling; otherwise his distant affiliation. Of course, it would be better for him to eschew tobacco in every form, and to take a frequent bath, and keep his face and hands clean, refinements which, it must be said with sorrow, are sadly lacking in married men. But, nevertheless, it is a law as old as the fundamental truths of the race that no woman will long be content without kisses and embraces. If she cannot get them

where they should be forthcoming, she will wish for them elsewhere; and wishing is the progenitor of infidelity to the marriage vows.

Learn this fact ere it is too late.

33. If you are a husband do not repose in the belief that your wife is dependent on you and your support, and, therefore, deny to her the refinements and the attentions that she craves. Do not let out your bad temper on her. Do not crowd her life into narrow limits by your selfishness, or by your thoughtlessness, which is the same as selfishness. She is not as dependent as she thinks she is. She may tell you, and she may believe at the time she says it, that she is dependent on you, and if you should leave her or die, she would not know what to do. But she will soon undeceive herself when the time comes that she can no longer endure your boorishness and inattentions, or your selfishness and narrow treatment of her. The spirit of domestic liberty is in the air, and she will inhale it sooner than you would believe. Children hold some wives to husbands who are too mean to live with; but the history that is making itself every day in this age is witnessing the annual exodus of thousands of wives from their homes, despite the fact that they have children. The wife who kills her children and herself has her husband marked for life as the guilty party. In most cases he is to blame. It is an awful remorse to take to the grave. Better turn over the new leaf now. You may think your wife is not the one who would do such a thing; but minds give way suddenly when they are compelled, as many wives are in this land, to live with men who are selfish, boorish, lacking in that kindness that they promised in courtship, and stayers away from home, where they are needed to help bear the burdens of work. You who drink may all too soon be made fatherless and a widower by the hand of an insane woman, whose love you are now trailing in the dust of life.

34. If you are a married woman, do not repose in the belief that your husband does not dare to leave you, for fear the courts would have him punished for neglect of his home and family. The courts have control within the State lines, not beyond, and the husband who steps over the line may greet the court with a good morning salute and laugh in its face. Your safety is in adopting the teachings of this book, and rais-

ing yourself to a higher level in life, and to that level he will be drawn if you have magnetism.

35. Every wife can make herself a better woman, and she can in time draw up to herself the husband that is curable of his faults and unrefinements. The better way is to induce the husband to study this book with you. Do not be afraid that he will think you are exposing him, for he will not take seriously any charge herein made. He really does not know how he looks in the eyes of those who know him best. But if he has any true manhood about him, he will ask you to write down each day a fault for him to correct. You can tell him it is a very small fault, almost too insignificant to mention; but as he asked for it you feel compelled to write it down. Then make it in strong letters bold enough to enter his head. He would be a man of a very low grade of intelligence who could not read his needs in that gentle list.

36. Most women lack sensible value and practical judgment. They can make themselves of value by mastering the greatest of all problems in the home, and that is the laws of food selection and of cookery. Sickness and ill temper both come from the neglect of this duty, and what is worse in a home than sickness and bad temper. The wife who is to hold the greatest power in the future is the one who will learn how to combine palatability and health in the diet. Today a palatable diet is decidedly unwholesome, and a wholesome diet is decidedly unpalatable. If woman wants to prove to the world that she is intelligent and civilized, she must master this problem. It is in her domain, not man's. Yet man, for his protection, acting under the rule that self-preservation is the first law of nature, is forced to study this problem himself, and to compel woman to adopt it. On the other hand, she is pretending that she is making progress in the same direction by her domestic science schools.

37. What is a domestic science school? Let us take the facts: Any woman, by witnessing the cooking done by a teacher for a certain number of weeks, and then braiding some hats, is given a diploma as a domestic science teacher, and she is then a candidate to become such a teacher. We know what we are saying, for the reason that we have purposely had some of our lady friends take the most thorough courses in domestic science,

and receive their diplomas or certificates. But there are some skilled teachers in domestic science who are skilled cooks. What do they cook? The height of their art, represented by tables full of food all ready to eat, has been preserved in photographs, and contain a collection of the very things that ruin the stomach, bring on sickness, add to irritability, and end in misery from all points of view. The foods are palatable, but not safe. There will never come a time when pastry, cake and fried foods will be safe for the human stomach, for the reason that the stomach cannot digest them, and will set up virulent poisons when nature tries to throw them off. What is needed is domestic science with an entirely new science. There is but one problem to be solved, and it is this:

a. How to get palatability without indigestion.

b. How to get wholesomeness with palatability.

Domestic science does not solve this problem, nor has it solved one iota of it. There has not been the slightest attempt to solve it. It is, as one of its chief critics has said, "a mountain of indigestible cookery."

38. In the wide world there is the hope of some person here and there to rise up above the heads of the throngs, and become great by reason of a mighty achievement. Men reach fame through war, or in statesmanship or the professions. To women the doors of high attainment are closed, or have been in the past. But now an opening is found for the first time since women were made free. That woman who will show the way to provide food that is nourishing, wholly free from indigestibility in a normal stomach, and at the same time palatable, will be the greatest personage on the stage of modern history, and her name will go down to succeeding generations as the bright particular star of this era, if not of all eras.

Why?

Because the human body is made up of what is eaten, and the brain, nerves, mind and all are dependent on the material that enters the body. Therefore, what we eat makes us what we are. If sin is to be punished, and irritability, temper, crime and the results of an uncontrollable ill nature are charged against people as sins, then the present-day diet, being the cause of these erratic conditions, must bring the blame home to woman who refuses to reform the diet.

39. It has been said that man is lacking in many little refinements and attentions that wives crave. On the other hand, woman is lacking in stamina. She may be active in body, but she is lazy in mind. If she were alive and strong in her mind, rather than in her talking powers, she would take up this problem of making wholesome foods palatable. But she contents herself with new bread, hot rolls, muffins, cakes, pastry, ice creams, fancy dishes, and all that train of barbarous products for furnishing her the power to attract the attention and appetite of her husband. He may praise the food while it is passing down his throat, for the most indigestible food is the most palatable; but when it gets to his stomach, and there sets up its ferment and its poisons, little wifey is horrified to see how touchy he is, and she climbs behind a sofa pillow with the exclamation that he does not love her as much as he did, and she is not going to slave any more to please him.

Where is the mental power in that woman? She is the type of the great army of brides that are stepping into the vortex of trouble.

40. Brides who are past twenty-five years of age, and especially those who are in the thirties, as a rule know how to cook much better than the young things; but they need just the reform that is mentioned herein. The world must have, and the man awake is going to have, wholesome food properly cooked and palatable.

41. If wives would hear themselves talk they would wonder what man can think them mentally attractive, as a rule. It is better to speak to yourself the things you are to speak aloud; listen well and absorb what you have said; then ask yourself if it sounds like the emanations of a good mind to say those things to your husband. Let it be your ambition to be sensible, and let him know you are sensible. A wise woman has a great hold on the heart of her husband; whereas a shallow woman is regarded by him as a toy if she is good-natured, or as a termagant if she is a hereditary scold.

42. If you are unmarried, hold the engagement off until you have ascertained what is the temperament of the other party. You can learn all about it by following the teachings of this book.

43. If you, are married and cannot agree, do not separate.

Go on to the principles taught herein, and find out the cause of the trouble. It may be that you have been touching the wrong spring all the time in the nature of your consort, or that your consort has been touching the wrong spring in your nature; but there may be a remedy. Just as sure as you two once saw something in each other to like, just so sure is there something still left of the likable, if not lovable. You have not been revolutionized by marriage, nor has your consort. When you thought each the best people in the world, you had the same devil-nature that you both have now, but you did not touch the wrong springs then, as now.

44. The easiest people to learn to hate each other are relatives of the same blood. An enormous percentage of people who are sisters and sisters, or brothers and brothers, or brothers and sisters, or parents and children, especially parents and sons, are estranged, and would sooner leave their property in case of death to any freak than to each other. This hatred is due to the closeness of their relationship. They know each other; and, as the relationship permits the utmost freedom of knowledge, they set up friction of feelings very easily, and this touches the wrong spring. Next to blood relations, the easiest people in all the world to learn to hate each other are husband and wife. The difference is, however, marked in the intensity of the hatred, for husbands and wives reach the utmost confines of diabolical malignity when they are thoroughly aroused. The courtship that was smooth in large degree, and that weathered the gales of misunderstandings, coming into the port of marriage with sails flying and banner at the masthead, is wrecked on so small a rock as a bit of temper that friends would forgive or not even notice. But married folks in their first months of wedlock are super-sensitive, and then fall apart, or else settle down to a steadfast warfare that has its intervals of peace and quietude while the campfires are shining in the background. It is a life of endurance for a while. Then when the time comes for the great battle there is no malice so black as that which drives these one-time lovers into court.

45. It is supposed that the mutual hatred is incurable.

Let us see.

The devil has been seen, and is out, and each thinks that no amount of veneering in the shape of promises or good nature will house his majesty again. "I have seen just what my husband is, and I can never think of him again as anything better than he is," says the wife. The husband says: "My wife is a tigress, all claws, and a she-devil combined. If we make up and go to living together again, I can never think of her as anything different from what she is." Many men and women live together in marriage for the sake of the children, all the time entertaining these regards for each other. Now, let us look at the facts as they are. That man had just the same nature in him that he has now, and he is no worse than millions of men who are married, some of whom are models of noble character. That woman had the same nature when she was being courted that she has now. She might have been the sweetest angel in all the wide world if the right spring had been touched all the time. All lovers in their halcyon days are just as much possessed of the evil nature as they are afterwards; and it is a true, if an old, saying that it takes marriage to bring out the devil in both man and woman. But it comes from touching the wrong spring. It is better to get together and understand this fact. The husband has a good defense, in that he was born with no more bad in him than the average man, and that any other man would be just as bad in disposition if he had his wrong spring sprung on him all the time. The wife has the same good defense. Just human, that is all. When they once understand the cause of it all, and are convinced that all men and women have the bad in them, they can bring about a peace; and, being married, they should change the methods of fighting; let them battle against their deficiencies. It is worth while. Breaking homes and wrecking lives must cease. Civilization cannot stand any more of this breach of her best purposes.

46. Do you know that there are millions of wives today that are like little fleas—all the time biting at the temper of their husbands? Others nag and nag. Then still others scold out loud. The great cause is the hasty marriage. Of all the weddings that have occurred after the parties, or one of them, had passed the age of twenty-five years, and had been in love for three or four years before, not one in fifty has been the stepping stone to trouble. It is the pretty girl or the handsome man that walks into an ill-assorted union. The lesson to be learned is that a long courtship is necessary. The lovers do not think so, and

can never be made to believe it, for they assert they are to become exceptions to the general rule of mis-mating. But they soon join the grand sea-wash of wrecked mariners, all too late to be saved. Deliberation and delay are necessary.

47. Find out the temperament of the other party before marriage; and this can be done in every case by the methods already stated in this book. If you are balked in your effort to do so, give yourself the benefit of the doubt. In a criminal case the defendant is given the benefit of every doubt that is reasonable; but in an anticipated marriage the rule should be stricter. You will be the criminal if you endanger the happiness of two lives, and possibly of children, as well as the happiness of relatives by a mis-mated union. In nearly every phase of life the motto, "Be sure you're right, then go ahead," applies; but what can more need this motto than marriage? And what gets its benefit less than marriage? It seems strange that in business transactions people wish to be sure they are right before they go ahead, and yet in matrimony they wish to go ahead in order to see if they are right, like the man who jumped into a basket of eggs to see if they were real.

48. In courtship that woman is wisest who holds back the goal to the man. In football when the goal is made that play is ended. In courtship when consent is won the goal is made, and that part of the play is over. What does she gain by giving consent? She thinks she has secured him from other women, but what is the use of securing a man who, in ninety chances out of a hundred, will be unworthy of having? Let the other girls have him, if he is that fickle. But if he loves you and you do not tell him that you love him, you are doing him the greatest service that one human being can bestow on another. You are keeping him at his best. You think that perhaps your charms will fade in a long courtship, but they will not fade then to such an extent as they will after marriage; and they will rather increase before matrimony if you follow the practice of magnetism, for this art keeps the eyes growing brighter all the time, and the features more beautiful. A beauty that is more attractive than complexion or velvety skin will be yours. You will have a better man if you test his power of remaining steadfast, if you keep him on his good behavior, and if you do not reach the goal.

49. It is not good for man to be alone. He should have a woman. If he is married, that woman should be his wife. She should be made to understand that he regards her as the greatest of all persons in the world. He should so regard her, and she should know it. If he cannot look upon her as the most important individual living, as far as he is concerned, he should school himself to learn to so estimate her. This is his duty to her and to himself. She may not be worthy of such opinion, but that makes no difference. If, when he married her, he so valued her, it will be easy for him to learn to do so again; and if he did not so value her, then he has a greater task to perform. It is not very hard for a magnetic man to relearn to love his wife.

50. If the man has no wife, and cannot get one, then he should have some woman in his life. His mother, his sister, his daughter may, perhaps, fill the void; or he may form the acquaintance in a general way with the sex at large, and be cordial and social with them. But he should submit himself to the refining influences of woman somewhere and somehow. He should be lifted up to the standard that requires him to be attractive to an excellent woman of high tastes and select mind.

51. It is not good for woman to be alone. She should regard her husband as the greatest man in the world; and if she knows he is the smallest, she should set about making herself believe more in him, and he will in time respond. "My husband? He? Make him think I believe he knows anything? Well, well, of all things, I should say I have not gone daffy yet. Why, he don't know enough to come in out of the rain," was the send-off a wife gave her husband some years ago. The man looked all the woman said. But as an experiment we induced her to gradually pretend to respect his judgment, to ask his opinion from time to time, and to generally expand his opinion of himself. She then asked him what he knew about certain matters. When she wanted to find out how to spell a word, she asked him, just to set him looking into the spelling book and dictionary. Then, later on, she asked him about grammar, and about adding and subtracting, and fractions, and led him to take an interest in studies. In four years she had a man whom she really respected.

52. Every woman should have a man. If she has no husband

let her cling to her father, son or brother. If these are lacking, let her entertain in a social way, and have men and women call to see her, and call upon men and women. It is not good for women to see only women, for they soon become yellow-hued gossips.

53. Every woman by magnetism, as taught in this work, can in time secure complete control over her husband.

54. Every man by magnetism, as taught in this work, can in time secure complete control over his wife.

55. This kind of control is not hypnotism, but is exactly its opposite. The control is willingly given even by magnetic persons; and the result, if both are magnetic, is that both will seek to yield subjection to the other. There has never been a great man who has not gloried in the fact that his wife could lead him like a little child. Yet she obeyed his slightest, as well as his greatest, wish.

56. This book shows the nature of woman to man in knowledge that he can never find elsewhere.

57. It shows to woman the nature of man in facts that cannot be obtained from any other source.

58. It lets each sex know all about the other sex, and is absolutely sure to DISCOVER TEMPERAMENTAL UNFITNESS.

59. What every woman ought to know about a man has been disclosed here and laid bare.

60. What every man ought to know about a woman has likewise been made clear.

61. Man places too low an estimate on woman.

62. Under the influence of this training course, if pursued diligently and faithfully to the end, and mastered thoroughly by repetition until every law and doctrine has been absorbed and brought into the pulsing life of the student, Sex Magnetism will lead the way to the grandest existence which is possible on earth. It is not difficult. It is practical. It is worth while.

MAGNETIC PASSION

FROM the cradle to the grave; from the hours of childhood's prattle to that sweet companionship of the aged couple sitting with clasped hands and looking out upon the autumn sun just dropping behind the gray hills; from the years of hope and progress to that last footfall on the threshold; from the planning that looked forward through the unopened years, to the closed book now shut forever; from the farewells of young hearts going out into the thick of the fray, to the benedictions of ripened age; from the gayeties and fancies of the bright hours that have been frequent visitors in the past, down to that last walk in the rose garden which will see the aged form no more; from all the up-reaching years of life's best work to the final days of rest; from first to last; from the cradle to the grave, life makes its span and is done.

When a young man falls in love with a young woman; when two persons stand face to face with the possibility of a union of lives; when home ties are about to be broken that have held the family together, and new associations are sought; when the all-important step is to be taken that shall bring man and woman into a new companionship, let them stop and ponder over the final picture as they would like to have it set in the framework of life.

In the time of sowing the harvest may be chosen.

Who is there that will go forth into the field and sow blindly, not knowing the seed and the soil? The simple rule of nature is as true in human life as in the cultivated land.

Victory at every endeavor comes to that person who will study the end of the span at the beginning; for, between the first step and the last in every history, there is the long road and the dangers to be passed. He is wise who, before entering wedlock, will seek definite knowledge of its final consummation.

From the age of impetuous blindness in matters of love, out into the better age of wisdom is not a long step; all that is needed is the mainspring of good sense and a masterly will power to resist the two demands; one for support, and the other for animal mating. The woman of all time has been too eager to win a husband who will support her; and the man has been too eager to own and possess a mate. These two demands have led the sexes on blindly defying all laws of judgment and every maxim of business and sound principle; for nothing else in this world is so fearfully sacrificed to unreckoning haste as matrimony.

So urgent is the desire of youth that all other considerations must give way. It is useless to say, wait a few years. They do not want to wait, and they will not wait. But the young men and the young women who are out of their teens should adopt a few simple rules:

1. Make love stand aside for a few years. It is not necessary to kill it, or to immure it, but let it stand without. If love is all that you are to depend upon for the stability of marriage, you will fail in short order and end ingloriously.

2. Learn the fitness of your chosen companion; and learn it before marriage. If there is one moment of hesitation during the prior acquaintance, or during courtship, no matter how slight it may be, let it be accepted as a mountainous obstacle. That brief hesitation or doubt tells the story of disaster to come. Learn the lesson in time.

3. Be deliberate. Do not be afraid of losing the one you want. If there is any danger of an escape from the alliance before marriage, accept it as a blessing in disguise; for if the bond of interest is held so lightly then, it will break quickly afterwards. Give the other party all opportunity for release. Favor the release, rather than insist on the betrothal. Every encouragement that is given to the possibility of the two lives falling apart, is an advantage. Help it along.

4. Proceed on the theory that nineteen unions in every twenty are illmated, and that you are in the nineteen. Do not believe that you are the one in the score that will succeed. If you are really intended for each other, you will find it out better by

delay than by blind haste; and you should quietly make up your mind to ascertain the truth before a decisive step is taken.

5. When you have found the one person in all the world that is designed to be your life-companion, then cultivate

THE RED FIRE OF MAGNETIC PASSION

This is the genuine attainment of heaven on earth.

Let us look at it in a practical manner, laying aside all attempts at building the ideal in place of the real.

In the first place it is a matter of certainty that you can find the one person in all this world who is perfectly adapted to you. It will take time and care, as well as the application of the rules and tests laid down in this course of training. But you may avoid all mistakes.

In the second place, assuming that you have found the perfect counterpart for your life, begin to build the plans for a long future with that one person. Make up your mind, no matter how great and how grand some others are in this world, that one individual is the greatest and the grandest of all. Think this, believe it, and so act. Let every thought and every deed of your existence center around that one person. It is worth while a thousand times over.

You may have countless other interests, but let none be so great.

In the third place outline a long voyage through this life, and see in contemplation the final years as they roll on the last history you will participate in on this earth. Make up your mind what that history shall be. The most magnificent law of human existence is this:

Whatever you make up your mind to accomplish, that will come to pass.

It has been stated that what you think, will be; but thinking is one process and a fixed determination, such as is taught in universal magnetism, is another. In other words, as applied to this work, you may and you will build that future which you set about achieving with a fixed determination to attain.

The man or woman with a magnetic goal ahead, is the one greatest power in life. Most people are adrift on an unknown stream and they have no port to which they sail. They are

brushed aside. Look out for the person with a definite and
determined purpose. Discouragements and failure will come,
but they will always be stepping stones to further progress; for
that is the method of success.

Here you are now, we will say, with a chosen companion
whom you have selected out of a score of others; and your
choice is perfect. This is the starting point. Next you have
your plans for the whole future; and, third, you are magnetic
enough to know how to make up your mind to accomplish what
you will in the world. You now have become an irresistible
force in the moving masses of humanity. Let all others stand
aside.

In that beautiful future that shall shine for you on this
earth, your chosen companion is the central figure and the
leading power. Homage and worship, exaltation and adoration are for that one alone, of all those who dwell on this globe.

Fit yourself for such an existence. It is not ideal, except
that it is best; but it is real in that it is possible and is being
today accomplished in many lives. You may at first thought
believe that no human being is good enough for your best regard and best care; but stop here a moment and look at the
picture that is being enacted in thousands of homes at this
very minute.

She is a beautiful maiden. The flush of the rose is on her
cheek, and the diamonds glitter in her eyes. Appareled like a
princess she receives the attentions of a gallant young gentleman who looks like a royal scion of a noble line. But they are
just plain people taken out of the hurry of life and made as
attractive for each other as care and interest will permit. They
are meeting now for the first time after there has been some
faint encouragement to the suit. He is all doubt and all wonderment. She is timid and fluttering like a bird let loose for
the trial flight. As he gazes upon her, there comes over him
the feeling that nothing so divine ever trod this earth before,
and she thinks of the grand heroes of her books that were so
different from other lovers that only the elect of heaven could
be good enough for their attentions.

Nature is at work. This is her magnetic spell.

You say it is not real, for it all vanishes. But it is real, and
is being lived in the first meetings of lovers at this time wher-

ever civilization holds sway; and it has been lived countless
millions of times in the past. You cannot say a thing is not
real that has been the one uniform history of every life. The
fact is, nature gives a brief touch of the red fire of passion, and
then she lets things take their own course, on the principle that
all streams will settle to the level of their fountain heads. It
is to realize that level that this work has been written. There
and there alone is the whole secret.

You can see for yourself that your chosen companion can be
no greater in your estimation than your own regard and opinion decide. If you are to consider yourself first, then the plan
will fail. The other party must always be first, and you must
always be second; and it is more than likely that in the eyes
of that individual you will be first and the other party will be
second; so there will be two firsts. This is the way it should
be; for it is the way nature sets up the standard in those glowing hours of the first feelings of love.

How feeble and how futile are all attempts to assume a charm
that is not real!

The woman dresses the best she can, in the hope that dresses
will prove a charm. She puts up her hair with hours of
thought and much attention, looking a thousand times in the
mirror to see if her face is framed in attractive beauty. She
has been known to brighten her eyes with bella donna to give
them the brightness that comes naturally only through magnetism. Just as she enters the room where he is waiting, she
gives her face a few pinches to plant the hue of the rose there,
never dreaming that magnetism paints better and more endur-
ingly. Now as she comes into his presence, she is all life, all
vivacity, all blushes, all afire with charms that burst forth in
every word and every expression of the face. Her smile is most
fascinating. Her voice trembles with the slightest fever of the
heart, and is full of the best quality that life has given it, while
her words are well chosen, and his every remark is the basis
of her zeal and solicitude. She is trying to be charming. Much
of it sincere, but it becomes artifice as her experiences grow.

He is just as eager to seem pleasing.

He is on his best manners; better than she will ever see after
marriage. He is attired to the full limit of his purse, in most

cases, and his words and manly utterances are attempts of nature to hold him up to the highest possible standard.

All this has been done more million times than you can count.

You say it is not deception. Of course it is not deception; but if it were, as it seems to be in some cases, it still remains the fruit of natural impulse. Have women ever tried to look better and be better than they really are, when they have sought to win the good opinions of men? Yes, millions of times. Women always do that thing. But why? On what principle will they seek to be sweeter and more pleasing in the first meetings with their prospective lovers than they would be in the presence of their own mothers whom they cherish? If women assume charms they do not in fact possess, why do they do so?

Even the deceits that men and women practice on each other to make themselves more pleasing, are part of the same plan of nature. There would be no sex calling if there were no demand for it.

Take this lesson into your life. Study this department of the present training course, and master it in every detail. Take time to do so, and do not hurry. Then make your lists of commonplaces and of margins. Having laid the foundation well, and proceeding with a determination to win, you will one by one drop all the commonplaces from your life; and, as you do so, you will enter step by step into Charmland; until, when all the dregs of existence are drained off, there will run the clear fluid of a new magnetism. On this build the many magnetic margins that have been taught; and you will be filled full with

THE RED FIRE OF PASSION

It is the nobleness of manhood, the truth of manhood, the upright honor of manhood, coupled with the sweetness, the purity and the lovableness of womanhood. May you and "yours" start at once making preparations for the great journey, and may you both enter into the full glory and the alluring delights of

CHARMLAND

CPSIA information can be obtained
at www.ICGtesting.com
Printed in the USA
BVOW06s1750210517

484772BV00006B/111/P